Taste Today

The Role of Appreciation in Consumerism and Design

Journal of related interest
Leonardo—Journal of the International Society for the Arts,
Sciences and Technology (ISAST)

Free sample copy available on request

Edward Duveen's concept of good and bad Taste depends on the avoidance of contrast. The 'bad' version of the Edwardian day dress differs from the 'good' only in the small added touches of red to the green ensemble.

CEILING

FLOOR

Red is, however, an approved colour for schemes of interior decoration, for example, that proposed by Edward Duveen for an art gallery. (Today, white would be universal.)

Taste Today

The Role of Appreciation in Consumerism and Design

by

Peter Lloyd Jones

Head of School of Three-Dimensional Design, Kingston Polytechnic, UK

PERGAMON PRESS

Oxford • Seoul • New York • Tokyo

UK   Pergamon Press plc, Headington Hill Hall,
Oxford OX3 0BW, England

USA   Pergamon Press Inc., 395 Saw Mill River Road,
Elmsford, New York 10523, U.S.A.

KOREA   Pergamon Press Korea, KPO Box 315,
Seoul 110-603, Korea

JAPAN   Pergamon Press, 8th Floor, Matsuoka Central Building,
1-7-1 Nishi-Shinjuku, Shinjuku-ku, Tokyo 160, Japan

First edition 1991

Library of Congress Cataloging-in-Publication Data

Lloyd Jones, Peter, 1940–
Taste today: the role of appreciation in consumerism and design by Peter Lloyd Jones—1st ed.
p. cm.
1. Aesthetics.   2. Design—History—20th century.
3. Consumers Psychology.   4. Visual communication.
I. Title.
NK1520.L46   1991   745.4′442—dc20 90-29081

British Library Cataloguing in Publication Data

Lloyd Jones, Peter
Taste today: the role of appreciation in consumerism and design.
1. Aesthetics
I. Title
111.58

ISBN 0-08-040251-8

Printed in Great Britain by BPCC Wheatons Ltd, Exeter

Dedication

In gratitude of my contact with three great teachers, without whom this book would never have seen the light of day:

Derek Farndell, my first art teacher, whose ironies on the foibles of consumer society first alerted me to the importance of design as symbol and value. From him too I first learned of the pleasures of jazz and thereby came to appreciate the plurality of contemporary cultures and of artistic standards.

William Hallé, artist, whose gentle canvases showed me the true poetry of everyday things, those collections of very ordinary items that everyone keeps on the bookshelf, mantlepiece or bedside table, not for their use, but for their meanings.

Sir Ernst Gombrich OM whose books and lectures on art provide an inspiring example for anyone who seeks to comment usefully on the role of the subjective in design—and whose early encouragement led me to try.

Foreword

In 1986, the Royal College of Art celebrated its 150th anniversary. This marked 150 years during which concepts of design founded in Victorian values became transmuted through the stresses of economic growth and the challenges of the modern movement to the diverse international professional activity it is today.

These developments in design have been accompanied by the growth of complexity, of factions, of fashions, and of some disillusionment but, I suggest, no corresponding growth of understanding.

Serious writers on design from Ruskin and Morris onwards have tried to analyze and explain the phenomenon of design but over recent years serious design writing has declined and largely been replaced by ephemeral journalism, a sad neglect of the underlying truths of a vital matter in human affairs.

This was why, in commemoration of the 150th anniversary of the Royal College of Art, we decided, with the generous sponsorship of Mr Robert Maxwell to launch the International Robert Maxwell Prize for New Writing on Design Thinking.

We hoped that this would focus attention on the need for some new and critical thought on the philosophy, theory and practice of design, and would encourage new writers and discover important work already in being.

All these objectives were fulfilled, a large number of fresh and original submissions were received from authors throughout the world. The winner, *Taste Today* by Peter Lloyd Jones is here and I believe its importance to be very great.

Confronted by the complexity of modern design and by the trail of abandoned visual movements and styles which litter the history of the twentieth century, the task of discussing those elusive and subjective values of design which Peter Lloyd Jones classifies under the heading of 'Taste' is enormously daunting. It is the difficulty of discussing these values which frightens potential authors but it is precisely those values which need, more than ever, to be confronted head-on if we are to begin to develop any useful terminology, frame of reference and dialectical method for the discussion and analysis of the deeper meanings of design.

This book tackles the matter bravely and unsentimentally, seeing both the real and the spurious in design and being generous in recognizing the essential pluralism of twentieth century design.

The author, himself being a polymath, uses his broad understanding to bring in the fields of linguistics, anthropology and semiology to demonstrate the intellectual effort and growth of understanding occurring in other, but related, fields of human life. This breadth of reading and the illustrations and reference material provided, on their own, make this a seminal work.

Design has long passed its pioneering and heroic phase. In many ways it has now passed its period of assured professionalism and is torn by doubt. This faltering of confidence is not helped by the present shallowness in the understanding of design.

Design needs to be reclaimed and this reclamation must be found in premises that have been thought through to greater depths than those of the perceived superficialities of today. Peter Lloyd Jones under the deceptively slight title of *Taste Today* has provided a solid foundation for new design speculation in the most difficult area of all—style.

Frank Height
Professor Emeritus
Royal College of Art

Preface

Taste—the acts and arts of appreciation, discrimination, critical judgment and the pleasurable savouring of man-made artefacts—has so long been absent from the agenda of public debate that many have supposed the matter dead. Not only are the philosophical arguments about what exactly constitutes Taste tedious, abstruse and unrelated to secular realities as most people sense them, but the whole issue invariably stirs political passions. Anyone foolish enough to raise the subject immediately faces indignant accusations of élitism. For we live in an increasingly pluralist (not to say populist) society, a free market in which *chacun à son goût* and a plenitude of idiosyncratic possessions exist to prove it. To many, there is something intrinsically offensive about the idea that some people have more or better Taste than others or, to put it even more starkly, that some people have Taste and others simply do not. Who are those that take it upon themselves to pronounce on such matters? What qualifications have they? In any case should not one's Tastes be a private affair and is not interference in such matters sheer impudence anyway?

But even among those that do not sense this rancorous social division there is a feeling that, in a world of real problems such as the nuclear threat, unemployment, pollution and famine, that Taste is just a massive irrelevance. Yet Taste obstinately refuses to disappear. Indeed, submerged just below the surface of secular discourse and political battle, it survives and flourishes. Recently, there have been many spectacular cases (Prince Charles' controversial television programmes on modern architecture in England and the controversy over the late Robert Mapplethorpe's photographs involving the United States government would be good examples) where Taste has emerged as a live issue in controversies which raise all the same confused passions as it did a century ago when reformers of Taste such as John Ruskin and Henry Cole held confident sway over the preferences of multitudes, proffering minatory judgments over such minutiae as the citizen's choice of wallpapers.

There are several reasons for this Renaissance. First, Taste turns out to be inextricably mixed up with public policy in ways which affect the ordinary man and woman. Censorship—the selective curtailment of culture—or its opposite, propaganda—the selective promotion of culture—are clearly matters of public concern. Both depend on judgments which often turn on matters of Taste. Each is of considerable economic and social import. In a democracy what should govern the purchase of modern art for the state museums or determine the preservation of cherished buildings or neighbourhoods against ruthless developmental pressures? The former issue will usually be considered merely a matter of wasting the taxpayers' money (and in amounts which are in global terms trivial) while the latter invariably arouses deep passions. A substantial portion of the public purse is allocated on the basis of judgments about such matters of Taste and much of the quality of the environment is determined likewise. But who is qualified to make such judgments? Experts no doubt, but what precisely is their expertise? How does one qualify to advise ministers on issues of Taste?

Still more difficult in a democracy that relies on votes is the fact that Taste is clearly a subject on which great differences exist between the various social groups. It is difficult enough to obtain universal endorsement or assent even on fundamental matters of equity and social justice where there are at least some more or less explicit principles on which most men can agree. In the field of Taste this is not so. Indeed, Taste is an area where the views of the majority are frequently in disagreement with the so-called experts. Popular culture is in regular collision with high culture. Why should the majority be taxed to finance the Tastes of an already wealthy élite? And how can we justify expenditures on Taste education by government agencies when the majority of the population considers itself already satisfied? One could endlessly multiply these conundrums. And of course these same dilemmas and paradoxes were prominent in discussions of Taste going back to the eighteenth century. Today, what was once purely an abstract dispute in an unimportant branch of philosophy has become the province of big business and the occasion for intervention by central government.

Even more significant than its involvement in the problems of supporting and managing culture and the arts generally and of defending the boundaries of the socially and environmentally acceptable, is the role that Taste plays in the economy at large. Once an economy moves into a stage of relative affluence the abundance of necessities can be assumed. Consumption then becomes more and more removed from the business of satisfying primary physical needs and increasingly becomes the indulgence of our Tastes. Obviously, there are still many goods that are consumed on the basis of their performance or price. Capital goods, scientific equipment and computers are all examples of items where Taste is rarely the salient factor in decisions to purchase. Yet even here there is usually a choice of several competing brands which are more or less alike. This is the phenomenon of technological convergence which affects all advanced industrial economies. In such cases subjective factors are more important than we might initially suppose. (Even advertisers of such ostensibly technical products as personal computers have never doubted the power of those intangible behaviours that we call Taste.)

In any event, with most industrial products performance is simply taken for granted. And in many cases performance is far greater than is ever needed for daily use, for example, most cars are capable of speeds far in excess of the legal limit and most audio equipment is capable of noise levels which can severely damage the hearing of its users. In all such cases consumer choice is determined by more intangible subjective and social factors, in short, by Taste. Consider this in the context of the endless internecine economic warfare between companies and nations and the importance of an adequate understanding of Taste is hard to underrate.

Ironically, Taste is little understood by business. It is rarely considered a central issue in company affairs. While the gut feeling in the marketing department may often play an important part in major decisions such as whether to purchase or manufacture particular products, conventional marketing theory has little useful comment to make about Taste which might relate it to the ways in which it is actually exercised by consumers. This is especially true in the case of those consumer products such as furniture and domestic utensils and decor which affect the interior environment of everyone. Here the crucial element is symbolic imagery. But this is precisely the area where conventional marketing is at its weakest and where the establishment of a creative relationship to critical discourse in those areas such as art and design is long overdue.

At a national level, the importance of an understanding of Taste and, crucially, of an appreciation of differences in Tastes, is invariably overlooked in discussions of economic performance. At the present time there is a welcome upsurge of interest by the government of the United Kingdom in design. However, what is meant by design all but excludes the subjective, focussing instead on questions of practicality and utility. Of course, these are all important matters. More to the point they are uncontroversial and therefore eminently suitable topics for pronouncements by civil servants. The doctrine of functionalism in design is thus still promoted with special zeal by the official organs of governmental interest in design. Few outside these circles believe in functionalism today. Yet with the demise of functionalism, the theory of design is left vague or silent on precisely those issues which determine good design. Indeed, to take it at its most general and important level, it is silent on the issues which determine the imagery of the entire man-made world, central to which is that complex and subtle mix of human passions, preferences and prejudices we call Taste.

Taste Today is not however an account of contemporary Tastes. Such may be found in the innumerable magazines and papers concerned with consumption, homemaking, fashion, leisure and the arts. Ample documentation on the constant changes in Tastes already exists embalmed in the countless advertisements which crowd publications in every medium. And while the scribes and prophets of commerce are constantly discovering (and promoting) new trends in the marketplace, their academic confrères, the cultural historians, perform the same task for the art gallery or concert hall. Yet all this continues without any clear understanding of Taste as a general concept.

Taste Today is rather a study of the concept of Taste as it actually operates in contemporary society—of how general ideas invariably acquire their characteristic flavour and concrete content from the nature of the problems on which they are put to work. No longer confined to the pages of the eighteenth century gentleman's dispute on the nature of the beautiful in art, *Taste Today* takes life in the turmoil of consumer culture. And the disputants are no longer a few wealthy amateurs but professional psychologists, sociologists, anthropologists, marketing men and designers of all sorts. *Taste Today* brings together insights and ideas from all of these fields. It is illustrated with examples drawn from all levels of contemporary culture from the undoubted achievements of twentieth century high art and big design to the crassitudes of the global High Street. It aims to show that if the marketing professional has much to learn from traditional modes of discourse on high art then the contemporary critic has much to gain from a contact with those technical disciplines which aim to understand (and hence to exploit) the fluctuations and caprices of consumer society.

Above all, *Taste Today* discusses issues that can only be illuminated by the light of historical example and precedent. We are not the first to ponder these matters. Designers, marketing men, consumers or even the curious observer of modern consumer societies, all need to realize that appreciation or social judgment in the field of consumption is as old as man himself. And the resonances which attend each daily act of judgment, be it as trivial as choosing a tie or a restaurant, reverberate back into the past as well as across the many dimensions of complex contemporary societies.

Finally, it should be noted that the word Taste has been used freely in the sense of both the actual exercise of appreciation—of discrimination, critical judgment and pleasurable savouring—and more generally as a collective noun signifying that whole clutch of discriminations and judgments that characterize a person or group.

Acknowledgements

The present book started life when I was invited to give a short series of talks on BBC Radio Three during the year of the Royal Jubilee. I chose as my theme the 'Englishman's Home' and gave an account of what seemed to me to be the real history of design over the previous twenty years. These years—the Jubilee period corresponded roughly to the years which had elapsed since the Festival of Britain—were regarded by many as the final dawning of a truly Modern Movement in design in the United Kingdom. To me, however, it seemed patently obvious that this was not the case. Despite the spectacular success of a few retailers of modern furniture and appurtenances, the average British home was manifestly very different from the image of good design as purveyed by establishment organs such as the Design Council. Moreover, the confident Modernism that saw fit to denounce the majority view as merely bad Taste, tractable only to further massive doses of state-subsidized propaganda for Modernism, seemed both arrogant and doomed to failure. But what was good Taste?

The theory behind the Modern Movement, or functionalism as it is often called, dodged this issue altogether. By insisting that design was nothing to do with Taste but was, on the contrary, a technical matter concerned with fitness, economy, ergonomics and the appropriate use of materials, the theory entirely avoided the issue of social judgment. I argued that Taste must once more be brought back onto the designer's agenda—not least because, with the collapse of belief in functionalism, teachers of design needed to have some valid discourse with which to engage their students, discourse that went beyond mere judgments *ex cathedra* dished out on a more or less random basis.

The producer who commissioned the series was Leonie Cohn and I am grateful to her for her patience in helping me turn a tumult of observations and impressions into a legible pattern. Even then though it became inescapable that, as a designer and teacher, I really knew very little about the social sciences that must provide the basis for any serious study of Taste. Nor was the discovery that Taste was not really considered a proper or even a unitary subject by orthodox thinkers in these fields long in coming. Appreciation (or social judgment in the field of consumption goods) has been treated widely, but the material is scattered about in many different subjects and the prospects of mastering even the basics of all these looked daunting. And besides, it all seemed so dry!

I was overjoyed therefore when my colleague in the School of Sociology, Keith Weightman, pointed me in the direction of Thorstein Veblen, surely one of the funniest writers since Swift. It was Veblen that kept me going through daunting shelf-loads of books on economics, marketing and social theory in my search for material which might illuminate such mundane matters as the real reasons for a man's choice of car or carpet—or any other issue of practical judgment, poignant or profound, curious or absurd, which falls under the heading of Taste.

Many colleagues have helped to shape the form of the book. Professor Michael Podro of the University of Essex Department of Art read an early version and suggested that radical surgery was necessary. He was right and the final version owes much to him. Brigit Towers and Gill Rolls-Wilson have read over the manuscript and helped me to avoid at least some of the inevitable errors of a beginner in the fields of sociology and marketing. Stuart Durant has been endlessly useful in suggesting apt images and his encyclopedic knowledge of nineteenth century design history has been made available to me on many occasions. I must also thank Susan St. Clair, research librarian at Kingston, who has been prodigal of time and effort in chasing and verifying bibliographic data.

Many people helped to source material for illustrations and I am grateful in particular to my colleagues Bastiaan Valkenburg, Allan Philips, Jon Wealleans and Brian Kernaghan and to Antti Nurmesniemi in Helsinki and George Sowden in Milan all of whom were kind enough to let me use original photographs. Many people in several countries were brave enough to let me photograph their business premises and, even more valuable, their homes and their most precious objects and I would like to record here that it is an honour to have been allowed to invade their privacy in this way. Acknowledgements to all those who generously permitted the use of copyright material are listed separately on page xvii.

The Faculty of Design Research Committee gave a small grant towards the purchase of desktop publishing facilities and for picture research and I am grateful to them. Several secretaries helped to translate my handwritten drafts into readable form in the early days before the word processing revolution arrived and I could cope on my own. I am particularly grateful to Rae Higgins and Melissa Comfort. In addition, I would like to thank the staff of Pergamon Press and in particular Karen Giles for her diligent editorial work on the preparation of the manuscript.

No work of any scale or substance would be completed without the support of long suffering spouses and I must thank my wife for her patience during the years when I was burning the midnight oil.

Peter Lloyd Jones
Kingston Polytechnic 1990

Picture sources

Plate section

Antti Nurmesniemi, Plate 15
Bastiaan Valkenburg, Plates 8, 9 and 19
International Colour Authority, Plate 20
Konde Shobo, Shinsha Publishers, Plate 21
M. J. Pover, Plate 23
One-Off, London, Plate 17
Promostyl, Plate 22
Richard Bryant, Plate 13
With the permission of the Trustees of the Wallace Collection, Plate 11

Black and white photographs

Alison Britton, 4.9
Allan Philips, 6.11
Antti Nurmesniemi, 6.10
Architects Journal, 5.11
B. T. Batsford, Ltd., 5.20
Bastiaan Valkenburg, 2.25, 3.22, 3.24, 8.7, 8.8
Bentalls PLC, 1.12
Brian Kernaghan, 6.12
Charles Jencks, 5.14
Corporate Industrial Design—N.V. Philips, 2.12
Courtauld Institute. Reproduced by kind permission of Lord Egremont, 4.2
Croom Helm, 7.3, 7.4
Cuisines ABC, 3.21

Daily Mail Ideal Home Exhibition, London, 3.28 (top), 6.20
David Sillitoe, *The Guardian*, London, 2.16
Design Museum, London, 5.7, 5.8, 5.9, 6.4, 6.22
Dover Publications Inc, USA, 1.2, 3.8
Editions A et J Picard, Paris, 2.5
Falmers Jeans, 7.9
Fitch Richardson Smith, 2.13
Gallaher Tobacco Ltd., 4.8
George Sowden, 6.22
Henry Poole, Tailors, Saville Row, London, 2.7
i-D Magazine, 3.2
I.S.A.S.T. 1990. Translated and reprinted by permission, 7.2
IIT Design Process Newsletter, Volume 2, Number 4, 5.4
J. L. Wright, 3.13
Jon Wealleans, 2.15, 6.5
Leo Burnett Ltd, 1972, 1.11
Louis Hellman, 5.13, 6.1, 8.3
Next PLC, 3.18
Nick Clements, *The Independent*, London, 8.4
Oxford University Press, 3.10
Paris Match, 7.1
Pion Ltd, 2.10, 7.6, 7.7
Reinhart Butter, Director of Transport Studies, Ohio State University, 2.14
Routledge and Kegan Paul, 5.17, 5.19
Salama-Caro Gallery, London, 8.2
Sunday Telegraph Magazine, London, 8.11, 8.12
Town Hall Art Galleries, Burnley, 4.3
Warburg Institute, 1.13

Contents

Contents

About the notes

The scope of the study of Taste is so large that the list of possible references is potentially vast. Most, if not all, readers will approach the subject from one of the many disciplines which embrace the issue from a particular viewpoint. They will find much that is familiar, if not obvious. I ask their indulgence for I have tried to give reference material which would enable the layperson, unfamiliar with a particular topic or even a whole discipline, to break into their particular field of interest. This has inevitably led to references which include textbooks, reviews, secondary sources as well as primary material where this is relevant. The aim throughout has been to include sufficient detail about each field of enquiry to give the reader a 'feel' for its central insights and methodology. In some cases, textbooks which include up-to-date reviews of a wide range of literature are a positive advantage. Much marketing literature, for example, is very subject specific, usually proprietary, and covers a restricted range of commercial products. Drawing general insights from this disparate body of research is arduous, even for those who specialize in such analysis. For the layperson it is overwhelming. In areas such as the history of art or design, the notes and references include more primary sources. Throughout, citations are to recent and easily obtainable editions.

1. What is Taste?

Taste yesterday

Taste is the power or faculty of distinguishing beauty from deformity and is shown in the preference a rightly constituted mind gives to one object above another. It is in some degree constitutional but can also be improved by careful study of beautiful objects, for by comparison alone can we arrive at the knowledge of what is most perfect of its kind. It is by the study of the best, and the experience gained by noting its beauty and its accuracy that the mind acquires refinement and an instinctive appreciation of excellence.[1]

This resounding and confident definition of Taste comes not, as one might suppose, from the eighteenth century, but from our own. It happens to be the opening paragraph of Edward Duveen's *Colour in the House—with notes on architecture, sculpture, painting and upon decoration and good taste*, published in 1911. Here, with all the uncompromising solidity of the upper class Edwardian (Edward was a brother of Joseph Duveen, the picture dealing millionaire), is the classic gentleman's definition of Taste. It was almost the last time that such confident pronouncements could be made. Revolutionary movements in art and architecture (Dadaism, cubism and futurism) were about to burst upon the tranquil world of the connoisseur, initiating a period in which the distinction between beauty and deformity was entirely to be subverted. Moreover, the social position of the connoisseur himself has also been subverted in the populism of modern democracy. In place of such élitist declarations we now have an embarrassed dissembling against the accusation of snobbishness. Duveen's advice was a rehash of Victorian views leaning largely on Owen Jones. His own

recommendations are conventional. However, his definition of Taste is a useful starting point since it gathered together many traditional themes which today would be scattered about in many different writers.

Many questions arise at once from this definition of Taste which are the very stuff of traditional aesthetics. To begin with, there is the problem of discrimination, or as Duveen calls it, the faculty of distinguishing. What kind of activity is this? How does it relate to other mental faculties? Again, Taste is connected immediately to the idea of beauty and its opposite, deformity. How do we define and recognize each when we see it? To what extent can we say beauty is immanent in particular objects or settings, or must we admit that it lies in the eye of the beholder? There is also the question of what qualities are needed for the rightly constituted mind. Is this a matter of heredity or can one acquire it? If so, how? Or if we come to the idea of the collection of beautiful objects, each of which is the most perfect of its kind, who is to make such a collection? How do we know that it is indeed a collection of the best? And even when we have a collection, how do we know what comparisons to make? And how too does the act of comparing enhance the refinement of the mind or the appreciation of excellence?

Taste Today will not follow the traditional path of philosophical aesthetics which seeks to answer these, and related conundrums, through logical and linguistic analysis, referring perhaps to some current view of human nature. Controversy over the nature of beauty (or deformity) has not hitherto been very rewarding, consisting for the most part of overt or hidden justifications for a particular form of high art. The present enquiry seeks to approach these complex and subtle matters from a more empirical direction, broadening the scope of Taste to include the appreciation of everyday objects and settings as well as works of art.

There is no doubt, however, that appreciation is closely linked to critical judgment or discrimination, and that discrimination is in turn based on comparison. Clearly, for discrimination—the power or faculty of distinguishing—to be possible, we must have a range of objects amongst which to discriminate, for choosing implies both surplus and diversity. However, comparison (of one object with another in order to assess their respective qualities) also implies a conscious collecting or grouping together of objects for this purpose. Only if a collection (physical or mental) is made, in which objects are in some way related or similar, can significant differences be noted and savoured.

It is clear that works of art were collected and valued for these reasons in ancient Greece.[2] Extraordinary sums of money were spent on indulging them, especially when an aesthetic element such as their vivid realism shaded over into something akin to magic. In Roman times, works of art (often plundered from Greece) were avidly collected, these included the useful and decorative arts—ivories and vases, silver and gold platters and embroidery. By the time of Cicero auctions were held regularly and shops specializing in such antiquities opened. No doubt the result of a lust for hoarding, and the convenience for easily embodied wealth in the days before banking, vied with a fondness of art itself. Nevertheless, market prices surely reflected Taste as well as the intrinsic value of gold, silver or precious stones. Pliny's account of the relative popularity of different artists from the ancient world is an account of Tastes for different types of cultural product.[3]

The Renaissance saw the rebuilding of collections of diverse cultural artefacts, particularly Greek and Roman antiquities but also artefacts from the Near and Far East and other exotic lands. The origin of the Renaissance hierarchy of genres: history painting, portraits, animals, landscapes, still life, lies in these Greek Tastes described by Pliny. Once collection goes beyond mere accumulation, the process of classification—what goes with what —begins, however haphazard contemporary arrangements might seem to our eye. Giorgio Vasari as art historian is also the first modern critic when he discusses different styles and manners in the making of works of art.[4]

By the end of the Middle Ages, cities, in particular London, which had the most spectacular population growth of all, saw the beginning of something like modern commercial life with an unprecedented number and variety of objects available in shops and markets. Comparison between goods in shops was now commonplace. In such cities, emulation and rivalry in display among the aristocrats who had newly acquired city homes (they had rarely met in the country) led to rapid stylistic development in dress and other consumer goods. Many examples of cripplingly elaborate costume from the period testify to the power of Taste once comparison and discrimination extended to wider circles of wealth and influence among merchants and bankers.[5]

Of course, exaggeration in itself was not new. During the Middle Ages there were (as Johan Huizinga has described[6]) fantastic excesses during feasts and festivals such as whole orchestras hidden inside gigantic pies. These

1.1 *Shoes from the fifteenth century show increasingly pointed and lengthened toes—to the point where a chain is needed to tie the tip to the knee to avoid tripping the wearer.*

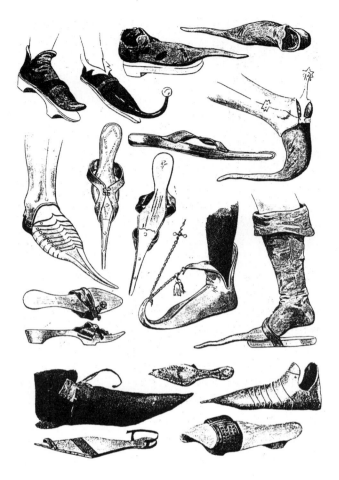

were designed to show the wealth and splendour of the Court, overawing the populace and dazzling rivals. It is in the translation of such sentiments into the secular, everyday life of the citizen that we see the flow of what we now call fashion—the shift of Taste over time—in its modern form. The rational, enquiring side of the Renaissance mind looked upon all this quite novel diversity of form and expression, not as something to be denounced, but to be understood. In analyzing both works of art, and our responses to them, Taste became a matter for enquiry and systematic study.

Taste, in this particular metaphorical sense, enters fully into language at the beginning of the eighteenth century. The dictionary records a veritable explosion of metaphorical analogizing from the primary gustatory sense during the early years of the seventeenth century. At first such metaphorical extensions related to other senses, particularly touch, and from there to physical perception in a general way. From this latter meaning it is a short step to encompass the dimension of judgment or discrimination. When Mellefont in Congreve's *The Double-Dealer* of 1694 says 'No, no, hang him he has no Taste', we are fast approaching the modern usage. Taste entered explicitly into the discussion of the arts through the writings of the Earl of Shaftesbury and Joseph Addison, notably when Addison announced in *The Spectator* in 1712 his proposal to enquire into the 'Rules how we may acquire that fine Taste of writing that is so much talked of among the polite world'. In their employment of the term Taste, Shaftesbury and Addison are translating the sense of *goût* or *gusto* which had already acquired such overtones on the continent of Europe.[7]

Thus the immediate issues which gave birth to the word Taste arose in disputes about the qualities deemed to be essential for the making and appreciation of works of art, disputes which date back to the seventeenth century. What began as practical wisdom during the early Renaissance soon rigidified into dogma in the academic concept of art, especially where influenced by a quasi-scientific rationalism. Particularly in the French Academy the view prevailed that art was made by reason and involved the just deployment of rules for composition and for the selection and presentation of theme. A counterview emerged which championed the merits of artists like Rubens and Rembrandt against the classicist Poussin. Both were artists who stressed 'painterly' brushwork and above all colour. Their style might be more informal, yet we can immediately feel an inner order.[8] It is this power or faculty for apprehending beauty intuitively (as we should now say) which is the defining characteristic of Taste. However, if sentiment, an essentially non-rational faculty, is to be the touchstone of beauty, a number of important new problems are raised for what would now be called 'criticism'.

Many of these dilemmas relate specifically to the various philosophical positions then current, on such questions as the nature of mind. Taste was, for a man like Shaftesbury, a neo-Platonic intuition or inner sense, a sense which directly apprehended a pre-established harmony.[9] For a man of quite different philosophical temper, like David Hume, Taste was something totally removed from any kind of supernatural faculty. It was simply part of our psychological make-up. This he attempted to describe in his theory of the association of ideas.[10] The history of eighteenth century critical theory need not concern us here. What is important is to note that the problems which arise in this shift from a view of beauty as intrinsic to a work of art, to a view that beauty is rooted rather in the viewing mind (including that of the creator) are still with us.

Whatever the nature of the faculty which distinguishes beauty from deformity may be, it clearly involves an element of judgment which is somehow linked with pleasure. But this pleasure must be disinterested pleasure, arising from an attitude of detachment in which we contemplate something simply for itself. Aesthetic pleasure (the word was coined

1.2 *The continuing emphasis of Taste as embodied in the classical tradition. 'A student conducted to Minerva who points to Greece and Italy as countries from whence he must derive the most perfect Knowledge and Taste in Elegant Architecture.' Frontispiece from R. and J. Adam's* Works in Architecture, *1822.*

by Baumgarten) cannot be attained when our mind is clouded with desire. Here we can see the metaphorical connection with eating. Taste is unlikely to be a matter of concern to someone who is starving. Gormandizing demands serenity and begins where mere nourishing leaves off. Wine tasters must spit out their vintage clarets in order to savour their quality fully. Even for Hume, who stresses utility, the pleasure we get from utility must be as a spectator of it, even when the beautiful object is useful to the judge himself.[11]

If beauty is to be located in the mind rather than the object, does this mean that beauty is entirely relative? Hume is prepared to concede this: 'Each mind perceives different beauty. One person may even perceive deformity where

1.3 In the eighteenth century, aesthetic arguments unleashed powerful sentiments often expressed in satire or caricature. Hogarth's satire is an attack on the dictatorship of Taste by the circle of Lord Burlington. Alexander Pope is shown bespattering Lord Chandos while whitewashing the new gate which Colen Cambell had built for Lord Burlington in front of his house in Piccadilly. On the pediment William Kent is admired by Raphael and Michelangelo.

A. P.r a Plasterer white washing & Bespattering
B. any Body that comes in his way
C. not a Dukes Coach as appears by y.e Crescent at one Corner
D. Taste
E. a standing Proof
F. a Labourer.
Price 6.d

another is sensible of beauty; and every individual ought to acquiesce in his own sentiment, without pretending to regulate those of others.' Edmund Burke and Richard Payne Knight argued against this view. Since all human minds were similarly constituted, albeit with varying degrees of sensibility, 'it should naturally follow that all would be displeased more or less, according to those different degrees of sensibility with the same objects'. Knight, however, recognized that Taste was at least in part relative. Hottentots, he declared, clearly preferred black women with flat noses, fuzzy hair and breasts down to their navels. No doubt, he surmised, they would be quite

indifferent to the slender charms of an English society maiden in a muslin gown! That was part of their natural endowment and there was no point in expecting our standards of beauty to apply to them.[12]

Whether democratic or not, all the eighteenth century philosophers who started the discussion of Taste, naturally assumed that there were indeed standards of Taste. The cultural norms of the day were not to be challenged. By standards were meant criteria which would account for our judgments between good and bad Taste. However, since beauty was supposed to be attached to subtle sensations in the mind, it was very difficult to decide how to determine such standards. Two complementary difficulties arose. First, assuming that you possessed a rightly constituted mind with a suitable delicacy of Taste, what qualities in objects were fitted to arouse the faculty of pleasurable discrimination? Answers to this question were often rather lame and tautologous (greatness, novelty and beauty, according to Addison). Second, how could you account for the fact that people who were manifestly not coarse or insensible, did nevertheless show an embarrassing variety of Taste. That Taste is educable by exposure to, and careful study of, beautiful objects, was widely believed then as now. It is the foundation of all cultural uplift propaganda to this day. Yet it is the subjective nature of beauty that is embarrassing here. If beauty is only what some people think is beautiful and, on the other hand, 'one man's meat is another man's poison' how are we ever to decide whose Taste is worthy of general consideration?

Paradoxes such as these, which date back over two centuries, are still at the centre of disputes on cultural policy today. When the

1.4 *Many aesthetes were appalled by the Great Exhibition of 1851 and a wealth of published argument on Taste followed including*, On the Necessity for a General Diffusion of Taste among all Classes *by Sir J. Gardner Wilkinson, 1858. For Wilkinson, good forms* (left) *are characterized by the absence of decorative detail and the avoidance of opulent, bellying curves demonstrated in the bad examples* (right).

state pays for the spiritual banquet, who chooses the menu? And how are they going to explain their choice to those who do not share their Tastes? These are difficult questions in a modern democracy particularly when they are associated with moral improvement. Improving the level of national Taste has rarely been seen gastronomically—as educating the population to enjoy its portion to the full or as instruction in the most effective techniques of hedonism. Quite the contrary, it is precisely licence and luxuriousness that have been most feared. Those who urge restraint as a virtue in consumption seldom do so on the grounds that, on occasion, by contrast, it stimulates the appetites to keener pleasures. Delicacy of Taste is seen not as an aid to the voluptuary, but as an aspect of moral refinement. From Shaftesbury on, the struggles of one social group to foist its own cultural norms on to others have usually been undertaken in a spirit of militant ethical evangelism.

Discriminating palates and keen eyes

Sense, as a metaphor in the discussion of beauty, encourages us to focus attention on the immediate organs of sense. We speak of a discriminating palate, a good nose, an ear for music, a genuine feel, above all, an eye for beauty. Educating Taste envisaged in this way becomes a matter of training the organs of sense in the direction of greater acuity. Discernment is seen as a perceptual matter, the ability to notice fine-grained detail, to detect small variations, to respond to nuance. If successful, Taste education in this form would enable someone more easily to see the point in a story or painting.

1.5 *Most aesthetic experiences are so complex that initially we need a guide to show us what to look for. A tour guide points out the notable features of the historic confection of Randolph Hearst's* Casa Grande (*Hearst Castle*), *San Simeon, California.*

Inherent in this approach is the tacit assumption that if someone doesn't appreciate or admire something it is because he is unable to perceive whatever it is that is admirable. Explanation consists of identifying the features which are admirable, drawing to his attention aspects of form or colour, or plot or rhythm, he may not have seen. There is no doubt that there is much that is valuable in this technique. We are all aware of the need for a guide to complex experiences, someone who enables us initially to grasp a few salient features, and then points out subsidiary detail and unnoticed relationships. Most great art is so complicated that we can easily be overwhelmed. Unless we are primed on what to look for, we can come away convinced that we failed to see the significance of an object that by all accounts was a miraculous piece of work. When we listen to the cicerone in a great cathedral directing the gaze of tourists to certain figures or architectural detail, or when we brief our students on points to look out for when they visit an exhibition, we are endorsing the model of discrimination as acuity of perception.

Modern theories of perception provide good warrant for this approach.[13] In place of earlier passive theories of perception, which showed the eye as a kind of camera registering impressions, we now speak of the eye-brain system as an active computer-like analyzer of visual information. Because of the overwhelming quantity of information constantly presented to the eye, we must be selective in our attention. This is done by first discerning certain significant features which enable us to construct perceptual *figures*.

A figure, once established, causes the brain to suppress other information which is seen as generalized and vague, a mere background. In viewing works of art which involve a complex hierarchy of interlocking orders we necessarily need to limit our attention. It must initially be focussed on to certain central orders which we see as figure. Once these are established in our minds we can analyze the ground, seeing it as figure in turn. We can progressively decode images with enormous quantities of visual information by grouping together millions of tiny *bits* into whole units or *chunks*. Help in suggesting appropriate figures is all the more important when the complex orders are those of abstract relationships, proportions or ratios, or the interconnection of features rather than discrete features themselves. Many significant features are small; to perceive beauty or quality in a product may require simultaneous scanning for many tiny features. The craftsman or connoisseur runs his eye quickly over an item and pronounces upon its merit at once. Such diffuse scanning can only be learned by example and training.

Even having a name can help us notice something. This is especially true of colour where an ability to discriminate between (tell apart) small intervals of hue varies around the colour circle, being most acute in those areas where there is a large vocabulary of colour terms. Compare and contrast—the old staple of the lecture room exposition of Taste—is the key to Taste education viewed as a matter of increasing perceptual acuity. It is very difficult to establish standards except by comparison. By comparing artefacts which are progressively closer in appearance we can focus more and more attention on minute differences. This technique may be transferred to the activity of gormandizing. A gourmet trains his palate to savour greater and greater refinement, to relish smaller and smaller nuances. Wine tasters in competition bracket a particular vintage by narrowing the comparisons which frame a particular flavour or taste. Moreover, verbal description and classification, even anecdote, may help to recall past sensory experiences for present comparison. A skilled gourmet can compare his present pleasure with the liveliest memories of comparable instances. But who are the gourmets of art, the wine tasters of the beautiful? How do we learn to discriminate what is best once we remove Taste from its anchorage in the pleasures of the table?

1.6 *Complex aesthetic experiences are approached piece-meal, with certain elements seen as figure while the remainder are relegated to back-ground attention. Computer simulation of the figure/ground effect in the perception of a painting by Mantegna.*

An interesting early attempt to decide such matters on a quasi-scientific basis was made by Margaret Bulley.[14] In her book *Have You Good Taste?* of 1933, she asked a panel of experts ('the Director of the Courtauld Institute, the Director of the National Gallery, the Director of the Victoria and Albert Museum, the Director of the Central School of Arts and Crafts, the editor of the *Burlington Magazine* and Mr Roger Fry') to choose pairs of photographs of particular product types: chairs, carpets, wallpapers, etc. Within each set one item was judged the better of the pair. Readers were invited to try their own hand at this paired-comparison test. They could check their scores at the back of the book where they could also read the experts' explanations for their particular choices.

Later, a selection of nine pairs of products was printed in *The Listener*, in a pioneering use of the radio audience as a population for a sociopsychological survey. Listeners were

1.7 Have You Good Taste? *Listeners to a national radio service were invited to choose between the paired comparisons (good and bad) in the first national survey of public Taste. Contemporary examples of industrial artefacts mingled with historic prototypes but the unspoken assumptions about what features characterized good Taste were identical with those of Wilkinson nearly a century earlier.*

invited to write in with their own judgments which were subsequently analyzed. Cyril Burt, Professor of Psychology at the University of London, evaluated the results. They make fascinating reading today. Of those who replied, 'it will be seen that those who had enjoyed a university education were distinctly superior in Taste to those who had received an elementary education only'. (Of the university men the psychologists were most superior.) 'Among those at the other end of the scale . . . the best are those who described themselves as artists, even they however are below the general average of the whole population . . . the poorest of all are those we have roughly classified as labourers.' Moreover, Burt continued, 'Men of the highest eminence in their own respective spheres were good enough to send in their judgements.' (He gives a list which includes great names like Bertrand Russell, James Jeans, Oliver Lodge, Julian Huxley, Clive Bell, Eric Gill and Walter de la Mare.) 'It is extremely interesting to note that persons of this eminence no matter what their sphere of work send in replies that are invariably superior to the replies of others following the same calling.' Burt noted that it was a pioneering test, but regarded it as a promising demonstration that Taste could be measured under controlled conditions, and called for more empirical research.

It would be easy to pour scorn on such efforts. Much additional research has been undertaken in the years since, alas most of it contradictory and inconclusive. Given the social basis of the university population at the time, it is hardly surprising that they, and the experts, came from the same, more or less homogeneous, cultural background. Certainly, university men as a whole are not notoriously given to discrimination in the arts, whatever skills they may have acquired in discriminating other offerings at High Table! Nevertheless, the results, meagre as they are, can be interpreted at face value. Those whose occupations are of a humbler nature may well be lacking in particular consumption skills, being culturally unfamiliar with gormandizing in the particular areas chosen by Bulley and her team of experts. Abundant evidence exists that working class people are just as capable as professors of minute discrimination in areas that are culturally valid for them, for example in the many hobbies which involve breeding and rearing animals or the cultivation of garden produce and flowers (Plate 1). Gormandizing in the field of interior decoration is probably not culturally valid for certain

social groups and it is a question of serious debate whether or not Taste in this area should be subjected to efforts at improvement.

Approximately fifty years later, in the United Kingdom, the BBC, now using television, broadcast a contemporary version of Bulley's early effort, this time using current designs for a series of national design awards. Again, items were selected by a panel of experts, but this time they were subsequently presented as a series of exhibitions around the country. Members of the public then voted on their best design. Not surprisingly, in the first series of awards, there was, as before, little correlation between the public's favourite and that selected by the experts.[15]

It appears Hume was right, Taste is relative. While experimental psychology may be able to show universal agreement on simple matters like preferred colours or the most harmonious proportions of rectangles, all the evidence is that, in anything more complex, more close to the objects of everyday secular use, discrimination, judgment, preference and pleasure are highly variable, both between cultural subgroups and individuals within them. Taste is certainly not a unitary faculty which one either has or has not. Purpose and intention must also be included. Connoisseurs, collectors, critics or dealers may well need the keen eye and discriminating palate. But many people use their interior decoration for other

1.9 *Johan Kaspar Lavater's physiognomic characterizations of the four Temperaments, an early attempt to relate internal emotional states to external appearances.*

purposes. Perhaps they quite like choosing furniture but they can't see any point in making a meal out of it.

Taste and temperament

What, however, of those who simply beg to differ? What happens if a paired-comparison test suggests a split of opinion even within a particular social group? Many individuals invariably disagree with the official position on a particular matter of Taste. They can perfectly well see the point being made, but demonstration does not elicit agreement. When such issues arise, men must take sides. But what draws a man to one side or the other? Is it mere chance? Most people would think not.

With hindsight, at any rate, we can usually see that somebody was bound to feel as he did. Even though we may have no previous evidence of his opinions on a particular matter, we can see that to do otherwise would have been for him completely out of character. We do have some intuitive sense of a close connection between the particular judgments an individual might make and his general behaviour, between his Taste and his temperament. It is a commonplace to say of a man that his choice of clothes, car, or wife was characteristic, or that they were typical expressions of his personality. If, however, we are to say that someone's Taste is related to his temperament, we first need a proper account of temperament and, second, an explicit account of the precise nature of the relationship between temperament and Taste.

The attempt to classify mankind into different temperaments or personality types goes back to the beginning of natural philosophy.[16] Galen, echoing the earlier ideas of Hippocrates, the great physician of the fifth century BC, proposed to relate different types of men to differences in physical constitution. In his theory of the bodily humours (or fluids) he suggested that a preponderance of one type of fluid over another caused differences in behaviour. A sanguine person, full of enthusiasm, was supposed to owe his temperament to the strength of the blood. Black bile lay behind the sadness of the melancholic. Irritability in choleric temperaments was excited by an excess of yellow bile, while the dullness of the phlegmatic was due to the influence of phlegm. There are two parts to the theory: first, a notion of personality types in the sense of characteristic bundles of traits or behavioural stereotypes, and second, a physical explanation of these types.

Plato attempted a rather different description of personality from a purely psychological point of view.[17] According to him the soul was tripartite, being based on reason, the fighting spirit (passion) and desire or appetite. Men may be divided into three primary kinds depending on whether reason, passion or desire predominates. This particular typology surfaced again much later when Hume writes of 'the Epicurean—the man of Elegance and Pleasure, the Stoic or Man of Action and Virtue, the Platonist or Man of Contemplation and Philosophical Devotion'.[18] There are echoes of these ideas in more recent typologies devised for marketing research.

Modern theories of the temperaments date back to Kant's reworking of the eighteenth century legacy of the physical ideas of Galen.[19] For Kant, the important differences were between the sanguine and melancholic temperaments which are predominantly volitional. This particular division, in which there are only four types, does not correspond very adequately with the facts. A more subtle division was later devised by Wundt who suggested strength of feeling or effect as primary criteria, with the speed of change of the emotions as secondary criteria. Cholerics and melancholics have strong feelings. Phlegmatics and sanguine types have weak ones. A high rate of change occurs in sanguines and cholerics, a slow rate in phlegmatics and melancholics. With Wundt we move from a classification system envisaged in terms of fixed categories—separate boxes or pigeonholes—to the notion of continuous variation and a two-dimensional map. The four temperaments correspond to the four quadrants of the compass.

A significant development of the traditional Galen-Kant-Wundt school of thought concerning personality types is the work of Jung. According to Jung, the major cause of differences in temperamental type was what he called *introversion-extroversion*. These terms refer to the tendencies of a person's instinctive energies to be directed outward, towards the objects of the external world, or inward towards inner mental states. Introversion-extroversion is the major axis of orientation of the personality. It may, however, be expressed in a number of functions: thinking, feeling, sensing, intuition. The first two are called rational functions because they involve judgment, the last two are irrational. Since the work of Jung, which established this major axis of orientation, research into personality types has been vastly aided by the invention of the computer. So-called *factor analysis* enables bundles of correlating traits to be extracted from the statistics of survey and questionnaire material.[20] Although the process of factor analysis has enabled many, more or less autonomous, personality factors to be identified, it is still considered that these can be subsumed under the broad introversion-extroversion scale, together with another independent scale; neuroticism versus stability, relating to the strength of the ego (Eysenck).

What do these exercises in classification offer for the study of Taste, in particular for the study of the ways in which we choose and savour our goods? Here we immediately run up against the problem of obtaining a clear understanding of the relationship between Taste and temperament. Unless both Taste and temperament can be independently and objectively described, any relationship between them is liable to be based merely on tautology. Certainly the relationship between a person's system of preferences—his Taste—and his

1.10 Illicit projection of human emotions on to inanimate objects ('the pathetic fallacy'). Joan Evans used the later emotional typology of Jung in her efforts to attribute expressive temperaments to works of art themselves. 'Quick introvert' expressed on the frieze on the west door of Notre Dame in Paris (left) 'Quick extrovert' expressed on corsage ornament by Réné Lalique (right).

temperament (perhaps defined by the scientific methods of analysis described by Eysenck) is not one of cause and effect. A man's choice of loud ties is not caused by his extrovert temperament. Rather it is symptomatic of it, part of the bundle of traits and characteristics that lead us to judge him an extrovert.

Joan Evans' book *Taste and Temperament* is a classic case of circular argumentation.[21] She proceeds from the Wundt-Jung typology to label both artists and their work as slow or quick introverts or extroverts. Since most of the artists she describes are dead, and our knowledge of their personality scanty and anecdotal, these attributions lean heavily on the works themselves. In turn, these acquire personality labels so that, for example, a piece of decorative frieze from the west door of Notre Dame, Paris, becomes 'quick introvert'. To project the typology of character onto works of art is, of course, the ancient pathetic fallacy. It is only harmful once we forget that we are using a convenient verbal shorthand

and come really to imagine that a particular type of foliage can be introverted or extroverted. Raised to the level of grand generalization about styles in art, the Jungian apparatus plainly yields nonsense: 'the highly organized conditions of modern city life have recently given the slow extroverts fresh fields to conquer. Reinforced concrete is an ideal material for their use; and the modern skyscraper and the modern block of flats, plain as a box and huge as a cliff, are their creations.'[22]

More interesting than such curiosities are recent attempts to apply more or less respectable research techniques to the study of discrimination and preference. Many years ago, Burt used the two scales of the Wundt-Jung typology to classify a group of subjects who were then asked to indicate their preferences for various types of painting—Romantic, Realist, Impressionist and Classical. He was able to show some moderately convincing correlations. His unstable extrovert liked emotional pictures, dramatic events or scenes with a human interest. Stable extroverts preferred representation, utilitarian or functional criteria expressed or implied.[23] Eysenck has done some similar work with poetry. A division of poems, into complex and simple, correlated highly with the introvert-extrovert scale, extroverts preferring simple poetry.[24]

In recent years there have been many attempts to put this characterological approach to work in the field of consumer goods. Marketing specialists have tried to identify correlations between preferences for given styles in, for example, household furniture, with personality types. Mary Blackburn was able to show, at least among the college graduates she studied, that there was a correlation between personality types and choice of

15

Andy

He's young, he's got money to spend. Andy seeks his own pleasures quite selfishly and has few moral scruples. He's educated and ambitious in his job.

Age 34, up-grade. 16%

Brian

The conventional busy Dad. Brian works hard, both at his home and his job. He's well-off, outgoing and liberal.

Age 41, average grade. 18%

Charlie

A disappointed and resentful working-class man. Charlie is bored and badly paid. He hopes his children will do better than he did. He's the strongest labour supporter.

Age 43, down-grade. 17%

Dennis

Uninvolved and depressed. Unable to take much interest in anything. Dennis just about gets by. He likes sweets and does not care for savoury things.

Age 44, average grade. 21%

Edward

Self-disciplined and independent. Edward is suspicious of the consumer society. He's quite well-off and tight-fisted. He has few worries or regrets.

Age 52, up-grade. 15%

Fred

The traditional older working-class man. Fred is pernickety and is sorry that the good old days are gone. He's struggling with old age and a low income, but with good humour and grit.

Age 53, down-grade. 13%

1.11 *Contemporary physiognomy uses caricatured stereotypes to depict the classification of populations into 'Lifestyle' categories. These derive from questionnaire material on subjects attitudes, interests and opinions, correlated with demographic information on age, occupation and education. As a marketing tool Lifestyle is alleged to be superior to purely demographic classifications in locating patterns of Taste in a population. British men by Leo Burnett Life Style Research.*

living room furniture.[25] She showed her subjects cards on which there were line drawings of chairs, tables and other items in various broad stylistic categories (Early American, Contemporary, Mediterranean, Modern and Provincial). Such drawings form a test instrument called the Turner Furniture Style Preference Test.

Blackburn was able to show that, in two cases, there were definite correlations between a preference, as shown on the Turner Test, and personality, as registered by another pencil and paper questionnaire test called the Myer-Briggs Type Indicator. This scores personality along four different indexes: extrovert-introvert, sensory-intuition, thinking-feeling and judging-perceiving. According to Blackburn, 'those preferring Provincial style furniture were found to be sensors, while those preferring Modern style furniture were intuitors and thinkers. Those subjects having a preference for Mediterranean furniture were classified as feelers.' Statistical significance, though real enough, was not spectacular. In addition, results were dependent on the subjects' abilities to evaluate crude drawings which attenuated or degraded the stylistic features of the artefacts drastically. Moreover, it is not clear that potential purchasers of household goods actually rely on this particular stylistic classification at all. (We shall come to the problem of individual taxonomies later.) Apart from this poverty of presentation which leaves out the details of materials, surfaces, finishes and colour—the very imagery which, in reality, seduces a potential buyer into the act of purchase—there is a basic problem about such laboratory research.

Human typology at this level is just too remote from the details of making a choice to be usefully predictive. We can see after the event that so and so's tie was typical of his extrovert personality, but we couldn't have been sure that he would have bought it beforehand. Brillat-Savarin wrote in *The Physiology of Taste*: 'Tell me what you eat and I'll tell you what you are.'[26] It is not so easy to effect the reverse proposition: 'Tell me what you are and I'll tell you what you eat.' Personality variables have proved their worth in market research but only when incorporated into much more complex surveys of patterns of social and consumer behaviour, so-called *lifestyle profiles*.[27]

Attitudes, beliefs and choices

What then governs our behaviour when we choose?[28] Traditional aesthetic theory suggests that once we can perceive the difference between beauty and deformity then the pleasure which attaches to the former will naturally cause us to prefer it. We would actively choose it, buy it, or collect it. In fact, our behaviour when we choose is much more complex. Any advertiser knows that merely pointing out the respective beauties and deformities of particular products by no means ensures that potential customers will choose accordingly. Every teacher of art or design knows that this is also true of the teaching process. Students do not shift their allegiances on receipt of information about beauty or deformity, even when this is accompanied by sophisticated techniques for calling their attention to details of form or symbol. Our preferences are bound up with our attitudes and beliefs, not only to the product in question, but also to the act of choosing. What must be shifted is not just our attention, but our value system.

Rhetoric, the art of persuasion, is designed for just this purpose. Advertising is rarely concerned to point out the various beauties and deformities of the products. Advertisers deploy a vast and sophisticated visual rhetoric, not to inform, but to influence. Persuasion as an industry extends from selling soap to political indoctrination. It can be benevolent, as in health propaganda against the perils of smoking, or maleficent, as when it stirs desires that cannot be assuaged by the product in question—the stimulation of sexual fantasy to sell cigarettes would be an example. Vast sums of money are involved in these activities. Consequently, a considerable research effort has been mounted to attempt to unravel those factors which are involved in forming and maintaining our attitudes and beliefs. Once these are understood then the efforts to change them can be focussed more accurately.

Because it is so important for the advertising industry, *attitude research* is an active and fast moving area of social psychology. Many rival schools abound, each of which promises something for the salesman. That which currently claims the greatest operational validity, in the sense of predicting behaviour most accurately, is based on the work of Martin Fishbein.[29] According to his formulation, our actual behaviour in any situation follows from the prior formation of a *behavioural intention* towards the particular act. This behavioural intention in turn follows from our *attitude* towards the act in question. Finally, our attitude towards the act derives from *beliefs* which we hold about it. So much seems commonsense, even commonplace. What this separation does, however, is to enable Fishbein to give precise operational meanings to the various stages from belief to act. Of course, we

all have countless beliefs about objects and potential behaviours. However, according to Fishbein and his followers, this doesn't matter. If we are asked about our beliefs, then, because of inherent information processing limitations in the brain, the first seven that we identify are the ones which are salient. These, for all practical purposes, determine our attitude to the object in question.

Using suitable questionnaire design, and techniques for scaling the degree or strength of our beliefs, our attitudes can be given a numerical value. There are two components to the complete Fishbein formulation, an attitudinal component (just described) and a normative component representing beliefs about social norms—what we think about how other people feel about the act in question—together with our motivations to comply with them. These again can be measured. The simple (algebraic) sum of the two components gives the behavioural intention. Many experiments have shown that subsequent behaviour is highly correlated with this particular measure. Our small set of salient beliefs form the inferential base against which newly perceived information is evaluated.

There are all sorts of problems in the application of Fishbein's measures. Clearly the level of specificity of the measurement must be the same as that of the behaviour it is hoped to predict. A high positive attitude towards art doesn't necessarily mean one will buy a postcard of a particular artist on any given visit to the museum. Other unforeseen factors might supervene if the execution of the act is long delayed after the measured intention. And there are, of course, many critics of Fishbein. Many refinements and rival models are on offer. Nevertheless, the technique does enable

1.12 *'Is this really me?' The process of choosing is complex and invariably involves the mental matching of potential purchases against existing self-images.*

the market researcher to unpack the attitudes of potential customers and enable their salient beliefs to be isolated. Persuasion works, it would seem, by shifting a small repertoire of salient beliefs. It may be easier to do this by displacement than by refutation, that is by installing a new belief on our limited agenda at the expense of another, either one weakly held or even perhaps one about which our beliefs are negative. Taste education as an exercise in persuasion seeks to set the agenda of salient beliefs about particular products.

Until now, the scientific approach of the market research psychologist has not been employed in such non-commercial areas as discrimination between the beautiful and the deformed. Yet throughout the educational process, certainly in such fields as architecture and all aspects of design, the inculcation of Taste is a prominent part of the curriculum. Here, as in the wider field of consumer education or the appreciation of the arts, the techniques used are, compared with those at the disposal of market research, amateurish. This is not to say that they are ineffective—we simply don't know.

Knowing what you (don't) like

What actually goes on in our heads when we choose a new outfit to wear or, on much rarer occasions, a new set of furniture for the living room? We start by choosing a shop or range of shops that seems intuitively 'us'. An overall imagery, the architecture of the facade, the shop windows, the display that catches our eye from the street as we walk by, seizes our attention as somehow possible. For many people the person-to-person encounter with the shop assistant is daunting. We run the risk of embarrassment and so we do what we can to minimize it by choosing the shop that corresponds in some way to our self-image, our picture of ourselves as we are and, perhaps, as we aspire to be.

We may want, perhaps, a jacket or skirt. We describe our rough and provisional ideas in general terms: I like brown, or perhaps grey, not navy blue. We may point to something that has caught our eye in the window. The shop-keeper brings us some things to try on. We retire to the changing room and proceed to change identities in front of the encircling mirrors. Some garments are quickly rejected.

They are not us at all. We may end up with several which form a short-list from which a final choice is to be made. From here on, the process of choosing what we like becomes complex. We may discuss the various positive and negative features of perhaps three competing models, noting differences in their perceived desirability and comparing this with price. (Unless we are very wealthy this is usually a measure of their undesirability.)

Our shopkeeper, or his assistant, may make suggestions stressing good points that perhaps we hadn't picked up, and reinforcing any doubts by assuring that our choice is absolutely *à la mode*. We eliminate one of the last three and then, finally, run-off the last pair against each other. Sometimes we are stuck. No one outfit seems just right. We may leave the store altogether with apologies to the shopkeeper and try elsewhere. We didn't really know what we were looking for but we knew it wasn't there. Someone looking for furniture has an even more difficult task. They can't try it on, usually they can't even take it home in photographic form. Choosing what suits you entails the difficult task of abstracting the object from its physical location in the shop and mentally inserting it into a memorized image of the room in which it is to go. It is not surprising that many people express dissatisfaction with their choice of furniture.

Evaluation, inference and choice are aspects of an extremely complex sequence of behaviour. A considerable amount of evidence exists to show that people have a wide variety of choosing strategies which they selectively deploy depending on the nature of their problem, their familiarity with it, and their own current predispositions. Choosing behaviour may be simple—selecting one from a small number of similar items on the basis of one criterion. It may, however, entail checking a list of alternatives against several attributes. These may be differently weighted, both positively and negatively. Finally, we may be in the much more complex situation of trying to evaluate complex trade offs between different attributes, which are no longer seen as independent variables but variables which interact. Psychologists have attempted to model the various possibilities in mathematical terms and then test the models under controlled conditions. Despite a great deal of sophisticated work, the predictive capability of this branch of science is still relatively meagre. Not only is the repertoire of possible judgment routines large, but there is, at the moment, no clear way of predicting which predispositional variables will become salient in a particular decision.

Hamsen, in his review of the then current state of the art, distinguished four levels of predispositional variables ranging from broad personality categories at the most general level, to choice-specific predispositions such as preferences and intentions.[30] We have seen already that general personality tests have but a modest predictive power when it comes to consumer choice. At the other end of the scale, predictions about likely behaviours can become expensively tautologous—the man who prefers Snook's beer is likely to choose Snook's beer. Fishbein's belief, attitude, intuition and behaviour analysis (Hamsen discusses a great number of variations on this theme) comes usefully between these two extremes.

There is an equally wide range in the level of the stimulus which sets up the conflict situation in which we must choose. This can vary from a simple physical stimulus such as colour (which can be described objectively in physical terms)

1.13 *Taste as a metaphor. The senses have always been used as metaphors for other more abstract human emotions. The gustatory is here allied to the emotion of love in this eighteenth century allegory by B. Lens.*

TASTING

Represented by two Women in a Garden, of one seated & eating an Orange, expressing by her gay air of pleasure afforded her by that noble sence, the other is the figure of a Woman pulling some fruit, in order to eat it; there are also Cupids eating Oranges, to shew the pleasures of love, consist chiefly in Tasting.

street for a questionnaire session. This will always be expensive. At the present time, beyond the small but useful predictive success that can be demonstrated, psychological theories of choice do at least serve to provide an empirical thrust to wider speculation about our Tastes. We must make what real gains we can. For we must remember that all of the intractable problems of the relationship between situational variables and predispositions were there in the more prosaic language of those eighteenth century philosophers who pondered in which way Tastes were relative and what particulars characterized the man of delicate sensibility.

The pleasures of the table—Taste as a metaphor

So familiar are the myriad metaphorical extrapolations that we forget that Taste is a metaphor, a metaphor that depends for its effect on latent resemblances between the phenomenon in question and the pleasures (and pains) of eating, or our affections and aversions among items of nourishment. Regarded literally, eating is merely part of a cybernetic machinery designed to maintain necessary levels of nutrition. We use energy, burn up our stored food, feel hungry and act accordingly. We stop feeling hungry when the balance of nutrition is restored. But eating is not just about sheer quantity. Nor is Taste related in any clear fashion to the gratification arising from the periodic abolition of the feeling of hunger. Our taste-buds can be stimulated in very diverse ways. Four basic dimensions of flavour, plus some textural sensations,

to complicated internal perceptions of novelty and complexity. No doubt market research techniques will become progressively more effective, not least because the elaborate models of choice behaviour, provided by psychological theory, become progressively easier to apply as computer power becomes ever cheaper. Finally though, someone has to knock on doors or stop the passer-by in the

combine to create the entire gamut of gastronomic experiences. We rate these experiences
along a scale between gratification and aversion, pleasure and disgust. We soon learn
(from our parents, if not from unpleasant
biological reminders in ourselves) that what
strikes us as particularly pleasurable is not
necessarily good for us or even calculated to
allay hunger.

A vast and complicated cultural apparatus
is designed to shape our appetites and the
pleasures that go with their satisfaction. As
children we start with a small (and sometimes
surprising) repertoire of acceptable foods,
usually preferring sweet things. Persuasion,
and encouragement from those in authority, or
from the leaders in our peer group, tempts us to
try strange foods and overcome our initial
aversion or disinterest. We thereby enlarge our
Taste and acquire a more sophisticated palate.

Equally importantly, we are educated in
the ways of maximizing the pleasures of eating
by adopting a regime of alternate fasting and
feasting (especially in the normal circumstances of chronic food shortage for most of
mankind). In medieval Europe, for example,
this regime became ritualized and the calendar
became a patchwork of alternating fasts and
feasts. The gourmet is little impressed by sheer
quantity, nor is he satisfied with sheer quality—though both help. As David Berlyne has
reminded us, taking up an old theme of Wundt,
equilibrium—even the equilibrium of satiety—
means not pleasure but boredom and, conversely, pleasure necessarily entails some
discomfort to provide the essential stimulation
of contrast.[31] Crucial in that constant shifting
towards and away from the optimum stimulation which yields most pleasure is surprise.
Not too much surprise of course, but variety

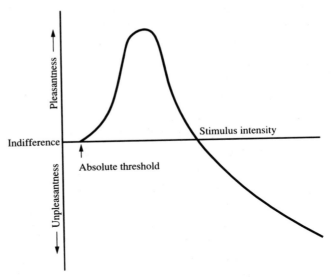

1.14 *The Wundt curve represents a very general finding that stimulation is pleasant at medium intensities but unpleasant at higher and lower extremes.*

and novelty; periods of tranquillity followed
by renewed agitation of the senses. This is the
best regimen for the sybarite.

Maintenance of relish or savour also requires subtle and unexpected combinations of
flavours, contrasts between successive dishes,
deliberate stimulation of the taste-buds by
foods which may have little or no nutritional
value but which spice others or act as appetiz-
ers. In the Middle Ages, sudden variation in the
kind and quality of the gustatory sensations
was much appreciated during long feasts,
leading to the development of the entremets—
little dishes interspersed between main
courses—whose function is well described by
their English name, 'sotelties and surprises'.[32]

Visual appearance is also important.
Brightly coloured, smooth and symmetrical
fruits are more tempting than irregular or
blotchy ones, which are perceived as blem-
ished. Size itself may be a symbol of tastiness.
When Apicius, the famous Roman gourmet,

sailed from Italy to Libya in search of ever larger prawns it was because size itself excited. An equivalent weight of smaller prawns would not have had the same effect.[33]

In all cultures, and all ages, food has been decorated to make it visually attractive and, in consequence, seductive to the palate. There are usually complex rules and conventions for what may be coloured or adorned. For example, we would not like blue meat or green milk. Sweet things on the other hand seem to inspire decoration. Elaborately decorated little sweetmeats or cakes may become important symbols in a particular social code concerned with hospitality. So universal are the cultural arrangements for the shaping of our appetites that Tastes invariably become vehicles for all manner of different social messages, as identified in the work of Claude Levi-Strauss.[34]

When we use the word Taste as a metaphor of pleasurable discrimination in other fields we carry over with it all these associations from the relishing of our physical appetites. There is one vital aspect of the gastronomical analogy which is surprisingly little studied. This is the menu. We have seen that choosing one item: a jacket, a beer, a nice chair, is complicated enough. What then about the whole sequence of interrelated decisions entailed in choosing a meal or, by analogy, an entire decor for a room? We can see at once the crucial role of the menu with its categorical groupings—hors d'oeuvres, soups, entrées, desserts—in setting up the structures within which our choices are exercised. Once there is a menu, choice becomes a matter of arbitration, not between the claims of single dishes, but of sequences. Not only must each dish be tasty, but a succession of such stimulations of the palate must be orchestrated into a convincing whole. A host of conventions and taboos tell us what, within one category, may or may not go with something in another. The sequence is also fixed by convention.

These rules drastically reduce the size of the information handling problem presented by a menu. Paradoxically, once the waiter shows you the card it is not difficult to choose a good dinner. Moreover, as every successful restaurateur knows, our choice sequences are also predictable. Yet it is curious that the notion of a menu has not been more widely explored in the application of the metaphor of Taste in other matters. Choosing furniture which goes together for a living room is surely close to choosing a dinner.

We shall return to the idea of a visual menu as an aid to the education of Taste later. For the moment let us remember that some gastronomic pleasures are simply not to be had. Too much of anything soon palls and eventually sickens. Some combinations do not work. Ice cream and mustard together would revolt most people. So it is with our choices in art or in the humbler fields of furniture and household goods. Taste here, as elsewhere, involves menu planning; the imposition of structure on our choosing. Distinguishing beauty from deformity in the sense of effecting simple and unitary either/or judgments is but a minor part of it.

Ice cream and mustard is a persuasive, if not loaded, example of gustatory incongruity. By pointing to the clash of diametrically opposite sensations—hot and cold, sweet and sour—and to the disjunction between real coldness (low temperature) and chemical hotness (burning sensations due to overstimulation) it emphasizes that there are indeed natural categories within which we make Taste judgments. By using such examples we address ourselves to an argument based on universals of Taste which operate at a biological level or, at any rate, on examples which are not merely a matter of habit or culture. We should be surprised to hear of people who ate mustard and ice cream as a matter of course. But how many of our gastronomic judgments are like that? In fact, less extreme examples are quite commonplace, for instance, the eccentric but pleasing combination of hot pastry and cold ice cream in the so-called 'Baked Alaska' pudding. Given less extreme examples though we are soon back with the obvious fact that Tastes vary from individual to individual and more broadly from one social group to another. This is even more the case in those metaphorical extrapolations from gastronomy— our aesthetic Tastes, and our Tastes in domestic goods and settings.

So what can usefully be said about Taste at this universal level? Deriving accounts of particular behaviours—especially behaviours concerned with the minutiae of Taste judgments—from the generality of human nature has not hitherto proved instructive. Explanations at the level of instincts or natural passions explain far too much. Avoiding obvious nonsense on one hand, and platitude on the other, means hedging them about with just such reservations as Duveen's rightly constituted minds, reservations which beg the very questions they set out to answer. Since matters of Taste are, in the end, social matters, it is far more useful to build an account of the operation of Taste on a deeper understanding of society itself.

How different Tastes are located in different parts of society and, in particular, how different Tastes relate to the socioeconomic arrangements of modern industrial economies are the subjects of Chapters 4, 5 and 6. But before we come to them, we need to enlarge our understanding of the nature of Taste. Clearly, if we are to tackle the issue of critical judgment in pluralistic societies like our own we must move away from the view of those who think, like Duveen, that Taste is concerned with the perception of beauty or deformity in certain objects and settings. To pursue this line runs straight into the objection with which we began, that there is today no general agreement on which artefacts are the proper object of study, even within the fine arts themselves, let alone among the innumerable artefacts of commerce. Nor is it acceptable any longer to leave the selection of certain beautiful objects as uniquely appropriate for the purposes of comparison to experts, whether these are the old aristocratic élites or new university-trained aesthetes and culturati.

One way out of this impasse is to treat the issue as a practical one and to study as scientifically as possible how we make critical judgments. Paradoxically, in the recent past, this has been regarded, for the most part, as a matter, not of how to identify the beautiful in works of art, but of how we choose between one consumer product and another. Published studies have been heavily influenced by the needs of commerce and especially of marketing. Taste, however, is not limited to registering a preference for one or even a few objects, whether these are works of art or ordinary items of commerce. Taste is concerned with wider patterns of likes and dislikes. It is concerned with the integration of individual critical judgments into enduring patterns of behaviour which shape individual and group lifestyles and cultures.

One area of scientific enquiry which has fruitfully influenced recent views on the nature of Taste is the study of language. At first sight perhaps, the study of language does not seem especially relevant to an understanding of the nature of appreciation or the exercise of critical judgment—even though we discuss continually our likes and dislikes in language and, indeed, for many groups in so-called consumer societies, such matters dominate most conversation. Yet there are some important features of Taste which make the analogy with language persuasive. Taste, like language, is structured, it is governed by some sort of organizing rules or principles even though it is often difficult to be precise about their nature. At the same time, like language, Taste is open-ended and creative. Previously unknown objects and situations can be effortlessly incorporated into existing ensembles without rupture. We can extend our present Tastes into unknown futures. Like language, Taste is recursive—we can always add new distinctions, create new relationships, establish new saliencies or insist on new emphases within a particular congerie of choice. And, although modern linguistics has sharpened the analogies that can be drawn, such observations as these are, as we shall see, by no means new.

Notes and References to Chapter 1

1 E. J. Duveen, *Colour in the House—with notes on architecture, sculpture, painting and upon decoration and good taste*, London: G. Allen, 1911.

2 See A. Wittlin, *Museums in Search of a Usable Future*, Cambridge, Mass: MIT Press, 1970, for an account of the evolution of collections.

3 K. Jex-Blake and E. Sellers, *The Elder Pliny's Chapters on the History of Art* (Naturalis historia selections), Chicago: Ares Publishers, 1982 (facsmile of the 1986 edition).

4 G. Vasari, *The Lives of the Most Eminent Painters, Sculptors and Architects* (trans. A. B. Hinds, revised edition, London: Dent), New York: Dutton, 1963.

5 See J. Dover Wilson, *Life in Shakespeare's England*, Harmondsworth: Penguin, 1968. (Originally CUP, 1911.)

6 J. Huizinga, *The Waning of the Middle Ages*, London: Penguin, 1955, p. 249.

7 W. J. Hipple, *The Beautiful, the Picturesque and the Sublime*, Carbondale: Southern Illinois University Press, 1957, is still the best general introduction to the work of these eighteenth century aesthetes.

8 For a discussion of the issues raised by the 'battle' between the Poussinists and the Rubenists for the teaching of art see N. Pevsner, *Academies of Art*, Cambridge: CUP, 1940, p. 103. R. G. Saisselin, *Taste in Eighteenth Century France*, New York: Syracuse University Press, 1965, p. 15 *et seq.* deals with the background to the 'quarrel of the ancients and the moderns' in more detail. The issue has persisted over the centuries in one form or another. In recent times, H. Wöllflin, *Principles of Art History—the development of style in later art* (translation of *Kunstgeschichtliche Grundbegriffe* 1929), trans. M. D. Hottinger, 7th edition, London: Bell, 1950, saw much the same contrast between stylistic approaches in terms of the polarities 'linear' versus 'painterly' and 'clear' versus 'unclear'.

9 On Shaftesbury's idealism see K. Gilbert and H. Kuhn, *A History of Aesthetics*, London: Thames and Hudson, 1956, p. 236. An easy access to Shaftesbury's thought is the extracts collected in A. Hofstadter and R. Kuhn, *Philosophies of Art and Beauty*, Chicago: University of Chicago Press, 1964, p. 239.

10 See W. J. Hipple, *op. cit.*, p. 37, for a discussion of Hume's aesthetics and its relation to his doctrine of the association of ideas.

11 W. J. Hipple, *op. cit.*, p. 39 discusses Hume's ideas on the relationship between utility and beauty. Although Hume stresses utility he does so within a broad sense of the term and is ready to concede the fact of the immediate perception of beauty prior to any realization of possible usefulness.

12 R. Payne Knight, *An Analytical Enquiry into the Principles of Taste*, Westmead, Kent: Gregg International Publishers, 1972 (originally published in 1808), pp. 13-14.

13 For example E. H. Gombrich, *Art and Illusion*, Oxford: Phaidon Press, 1960 and E. H. Gombrich, J. Hochberg and M. Black, *Art, Perception and Reality*, Baltimore: Johns Hopkins University Press, 1972.

14 M. Bulley, *Have You Good Taste?* London: Methuen, 1933.

15 *BBC Design 1990*, Redwood Publications Ltd, London, 1990. In the 1990 series there was again a marked difference between the views of the experts and those of the voting public, only the entry for the graphics section (a series of comic postage stamps) scored a partial overlap.

16 For a brief history of the theory of temperaments see J. Evans, *Taste and Temperament*, London: Jonathan Cape, 1939, p. 17.

17 Plato, *The Republic*, Book 9, in E. Hamilton and H. Cairns (Eds.), *Collected Works*, New York: Bollingen Press, 1961, p. 807.

18 D. Hume, *Essays Moral, Political and Literary*, XV–XVIII, Volume 1, 1875 Edition, p. 197.

19 For references see J. Evans *op. cit.*, p. 21.

20 Guildford and Cattell are two of the prominent workers in this field. For a review see H. J. Eysenck, *Personality, Structure and Measurement*, London: Routledge and Kegan Paul, 1969. H. J. Eysenck (Ed.), *The Measurement of Personality*, Lancaster: RTP, 1976.

21 J. Evans, *op. cit.*

22 J. Evans, *op. cit.*, p. 101.

23 See C. W. Valentine, *Experimental Psychology of Beauty*, London: Methuen, 1962, p. 167.

24 C. W. Valentine, *op. cit.*, p. 346.

25 M. Blackburn, *Preferences for Furniture Styles as related to Personality Type and other Selected Variables*, Ph.D. thesis submitted to the Faculty of Graduate Studies, University of North Carolina, Greensboro', Carolina, 1978.

26 J. A. Brillat-Savarin, *The Physiology of Taste*, with an introduction by A. Machen, New York: Dover Publications, 1960 (a reprint of the English edition of 1925).

27 See W. Wells (Ed.), *Lifestyle and Psychographics*, Chicago: American Marketing Association, 1974.

28 For a useful general introduction to the subject of consumer choice behaviour, see M. Tuck, *How Do We Choose*, London: Methuen, 1976.

29 M. Fishbein and I. Ajzen, *Belief, Attitude, Intention, Behaviour*, Reading, Mass: Addison-Wellesley, 1975.

30 F. Hamsen, "Psychological Theories of Consumer Choice." *Journal of Consumer Research*, Volume 13, December 1976, p. 117.

31 D. A. Berlyne, *Conflict, Arousal and Curiosity*, New York: McGraw-Hill, 1960, p. 200.

32 B. A. Henisch, *Fast and Feast—food in mediaeval society*, Philadelphia: Pennsylvania University Press, 1976, especially Chapter 8.

33 Atheneus, *Deipnosophists*, London: Loeb Classical Library, Heineman, 1927–41, Volume 8.

34 C. Levi-Strauss' three volumes of Mythologies, 1. *The Raw and the Cooked*, 2. *From Honey to Ashes*, and 3. *An Introduction to the Science of Table Manners*, trans. J. and D. Weightman, London: Cape, 1970, 1973, and 1978 are an astonishing attempt to unravel the metaphorical systems in the myths of indigenous South American Indians on the basis of certain primary metaphors concerned with the preparation and consumption of food. These systems, Levi-Stauss asserts, provide the structural schemata which carry other social meanings within the social structures of the tribes concerned. For a critical review of this undertaking see E. Leach, *Levi-Strauss*, London: Fontana (Modern Masters), 1970.

2. Goods and Language

2.1 *Many visual 'grammars' were published in the nineteenth century. These were collections of typical decorative forms reduced to a standard scale and drawn in a uniform style which were classified by nationality and period. Racinet's* L'Ornament Polychrome *is a French example from which the images for* Primitive (top left), *Egyptian* (top right) *and Renaissance* (bottom) *are drawn. There is invariably no information on the rules for syntax within a given style, the reader is left to deduce these for himself.*

Purifying the dialect of the tribe

From the time of the Roman rhetoricians, the metaphor of language has been widely used in the analysis of non-verbal expression in many fields, including Taste. For much of this time though, the metaphor of language was used in a non-technical manner as the study of language was itself in a pre-scientific state. However, in recent decades, the study of spoken and written language has advanced rapidly, stimulated in large part by theoretical work on linguistic structures in formal languages, especially those devised for computer programming. The success of this enterprise has inspired workers, in many ostensibly unrelated subjects, to a new interest in the application of the metaphor of language to their own field. Just how far other, non-verbal articulations of thought and feeling may be regarded as 'language-like' is a matter of complex philosophical analysis and difficult empirical enquiry. Certainly, for many critics, a brief preliminary survey of contemporary linguistic theory is merely a prelude to a conventional pre-linguistic discussion of Taste.[1] But for all the many purely ritualistic references to the creators of modern linguistics, Ferdinand de Saussure and Noam Chomsky, that abound in the literature there is, nevertheless, a considerable body of work that draws real strength from the analogy with language.

Each of the two primary categories that constitute a language—the grammar and the lexicon—has served as the starting point for somewhat different lines of critical enquiry into matters of Taste. In previous generations it was the grammar or syntax that attracted the most attention. It is easy to see why grammar—the rules for what goes where—is popular in academic circles. A grammar systematizes, and thereby fixes, the numerous and diverse, often overlapping rules for composition which are normally transmitted as disparate pieces of craft 'know-how' in the daily transactions of a master-apprentice relationship. In a craft tradition, it is not only the technical and manual skills that are passed on by demonstration and imitation. Hand in hand with these go skills of design, in the form of procedures for forward projection: bundles of strategic and tactical plans for elaborating elementary schemas step-by-step into structures that are too complex to grasp as a whole.

In contrast to these pragmatic and *ad hoc* procedures, a visual grammar establishes a well understood hierarchy of routines for the assembly of elements into a complete composition. However, it is wrong to suppose that grammatical rules were ever widely regarded as mere restrictions on otherwise spontaneous utterances. It is clear that the two famous nineteenth century grammars—Owen Jones' *The Grammar of Ornament*[2] and Charles Blanc's *Grammaire des Arts du Dessin*[3]—and, indeed, the whole *beaux arts* tradition, envisaged the use of grammar in a modern generative sense. For them, syntactical rules were conceived as something positive, as standard procedures which yet create novelty—much as, many years later, Chomsky described the creative character of sentence formation by the grammatical apparatus of natural language. That anti-academicism, which sees in rules only restrictions, is a much more recent development. A measure of the success of that earlier tradition can be seen in the fact that, in many areas of design, the contemporary student, who wants to learn 'how to do it', must still have recourse to Victorian grammars such as the treatises on pattern design by Lewis Day, himself a follower of Owen Jones.[4]

In previous centuries, it was usually changes in grammar that were crucial in the development of new styles. Changes in the rules for putting things together were immediately recognizable and telling, even when the elements—what might be termed the visual vocabulary or lexicon—were unchanged. On the other hand, the ability of a style to incorporate an incredibly disparate collection of items from a lexicon of symbols into an existing grammar is commonplace. We can see this even in an austere idiom, such as neo-Classicism, where the grammar is limited and rigorous. As it evolved during the eighteenth and nineteenth centuries, neo-Classicism smoothly incorporated oriental and primitive images alongside the conventional classical repertoire—the Egyptians and Etruscans soon sat down happily with the Greeks.[5]

However, neo-Classicism was only the beginning of nineteenth century eclecticism. The nineteenth century was a time of unparalleled social mobility and demographic upheaval. New social groups and institutions were continually being created by emerging technological and economic forces. Moreover, through trade and conquest, the discovery and diffusion of exotic and alien imagery occurred on a scale without precedent. In the welter of style, the Egyptians and Etruscans were soon joined by Red Indian and Hottentot, Persian and Hindoo, and later, by Chinese and Japanese (not to mention Goths, Vandals and Byzantines from nearer home). All this imagery was digested, without distinction, in the ecumenical workshops mass-producing new types of goods for new mass markets. The social impact of this stylistic 'Tower of Babel' was

2.2 Exaggeration of decoration to the point of distortion characterized many of the exhibits in the Great Exhibition of 1851. The resulting controversy relaunched the perennial Taste for simplicity and lead eventually to the position of Adolf Loos, 'Ornament is crime'.

2.3 Extreme simplicity and the avoidance of any extraneous decoration whatsoever is a defining characteristic of much 'modern' design. Never widely popular, it can lead in its turn to similar visual exaggerations. The chair by Eric de Graaf is surprisingly comfortable although it looks the opposite.

predictable: existing cultural patterns, embodied in traditional images and practices, simply collapsed under the load.

In the teeming new cities, as in the remote new colonial hinterland, it became harder and harder to know who you were talking to, or dining with or—horror of horrors—marrying! Problems of identification became acute and, in all areas of life, explicit rules for 'what goes where' became an urgent necessity. Strident cultural propaganda, minatory pronouncements on etiquette, authoritarian guidebooks on manners, tried in vain to replace what custom and convention had once achieved, unseen and unsaid, in the nursery, dressing-room or at the family dinner table.[6] Today, the very violence of those far-off cultural polemics—the passionate rhetoric of John Ruskin, or the sarcastic vituperation of Matthew Arnold or Charles Dickens—is striking evidence of the threat that established cultural élites perceived in these illicit appropriations, distortions and conflations of previously hallowed symbols.[7] A new obsession with symbolic purity, with keeping disparate images apart, grew hand in hand with a new social exclusiveness, an exclusiveness that physically separated servants and served in the incredibly complex architecture of the Victorian country house. How this revulsion against symbolic pollution, which began after the confusions of the Great Exhibition of 1851, led on from the clamorous denunciation of ornament as a 'sham' to its final extirpation as a 'crime' is a familiar story in histories concerned with the design of consumer goods.[8]

In the visual arts, concern with grammar progressed from an obsession with order to a complete 'purist' abstraction, free from all references to external imagery. In true purist art the only symbol permitted is the geometric structure itself: beauty is presented, as it were, naked. Whatever its immediate sources in local traditions and particular (often religious) beliefs, that confluence of ideas and images that constitutes modern abstract art expresses a fundamental revulsion from symbolic pollution and a desire to return to unpolluted wellsprings. Stéphane Mallarmé described his efforts to create an uncontaminated contemporary poetry as 'purifying the dialect of the tribe'.

For most contemporary artists and designers, the long affair with abstraction is over. Stirred once more with a desire to communicate with a real (and restive) public, their dominant concern is not with grammar but with the lexicon. However, once design has been stripped of its original conventional references, they are very difficult to replace. It requires a willing partnership between different social groups to attach specific meanings to particular forms. Artists and designers, however creative, cannot do it alone. This painful realization has led many designers and architects to adopt a new interest in the academic study of meaning. How forms carry meaning is the province of semantics, which is today what syntax was for the theoretician of the nineteenth century. Semiology is currently one of the intellectual growth industries in fields such as architecture, which are particularly exposed to the vocal public criticism of earlier abstract styles now denounced as meaningless.[9] Taste is, in our time, ineluctably bound up with the problem of communication, the communication of a sense of place and of personal and cultural identity.

What goes with what?

In this context, Taste, the choice of symbols and settings by an individual or a group, is crucial in establishing a sense of normality, an understanding of 'what is going on' in any particular scene of which we may be part. Because our lives are conducted as a series of encounters with others which occur in 'real time', we do not have the opportunity of extensive and leisurely deciphering of the

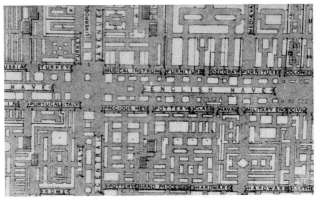

2.4 *The exhibits in the first great exhibitions were invariably laid out according to the technology of their manufacture rather than how they would be used. Plan of the Universal Exhibition of 1862.*

'goods' in the environment of any particular action scene. Instead, we have to assure ourselves at a glance that all is well in each particular setting. Yet, settings for certain action scenes invariably involve a large number of goods in a previously unseen arrangement. How do we know what goes with what—and where—so that we are able to interpret, virtually instantaneously, this previously unknown situation? Or, to take another illustration, if we propose to introduce new goods into an otherwise familiar situation—for example, new curtains in a living room—how do we know what will go? Do we have some kind of internal catalogue which tells us that this will never go with that? What would such a catalogue be like? What would be relevant axes of its categorization?

Classification, known technically as taxonomy, is an activity that flourished enormously at the end of the eighteenth century and the beginning of the nineteenth. Our first encyclopedias: the biological system for grouping flora and fauna that followed the pioneering efforts of Linneus, whose system for classifying plants was published in 1733; the universal system for classifying English words started by Roget in 1805; even that eccentric, but enormously

2.5 *Early large scale retailers faced the same problems of 'what goes where' as the great exhibitions. In this example, soft furnishings (armchairs and sofas) are grouped next to bedding. Contemporary illustration of* Aux Colonnes d'Hercules, *Paris, France, 1861.*

influential, classification of human facial appearances, Lavater's *Physiognomy*, all stem from this urge to categorize, characteristic of the Enlightenment. Later, this need to classify and to catalogue assumed a practical form when, in the middle of the nineteenth century, the problem arose of how to organize the layout of the first great *omnium gatherum* of industry in the Great Exhibition of 1851.[10] To a great extent, the arrangement eventually adopted merely continued the traditional geography of early markets, where people largely sold what they made and the stalls of one particular trade, based on a certain technology (for example, wood, metal, leather, pottery and glass), were grouped together into rows and streets. The process of manufacture, not of utilization, was the criterion chosen for the organization of the Great Exhibition. This system was very influential and still survives in Dewey's universal system for cataloguing library books.

As retail shopping developed in the later nineteenth century, a similar problem was faced by the first department stores. (William Whiteley's store in Bayswater opened its doors in 1863, *Bon Marche* followed in Paris in 1876.)

Large shops, which aspired to become 'universal providers' (the term was Whiteley's), had to organize the layout of a vast range of disparate goods so that closely related items were kept together (all the china, all the glass, etc.), yet each department had a natural set of neighbours (all the tableware—glass and ceramic—next to the cutlery and silver). Ideally, someone strolling around the shop should be encouraged to notice and desire further goods by virtue of being constantly nudged with visual suggestions which follow 'naturally' in the course of his perambulation.[11] Mail order catalogues, a more recent development, have to make a related series of decisions concerning layout, constrained by the limitations of the sequential nature of the pages. Few will read the catalogue cover to cover. Fewer still will read it in the right order. So how should the designer of such publications group items in a logical, categorically unconfusing manner yet, at the same time, encourage browsing into areas beyond the immediate interest of any one reader? Whatever the theoretical problems of achieving such categorizations, it is possible, in practice, to contrive some effective layout or pagination. It is partly a matter of tradition, but must also depend on some universally shared internal taxonomy of goods.

That such a thing exists is obvious.[12] If you ask someone to free associate words, given a starting word, knife, he will invariably respond with a series such as, fork, spoon, plate and tablecloth. There is a wide measure of agreement in the articulation of such series. We can all generate, around any word, similar sets of related words with which it has progressively diminishing affinity. The popular parlour game, *Twenty Questions*, testifies to the fact that we can partition the entire universe of possible words and concepts and arrive at just one by applying simple principles of classification.

But how do we obtain this internal structured lexicon, especially the lexicon of all man-made goods in the world, past and present? Presumably we construct our categories of goods in infancy, starting from the very specific inventory of items in our immediate domestic environment. Our first bedroom, our first home, our parents' clothes, our first familiar journeys in the pram, all presumably enter our consciousness and provide the data for the endless naming exercises which occur as we learn to speak. 'This is a clock', our mother says, and we gaze, following her finger as she points at a particular object on a particular wall. When we see a drawing of a clock in a picture book, it is that first clock that enables us to recognize the object from the drawing. These early images, of objects and pictures of objects, provide the mental scaffolding of *prototypical categories*, categories we use in ordering all later candidates for naming.[13] In some way that is little understood, the acquisition of grammatical competence enables us to exercise the logical operations of classification—inclusion and exclusion—and order the plenitude of goods into homologous collections of different types. Homes of every kind (real and pretend) provide the child with examples of canonical ensembles of what goes with what in a given physical space devoted to the activities of the family.

Usually one part of the house is heavily used living space and the goods in it may constantly be shifted in apparent confusion. Equally often, other zones will be reserved for special occasions, the goods in them remaining relatively undisturbed. We may

2.6 Prototypical categories are acquired early on in life and include only the salient defining features of a concept. Child's painting (aged 3) of a person.

venture unnoticed (and perhaps with some trepidation) into the silent and empty front room, all precisely laid out, 'everything in its right place', in a solemn and hieratic symmetry (Plate 2). When we visit someone's house it is their front room that draws us. What will it be like? If we discover that they have exactly the same layout of the same sorts of furniture and ornaments, we conclude that there is a natural order of objects in houses. Our first picture books (especially those concerned with naming) and stories are very influential in establishing a normal order of objects and a normal place for each object in relation to others. We might call these 'prototypical arrangements'. So influential are these first graphic images, that even children who live in apartments continue to draw 'home' with a pitched roof. Physical replicas in the form of doll's houses, in which minute versions of useful artefacts can be arranged and rearranged, are widely popular toys which occur in many cultures.[14]

Later, when we are older, images of the homes of famous people in books, and visits to historic houses, add to our tacit knowledge of what goes where. For those who do not spend their leisure visiting stately homes, there is always film and television which is intensely alive to the importance of characteristic settings in attracting audiences. Exposure to the media thus brings an enhanced awareness of the 'proper' furnishing of a room, or the 'proper' arrangement of clothes for an outfit, to everyone born into a modern industrial society. This awareness is constantly reinforced in play, importantly in the endless dressing up games or 'mothers and fathers' in which children adopt a space and convert it to a make-believe setting of their own choosing. During adolescence there is usually a considerable exposure to dedicated magazines, which provide an informal education in the combinatorial logic or 'language' of, for example, dress or motor cycles, incessantly reinforcing variations on a few narrow themes. Ironically, the combinatorial skills of home making, of choosing the 'right' furniture and equipment, are not pursued with anything like the same vigour, even vicariously. Nevertheless, the pursuit of seemly combinations, of objects which are to be viewed together being 'in keeping', is widely recognized as the essence of Taste in everyday life. Yet the sense of Taste is manifestly intuitive. People clearly do not go around with

formally structured taxonomies in their heads. So how can they know what will go with what—even in some future situation? It is the manifest inadequacy of the 'filing cabinet' model of taxonomy that has given a new impetus to the effort to develop a more fruitful analogy between Taste and language.

Structuralism and the world of goods

By far the most important contributors to this enterprise are two French theoreticians, Claude Levi-Strauss in the field of anthropology, and Roland Barthes in the field of literature and popular culture. They are the founders of the structuralist approach to the appreciation of art and artefact. Based on the differential aspect of language, Barthes and Levi-Strauss both developed their analogies from the structural descriptions of the vocal sound system (phonetics) elaborated by Roman Jakobson and his followers.[15] Fundamental to Jakobson's system was the definition of an ultimate 'unit' of vocalization. This he found in the phoneme.

Phonemes are defined in terms of bundles of acoustic features: voice, nasality, labiality and dentality. Each phoneme could be characterized by listing the features and marking them either '+' or '−' depending on whether they were voiced or voiceless and '0' if irrelevant. Armed with such tables, phonological researchers were in a position to discover the rules for the combination of phonemes into strings. Not all combinations are possible since certain features may not occur in the neighbourhood of others (it may be mechanically impossible to produce the sound combinations concerned).

Levi-Strauss began with combinational lists of features modelled on the phoneme tables of Jakobson. His task was to identify contrasting elements that could be considered as ultimate units in a variety of fields where goods, and our transactions with them, carry some sort of cultural code. He was able to find a great many, including behaviour, ceremonies, kinship relations, marriage customs, cooking and totemic systems, which were analyzed by means of 'paradigmatic' tables of features. Cooking, the field that provides the primary metaphors of Taste may, for example, be characterized by what Levi-Strauss called *gustemes*, organized into the now familiar tables of contrast and correlation.[16] According to Levi-Strauss, one might be able to distinguish between English and French cooking by means of three oppositions: endogamous/exogamous (national versus exotic ingredients); central/peripheral (staple food versus its accompaniments); marked/not-marked (savoury versus bland).

We should then be in a position to construct a chart with + or − signs corresponding to the particular pertinent or non-pertinent character of each quality.

	English cuisine	French cuisine
endogamous/exogamous	+	−
central/peripheral	+	−
marked/not-marked	−	+

Other oppositions would be necessary to account for the particular character of other cuisines, for example, the sweet and sour nature of Chinese cooking. Levi-Strauss has developed the ramifications of his gastronomic 'languages' in enormous detail in his many books on structural anthropology.

Barthes, working over the same years, developed a parallel schema for unravelling the structure of languages in fields such as motor cars, furniture and, in most detail, dress.[17] In his book *Systéme de la Mode*, he worked out the combinatorial games within the language of fashion terminology in terms of three sets: objects, support and variation (O, S, V).

Various permutations of these three elements generate the characteristic expressive possibilities of fashion, for example:

cardigan • collar • open ≡ sporty
cardigan • collar • closed ≡ dressy

His analyses are enormously detailed and very suggestive. Long tables of genres—of objects, supports and variations—are mapped onto equally detailed descriptions of the occasions and places which are suggested or implied by a particular combination of elements in a given garment. His raw material was the laconic phraseology of fashion journalism (apparently technical but in reality highly emotive) which he culled from magazines such as *Elle*.

'gauze, organza, voile and cotton muslin, summer is here'

'a little braid gives elegance'

'She likes studying and surprise parties, Pascal, Mozart and cool jazz. She wears flat heels, collects little scarves and adores her big brother's plain sweaters and those bouffant, rustling petticoats.'

Evocative sentences were mapped out as syntactical 'trees' which highlight the underlying 'grammer' of fashion, for example:

2.7 *In a 'proper' gentleman's suit all the 'objects' and their 'supports' are mandatory. At the level of 'variation', tiny nuances of shape and construction mark out an extensive range of expressions in suits for different social occasions. These nuances vary somewhat from year to year but the relationships between them remain the same over long periods. Gentleman's suits from Henry Poole, tailor of Saville Row, London, England, Autumn/Winter 1899-1900 (top), Autumn/Winter 1919-20 (centre) and Autumn/Winter 1921-22 (bottom).*

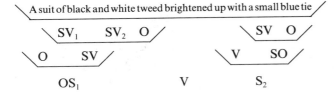

This analysis is devised using examples from natural language, albeit the language of fashion discourse. All these journalistic aphorisms on the social implications of particular style markers add up to a total universe of possible fashion implications—a fashion 'utopia'. Barthes' fashion utopia is in this respect analogous to the concept of linguistic competence developed by Chomsky. Particular ensembles of dress as worn are subsets of the total universe of possibilities realized in practice. A further analogy can therefore be drawn with Chomsky's concept of linguistic performance.

To see how this system fares in the description of dress itself, let us take a common example, the conventional man's three-piece suit. The standard gentleman's attire can be regarded as a set of elements together with a number of rules for putting them together. A properly turned out gentleman will wear only the correct or allowed combination of elements. Incorrect or incomplete combinations are immediately noticed and read as solecisms, as infractions of the normal codes of dress and, by implication, much more besides.[18]

We can easily make a table of the main components or objects: jacket, trousers, waistcoat, shirt, collar, tie, socks and shoes. Within each object there is a set of possible subunits, the supports. Each of these in turn may be presented as one of a number of variations. The theoretical number of these elements is, of course, enormous. In practice, the operation of the rules which determine allowable combinations drastically reduces this number. We may represent all these innumerable permutations as a schema in the form of a multidimensional space. Each element may denote one cell in this space, which may be filled or empty depending on whether or not that particular element is expressed. Rules for proper dress amount to stipulations as to which cells may be occupied. The simplest rule concerns completeness. At the level of the object it simply states that, to be a proper suit, all the cells in that part of the space must be filled. It is this rule that causes the wearer to suffer in silence the discomforts of a proper suit in hot weather.

More interesting though are the rules which specify allowable combinations at the level of the support. First, to be recognized as a suit, the material of the jacket and trousers must be identical. In the strictest application of the rules, this also applies to the waistcoat. Moreover, there is a limited range of materials from which the garments may be made and still be read as 'suit-like'—colour, pattern and texture must be restricted to a narrow range of possible types. Where a waistcoat of a different colour is allowed, there are analogous restrictions on the range of textiles from which this may be made and still be considered 'waistcoat-like'. The material from which the collar and shirt are made must be identical unless the material of the collar is white. Ties must be quiet, socks must be dark and shoes must be black. For all formal occasions, these rules are stringently applied.

At the level of the variation, the rules are somewhat less rigid though no less significant for meaning. On the jacket for instance, minor changes in the number of buttons on the front

2.8 Tiny variations at the level of collar forms are named after the venues of different sporting and social occasions and signal different degrees of 'dressiness'.

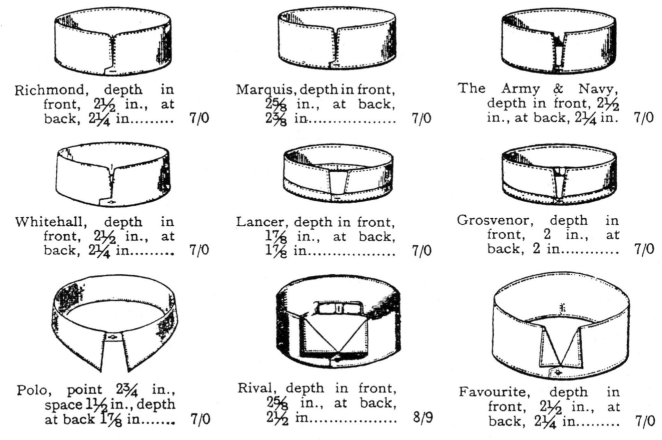

Richmond, depth in front, 2½ in., at back, 2¼ in......... 7/0

Marquis, depth in front, 2⅝ in., at back, 2⅜ in.................. 7/0

The Army & Navy, depth in front, 2½ in., at back, 2¼ in. 7/0

Whitehall, depth in front, 2½ in., at back, 2¼ in......... 7/0

Lancer, depth in front, 1⅞ in., at back, 1⅞ in.................. 7/0

Grosvenor, depth in front, 2 in., at back, 2 in............ 7/0

Polo, point 2¾ in., space 1½ in., depth at back 1⅞ in....... 7/0

Rival, depth in front, 2⅝ in., at back, 2½ in.................. 8/9

Favourite, depth in front, 2½ in., at back, 2¼ in......... 7/0

or the cuffs, or changes in the cut of the front overlap (single or double breasted), in the treatment of the rear (single or double vent), or even in the details of the stitching, all mark out frequent changes in fashion within this otherwise restricted domain. Similar variations exist in the cut of the trousers and, of course, there are important rules governing the forms of jacket and trousers which may properly be worn together.

All these rules can be described as prescriptions about the occupation of particular cells in the multidimensional space. These may be either mandates—if this cell is occupied then so must these others—or they may be restric-tions—if that cell is occupied then these others may not be. We can think of these as 'combination' or 'exclusion' rules respectively. It is obvious that some rules are more rigidly drawn than others. For example, the rule that 'shoes must be black' excludes all colours except one. That which states that 'socks must be dark' is somewhat looser: while it excludes all but a certain range of materials with a low bright-ness, it says nothing about the hue. To state that 'ties must be quiet' is a looser restriction still, in that it merely excludes colours, and combinations of colours, which are both saturated and bright and therefore, perceptu-ally dominant. To make the matter more complicated still, there are clearly various degrees of control which operate in more or less self-contained regions of the space. Rules which concern the objects control whole domains within the space but there are usually interactions between one region and another. Some rules are more 'context sensitive' than others, their operation depends on a more complex description of the local situation than the simple 'if this: then that' format allows. Within a sartorial ensemble of any complexity, it soon becomes extremely difficult separately to tease out all the rules.

Nevertheless, it is analyses of precisely this kind which underlie the analogy with language. Barthes' schemas amount to the proposition that we can indeed 'parse' a suit, just as we can parse a sentence. But can we? How close is the analogy? Obviously there is a formal similarity between the trees which Barthes used to analyze costume phrases and the familiar structural diagrams which are used to show how a sentence is constructed from its parts. It is closest in the type of grammar called *immediate constituent analysis*, in which sentences are broken up into constituent parts such as noun and verb phrases. This grammar is still taught in schools and is simple enough for the analogy between the two types of structural tree to be persuasive, at least at first sight.[19] Yet the enormous number and diversity of the structural possibilities, even within a simple ensemble such as a suit, limits the usefulness of the schema for any predictive purpose. In any case, we should have to devise another schema for each new type of outfit. More profitable, at least in principle, is the possibility of developing analogies with more modern methods of linguistic analysis, in

particular those which use more sophisticated structural devices.

We might then be able to move to an account of dress in general and not merely a few more or less arbitrarily chosen cases. One important model discusses language terms of several 'levels'. The type of immediate constituent analysis used by Barthes would be the first 'surface' level. Beneath this is a deeper level in which are located the semantic structures and categories which give the meaning to surface utterances. Perhaps there are useful analogies to be made between the underlying meanings which we derive from the system of dress and these so-called *deep structures* in sentences. This line of argument takes off from the work of Chomsky, who showed how fundamental categories of meaning could be mapped onto the enormous variety of more or less equivalent sentence structures in everyday spoken and written language.

Theories of language in this tradition postulate the existence of semantic structures analogous to the syntactic structures of surface language. These are the rules for combining categories of meaning into consistent and coherent organizations, which reflect the logic behind our understanding of the world including, of course, our understanding of the social world. Fundamental semantic categories are: entity/non-entity, concrete/abstract, animate/inanimate, human/non-human and male/female. These can be arranged in trees with categories at one level dominating those beneath them. Deep structure rules connect these categories along logical, allowable paths. Violation of these rules generates nonsense. Chomsky's famous neologisms (for example, 'colourless green ideas sleep furiously') vividly show how this happens in English. We can postulate analogous semantic categories in the field of dress which enable us to interpret the infinite variety of costume in terms of social and sexual significance.

Semantic categories in dress might include: intentional/neutral, practical/impractical (more or less equivalent to functional/symbolic), literal/ironic, sexually provocative/sexually neutral, extravagant/restrained, formal/casual, sober/playful, aggressive/friendly and non-socially conformist/socially conformist. Deep structure rules for dress would ensure allowable combinations of features such that these categories occurred in 'sensible', socially meaningful and coherent, sartorial strings. We can easily postulate nonsense costumes which are the analogue of Chomsky's neologisms to emphasize this. Indeed, one way in which we can establish these categories for a particular culture, is to generate unlikely combinations and identify those which strike us as nonsensical. And, just as the semantic structures of spoken language are mapped onto the diverse and changing surface structures of everyday speech, so in dress the underlying semantic structures are mapped onto the endlessly changing and disparate surface features which are the staple of fashion.

These underlying categories and the relationships between them, not the particulars of any one ensemble, are important in the process of understanding what is going on. Without a structured set of more or less universal semantic categories, we should not be able to make sense of each new costume as it is presented to us, and thus interpret the wearer's attitudes towards us and society in general. In reality, we do this daily at first glance. Similar sets of semantic categories can be constructed for other types of goods—furniture and interior decoration, gardens, automobiles and other personal transport—which in some sense make up a visual language. Intuitively, it seems probable that many, if not most, of the semantic structures will be similar across the many different symbolic domains. Such decipherings are fundamental to judgments about a person's Taste.

There are, of course, some serious theoretical difficulties with all such structuralist approaches to the language of goods. To begin with we can only construct a logical system which shows how such decipherings could be possible. There is no way of knowing whether our theoretical scheme bears any relation to the actual mental software which may be operative in any particular case. In Chomsky's terminology we can define linguistic 'competence' but not 'performance'. In addition, many linguists belittle attempts to extend their theoretical techniques into areas for which they were not originally designed.

There are other difficulties beyond those which the language of goods shares with natural language. A particular problem concerns segmentation: outside of natural languages, there is usually no obvious and agreed way of breaking up the field of study into 'parts' and 'wholes', no natural equivalent to the sentence that can frame a convincing structural analysis. For example, the parts which make up the whole in our mental image of a suit may not correspond to the physical components from which it is made. Moreover, the rules for connecting semantic categories into structures cannot be formulated precisely enough to be used generatively, for instance, to construct new garments or furniture which are recognized as a novel but acceptable design by a given culture group. Philip Pettit for one, insists that schema of the type proposed by Barthes can only tell what is physically possible and not what is fashionably possible.[20] According to him, without a hard, universally shared notion of grammar, framed within commonly agreed segments, such as sentences, we are left only with the fickle notion of the Gestalt. As we shall see though, the Gestalt is not so fickle—nor is it so removed from the problems which attend the understanding of natural language.

Despite these reservations, there is much practical benefit to be gained from the structuralist unravelling of meaning in the world of goods. Designers are accustomed to dealing with the imagery of their field in terms of what we have called semantic deep structures. This is how they are able to manipulate form and material into images that are accepted in markets. Within any given idiom, designers are keenly aware of the semantic markers that signal this or that semantic category or combination. Variety is thus generated within an overall 'look'. It is also a matter of observation that, in the studio or drawing office, the details of surface structures are mentioned much less frequently than the underlying semantic categories, which are often used as a kind of short hand for actual visual features themselves. Artists and designers invariably start from highly generalized, undifferentiated concepts which to them are expressive of deep meanings. These concepts are readily transmitted in their attenuated form as sketches and diagrams which are understood within a particular community. Nor is this an especially private discourse. Abbreviated sketches are the staple of fashion magazines with wide circulations and they are clearly read by the fashion conscious public as expressive of precise social and sexual meanings. The same is true in many other areas

2.9 *Highly generalized concept sketches indicate an overall look. Including only the 'deep structure' relationships between the components of dress they leave out all detail which will be worked out later.*

of consumer goods. There is also a serious sense in which we can say that we use a grammar of clothes whenever we choose an appropriate outfit to match a particular social occasion or partner. One has only to listen to people discussing what to wear to a difficult social event to realize how explicit these semantic categories are and how fine are the symbolic distinctions in everyday use. There is every reason to suppose that a better understanding of the rules which govern such choice making would enable everyone more satisfactorily to perform it.

Certainly, marketing professionals would gain a great deal. We live in a world that is already surfeited with standardized products. Markets for many types of consumer goods are reduced to replacement purchases only and there are limits to what may be achieved by planned obsolescence. Today though, the computer control of manufacturing processes makes the mass production of diversity possible. Given this facility, there are increasingly compelling reasons for marketing departments to attack local and transient symbolic cultures, till now the last territories inaccessible to the great producers. In some countries (notably Japan), which have already anticipated an end

2.10 *The language of the prairie. Houses such as these form the corpus from which the 'grammar' of Frank Lloyd Wright's early architecture was extracted. Houses in Oak Park, Illinois, USA.*

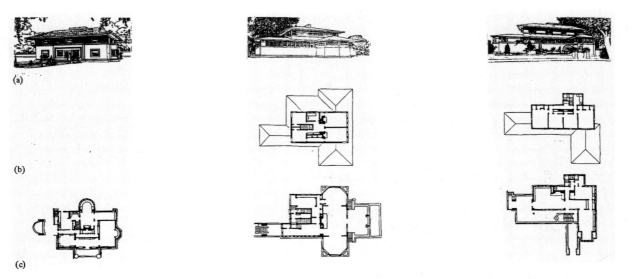

Shape grammars are written as computer programmes which generate complex wholes from primitive elements plus a set of syntactical rules for their proper combination. Koning and Eisenberg have extracted the elements and teased out the grammatical rules which underlay the design of Frank Lloyd Wright's early Prairie houses.

Winslow house, 1898   Henderson house, 1901   Thomas house, 1901

The corpus: three of the prairie-style houses designed by Frank Lloyd Wright. Shown are (a) exterior view, (b) bedroom floor plan (Winslow House not available), (c) main floor plan. (Exterior views are from Wright, 1910.)

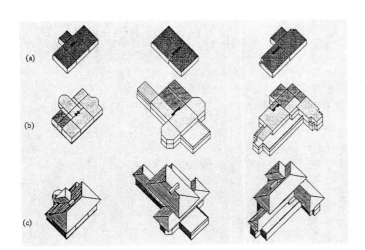

The Winslow, Henderson and Thomas houses defocused and reduced to four function zones: living, service, porch and bedroom. Shown are (a) the bedroom level, (b) the main floor level and (c) the external form.

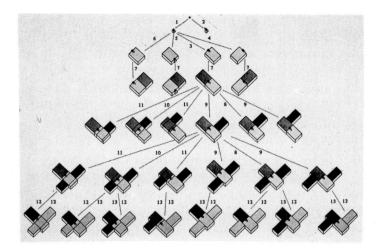

Starting from the hearth as the kernel of the scheme, the computer programme generates new plans using syntactical rules discovered in the corpus of existing houses.

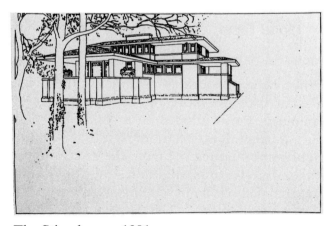

The Stiny house, 1981

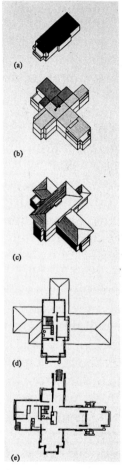

Stiny house

New design as generated by the grammar: (a) bedroom level, (b) main floor level, (c) external form, (d) bedroom floor plan, (e) main floor plan.

45

of the era of mass-produced standardized goods, a great deal of research is proceeding to attempt to understand how the semantic systems of the various languages of goods actually work. If this is successful, the large multinational producers will be able to cater for ever smaller groups of consumers and penetrate the most private of symbol systems. Our Tastes will be no defence against the global salesmen. What seems at present an arcane area of theory could provide the tools for a new and highly effective stage of economic aggression.[21]

An example of the way that the visual language, of even a highly individual artist, can be 'unpacked', will serve as a pointer to what might be achieved given a coordinated effort. It concerns the 'prairie houses' of Frank Lloyd Wright. Koning and Eisenberg studied a corpus of the early houses of this most organic of architects in order to isolate the characteristic features of his plans.[22] His prairie houses show an arrangement of interlocking spaces which, while they eschew any of the standard *beaux arts* symmetries or other academic devices for ordering the spatial elements, nevertheless communicate a powerful sense of an underlying order. From this analysis, and taking into account what is known of the architect's compositional procedures, Koning and Eisenberg were able to construct a *shape grammar* which, run on a computer, would not only generate plausible replicas of the existing corpus of houses, but also create new ones, houses which Frank Lloyd Wright might have designed but, in fact, did not.

A shape grammar is a set of syntactic rules for composing simple building blocks into a whole by means of a series of recursive operations on a simple starting element, in this case the central fireplace which the architect himself often used as the pivotal element which generated the entire plan. To the extent that the computer can generate not only plausible replicas, but also new works in the style of a particular artist or designer, it can be argued that the grammar gives a plausible account of the actual processes of composition. The results are indeed impressive: the new houses are very convincing simulations of the work of Frank Lloyd Wright. They are certainly much more believable than the computer generated Mondrians of a few years ago. How far this approach can be extended to other areas of design has yet to be demonstrated but, given the level of complexity in the three-dimensional architecture of the prairie houses, its application to, for example, the man's suit, should not be too formidable. Different styles or Tastes within a particular genre would then be described as variations within an overall shape grammar.[23]

Good form, Gestalt and the nature of nuance

When he unfavourably contrasted the fickle Gestalt with the more rigorous structures of language, Pettit alluded to a somewhat slippery concept. It is one, moreover, that is at first sight somewhat remote from the discussion of Taste, for the original studies on the Gestalt were carried out by psychologists interested in visual perception.[24] Gestalt simply means 'form', and the Gestalt psychologists were interested in the way that the brain organizes the raw input to the visual system into perceptual wholes or forms. Many years of ingenious experimentation led to some generalizations about the transformation of the visual input during the processes of perception. There is a tendency to regularize, smooth out and simplify irregular and complex figures, to close up open shapes and generally to distort images presented to the eye in the direction of greater symmetry and completeness. These generalizations form the *Laws of Good Gestalt.*

Modern explanations for the phenomenon of the Gestalt are based on insights drawn from information theory and, in particular, on computer models of the mental processes of pattern recognition.[25] In this picture, the Gestalt is the mental grouping or aggregation of visual information from the sense organs into larger units for the purposes of more economical coding. This regrouping has the benefit of reducing the amount of information that has to be handled at any one time. Sometimes called *chunking*, perceptual aggregation can be conceived as similar to the formation of *macros* in a computer programme. Macros are the names given to whole sequences of codes which are kept together under a simple filename. Using this filename enables the entire sequence to be recalled at once. In computer drawing for example, the use of macros enables whole sections of a complex plan to be filed, recalled and manipulated as one. We can regard macros of this kind as a sort of electronic template. In many common types of pattern recognition programmes, the computer is given a vocabulary of such templates which it attempts to fit onto the data. If the brain does indeed work in a fashion which is analogous to artificial pattern recognition, then it seems likely that we are also equipped with templates as part of our mental software. This may be innate, or it may be generated internally as a result of the interaction of learning with higher level soft-

ware that is innate. The Laws of Good Gestalt refer to economic templates and routines which ensure that information handling is done as efficiently as possible.

There are a number of features of pattern recognition computer models which provide useful insights into discrimination—an essential preliminary to judgment in the exercise of Taste. In artificial pattern recognition, the image to be recognized is projected onto a grid or screen, each cell of which reports separately as to whether it is being covered. The size of the cells determines the ultimate resolution of the device, that is, the smallest detail that can be discriminated.[26] We can extend this notion to the brain. Although, of course, there is no actual geometric grid, we can imagine its mental equivalent deriving from the operation of the many patterned mosaics of brain cells. This in turn enables us to give a more precise meaning to the idea of discrimination. Sensitivity entails a fine mesh to the perceptual grid. Coarseness arises from the opposite.

In reality, in order to achieve maximum efficiency, the size of the perceptual net needs to be varied, the level of resolution being adjusted to that necessary to capture the smallest significant detail. Too large a grain and detail will be lost as information goes 'through the net'. Too small a grain and large amounts of redundant information will needlessly be processed. We can imagine a close mental analogue to the process of *windowing*: the ability of computer graphic devices to isolate one portion of the field and blow it up to a larger scale in order to discriminate finer detail. In good programmes, windows can be moved around at will and the image within the window zoomed up to any scale. Subtlety is the sensed characteristic of those organizations that demand constant changes in the size of the perceptual grid as it becomes clear from the nature of the pattern that fine grained detail must be taken as significant, an intended nuance to which attention must be given, rather than unintended 'noise' that may safely be disregarded.

One of the most difficult tasks in the act of interpretation is to decide what is in fact intentional and what is accidental. There is no point in reading intention into every mark on an artist's canvas once we have perceived that some are scratches which appear to have arrived there accidentally. Similarly, there is no point in reading stylistic significance into the ensemble of objects in someone's living room once we perceive that some have been dropped there at random. Only if we know what is intentional can we gauge the minimum level of discrimination required to catch all the different meanings in a message without wasting large amounts of mental effort on processing noise. But how do we make such interpretations? How do we decide between intention and accident? What processes enable us to decide that some aspects of a message are mere noise in relation to intentions of the sender?

It appears that initially we operate using interpretive procedures in which perceptual frames or windows are already established for the 'normal' forms of objects. Classification into groups for the purposes of comparison is decided by reference to the semantic categories we already have in the deep structure of our taxonomic understanding. From these we can generate at will the mental wholes or patterns of what is to be expected under normal circumstances. If there are no sudden discontinuities or inconsistencies, between what we are presented with and the patterns we generate under

2.11 'Garfinkeling' involves the intentional dislocation of the normal forms of objects by arbitrary rearrangment in order to probe the limits of the perception of normality in everyday behaviour. Ornaments which should be on the mantlepiece are spotted immediately if removed to an unfamiliar location.

the assumption of normality, we proceed with the presumption that our *prima facie* interpretation is currently valid. This is how we can glance around the room and see that all is in order without focussing on any particular item. Next, we check out the normal forms or patterns between especially significant objects, for example, those whose function and location is exclusively symbolic. The ornaments in a room may be presumed to be exonerated from the multitude of daily disturbances caused by activities of which we know nothing. If we confirm that the china dogs are indeed in place on either side of the mantlepiece then we may carry on under the operative presumption of normality and intention. If this is not so—we may find the dogs on the floor—we presume that this is not intention but accident and seek further interpretation of this event.[27] Beyond these global surveys and spot checks, we depend on windowing and on mentally generating appropriate grids on which to check internal relationships under the assumption of intention. Appraising Gestalt relationships under the assumption of intention is thus at the very foundation of judgments about Taste.

While in the first instance the study of the Gestalt was the province of psychologists interested in perception and, in particular, visual perception, it is a concept of much wider scope than the sense originally formulated. Indeed, the patterning of human behaviour into wholes—strings, sequences and clusters that cohere to produce units that are more than the sum of their parts—occurs everywhere. We can apply the same concepts to the semantic system itself for example. Meanings also cohere in clusters: local symbolic groupings that together signify more than the sum of their constituents. Thus we can envisage a grid or network with nodes and pathways in the field of meanings, with a unit cell denoting the smallest unit of meaning that can be discriminated.[28] Differences smaller than this are simply not registered. On this model, sensitive people would possess a fine semantic grid which enables them to be receptive of nuances: small but significant differences between meanings. This could be envisaged as an overall skill or ability, possibly related to the individual's capacity to handle the tasks of windowing and zooming. These matters are of considerable importance in the world of goods in relation to advertising and marketing. There is no point in producing marginal variations which are simply not perceived as different. And of course, there are considerable economic rewards for those who can identify persons or groups which have a high sensitivity towards particular symbols and images.

Again, there are easily observed differences between individuals in their ability to perceive patterns of relationships between separated items, whether these are visual stimuli or discrete meanings embodied in the symbolism of objects. Ability to discriminate fine detail depends on the prior ability to form wholes of which the details may be considered as parts. An important finding of the early Gestalt psychologists was that contiguity—actual proximity in space—constituted a significant factor in determining whether a grouping of items would be seen as a whole. Three dots close together on a piece of paper are more likely to be seen as a triangle than three dots widely separated. Furthermore, three items are more likely to be seen as a triangle if the items themselves are similar in character. Three dots are more likely to be perceived as a triangle than, for example, one dot, one photograph of a familiar person and one amorphous field of coloured blobs. This is not surprising since the task of spotting relationships of one kind is more difficult when these are overlaid by manifest differences of another. Analogous generalizations can be made about patterns between meanings which can be conceived as Gestalten in semantic space. Grasping relationships between concepts is easier when they are near than when they are remote from each other.

Similarly, the perception of a Gestalt is easiest when the concepts are presented in a

49

similar fashion, for example when they are all of a similar linguistic form or, in the case of goods, they are of homologous types or from similar epochs or cultures. Once more, this is not surprising since the task of seeing similarities is more complicated when the items to be correlated into one category are more obviously separated by differences in others.

In the case of visual perception, these regularities in our patterning behaviour seem to be innate and universal. There is good evidence that at least some of the semantic categories which underlie natural languages may too be innate, and very many languages appear to have a similar deep structure. However, in the language of goods, the idea of a more or less universal mental mechanism for the perception of Gestalten is much less plausible. Empirical research into mental pattern making is necessarily indirect and, even in the case of language, the outlines of the actual mental software responsible for the various Gestalt phenomena is still in dispute. Some believe it to be intrinsically undiscoverable.

It seems most likely, in the case of patterns between meanings embodied in the symbolism of goods, that the formation of Gestalten is much more variable between individuals and, in one individual, between different occasions and in different genres. Clearly much common ground does exist, otherwise the social codes expressed in a myriad of commonplace objects, such as the man's suit or living room furniture, could not function. However, to speak of a person as sensitive *per se*, as if discrimination and its concomitant pattern making were quite generalized activities, is needlessly to oversimplify. Even the idea of an individual's *bandwidth*, which is a metaphor borrowed from earlier sciences concerned with electromag-

netic radiation, does less than justice to the differences between individuals studied by market researchers.[29] Given the issues at stake, not least in the economic field, an attempt to expand our understanding of what is meant by discrimination and pattern making in the world of goods, by more seriously pressing the information processing model of the Gestalt would be well worthwhile. There is plenty of evidence that the ability to discriminate between forms and meanings, and to perceive patterns between both, can be altered by training. What Edward Duveen called 'rightly constituted minds' can certainly be enhanced, if not created, by the appropriate educational regime. However, in the case of Taste, there are few public facilities for developing the necessary attributes and skills.

In any event, the distinction that critics like Pettit are trying to make between the categorical 'either/or' of natural languages and the more blurry edges of the Gestalt, is exaggerated. The wholes within an assembly of goods may not be so neatly segmented as sentences in a flow of discourse. Our pragmatically generated grids may not produce units as discrete as words. Nevertheless, our ability to compare and contrast depends on our ability to correlate and group. That we can do this, and do it flexibly to any required degree of subtlety, is a measure of the power of the Gestalt processes in the brain. Our feeling that a certain cluster of items could be viewed as a whole may lack that hard intimation of grammar which pervades our use of written or spoken language, nevertheless, it is our intuitive sense of 'closure' or completeness, which we use to window the world, that enables us to interpret it at all.

Once we detach the notion of the Gestalt from its original anchorage in vision, we are left with usages which are, in varying degrees, metaphorical. The original hard-edged concept, embodied in the simple geometrical demonstrations of the first experimenters, becomes a much looser and more variable organizing schema. And once we move away from an innate, biological universality, we are faced with the difficulty that, on any particular occasion, the distinction between a schema and a nuance or detail, can only be determined by comparison with other comparable cases. Defining comparable cases is an operational matter, we have to rely on some sensibly attuned and experienced body of people, since such acts of perceptual judgment are never carried out in isolation. Only when we have saturated ourselves in the language of Frank Lloyd Wright or Mozart or Chippendale, or even of our host's Taste in dining room furniture, will we be confident that what we perceive as a whole will relate in any way to what the presenter intended or, indeed, to any other context that may be relevant. To discuss matters of Taste in terms of the model of language, or to borrow some of the formalisms of linguistics, does not permit us to bypass the issues of interpretation and judgment. However, there is much more to natural language than the simple formalisms of the early structuralists allow.

Product semantics

Perhaps the most tangible outcome of speculation about the linguistic aspects of the material world is *product semantics* in design theory. First coined in 1984, product semantics stresses meaning as the transcendant issue in design.[30] Eclectic in its sources in the behavioural sciences, it encompasses all aspects of the design process, and is indifferent to the nature of the artefact concerned. It subsumes the traditional emphases on physical performance, characteristic of functionalism, and radically transforms the conventional understanding of human factors as being merely synonymous with ergonomics.

Since 1984, an alliance of designers (for the most part industrial designers) with psychologists and communication theorists has extended the concept still further.[31] Under the new rubric, designers are, from the outset of their education, enjoined to develop a comprehensive knowledge of users' understandings of the artefactual world. Users' comprehension may range from direct perceptual messages carried in objects to the way in which objects and their settings act as cognitive structures, embodying the underlying myths which unite, motivate and console entire societies. At its widest, it entails a framework which extends beyond the influence of purely social and human factors to the ecological, objects thus enter into the relationship between human beings and their environment.[32] In view of this progression, it is timely to look at its pretensions and weigh its achievements.

The idea of product semantics emerged from earlier debates in architecture. Part of the growing reaction to the homogenized neutrality which had become the hallmark of the functionalist buildings of the Modern Movement, was a reawakened interest in the symbolic meanings embodied in the man-made world. From the time of Vitruvius, the classic texts of the past were dominated by accounts of the architectural principles which lay behind

2.12 *In an effort to design goods which have a definite identity and which therefore stand out from the world of electronic 'black boxes', Philips have made extensive use of product semantics. The 'Roller Radio' (left) was a pioneering example of forms which express complex ideas (roller skating, rock-and-roll) in a highly innovative visual form. An instant commercial success it has led to even more adventurous designs such as the zig-zag personal stereo (right).*

temples and palaces, types of edifice in which the symbolic expression of ideas—of religious mysticism and awe, or the exercise of temporal wealth and power—was of paramount importance. This tradition never entirely disappeared from discussion in scholarly circles, even during the heyday of Modernism. Not surprisingly then, the revival of interest in symbolism first emerged from academia. The seminal text was the collection of essays entitled *Meaning in Architecture*, which was first published in 1969.[33] This clearly demonstrated a continuity with the earlier history of architectural theory. Variously influenced by the linguistic metaphors of the day, the authors sought to cast this approach into the symbolic needs of the modern world, and to embrace contemporary building types. A new intellectual industry was born, and the search for ways to put meaning back into architecture has become one of the great justifying principles of the post-Modern movement.

Industrial design has never had this long tradition of intellectual speculation concerning meanings, growing as it did out of vernacular crafts on the one hand and production engineering on the other. Product semantics seeks to fill this gap. It aims to provide a contemporary rationale for the practice of industrial design and, at the same time, define the unique domain of competence of the designer. What then has been achieved so far?

As with architecture, the concern for meaning has provided a programme and justification for a movement of style away from the blandness of conventional functionalism. Its founders deny, however, that it is concerned with post-Modernism or any other particular style. Nevertheless, it has inspired some very significant shifts in the nature of the production of some major international manufacturing concerns, shifts which would not have happened without this theoretical

2.13 *Product semantics extends into a revolution in design for use. The Xerox Corporation in the USA, working with the Exploratory Design Laboratory of Fitch Richardson Smith, have revolutionized the design of complex electromechanical systems such as office photocopiers so that they become teaching machines, the manipulation of which enables operators to learn how to use and maintain them without the aid of elaborate instruction manuals. Xerox copiers before* (top) *and after* (bottom).

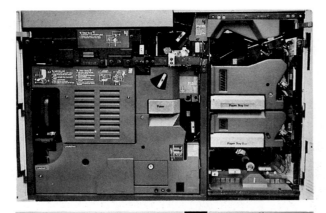

underpinning. The following two examples illustrate its scope.

Some time ago, Philips, one of the largest electronics companies in the world, realized that technological convergence had meant that consumers could rely on almost any supplier for more or less identical performance and price. In view of this, subjective factors, or Taste, would heavily influence the decision to purchase. Starting with the 'Roller Radio', at the time of launch a radical departure from the black box forms hitherto standard, they have developed a consistent search for forms for their electronic consumer products which, through their visual imagery, would reflect and, indeed, enable new lifestyle possibilities for their consumers.[34] In doing this, they have

powerfully influenced the form of competitors' products, and thereby effected an alteration of the appearance of all electronic consumer goods. Philips are even experimenting with a do-it-yourself decorative kit, to be sold with portable radio-cassette players, which will enable consumers to personalize the appearance of their sets, exercising their personal Tastes in the process—albeit within the genre established by the company.

In this project, Philips were clearly working with meanings at a cultural level, concerned with the expression of social status and gregariousness within youth subcultures for products whose function is obvious and whose man-machine interface is simple. Equally important is work at a more fundamental level, on technical products whose function is complex and whose man-machine interface is often baffling, even with the aid of an instruction manual. For example, how to operate an everyday machine, such as an office copier, is often far from obvious—especially when it goes wrong. Simple demands like the rapid clearing of paper jams are often difficult since, once inside the good looking outer case, the user is faced with naked engineering and the minimum of visual cues. Instruction manuals refer to the technical names of mechanical or electronic components of which often little is known.

Product semantics contributes to design solutions at this level in ways which expand on traditional ergonomics, focussing on the physical and psychological factors that enable an understanding of what a product is, what it does, and how the user is supposed to interact with it. Often inspired by Gibson's notions of *affordances*, it aims to contribute to the 'designing-in' of *self-evidency* to complex artefacts or machines.[35] With this approach, visual forms

53

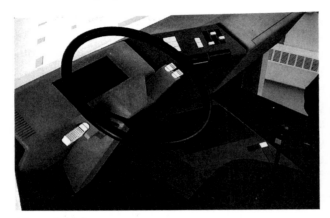

Functional.

Low-tech.

High-tech.

Contemporary.

Futuristic.

2.14 *Five different designs by students of Ohio State University Department of Transportation for the interiors of truck cabs designed from a brief written from the point of view of product semantics. Each image expresses a different meaning from a range of concepts distilled from the responses of truckers to questions about how they would like a truck to feel. In solving design problems, practical considerations are addressed in terms of the predetermined meaning.*

of interfaces, and internal components and systems, are contrived in such a way that they intimate directly to the user where, and how, to manipulate them in order to accomplish a particular task, and then what to do next when a particular step has been accomplished.

Here the work of John Rheinfrank for the Xerox Corporation has lead to a notable advance in the redesign of complex office machines. These are now much more user-friendly than the models they replaced. Design has been applied, not only to provide a few cheery colours for the buttons, but in a much more radical sense. By using colour and form throughout to provide affordances to the operators, the designers engage them in a learning experience with the machine itself. Its use gradually becomes self-evident. Understanding comes as a natural part of manipulation so that use becomes a motivating pleasure.[36]

There have also been exciting innovations in design education, notably from Reinhart Butter in Ohio and Michael McCoy in Michigan. They have each devised projects which expand the visual language of product design by emphasizing meaning as the determining factor in the brief for designers. Butter and his students have produced a range of interiors for truck cabs using a fivefold classification labelled by verbal descriptions—High Tech, Low Tech, Contemporary, Functional and Futuristic. These classifications, which derived from research into meanings currently employed by truck users, were then translated into contrasting vocabularies of form through a series of well defined steps. Beginning with the generation of lists of verbal attributes which corresponded to each of the semantic types, the student designers progressed to a systematic search for their metaphorical equivalents in existing artefacts. Characteristic forms and devices within these artefacts then acted as prompts for the design process within the technical and dimensional constraints of the truck cab. Once the detailed problem solving began, great care was taken to see that the semantic considerations remained paramount. Many of the techniques used, such as the exhaustive enumeration, ranking and structuring of lists of positive and negative attributes, resemble some of the procedures of Levi-Strauss, detailed earlier in the chapter.[37]

McCoy and his students have developed a visual language in which the bland geometric envelope of typical electronic consumer products has been exploded and replaced by an eclectic ensemble of forms which act as metaphors for the processes which go on inside a particular component or subsystem. Sometimes these translations are literal, for example, the cylindrical can which shows where a videodisc is located. Others are more obviously poetical, often involving the use of the visual pun, for example, the pages of a book symbolizing the electronic notepad-telephone, the bookcase representing the information modules within a personal computer or, even more rarified, the embossed grid, symbolizing logic on the casing of the printed circuit boards in the disc camera.[38]

Such images have rapidly become part of the *lingua franca* of younger designers and, unless used with understanding, will soon end up as superficial style clichés, like the black boxes they replaced. More important is the spread of a new generation of teachers who understand how to apply the premises of the theory in a truly creative way. Above all, product semantics creates the best opportunity since the Bauhaus in the 1920s, for scientists and designers, with their complementary modes of understanding, to work together on a coherent programme for the development of new product forms.

However, it is precisely at the level of discrimination, critical judgment and appreciation that we have called Taste, that the programme of product semantics is least developed. Perhaps this is because theories of signification at the level of use or affordances offer the most direct leverage on the process of shape making that designers love.[39] Possibly too, although theoreticians of product semantics are prepared to talk of 'evaluative conventions' and 'stereotypical ideals' (what Duveen called, more simply 'the beautiful'), there is still a certain residual commitment to the aesthetic puritanism of the Modern Movement, and the indulgence of Taste for pleasure is unconsciously disdained as sybaritic excess.[40] For the complete realization of its meaning however, product semantics needs the engagement of artists as well as designers, and they have hitherto been absent from the conversation. Aesthetics is still treated as somewhat of a side issue and metaphor, the key to creative extrapolation from the known to the unknown in design, as elsewhere, has so far no considered place in the theoretical structure.

Metaphor and the importance of context

Omitted from descriptions of visual language couched in terms of existing structural models, is the power of all natural languages to be articulated and understood, even when many of the rules are being broken. Surface rules—those which govern the production of good grammar—may be varied within a surprisingly broad band and still not frustrate understanding. Among different regional dialects, or in intimate or casual speech which, as any tape recording of everyday chatter will show, is amazingly fragmented and incomplete, grammatical differences or inadequacies are usually surmounted without great difficulty. More importantly, we can also understand language in which deep structure rules are violated. This is because we have alternative modes of interpretation which can be brought into play when the literal one appears to break down. Unless we are forewarned, we usually start from the assumption that discourse will be literal. However, if we are presented with what then appears nonsense, by virtue of manifest violation of the rules for semantic categorization, we can resort to other possible interpretations under the overriding assumption that our interlocutor must have meant something.

Such non-literal interpretations are metaphorical.[41] In them, obvious semantic anomalies are reduced by projecting remoter sets of associations onto the words concerned, in a sequence of creative acts of interpretation, until we find one which, while it does not literally 'fit', does at least hold a number of suggestive associations simultaneously in play in the mind. In any 'near fit', there are inevitably a number of incongruities, or incompatible associations, also in play, and these demand further acts of metaphorical projection in order to reduce them to an acceptable level of understanding.

We select the 'next best fit' from among the stream of tentative interpretations by its superior ability to join coherently onto other parts of the discourse, and thereafter to square with the unfolding stream of events of which

2.15 *Visual metaphor. By making us interpret its unfamiliar ('nonsense') imagery as a metaphor, the* giant *coathanger-coathanger by designer Jon Wealleans forces us to reconsider the nature of the act of hanging our clothes.*

the discourse is part. Both the articulation and the interpretation of metaphor are creative acts, creative in the sense that, at least momentarily, new semantic categories are invented, categories which exist, as it were, in the 'cracks' between the everyday categories which guide us in literal speech. The function of this extra facility is to enable the necessarily finite and 'digitized' system of language to cope with an infinite and 'analog' reality. It is not surprising, therefore, that metaphor, far from being an occasional and abberant feature of language, is in fact universal. So much so that the creation of totally meaningless nonsense is virtually impossible. Even the most bizarre combinations of words, produced by the most

systematic infraction of the deep structure rules, combinations which at first sight present only an incoherent succession of semantic anomalies, can be given a more or less plausible interpretation as metaphor.

Consider the classic nonsense sentence of Chomsky quoted previously. 'Colourless green ideas sleep furiously' could be taken to express the pent-up energy of seeds about to germinate in Spring, the emotional force coming from the violation of the deep structure rule that limits emotional adjectives or adverbs to animal agents. We could accept this perfectly happily in a poem, and only a little less so in ordinary speech—and, of course, most semantic anomalies are not as extreme as that.[42] In due course, a successful metaphor is used so repeatedly that it loses its status as a metaphor and becomes a cliché, warranting only a new entry into the list of meanings attaching to a word in the dictionary.

Much the same happens in other aspects of social behaviour, including our use of the language of goods. As in written and spoken language, where metaphor and its end result, polysemy, is a pervasive feature of all utterances, so in the social language of goods, ambiguity and equivocation are everywhere. The reason is the same: a finite and digitized system of interpretation—essential if we are to have logical inference—has to cope with an infinite and indeterminate analog social reality. As in natural language, it is always possible to find some explanation of events, however bizarre the combination of happenings or situations. Taste is never meaningless: this is true even when we are faced with violations of the deep structure categories of social behaviour. If the obvious interpretation of a social act is not immediately validated by an appropriate reciprocal act, then we can always switch to an alternative, albeit less plausible one. Defining an obvious interpretation is partly a matter of frequency. Something which has worked on many previous occasions will be the first to be tried on subsequent ones. It is also partly a matter of our understanding of the larger structure of affairs. Interpretations which are validated over long and structured sequences of acts will be maintained in preference to those which are validated only by shorter strings of reciprocal behaviour.

When metaphor is brought into play in ordinary discourse, the intention is usually signalled by special cues, a change in facial expression or the tone of the voice, or in the case of written language, by conventional expression marks. Such cues form a kind of parallel code which tells us the level of interpretation currently operative. The code tells us whether a particular utterance is to be taken figuratively. Without it we may often remain unsure just how we are supposed to interpret someone's remarks. (Of course, on occasion this uncertainty or ambiguity may be deliberate.) Moreover, since metaphor does indeed violate the deep structure rules of language it can easily disrupt the continuity of discourse—especially if the metaphors concerned are oblique and demand much mental time and effort to construe.

When many metaphors are strung together in a sequence as, for example, in a poem, then continuity of discourse can only be assured if special measures are taken to re-establish broken connections. In works of art, where a dense tissue of metaphor is the norm, the missing logical connections are supplied by means of other, parallel systems of formal integration—rhythm and rhyme in poetry, spatial and geometric symmetries in architecture, patterns of relationships in colour in painting, configurations of gesture in choreography, cadential and harmonic structures in music. In all of these instances, it is a variety of the Gestalt phenomenon which provides the missing 'glue' that sticks the parts of the work of art together when 'logical' structures of meanings are missing. Without this parallel architecture of form, strings of metaphor would rapidly cease to engage our attention. In all figurative language, it is the Gestalt which prevents the collapse of sense.

Figurative or 'poetic' discourse is, in this sense, a special kind of deviant language. The point of creating deviant languages seems to be 'that it enables poets to say not only things that can be said in Standard English but in a new way, but also things which cannot be said in Standard English at all—although they can only be understood by someone who does understand Standard English'. Extending this formulation to all figurative behaviour, including what Erving Goffman called 'the presentation of self in everyday life', the purpose of such new and deviant languages is to express qualities which remain hidden by the 'prose' of ordinary validated behaviour—although to understand the poetry we must first learn the prose of everyday life.

To understand the language of goods in practical situations, let us consider once more the humble gentleman's suit. The structured ensemble of possibilities, with permutations at the three levels of Barthes' object, support and variation, where infraction of any of the combination or exclusion rules result in the sartorial equivalent of nonsense and condemn the wearer to social stigma, is now too simple. True, the literal interpretation of the string of components which makes up the ensemble may well suggest 'non-suit', however, there may be other collateral evidence to prompt the thought that the wearer was perfectly aware of the rules and had decided to ignore them. These apparently forbidden combinations were being presented to us deliberately. It was for us to make the imaginative effort to decode his intentions, not as literally mistaken, but as consciously metaphorical. In so doing, we are involved in an effort momentarily to restructure the rules of dress and the world of social understandings of which it is part.

Take the question of completeness: we can all agree that at the level of the object, the ensemble must be complete. Lack of any of the elements immediately signals improper dress, and occasions outrage or mirth depending on the situation. Lack of trousers suggests that the unfortunate wearer has been debagged and the situation is interpreted humorously. Lack of a jacket declares that the most important marker of formality is missing and sets us off to seek an explanation. During very hot weather this could mean that normal social restrictions were temporarily relaxed, or that the wearer was perhaps not feeling well. In other circumstances, lack of a jacket is accepted as a compromise between the formality of the occasion, and the needs of the person not to be physically incommoded, for example, the use of the waistcoat as an outer garment by players in a snooker tournament. Clearly the players need their arms free for the delicate business of cueing the balls, however, further to distinguish it as a temporary exemption from normal proprieties, a bow tie is substituted for the ordinary variety in an oblique reference to evening dress.

In other temporary situations, lack of a jacket, or even lack of a jacket and a collar and tie, may be construed as a deliberate attempt to stretch currently accepted limits of fashion. The presence of a waistcoat implies a suit. From the manifestly coherent choice of fabric for the trousers and overcoat (not identical but closely and cleverly related), the wearer appears highly aware of formal or Gestalt methods of integration. We can intuit that the collar and tie are missing from choice because the exposed collar stud is a highly visible (and aesthetically validated) item which draws attention to the neck region. Other elements of the context—the wearer is a well known interior designer and the milieu is an artist's studio—guide us in our metaphorical attempts

59

2.16 *Drastic violations of conventions are also explicable from the context. Suspenders worn outside signal sexual provocation while the facial expression of the model together with the modesty of the high neckline tells us that this is merely an adventurous fashion image. Design by Vivien Westwood at the London Fashion show*

to restructure our concepts of what constitutes completeness in this particular subculture.

At the level of the support there are equally minatory restrictions on allowable combinations, especially those which specify consistency. To wear a jacket of manifestly suit-like material and trousers of a pronouncedly different textile is to invite immediate attention. The reverse is also true. In normal circumstances this leads to ridicule on the presumption that the wearer has acquired the items fortuitously—as a tramp might randomly assemble any selection of cast-off clothes that happen to fit. At the very least, we might imagine that the wearer has suffered an accident which has temporarily put his jacket or trousers out of use. Where the difference between the materials of the jacket and trousers is small, then the consistency rule may be relaxed somewhat. For example, a jacket of suit-like material may be accompanied by trousers of a plain black or dark grey material, however, in this case, the reverse does not seem to be accepted.

An interesting case arises where the textile used for both jacket and tie falls outside the range that is normally deemed to be suit-like. Ordinary commerce does not provide for such combinations. To achieve them means taking a non-approved material to a tailor and overcoming his objections. This is highly intentional and is read as such. Attention is attracted to the wearer immediately. Consequently, this is a ready device for showing-off and is much used for establishing character in the entertainment world. Worn on ordinary secular occasions, suits from materials outside the margin of the socially approved would give rise to comments about their 'loudness' and with them judgments on the character of the wearers, who may risk being stigmatized

accordingly. Similar considerations apply to the choice of material for shirt, tie, waistcoat, socks and shoes.

Infractions of the rules at the level of what Barthes called the variation are less drastic. Within the narrow field of the gent's suit, variations of shape and cut define the shift of fashion. Violations of current norms would be considered as unfashionable, but no worse. By the same token, deliberate violations of the rules carry metaphorical messages that are more subtle. A complete suit, proper in every way, but with the collar button open underneath the knotted tie signals, not that the wearer has unfortunately lost a button, but that he is a member of a fashionable 'designer' culture. How this is viewed will depend on whether the spectators are themselves more, or less, formally attired. Clothes play a crucial role in sexual attraction and its opposite. Innumerable nuances of incomplete or improper dress are used as a signals in the human mating games, games which themselves are conducted within a hierarchic and variously formal social world.

Indeed, as everyone is aware, the entire man-made world—for instance, furniture and interior decoration, houses and their settings, transportation and leisure equipment—is interpreted in a similar fashion, as variously expressive of complex social and individual realities. This is done 'on-line' in an infinite variety of novel situations. As in natural language, this is made possible by a system which combines surface rules of a Gestalt or syntactical nature, deep structure rules at the level of semantics, and that facility to create novel 'near structures' or 'next best fits' guided by our knowledge of the context which we call metaphor. Needless to say, formal models which attempt to encompass all these features are extraordinarily complicated, and necessarily combine more or less incompatible metaphors such as 'floppy networks' and 'fuzzy sets'![43] Once metaphor is properly taken into account, the contrast which Pettit tried to define between the categorical either/or of grammar and the fickle notion of the Gestalt is softened a great deal further.

Irony, sophistication and camp

Once we take metaphor properly into account, the formal neatness of early linguistic models of Taste vanishes, although what is left accords far better with our interpretation of the man-made world. Given the essentially creative, and hence, personal and provisional character of metaphor (even in natural language), and the even more tentative nature of metaphorical interpretation of the world of goods—which cannot talk back to us and tell us what we have got wrong—then it follows that with matters of Taste, we will always be faced, not with one or two 'well formed strings', but with a whole set of more or less permissible behaviours and plausible interpretations.

Within a population, individuals differ in their behaviour across a wide range of features. A penumbra of semi-acceptable or marginal behaviour surrounds that of the majority of the group, what we might call the central or modal form. Thus, many acts or interpretations will be seen as 'far-out' or 'edgy' by those in the modal group.[44] In turn, those on the margins see the symbols of the modal group as clichés or banalities. Someone outside of the particular culture group may well be unaware of these differences of interpretation. In negotiating action scenes with individuals in a culture group, we must develop a sense of the upper limit of permissible variations in particular symbolic norms. We can only decide that a certain behaviour or interpretation is too extreme or blatant when we receive confirmation that this limit has been exceeded. Given our knowledge of relevant contexts, we can make such judgments, even in situations we have never previously encountered. In the practices of each culture group there is a tacitly defined 'symbol limit', an outer edge to permissible expression (Plate 3). Within this peripheral band of the more or less acceptable, it is especially important to know the context of an action scene or symbol, since on their own these are almost invariably ambiguous or equivocal. And, where there are multiple readings in play, the door is open to irony.

Irony is the use of forms, 'that have an inner meaning for a privileged audience and an outer meaning for the persons addressed or concerned'.[45] Exchanges of irony, and the ability correctly to interpret *doubles entendres*, are the mark of those who are not only familiar with normal forms, but also with common contexts and with each other. 'Familiarity breeds contempt': an inevitable outcome of familiarity is boredom, in this case, with the 'stereotyped' or 'routine' nature of modal forms of expression. There is, therefore, a natural tendency to move away from the modal or natural form, towards those of a more complex or sophisticated nature. A fringe group might communicate its irritation towards the modal group by an ironic exaggeration of modal forms, 'sending them up' or making them deliberately 'corny'. This is a behaviour especially common in the field of dress where, for example, teenage subcultures often exaggerate to the point of caricature, the respectable fashions of their 'boring' parents.

The dictionary offers a wide range of meanings for the word 'sophisticated', highlighting a considerable social ambivalence about it. In particular, there is no clear view on the question of whether or not it is desirable. Whatever the moral consensus, sophistication is a universal phenomenon in the myriad transactions mediated through the world of goods. Private messages and 'in jokes' pass everywhere between privileged groups (privileged that is by virtue of their acquaintance with common contexts).

Whether multiple meanings, irony, and sophistication, are affectionate or aggressive, and whether in-groups are privileged in any other sense, or whether they are, on the contrary, truly on the margins of society, depends on the circumstances. A social group that feels its privileged exclusiveness threatened, when a rival (*arriviste*) group appropriates its symbols, may well react defensively by complicating and equivocating its behaviour. Only those who are truly 'in the know' will pick up the messages of social recognition hidden in the ironies of sophisticated language. An innocent parvenu will be spotted as soon as he misinterprets his first ambiguous symbol or enigmatic act.[46]

An important example occurs in the cultures concerned with art. Professional familiarity, with the formal and symbolic languages of art, enables those who share this culture to send each other covert messages carried on the manifest content of their work. Many artists carry on an invisible dialogue with their peers, or with artists from the past, on the back of images that the lay public imagines to be merely still life or landscape, love story or tragic melodrama. In our time, many of these secret messages are no longer secret. Meta-comment and critical explication have become the *raison d'être* of much modern art, which is intrinsically (and often intentionally) insignificant or banal when viewed from a wider social perspective.[47] To a great extent, the distinction between 'creator' and 'user' orientated Taste publics is erected on the basis of this tendency to exploit and render sophisticated the inherent ambiguity in the languages of particular behaviours.

This division may become extreme, for instance, when a particular creator group consciously adopts a language of studied and exaggerated ambiguity and multiple meaning. A calculated and affected language or behaviour, that is riddled with *doubles entendres* and puns, is often called *camp* or *high camp*.[48] Provocatively artificial, and insouciantly dissembling as to its intention, it is the language of the poseur (Plate 4). Camp styles flourish at times and places of transition between cultural norms. Indeed by insisting on multiple meaning as the common currency, camp prepares the way for a new modal form or norm, which coalesces out of what had been fringe or semi-private meanings.

Camp styles, whether in speech, or in the presentation of self in gesture or through the display of goods, appear to function as devices for 'role-distancing'. Distancing themselves from the immediate context of an action scene by means of linguistic devices, enables those who can master the techniques to dominate social interaction since their true purpose is constantly being masked or evaded. Mastery of a particular style of language (what Bernstein called an 'elaborated code'[49]) enables the

2.17 *When applied to more basic human functions, camp can lead to some bizarre images, the* Nautilus *sanitary ware being a good example.*

speaker grammatically to detach himself—and hence, by implication, conceptually—from the immediate context (in space or intention) of his remarks. However, there does not seem to be any clear characterization of camp in linguistic terms. Camp is often ambiguous by reason of a language of great syntactical complexity. A convoluted style, in which sentences are contructed of many subclauses held together in conditional relationships, detaches the speaker (or hearer) from an easy flow of intention carried on clear transitive verbs, active voice

and other affirmative structures. On the other hand, camp styles may equally often be expressed in disarmingly simple syntax, depending instead on punning, *doubles entendres* and meaningful insinuation and innuendo. All these different linguistic devices have their precise counterparts in behaviour and therefore in the world of goods when used as part of a person's presentational strategy.

Camp styles are often deeply offensive to the modal group, the majority users of the 'popular' culture. Inability to grasp the

2.18 *Pop design quickly picked up the techniques of pop art and recycled them into a commercial context. Exhibitions such as the 'Plastics Show' at the Victoria and Albert Museum display the Memphis derived clocks which George Sowden and Natalie Dupasquier designed for Lorenz with all the theatre previously reserved for high art. Thus legitimized, the clocks can then be sold in the museusm shop.*

intentions of a speaker (and artists, in particular, since they presume upon our attention) often leads to the imputation of hostility or contempt and provokes an aggresive reaction.[50] Paradoxically though, it was camp attitudes and styles which were particularly important in the one artistic movement which has sought to bridge the gap between creator and user-orientated Taste cultures. In pop art, which was deeply infected by the ambivalence of camp, the deliciously deplorable symbols of 'low' culture were enthusiastically embraced by 'high' artists. Transformed by stylistic alienation devices, which provided the necessary ironical quotation marks, familiar imagery from pulp fiction, advertising and mass consumption reappeared as the subject matter of the creator-orientated culture. Lichtenstein's paintings of comics, or Warhol's soup tins, were bought for small fortunes by museums, to be 'read' by a cultural élite that would never dream of using the originals![51] Soon however, designers (especially graphic designers) borrowed the pop idiom and recycled these banalities back into the commercial communication system, especially in advertising.

Contemporary advertising is both sophisticated and ironic, both artificial and elaborate, carrying incestuous private meanings between the privileged groups involved in its production. These messages are often deeply contemptuous of their ostensible audience—the mass consumer.[52] In this sense, pop is a malignant intrusion into popular. Between creators and users, the traffic in symbols is still one-way, but camp's relentless ironies and alienations are essential if it is to avoid confusion with its ostensible content—the imagery of the mass culture it despises. Those who don't see the quotation marks don't get the joke. The camp artist's problem is how to use *kitsch* without his art itself being mistaken for kitsch. The paradox is that kitsch also lives in two worlds and claims allegiance to two separate discourses. For kitsch depends for its effects on the robbery of devices and themes from high art.

What is kitsch?

There are many amusing compendia of kitsch, anthologies of the dire output of industries that mass-produce 'synthetic' emotion, 'simulated' art and a putative commitment to the most profound human values.[53] In the field of popular consumption it is hard to escape references to the passionate or sacred—to erotic arousal, to love and affection, to religious aspiration, to longing for homeland, to sorrow in bereavement or delight in infants, or merely to family togetherness and friendship. Films, television and pulp fiction provide the stream of stock characters and stereotyped situations ('soaps') which display these sacred feelings in their

65

simplest terms. Advertising picks up these themes and puts them to work in the business of selling. As any shopper, tourist or casual listener to television will know, nothing is exempt from kitsch. By a process of cultural inversion (itself a version of camp) the worst examples of bad Taste become collectors' items. First bought and sold in specialized markets, and finally ending up at Sotheby's, the exquisitely awful takes on a new significance. Eventually the whole field becomes a matter of academic study and philosophical analysis and critique.

Yet, although the classic examples (for instance, the Mona Lisa toilet seat cover) are well enough known to present themselves as a 'problem' to aestheticians and a standing affront to professional artists and designers, there is little clear understanding or analysis of kitsch. Some believe that the word itself derives from the English 'sketch'. More probably it stems from the German 'verkitschen'—to make do. Gillo Dorfles quotes with approval Ludwig Giesz's interpretation of kitsch as 'artistic rubbish'. The crucial elements in kitsch seem to be a cheapening of noble sentiments coupled with a gratuitous adoption of themes, devices and, ostensibly, values, from legitimate art. What emerges is sentimentality and not true sentiment, ersatz artiness and not true artifice, pervasive cheapness and not true worth or preciousness, as these would be expressed in real art.

Kitsch is a special category of artefacts that exists in a complex interaction (or 'dialectical relationship') with another special category of objects—that of 'real' art.[54] It is therefore no easier to define than real art. Clearly however, societies in which there is no separated cultural institution of 'art', cannot display its

2.19 *Religious kitsch from San Fransico, California, USA. The red light bulb replaces the sacred flame, Christ is a plastic injection moulding, the setting is a niche made from an abalone shell and sea-urchins painted with lurid fluorescent dye. The disparate elements are cheap and incongruous and the combination arbitrary. Visual reality clashes violently with the profundity of the religious sentiment leading to bathos.*

surrogate—kitsch—either. In such societies, variations in skill and in the investment of time and money will obviously lead to corresponding variation in the quality of goods, whether these are produced for practical purposes such as houses and tools, or whether they are made for social or religious ritual. Moreover, there may well be occasional inadvertent transgressions of the acceptable limits for the stereotyped symbolism of ritual objects. Such deviations would be condemned as incorrect or improper, just as corresponding shortcomings in the design or manufacture of tools would condemn them as useless or inefficient. The notion of bad Taste would simply not arise and kitsch would have no meaning. Native users of such flawed artefacts would fail to understand such adjectives as 'crummy', 'corny', 'phoney', 'tacky', or 'flakey' and those innumerable others that, in our society, serves notice that

2.20 *Knock-down Baroque. Again, the pretended sentiments (opulence and historical reference) collide violently with the actual construction of the table. Bathos is inevitable once it is realized that the supposedly luxurious legs are cheap die-castings which have to be bolted onto the imitation plastic onyx top.*

one culture group perceives a debasement of its expressive symbols by others.

Implicit in all these terms is a derisive tone that indicates that the speaker was not taken in by the attempted deception. Its perpetrator may have hoped to deceive us into thinking that his offering was poetry. We saw at a glance that it was prose, and very ordinary prose at that. For banality or prosaicness is the inner message of kitsch. Presented with what prima facie appeared to be art, we let our metaphorical imagination begin to play, but instead of novel insights arising from creative hypothesizing, our mental strivings were suddenly short-circuited into bathos. Hence our resentment at kitsch. Emotional let down is the inevitable result of this 'cathexis'—to use Freud's term—when what we took for a real metaphor turns out to be worthless.

In turning to Freud, we are returning to a much earlier (and simpler) brand of structuralism.[55] In his *Jokes and Their Relation to the Unconscious*, Freud was concerned to understand the expressive impact of jokes in terms of the interplay of surface language with what he perceived to be underlying structures of unconscious symbolism, commonly of a sexual nature. He was able to show that, behind the infinite variety of detailed narrative and setting in jokes, there is a limited range of stereotyped semantic structures. Indeed, virtually all jokes could be seen as examples of a few species of semantic association. *Substitution* occurs where one innocuous image or symbol stands for one of a more loaded nature (usually more sexually charged). *Displacement* is a technique that resorts to diverting our attention away from some charged area, while leaving the offending symbol at the periphery of attention. *Condensation* refers to the great variety of

verbal devices for forming more or less arbitrary associations between apparently unrelated items in the interests of humour.

Although this early work was concerned exclusively with verbal humour, the structural analysis was later applied to the analysis of dreams, and it can fruitfully be applied to other fields, such as the visual arts where it gives a good account of types of art, such as Surrealism, which depends heavily on visual jokes, that are difficult effectively to characterize with more traditional styles of art criticism. (Max Ernst's *What is a Phalustrade?* is a good inside account of the workings of joke structures in Surrealist art.)[56]

Any 'unlawful' shift which produces semantic anomalies may be taken as a joke. When a person is confronted with a manifest semantic anomaly, the possibility of humour— 'Is this a joke?'—is probably the first non-literal hypothesis. The subsequent significance of this hypothesis will be determined by the context, humour usually being signalled by other cues of voice, gesture and conventionally 'funny' goods. (Humour with only minimal collateral support has its own special flavour known as 'deadpan', although even here there is invariably enough contextual evidence to allow an eventual humorous interpretation to be sustained. Even if much of the force of deadpan humour comes precisely from the difficulty of deciding whether it is funny or serious, there must always be enough evidence for a final decision to be possible. In extreme cases there may be a lingering ambiguity of intention, but it is a rare artist or joker that can contrive to leave the issue totally unresolved.) It naturally follows, that if a speaker intends the deliberate introduction of a semantic anomaly to be interpreted, not as humour, but

2.21 Conflation is not condensation. The racing-car bed is a steady seller despite the fact that the imagery of the motor race has no relation to that of sleep.

as metaphor, then this too must be signalled by appropriate contextual clues. In circumstances where misreading might be possible, humour is excluded by surrounding the discourse or practice with forbidding seriousness. A writer such as Arthur Koestler might make much of the structural similarities between metaphor and humour, but in everyday circumstances it is important to distinguish between them quickly and fluently.[57]

Freud's effort was necessarily concerned with the explanation of why jokes were funny, rather than the interpretation of jokes that were meant to be funny, but were in fact not. In jokes which do not 'come off', it is only the surface rules that are violated, not the deep structure rules. This also appears to be true of metaphor. A 'dud' metaphor does not generate true semantic anomaly, although it may strike the reader or hearer with unfamiliar constructions or novel analogies.[58] Conflation is not condensation. We are not pressed into imaginative acts of interpretation or compelled to restructure the categories we use to make sense of the world. Superficial similarities do not make metaphors. This is what is meant by the phase, 'punning is the lowest form of wit'. In kitsch, visual punning of the crudest kind is the

most widely used device. Just as stereotyped surface transformations of prose do not make poetry, mere surface agglomerations of existing images fail to make a genuinely new poetic artefact. 'C'est pas la colle qui fait le collage,' said Ernst of his dreamlike combinations of nineteenth century prints, although they were literally stuck together. The artistic 'glue' was metaphorical and the almost unconscious combination of images by the artist suggests new and disturbing possibilities.[59] Where this is lacking we get only the banal would-be metaphor, one whose apparent artiness sends us off on a trail of creative hypotheses but quickly lets us down. The discharge of this mental energy into bathos is responsible for the irritation caused by the dud metaphors which characterize kitsch.

As an example of the way in which semantic anomalies can be used to create a kind of poetry based on metaphor, we may consider that least abstract of fields—eating. Levi-Strauss proposed to describe our eating conventions in terms of structures of basic units of Taste, the so-called gustemes. Rules for combining gustemes mark the final restrictions of concurrence—what may appear together with what—on the plate. Marinetti in his futurist cookbook devised all sorts of deviant combinations of gustemes with the intention of creating the gastronomic equivalent of Dadaist nonsense in fields other than art.[60] *La Cucina Futuristica* is deeply disturbing since it violates what are apparently deep structure rules for combining gustemes. Salami cooked in *eau de Cologne* and steeped in cold coffee does, indeed, appear to us as nonsense, but it is nonsense of a powerful kind. Pondering it may well lead to entirely new structures of Taste in food—and beyond.

We may compare the genuine, if odd, poetry of Marinetti's cooking to the prosaicness of the food described in the columns of the weekly cookery magazines. Here, in contrast to the deep structure deviancy of Marinetti, transformations are confined to arbitrary surface decoration. As Barthes perceptively noted, what are at first sight profound alterations turn out to be merely exotic glazings, disguising sauces and ornamental reshapings. In them, we discern a profoundly ambiguous attitude to the brute facts of food, raw meat and the dead bodies of beasts. Ornamental cookery 'on the one hand, flees from nature thanks to a kind of frenzied baroque (sticking shrimps in a lemon, making chicken look pink, serving grapefruit hot), and on the other, tries to reconstitute it through an incongruous artifice (strewing meringue mushrooms and holly leaves on a Christmas cake, replacing the heads of crayfish around the sophisticated bechamel which hides their bodies). It is in fact the elaboration which one finds in *petit bourgeois* trinkets (ash-trays in the shape of a saddle, lighters in the shape of a cigarette, terrines in the shape of a hare).'[61] This is a perfect description of kitsch.

Regressive symbolism, a childlike love of concreteness in imagery (abstract toys are bad Taste to most children), together with the surface appearance of creativeness (oddness and novelty or curiosity value) are the stock in trade of trinkets, geegaws and baubles everywhere. Preferences for such items are certainly not confined to any particular social group. Examples of aristocratic and *haut-bourgeois* kitsch abound in the published works. (The apparent predominance of down-market items from recent years is probably the result of the low survival rate of 'artistic rubbish' from the

2.22 *Coffee-grinder table lamp. Bizarre juxtapositions are commonplace in down-market furniture stores.*

lower social groups of earlier periods.) Nor are the particular quasi-metaphoric usages which characterize kitsch confined to any particular level of society. Primitive, childish or naive speech may be wildly rhetorical, as Adam Smith noted: 'There is nowhere more use made of figures than in the lowest and most vulgar conversation.' Similarly, in the world of goods, folk or ethnic products often display formal complexity and highly condensed symbolism. Neither is there any necessary protection against the commercial seductions of kitsch. Noble savages everywhere seem willing to trade their birthright for baubles and trinkets,

70

2.23 *Punning is the lowest form of wit. Kitsch invariably ensues when punning substitutes for genuine metaphor. In the 'golfer's teapot', five levels of pun are combined: the ball shape of the pot, the golfer on the lid 'teeing-off', the 'tee/tea' and 'for/4' jokes and the reference to the popular song.*

the artistic rubbish of an industrial society. But when the majority appears to prefer the ersatz to the real thing, who is out of step? Where does this leave social policies which seek to raise the level of public Taste? No wonder previous Taste reformers were grateful for functionalist theories of design, for these enabled them to bypass the difficulties raised by the brutal rejoinder of 'Who says?' from the populace at large.

Polluting the wellsprings?—the problem of mass culture

The charge against kitsch amounts to the fact that it is not real poetry, although it appropriates superficially poetic devices. Why should this be important? Why should the mass production of artistic rubbish be of concern if that is what people want? Two important strands in the indictment of so-called mass culture rest on the analogy with language and need discussing here. First, fake or sham

symbolism is held to be dangerous to genuine symbolism. By an analogy to the economic law which states that 'bad money drives out good', so it is alleged, kitsch subverts genuine art by corrupting the very language of art itself. True art then becomes impossible. Second, the unremitting consumption of 'phoney' or 'corny' items is supposed to have adverse social or psychological effects on the consumer, rendering him incapable of the full exercise of his humanity which essentially lies in communication. He may be denied the essential practice in the skills of expression, skills which enable him fully to assert his personal identity, and may, therefore, be tranquilized into acquiescense in injustice, repression or exploitation.

The critique of mass culture has been very well reviewed by Herbert Gans.[62] In reality, firm evidence for either of these propositions is very hard to find. High culture has generally fared as well as any other in the competition for resources (especially state subsidy). Indeed, in proportion to the numbers of consumers it is usually much the better resourced. As to the alleged corrupting effects of mass culture, factual evidence has been very hard to obtain, even in the extreme case of the supposed contagion of violence induced by exposure to regular brutality on television.

Most of the debate about mass culture has been concerned with the various 'high' arts such as music, theatre, literature and painting, which are seen to be threatened by contemporary mass entertainment. In the field of man-made goods, most attention has hitherto been focussed on threats to public amenity by visual pollution. This may be due to the spoiling of rural or urban landscape by the proliferation of artistic rubbish in the haphazard building of kitsch. It may simply be due to

71

2.24 Sometimes however punning can be amusing— especially when it is carried through on a a large enough scale. The Hotel Normande, Panne, Belgium imitates a ship.

an accumulation of a litter of discarded arte-facts. In recent times, less attention has been directed to the supposedly corrupting effects of kitsch indoors. Although the contemporary heirs to Ruskin and Morris still fervently argue for the moral improvement to be enjoyed by surrounding oneself with decent, well-made furniture, the matter has not stirred the passions of any wider circles. But even if we reject those arguments against kitsch, which are based on its alleged menace as visual pollution, there are other strong arguments for extending the influence of artistic culture into everyday goods and settings. These derive from the particular nature of artistic language, and are considered in the final chapter.

What of the argument concerning the corruption of language itself? That all the modern arts (relative to those of earlier preindustrial cultures) are poorer than they could be is so vague a proposition that it is hard to refute by means of examples. It is still more difficult to disprove the further assertion that this allegedly poor quality is due to an impoverishment of language. Any impoverishment has been wilful, the result of a conscious renunciation or withdrawal, rather than the supposed depredations of kitsch. The Modern Movement in design arose from a desire to 'purify the dialect of the tribe' by eliminating all extraneous symbolism, whether sham or otherwise. The result was certainly not a new visual lingua franca.

The decorated and exotic, the symbolic and the nostalgic, are still the most favoured styles in popular Taste for goods found in most homes. There have been many efforts to find compromising positions in the marketplace, often by offering styles which combine forms from simple peasant or folk traditions with modern rational production techniques. Occasionally, and among a limited range of social groups, these have had a considerable impact on design, as testified by the successes of the Conran empire and IKEA across Europe. But despite the fortunes that have been made, it is

2.25 Mass culture I. Does bad architecture or 'pseudo' art do any harm? Why should the intelligentsia worry about genuinely popular Taste? Entrance to a seafood restaurant, Lake Shore Drive, Chicago, USA.

clear that consumers of these styles are drawn from a narrow range of the upper middle class, and predominantly from among the youthful intelligentsia. Most other social groups have continued with traditional consumption patterns and time-honoured symbolic habits.

Whether or not the mass consumption of what would be termed by 'design-conscious' consumers as kitsch really has had any of the baneful effects that have been prophecied remains an open question. Certainly, little serious research has been done to evaluate the effectiveness of the propaganda for 'good'

73

Taste which, after all, accounts for a considerable portion of the budgets of government-sponsored institutions for the promotion of design. In any event, the fashion for attempts at social understanding using quasi-linguistic models is on the wane.

Basil Bernstein's suggestions that different social classes speak different languages, based on restricted and elaborated codes, ran into difficulties as it proved remarkably difficult to give the idea of codes any precise operational meaning, although certain differences in the extent and type of nesting and branching in everyday speech were noted.[63] Following up his suggestions that similar codes should be found in the world of goods has been even more difficult, although here again some tantalizing analogies can be found. Nevertheless, the idea that different Tastes should be seen as different dialects, if not different languages, is still attractive as it removes the pejorative overtones invariably associated with the discussion of Taste in terms of allegedly superior mental faculties of discrimination or judgment. All languages are successful adaptations to the particular environments of their speakers and Tastes should, on this analogy, be regarded in the same manner. It is clear that, at the present time, in the stratified society which prevails, no end to the stylistic Tower of Babel in which we live is in sight: 'them' and 'us' continue to be divided by our different Tastes.

To date we have discussed the metaphor of language only in terms of its hidden structures—syntax and semantics. However, there is, in the manifest, surface features of language production which is part of our on-going social behaviour, another level of analysis usually termed *pragmatics*. This level has also inspired critics and theoreticians of Taste yet further to

2.26 *Mass culture II. Does bad design corrupt? Does the influence of the infantile comic popularized by Disney really corrupt other visual languages? Mickey Mouse telephone, Dayton, Ohio, USA.*

develop aspects of the language metaphor. Traditional aesthetics has naturally been closest to pragmatics since this is the level which is most easily open to observation and introspection. In recent years, pragmatics has itself been subjected to much closer theoretical analysis and, in turn, this work has opened up new ways of understanding social behaviour in general. Needless to say, structures of whatever kind or level are not a conscious part of everyday life. Ordinary behaviour is, in this sense, transparent to structure. Nevertheless, models of behaviour which incorporate formal definitions of structure, especially 'split-level' models, with the observable features of everyday life—pragmatics—riding on the back of deeper levels, have much to offer to the understanding of Taste. We consider some of these in the next chapter, which surveys some traditional aesthetic issues, issues which can now be seen as aspects of pragmatics, the pragmatics of truth, mastery and surprise.

Notes and References to Chapter 2

1 For example, the otherwise excellent book, A. Lurie, *The Language of Clothes*, London: Heineman, 1981, Chapter 1, 'Clothing as a Sign System.' The author, a noted novelist and Professor of English, sets out a sketchy theory based on sartorial analogies to words, sentences, adverbs, and adjectives but does not develop the metaphor of language beyond mere suggestions in an otherwise perceptive analysis of fashion. Similarly, C. Alexander in *Pattern Language*, Oxford: Oxford University Press, 1977, says nothing that justifies the use of the linguistic metaphor. There is, in fact, a long tradition of linguistic analogy with the visual arts. For example, Alberti compares the standard Renaissance analytical schema for sentences with the 'parts' of a painting. See M. Baxandall, *Giotto and the Orators*, Oxford: Clarendon Press, 1971, p. 131 *et seq*.

2 O. Jones, *The Grammar of Ornament* (reprint of the 1865 edition), London: Van Nostrand Reinhold, 1972.

3 C. Blanc, *Grammaire des Arts du Dessin*, Paris, 1867.

4 L. F. Day, *The Planning of Ornament*, New York: Garland, 1977 (facsimile reprint of the first edition, 1887).

5 On neo-Classicism in the visual arts and architecture, see H. Homer, *Neo-Classicism*, Harmondsworth: Penguin, 1968. For a compilation of documents see L. E. A. Eitner, *Neo-Classicism and Romanticism*, Englewood Cliffs: Prentice-Hall, 1970. On the ways in which disparate and exotic styles were incorporated into the tradition of ornament see E. H. Gombrich, *The Sense of Order—a study in the psychology of decorative art*, Oxford: Phaidon, 1979.

6 For reprints of some salient extracts from Victorian books on etiquette see M. Douglas, *Rules and Meanings*, London: Penguin, 1973, p. 216. A further convenient reprinted source is AGOGOS, *Hints on Etiquette—with a Glance at Bad Habits*, London: Longman, 1836, reprinted London: Turnstile Press, 1947. Often these books were published anonymously in a small format convenient for the pocket so that they could be consulted unobtrusively during functions, for example *Mixing in Society—a complete manual of manners*, by The Right Honourable Countess of ***, London: George Routledge and Sons, n.d. For a contemporary view, see *Debrett's Correct Form—Social and Professional Etiquette, Precedents and Protocol*, London: Debrett's Peerage Ltd., 1986.

7 M. Arnold, "Culture and Anarchy" in E. H. Super (Ed.), *The Complete Works of Matthew Arnold*, Volume 5, Ann Arbor: University of Michigan Press, 1965. C. Dickens, *Household Words*, 1852, reprinted in *Architectural Review*, Volume CLXV, Number 984, Feb. 1979, p. 119 with a commentary by Jules Lubbock and contemporary drawings.

8 N. Pevsner, *An Enquiry into Industrial Art in England*, Cambridge: Cambridge University Press, 1937. See also *Pioneers of Modern Design*, Harmondsworth: Penguin, 1960 (originally published as *Pioneers of the Modern Movement*, Faber, 1936).

9 G. Baird and C. Jencks (Eds.), *Meaning in Architecture*, London: Barrie and Rockliffe, The Cresset Press, 1969, was a pioneering book in this area still much read today. Charles Jencks has gone on to write a whole series of books on contemporary architecture which explore the symbolic significance of buildings.

10 A tabulation of the classes in which the exhibits were grouped is given in

C. H. Gibbs-Smith, *The Great Exhibition of 1851*, London: HMSO, 1950, p. 14. *The Art Journal Catalogue to the Great Exhibition* (reprinted Newton Abbot: David and Charles, 1970) includes the essay by R. N. Wornum, "The Exhibition as a Lesson in Taste" in which the exhibits are compared in groups according to their technologies.

11 See A. Adgeburnham, *Shopping in Style*, London: Thames and Hudson, 1979, and D. Davies, *A History of Shopping*, London: Routledge and Kegan Paul, 1966, for accounts of the evolution of modern shops.

12 For an introduction to the issues which underlie the idea that there are (at least relatively) universal semantic structures, see R. A. Hudson, *Socialinguistics*, Cambridge: Cambridge University Press, 1987, p. 84 *et seq.* C. E. Osgood, C. J. Suci and P. H. Tannenbaum, *The Measurement of Meaning*, Urbana: University of Illinois Press, 1957, was the pioneering text which discussed techniques for measuring meanings in non-verbal contexts using the technique of semantic differential analysis which is still widely used today. See in particular p. 290 *et seq.*

13 On the acquisition of prototypical categories see E. R. MacCormac, *A Cognitive Theory of Metaphor*, Cambridge, Mass: MIT Press, 1985, especially p. 69 *et seq.*

14 See F. G. Jacobs, *A History of Dolls Houses*, London: Cassell, 1954. For a more recent selection from the European tradition see J. Latham, *Dolls Houses—a personal choice*, London: Black, 1968. Both books have useful bibliographies of earlier texts on the subject.

15 For a simple account of the way in which ideas from Jakobson's phonetics formed the basis for later structuralist thinking see E. Leach, *Levi-Strauss*, London: Fontana (Modern Masters), 1970, p. 27 *et seq.*

16 C. Levi-Strauss, *Structural Anthropology*, trans. C. Jacobson and B. G. Schoepf, Allen Lane: The Penguin Press, 1977.

17 R. Barthes, *Système de la Mode*, Paris: Editions du Seuil, 1971, especially Chapter 10. The English translation is by M. Ward and R. Howard, *The Fashion System*, London: Jonathan Cape, 1985.

18 A. Lurie, *op. cit.*, pp. 121-122 shows the range of minute formal and social discriminations possible within the narrow range of the Edwardian gentleman's suit.

19 An attempt to set out all the elements which in combination will generate the infinite variety of ensembles that mark the flow of fashion so that a computerized account can be made of those combinatorial possibilities actually used historically, has been made by R. Holman, "A Transcription System and Analysis for a Study of Women's Clothing Behaviour." *Semiotica*, Volume 32, 1980, pp. 11-34.

20 P. Pettit, *The Concept of Structuralism—a Critical Analysis*, Dublin: Gill and Macmillan, 1975, p. 64.

21 See C. Lorenz, "Globalisation—a two-edged sword." *Design*, Number 447, March 1986, pp. 34-37. (Excerpted from C. Lorenz, *The Design Dimension—product strategy and the challenge of global marketing*, Oxford: Basil Blackwell, 1986.)

22 H. Koning and J. Eisenberg, "The Language of the Prairie." *Planning and Environment B*, Volume 8, 1981, pp. 295-323.

23 Other convincing efforts at the computer generation of styles include: G. Stiny and W. J. Mitchell, "The Grammar of Paradise—on the generation of Mughal gardens." *Environment and Planning B*, Volume 7(2), 1980, p. 209. T. Weissman Knight, "The Generation of Hepplewhite Chairback Designs." *Environment and Planning B*, Volume 7, 1980, p. 227. G. Stiny and W. J. Mitchell, "The Palladian Grammar." *Environment and Planning B*, Volume 1, 1978, p. 5.

24 E. Boring, *Sensation and Perception in Experimental Psychology*, New York: Appleton-Century-Crofts, 1942, p. 252 *et seq.* is an historic account of Gestalt psychology written when the issues and controversies were still fresh. Rudolf Arnheim has spent a lifetime investigating the interaction between Gestalt

psychology and the visual arts, including architecture. His recent book R. Arnheim, *The Power of the Center*, Berkeley: University of California Press, 1988, reviews this work and contains a bibliography of his many writings.

25 Texts which are congenial to this approach, though from somewhat different points of view, include: U. Neisser, *Cognitive Psychology*, New York: Appleton-Century-Crofts, 1967, and J. J. Gibson, *The Ecological Approach to Perception*, Boston: Houghton Mifflin, 1979. Neisser stresses analogies between the mental processes of visual perception and feature detection software based on serial processing, while Gibson in his later work insisted on the importance of the detection of high-level structural invariants of a differential character in the ambient optical array.

26 For a simple exposition of these concepts see L. Uhr, *Pattern Recognition, Learning and Thought—computer programmed models of higher mental processes*, Englewood Cliffs: Prentice-Hall, 1973. In fact, all research since this early publication has indicated the true complexity of mental pattern recognition. One key issue is the precise relationship between Gestalt phenomena and what is known of the neural basis of information processing in the brain. See P. C. Dodwell and T. Caelli (Eds.), *Figural Synthesis*, Hillsdale: Erlbaum, 1984, and the discussion which followed its review by R. Arnheim in *Leonardo*, Volume 20, Number 4, 1987. The analogy suggested here is not meant to imply a position on these highly technical matters.

27 The intentional dislocation of normal forms in behaviour, by means of arbitrary rearrangement of expected items or sequences, can be used as an experimental technique to probe the frontiers of normal expectations. It is sometimes known as 'garfinkeling' after the inventor of the method. See H. Garfinkel, *Studies in Ethnomethodology*, Englewood Cliffs: Prentice-Hall, 1967.

28 For a discussion of various theoretical models of symbolic association see E. R. MacCormac, *op. cit.*, Chapter 4.

29 Sensitivity, as understood by aestheticians in terms of a generalized 'refinement of the sensibility', dissolves into a myriad different psychological factors studied by scientifically minded marketing researchers. See, for example, R. Markin, *Consumer Behaviour—a Cognitive Orientation*, New York: Macmillan, 1974.

30 The term 'product semantics' was put into circulation by K. Krippendorf and R. Butter, "Product Semantics: Exploring the Symbolic Qualities of Form." *Innovation*, Volume 3, Number 2, 1984, p. 4.

31 In particular, the psychologist G. Smets of the Technical University, Delft, Netherlands and the communication theorist K. Krippendorf of the School of Communication, University of Pennsylvania, Philadelphia, USA. The key papers on the subject have been published in a special edition of *Design Issues*, Volume V, Number 2, Spring 1989, and in the forthcoming *Proceedings of the 1989 Conference on Product Semantics at the University of Industrial Arts, Helsinki*, in publication.

32 The broadest statement of the scope of product semantics is that of Krippendorf. See K. Krippendorf, "On the Essential Contexts of Artefacts or On the Proposition that Design is Making Sense of Things." *Design Issues, op. cit.*

33 G Baird and C. Jencks (Eds.), *op. cit.*

34 See R. I. Blaich, "Philips Corporate Industrial Design: A Personal Account." *Design Issues, op. cit.* In fact, all the essential features of the design were manifested in a project by Graham Hynes completed when he was studying at Kingston Polytechnic. The brief was to explore lifestyle possibilities of a portable electronic product for a youth market and the 'Roller' solution was one of the more conservative proposals. Product development and the name, which is a crucial part of the marketing platform, was of course by Philips. Blaich makes it clear that the shift in marketing strategy would not have happened without the

supporting rationale emerging from product semantics.

35 See J. J. Gibson, *The Ecological Approach to Visual Perception*, Boston: Houghton Mifflin, 1979.

36 J. Rheinfrank, "On the Design of Design." *Proceedings of the 1989 Conference on Product Semantics, University of Industrial Arts, Helsinki,* in publication

37 R. Butter, "Putting Theory into Practice." *Design Issues, op. cit.*, p. 51.

38 L. Krohn and M. McCoy, "Beyond Beige: Interpretive Design for the Post-Industrial Age." *Design Issues, op. cit.*, p. 112.

39 On the usefulness of J. J. Gibson's theories of affordances to designers, see G. Smets, "Perceptual Meaning." *Design Issues, op. cit.*, p. 86.

40 For example, the dimension of values and conventions is the most abstract and at the same time most perfunctorily treated of the the six 'semantic dimensions' of space proposed by Lannoch. His visual examples are also expressed in minimal geometric forms. See H. Lannoch and H-J. Lannoch, "Towards a Semantic Notion of Space." *Design Issues, op. cit.*, p. 40.

41 On the difference between literal and metaphorical meanings see E. R. MacCormac, *op. cit.*, p. 53.

42 P. Pettit, *op. cit.*, p.115.

43 E. R. MacCormac, *op. cit.*, p. 85 *et seq.*

44 For a discussion of the shifting nuances of modal and marginal behaviour within socially marginal groups see D. Hebdige, *Sub-Cultures—the meaning of style*, London: Methuen, 1979.

45 Oxford English Dictionary

46 This behaviour is well documented, even in ancient cultures. R. MacMullen, *Roman Social Relations*, New Haven: Yale University Press, 1981, discusses some examples of Roman snobbery. A good example from the literature is the story of Trimalchio, the slave who inherited his master's goods but did not know how to use them 'correctly'. Petronius, *Satyricon*, Book 15, p. 45, trans. J. Sullivan, Harmondsworth: Penguin, 1965.

47 In this sense, the linguistic gamesmanship of conceptual art is the direct progeny of Marcel Duchamp's studied banality. For an account of twentieth century art as meta-comment, see C. Tompkins, *Ahead of the Game* (previously published as *The Bride and the Bachelors*), Harmondsworth: Penguin, 1968.

48 S. Sonntag, "On Camp" in *Against Interpretation and other Essays*, London: Andre Deutsch, 1987 (first edition 1961), p. 275 *et seq.* A camp masterpiece is Liberace, *The Things I Love*, New York: Grosset and Dunlap, 1976, copiously illustrated with images of his house and his many costumes it also sets out his views on Taste in camp aphorisms such as 'I love the fake—provided that it looks real'.

49 See note 63 to this chapter for references to Bernstein's many papers.

50 Much of the symbolic (and sometimes physical) struggle between rival groups found in more or less deviant youth culture such as 'mods' and 'rockers', or 'mod-revivalists' and 'skin-heads' turns on a wilful misreading of intentional aggressiveness in images seen as effeminate. These tensions have been exploited by many real or pretend 'bisexual' rock musicians who pose as 'gender-benders'. See D. Hill, *Designer Boys and Material Girls— Manufacturing the '80s Pop Dream*, London: Blandford Press, 1986, p. 135 *et seq.* for an account of this phenomenon and its commercial exploitation.

51 J. Russell and S. Gablik, *Pop Art Redefined*, London: Thames and Hudson, 1969.

52 For the way in which those who work in the commercialized world of newspapers and television distance themselves from the audience they despise, see K. Roberts, *Contemporary Society and the Growth of Leisure*, London: Longman, 1978, p. 48. For a structuralist unravelling of covert messages—often contemptuous—see J. Williamson, *Decoding Advertisments*, London: Marion Boyars, 1978.

53 G. Dorfles, *Kitsch—an anthology of bad taste*, London: Studio Vista, 1969. The best theoretical discussion of kitsch and its relation to contemporary culture is M. Calinescu, *Faces of Modernity*, Bloomington: Indiana University Press, 1977, p. 225 *et seq.*

54 The argument that there is a special 'dialectical' relationship between kitsch and the abstract art of the twentieth century *avant-garde* derives from an early essay by Clement Greenberg, "The Avant-Garde and Kitsch" reprinted in C. Greenberg, *Art and Culture*, London: Thames and Hudson, 1973. The issue is debated by M. Calinescu, *Images of Modernity—avant-garde, decadence, kitsch*, Bloomington: Indiana University Press, 1977.

55 S. Freud, "Jokes and Their Relation to the Unconscious." *Collected Works*, Volume 8, translated under the editorship of J. Strachey, London: Hogarth, 1960. Originally published 1905.

56 M. Ernst, *Beyond Painting*, New York: Wittenborn, 1948.

57 See A. Koestler, *The Act of Creation*, London: Pan Books, 1975, and its review by Medawar in P. Medawar, *The Art of the Soluble*, Harmondsworth: Penguin, 1969.

58 The approach outlined here gives a more technical meaning to the definition of Theodor Adorno who characterized kitsch as 'a parody of catharsis'. See M. Calinescu, *op. cit.*, p. 241.

59 Collections of Max Ernst's collages have been published, for example, *Une Semaine de Bonté*, New York: Dover Publications, 1976 and *La Femme à 100 Têtes*, Berlin: Gerhardt, 1962.

60 F. T. Marinetti, *La Cucina Futuristica*, Milan: Sonzogno, 1932. The English edition is *Futurist Cookbook*, trans. S. Brill, London: Trefoil Publishers, 1989. In combining such unlikely ingredients and techniques as salami cooked in *eau de Cologne* and soused in cold coffee, Marinetti is deliberately setting out to violate what he perceived as the natural combinations of gastronomy and create a gustatory shock—if only in anticipation—of the kind that we have previously attributed to ice-cream and mustard. Bizarre food combinations make up the art form of the German 'sculptor', Daniel Spoerri. See for example D. Spoerri, *Exhibition Catalogue*, Zuricher Kunstgesellschaft, Helmhaus, Zurich, April–May 1972.

61 R. Barthes, *Mythologies*, trans. A. Lavers, London: Jonathan Cape, 1972, p. 79.

62 H. Gans, *Popular Culture and High Culture*, New York: Basic Books, 1974. An excellent history of the concept of mass society is S. Giner, *Mass Society*, London: Martin Robertson, 1976. A collection of contemporary readings on the topic is B. Rosenberg and D. White (Eds.), *Mass Culture and the Popular Arts in America*, New York: Free Press, 1957.

63 Basil Bernstein's many papers on this topic are collected in B. Bernstein, *Class, Codes and Social Control*, London: Routledge and Kegan Paul, 1975. The issues and the evidence have been well reviewed by A. D. Edwards, *Language in Culture and Class*, London: Heineman, 1976, p. 81 *et seq.* See also H. Rosen, *Language and Class*, London: Falling Water Press, 1972, for a hostile review of Bernstein's ideas. An important review of the field is R. Hodge, "Linguistics and Popular Culture" reprinted in C. W. E. Bigsby, *Approaches to Popular Culture*, London: Edward Arnold, 1979, p. 107.

3. Critical Values and Social Behaviour

3.1 *The scenery of everyday life. Goods and their settings provide the essential background props for the role-play of family life. Domestic interior, Venice, California, USA.*

The nature of the social act

Attempts to derive accounts of particular behaviours—especially behaviours concerned with Taste—from generalizations about human nature have not been very instructive. Theories pitched at the level of biology, theories which appeal to instincts or natural passions for example, invariably explain far too much. We have to look for a level of explanation that is usefully wide, but not so wide that it ends up by explaining everything everywhere.

Matters of Taste are, in the end, social matters. It is far more useful, therefore, to seek an understanding of Taste in the analysis of social relationships and the way in which transactions with goods are embodied into the structure of society. Social mores are expressed in preferences and choices from among available goods in ways as many and various as societies themselves. If we want usefully general insights, we must look at the most fundamental level of human relationships—the social act itself.

In shifting the discussion of Taste onto social relationships at their most general level, we immediately encounter another metaphor which, like that of Taste, is so deeply embedded in everyday language that we rarely notice its original sense. Yet, when we speak of a social act, or a social role, or an action scene or a social setting, we are alluding (usually unaware) to the plays and players, scenery and stages from which these terms derive their meanings. Before we review how the dramaturgic metaphor is treated by modern sociology, let us note some of its more obvious deficiencies as a description of social behaviour in everyday life.

In real life there are no characters. Actors in a real life scene are not pretending to be somebody else—some pre-existing fictional personage invented by an absent author—the notion of a social role implies a personality that is made up by the actor as he or she goes along. As such, it is subject to constraints both looser and more general than those which are laid upon an author's *dramatis personae*. Again, in real life acting there is no script. The events in which we play a part are not written out or plotted. Instead, the social actor improvises his or her conduct in ways which are to a considerable degree unpremeditated. Moreover, there is usually no invited audience—often no audience at all. Social actors act for, and with, each other alone.

Despite these reservations, the dramaturgic metaphor is still persuasive. In fact, in its adaptation to the technical language of sociology, it is usually stripped of all these overtones of fiction, wilful contrivance and make believe, that animate its use in everyday speech. Yet it is precisely these ingredients, which are powerful and subtle elements in a variety of sociological analysis suggested by Erving Goffman, which take us closer to the social roots of Taste.[1] This perspective argues for a creative and constructive sense in which our goods serve as props or scenery in the drama of everyday life, a drama in which real or potential audiences are considered more often than is commonly supposed. From this perspective, Taste is part of a continuous effort in the scenic design with which we create the essential backdrop and costume for our intended social acts within our daily 'production'.

Crucial to our understanding of this perspective is the concept of social behaviour as essentially creative and open-ended.[2] It is an

83

activity that proceeds continuously and in real time, without a script. We can regard social interaction as the process of negotiating a succession of individual social acts. In a particular action scene, each participant articulates his or her behaviour guided by a continuous effort to interpret the intentions and meanings of the other participants. Each social act involves creative reciprocal interplay between persons. This process has been called *negotiated creativeness*, as each new tentative behaviour by one person is subsequently endorsed or validated only if it is met by an appropriate activity from another participant. Negotiated creativeness entails the continuous generation of possible behaviours and, equally, of possible interpretations of the behaviour of others.

How do we do this? Obviously, through all the familiar processes of learning in childhood, we acquire a knowledge of normal responses, approved routines, and likely outcomes to stock situations, as well as a repertoire of appropriate next moves. However, there is no way that knowledge of this kind could be used in practice if it is conceived merely as a store of behavioural data. Each social act is, at least in detail, novel and, because it occurs in real time, retrieving the data would not be possible, as the data files would necessarily be enormous and matching likely instances to a particular unfolding scene would take too long. Instead, each party to a social act employs a kind of hypothetico-deductive strategy, using clues to make guesses about the intentions and meanings of the other. In doing this, most features of a person's behaviour can be ignored and attention concentrated solely on those particular features which are salient for present purposes. Thus, appraisal of a comparatively

small number of features in the flow of events serves to maintain unbroken the assumptions and expectations upon which a particular interpretation and response is based. It is important that the flow of reciprocal creativeness should not break down; for this reason, this strategy has been called 'promissory'.

On a larger time scale, we memorize strings of interpretations and assemble them into a coherent and consistent storyline or scenario which accounts for longer sequences of social behaviour. We then use these to frame general strategies of our own. The element of pattern in behaviour makes this promissory strategy work. We are able to invent predictive guesses about another's intentions and likely next move because, despite the manifest novelty of any particular action scene, we know they are unlikely to be random, but structured. So long as events continue to unfold in a structured fashion, interpretation is possible despite the fact that, at least in its details, each social act is unique. This feature of social behaviour has often suggested the analogy with language— especially speech. So familiar are we with this particular reciprocal flow of negotiated creativeness that, within our own language, we can derive interpretation even from what is not spoken, from what exists 'between the lines'. Much the same is true of non-verbal 'languages' such as facial expressions and body gestures.[3] Goods and their settings provide vital clues to the meanings and intentions of others and enable us appropriately to guide our own behavioural flow. Body adornment (make up and costume) and interior decoration or scenery provide an essential background of circumstantial evidence which we use to direct the generation of tentative interpretations and, at the same time, cross-check other interpretations derived from speech and physical acts.

Each culture and, within it, each subcultural group, will have different sorts of behavioural patterning or social norms and, of course, different Tastes. Different types of behaviour and behavioural setting including, importantly, the selection of goods, will count as evidence in favour of a certain interpretation of another's intentions. Nevertheless, underlying all these apparent differences, there are a few features of behaviour which have to be communicated and understood if social interaction is to proceed. We can regard these as the necessary minimum conditions for negotiated creativeness. Expressed in their different ways, they form the basis for the many underlying similarities in the critical values, or Tastes, of very different culture groups.

Some sociologists, notably Aaron Cicourel have attempted to develop an analogy for social action with certain theories of language production.[4] Drawing on Noam Chomsky's ideas of a deep structure of language, in which are embedded the fundamental operations of understanding, Cicourel suggests that there are parallel deep structures in the mental operations which generate the interpretation and articulation of social behaviour. So-called *interpretive procedures*, perhaps inherited or, at any rate, acquired in early infancy, form the deep structure of social interaction which is fundamental to the ability to generate understanding of what is going on in endlessly novel situations. Just as the universal deep structures in the grammars of different languages are mapped on to surface structures of almost infinite variety, the interpretive procedures of social interaction are mapped on to social norms of equal diversity, each characteristic of the social structures of particular groups. Undoubtedly, this two level model does give a logical description of negotiated creativeness, that is, of our ability to generate (in language and social behaviour) endless novelty, novelty which is nevertheless understood. However, it is unclear how this model relates in practice to what we know of mental functioning. Whether our mental software has this sort of structure is unknown. At this stage, however, models such as Cicourel's would appear to have the minimum criteria required for a logical explanation for negotiated creativeness.

Pushing the analogy one stage further, we can suggest that underlying universals in the operation of Taste are derived from these deep structures. All the innumerable, diverse and often conflicting systems of critical values are generated by mapping these interpretive procedures on to the social norms of different cultural groups, in particular, on to the social norms which characterize the deployment of goods and practices in certain sensitive social, often domestic, settings.

With this theoretical preamble behind us, we can now consider the influence of the fundamental features of our interpretive procedures for social interaction on familiar debates in the history of Taste. Well known issues in matters of Taste, from classical times to the present day, will doubtless be familiar to the historian of art and design. However, by putting them into this new framework, we remove them from the abstruse argumentation of the philosophers and insert them into the centre of ordinary social life. We thus pave the way for an extension of the discussion of Taste in those areas which matter to most people—the purchase of consumer goods and their deployment in the conduct of everyday domestic affairs.

Previously known as the pathetic fallacy, the projection of human qualities and values onto external objects and settings has usually been seen as a rather special effort of the sensibility, involving the imputation of feelings and body-states of a physical kind, most commonly pathos and awe.[5] Associated with Romantic attitudes, and usually confined to natural objects or landscapes, it has often been regarded as a symptom of a lack of moral restraint or, at the very least, of intellectual confusion. We can now see the projection of human values on to objects and settings, including man-made ones, not merely in empathetic, physical terms—a kind of undifferentiated *frisson*—but as essentially symbolic, a crucial part of the normal flow of interpretive behaviour needed for daily life.

3.2 *'Say it loud with fake fur.' Ersatz materials are often advertised aggressively for what they are—fake—especially in the fashion world where the provocative is usually a good selling angle.*

Beauty and truth

Our primary task in social interaction is to establish the thrust of others' intentions. Everything in a particular action scene (including the man-made goods that usually form the setting) is used as potential evidence and searched for clues that might guide the flow of hypothesis and deduction, inference and act. Fundamental to all of this is the maintenance of the conviction of veracity. Only when we are sure that everything is really as it appears can the flow of negotiated creativeness proceed. Hence the vital importance of continuous checks for honesty. In a person's behaviour there are innumerable clues which we use to convince ourselves that what is being said or done really is what it appears. In sentences, we check for affirmative strength and clarity, for internal consistency and the absence of disjunctions. There are usually stylistic features which are used as indexes of veracity. Even on the telephone, we can attempt to pick up clues from intonation and the regularity or hesitation of phrasing. In face to face encounters, we can watch facial expressions—which often speak volumes. Body language—the range and nuance of gesture—also reveals whether the truth is being spoken.

A person's goods, their dress and immediate choice of surroundings, provide a vital source of collateral evidence in interpreting social interaction, therefore, it is not surprising that all the many adjectives for characterizing personal veracity are found in the critical appraisal of goods themselves.[6] Thus, we can

3.3 That natural materials equal quality is a myth that still sells goods—even when the material itself is ersatz (woodgrain printed plastic film on chipboard) and the setting (imitation 'wood' ends to the steel casing of a cheap electric fire) is irrelevant.

speak of styles in furniture as sincere or insincere, honest or dishonest. Similarly with candour or ambivalence, frankness or evasiveness. And, in making our judgments about the world of goods, we rely on the same sort of internal cross-checking that we employ for everyday speech.

An important viewpoint in discussions of Taste which centre on veracity, asserts that goods should be exactly what they seem, with no room for artifice. Materials and construction should be forthright and frankly disclosed for what they are. This is the doctrine of *truth to materials*. Of course, goods do not overtly express the logic of their production in a clear and unambiguous manner. Quite the contrary, making something to look like something else (usually more expensive) is as old as history, and the dishonest craftsman a creature of legend. The very proliferation of stories of the use of skill to deceive, of substitute and sham, not to mention the many laws attempting to prevent such practices, testifies to an abiding necessity for faith in honest craftsmanship and truth to materials on the part of the lay consumer.[7] Most people have some craft skills—usually of a domestic kind—and know well the tricks of 'bodging' and covering up.

Historically, attitudes to the covert transformation of materials and the creation of illusory resemblances to others are rather variable. Sometimes, a plain style emphasizes the qualities of a material near to its raw state or, at any rate, to its appearance in a blank form. At other periods, stylistic exuberance may endorse such skilful feats of camouflage that even stone carvers may convince us that they are dealing in a fluid material, infinitely malleable. To those accustomed to plain craftsmanship, this might seem like torturing the material beyond endurance. Even so, it would not have been considered illicit, merely perverse. It is the manufacture of illusion by large-scale industry that finally overwhelms the craftsman's view of the logic of production. From the early nineteenth century we begin to read denunciations of industrial fakery and sham, in a world where nothing is what it appears. Even those who are catholic in their attitude to form and technique eventually rebel against a world of simulated finishes. Today, despite the efforts of jolly advertisers to make us feel cheerful about 'mock-croc' or 'fake-snake' on our shoes or handbags, the epithet plastic is still a powerful term of abuse, signifying 'fraudulent'.

By contrast, natural materials, such as wood, still retain a potent appeal as symbols of honesty and worth. Today, for example, in industries such as the mass production of radios and televisions, cabinet making is a hopelessly uneconomic activity, as the casing must be very cheap compared with the electronic gadgetry that makes it work. Nevertheless, marketing men still feel symbolic craftsmanship to be essential. This is now achieved by high technology marvels such as structural foam moulded cabinets covered with a thin skin of plastic film which is printed to look like wood. Teak equals quality—even when the wood goes round a corner without any end-grain! Nor does the powerful symbolic value of the natural end with the surface. Injection-moulding enables complex forms to be made cheaply when they would be impossibly expensive to cut from a solid block.

The American economist, Thorstein Veblen, noted that the main characteristics of natural materials and honest craft processes were the innumerable small blemishes and defects of execution, a texture of minute deviations from the pure or ideal form that was, he supposed, what the craftsman had intended.[8] Veblen argued that only when industrial technology had raised standards of finish and accuracy to previously undreamt of heights could the natural become the object of special appreciation. Prior to that, hand finish was merely the best that was obtainable at the time. He was therefore particularly sarcastic about William Morris' arts and crafts production, especially his books.

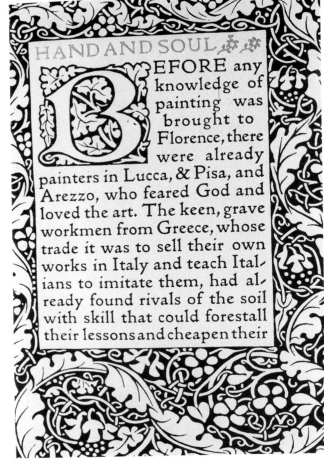

3.4 Hand-made works 'are expensive and less convenient ... (and) argue an ability on the part of the consumer ... to waste time and effort'. Thorstein Veblen's attack on William Morris. A page from Hand and Soul, *one of Morris's later works from the Kelmscott Press.*

The claim to excellence put forward by the later products of the bookmakers' industry rest in some measure on the degree of approximation to the crudities of the time when the work of bookmaking was a doubtful struggle with refractory materials carried out by means of insufficient appliances ... they are expensive and also less convenient ... they thereby argue an ability on the part of the consumer ... to waste time and effort.

Veblen's utilitarian irony would not be understood in many cultures. (The appreciation of Japanese raku pots, for instance, depends on a lively attention to

3.5 *In many subcultures 'stick-on' is noticed but nevertheless accepted. Expanded plastic foam mouldings are used to create an instant medieval style of 'realistic' timber beams and joints. Supplied in kit form with adhesive and applicator gun.*

defect and damage and antedates industrial finishes by centuries.) Nevertheless, his utilitarian view of honest craftsmanship is almost universally present at a subconscious level in our own.

What actually registers as dishonest or insincere, sham or fake, clearly varies widely from one Taste culture to another. One feature, which has often been the cause of profound division, is the combination of different levels and orders of reality into one object or ensemble. Pictorial illusion incorporated into useful artefacts has often been denounced as a sham. The trickery in *trompe l'oeil* is not usually held to be offensive provided that it is clearly demarcated from the real world. Conventional

devices like picture frames suffice. Henry Cole's strictures upon realistic decoration was vividly satirized by Charles Dickens in the famous opening pages of *Hard Times*. Poor Cissy Jupe attracted the wrath of the government inspector (supposedly modelled on Cole, organizer of the Great Exhibition and, thereafter, national Taste pundit) by admitting that she would like to carpet her room with representations of realistic flowers.[9]

> "So you would carpet your room . . . with representations of flowers, would you?" said the gentleman. "Why would you?" "If you please sir I am very fond of flowers," returned the girl. "And that is why you would put tables and chairs upon them and have people walking on them with heavy boots?" "It wouldn't hurt them sir. They wouldn't crush and wither, if you please sir. They would be pictures of what was very pretty and pleasant, and I would fancy—" "Aye, aye, aye but you mustn't fancy," cried the gentleman.

Dickens' inspector had previously voiced another objection to illusion, illustrating his point by assailing another pupil who admitted that he wouldn't mind decorating his walls with horses. As horses couldn't walk up and down walls in reality they couldn't be allowed to do so in illusion. 'You are not to have anywhere what you don't have in fact. What is called Taste is only another name for Fact.'

We can laugh with Dickens at Cole and the puritanical doctrines for which he stood. Yet the incongruities of different spatial schemes or varying degrees of verisimilitude still present problems—even to those who did not follow Cole into the aridities which ensued during the following century, when the only marker for honesty was plainness. Which of us from an upper middle class Taste culture would not

3.6 *The 'Berry Magicoal' fire* (left), *excoriated by Nikolaus Pevsner in 1935 for its fake coals and its flicker effect. Pevsner, a propagandist for the emerging Modernism, saw this as a deplorable example of all that was wrong with English industrial design. It is still going strong over half a century later. In the 1980s the dilemma of how to create a 'living fire'—symbol of hearth and home in smokeless cities—in centrally heated houses was resolved with the 'gas-log' or 'gas-coal' fire (right).*

falter as he pasted up a photomural of the Pacific (Plate 5) in his daughter's bedroom? Who would not feel a qualm at the revelation that his dinner guest had just spent a happy afternoon at the waxworks? Cissy Jupe's innocent admission signifies a total indifference to such matters. She can perfectly well see the difference between fact and fancy, for her though, it is not a moral issue, a necessary marker of veracity in social interaction. As we shall see, it is the Cissy Jupes who make up the vast majority of most Taste publics—now as then. For them, incongruities between reality and illusion do not register. The perceptual shifts which would enable illusion to be read abstractly *as* illusion—and hence be seen as separate and possibly dangerous or threatening—have never been rehearsed.

It is, however, among the middle class Taste cultures that we so often discover the particular confluence of ethics and aesthetics which equates honesty and forthrightness of character with visual plainness and the unequivocal demonstration of construction in household goods. Everything must be exactly what it appears—and no more.

For us to work to imitate the minor vices of the Borgias or the degraded and nightmare whims of the blase and bankrupt aristocracy of Louis the Fifteenth's time seems to me merely ridiculous. So I say our furniture should be good citizens' furniture, solid and well made . . ..

Thus William Morris.[10] (It was, of course, the contrast between Morris' theory and his practice that attracted Veblen's strictures.) Perhaps the most complete and perfect expression of the idea of plainness as veracity and, by extension, the unadorned as both beauty and truth, is seen in the great Shaker products of nineteenth century America. Shaker maxims stress the need to avoid superfluities—any appearances which go beyond the necessary minimum to achieve some useful end. 'Odd or fanciful styles of architecture may not be used by Believers. Beadings, mouldings and cornices which are merely for fancy may not be used by Believers.'[11] It is notable that the great twentieth century denunciations of superfluities were scarcely less Messianic—'ornament is crime' (Adolf Loos).[12]

3.7 *Illusionist wallpaper showing the Great Exhibition of 1851. Realistic perspective must be read from one viewing point only as repetition destroys the illusion. At the same time the realism of each pictorial unit is sufficient to prevent the generation of a true 'all-over' surface pattern.*

However, human conduct is not logic. A meaningful proposition may be either true or false; there are no other alternatives. Not so in life: not all untruths are lies, even when they are, they may vary from white to black. Besides, 'communication techniques such as innuendo, strategic ambiguity and crucial omissions allow the misinformer to profit from lies without, technically, telling any.'[13] Recognizing this, the law allows for innumerable fine shadings of graduated dishonesty in conduct, taking into account varying degrees of effectiveness and culpability. Much depends on audiences. What would be lies for one would be acceptable (perhaps unnoticed) rhetoric for another. The *art of appearance management* is Goffman's name for the myriad ambiguous social activities which operate in this grey area between truth and falsity, fact and fancy.[14]

Good manners

To be successful—that is, to be sustained—all our social interaction with others must elicit, not only a flow of verification, but also reassurance. We must recognize aggressive or other hostile behaviour and accordingly modify our own acts. All social behaviour is therefore invariably accompanied by a stream of signals, including facial expressions and body gestures, vocal noises and modulations of the tone of speech, which constantly transmit messages of intent to others. The 'ugh-ughs' of speech, the nods of the head, the nuances of eyebrow or bodily stance, the character and speed of our gait, all tell a vitally important story to others which they in turn reinforce by reciprocal gestures. This is often called *phatic*

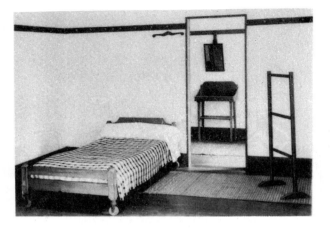

3.8 *Shaker furniture eschews all extraneous detail ('mouldings and superfluities') for religious reasons. Ornament was perceived as the province of the ungodly. 'Stripped-down' imagery in everyday artefacts is characteristic of Puritanical cultures throughout the world.*

communication.[15] In all societies, these more or less instinctive signals are further developed by acculturation into the myriad ritualized acts which accompany exchanges with others. These rituals are often highly specialized, reserved for particular occasions and events and for particular individuals or groups. Greetings and dismissals; gestures of deference or authority, of welcome or withdrawal; the sharing of tenderness or grief or hilarity; intimations of seduction or rejection; the communication of enthusiasm or weariness—all these and many other familiar transactions of social life are based on a series of stereotyped ritual behaviours.

It is not only our intentional signals that are read by others as indicators of our feelings and intentions towards them. All behaviour is potentially symptomatic. For this reason, all societies sanction an equally extensive range of inhibitions and prohibitions of behaviour that might be construed as hostile or inappropriate to a particular role-relationship. There are rules for the appropriate conduct of bodily movements which might be misinterpreted as potentially violent or offensive or give rise to misleading inferences of sexual response.

3.9 *Appearance management. Modern homes invariably present large amounts of electronic equipment such as televisions and hi-fi which blend ill with traditional furniture designs. Hence the market in pseudo-Chippendale cabinets which enclose the offending items when not in use and are accepted even in designers' culture. Living room, Phoenix, Arizona, USA.*

There are especially detailed and severe interdictions on those most basic biological activities—those involving ingestion and the various bodily excretions—'Eat with your mouth shut!' 'Don't pick your nose!' Appropriate conduct in such matters marks out what is decent or proper for a member of any particular social group. Social rituals and taboos are infinite in their variety, the stuff of anthropological study. The role of man-made goods is also important: good manners and social graces often determine the character and design of goods. Dress, in particular, is sensitive to changes in propriety. Even quite modest deviations from an expected or customary design or manner can strike us as quaint, risible or even offensive.[16]

All societies go far beyond the control of such small-scale behavioural acts, the routine exchanges between parents and offspring, host and guest, spouses, lovers, friends and strangers. For it is vital to assure proper conduct from the individual towards the group. What kind of personal conduct will promote the happiness and prosperity of the group? Conversely, what kind of rule will best promote the happiness and prosperity of individuals? Since Plato, philosophers have sought to define the relationship between individual conduct and public welfare. Law, ethics and politics are disciplines which emerge from these early debates. Each attempts to connect an account of individual psychology (the passions) with that of the structure of the various societies known at the time. Our language carries, in many words still used everyday and especially in the discussion of matters of Taste, the values considered appropriate to members of those early societies. Politeness, civility and urbanity are the mark of those who belong to the city (or rather, to those who rule the city, for often, the majority were slaves whose interests were not highly considered). Inevitably, it is governance and good order that dominate the consideration of rulers. Education—including the education of Taste—is instruction in citizenship for the many and in the correct exercise of power by the few.

Philosophical discussions are not particularly useful as guides to daily conduct.

Instruction in everyday behaviour of the more intimate kind—on manners, deportment and what we have come to call etiquette—dates from much more recent times. Although some texts from classical antiquity (for example, Cicero's *De Officiis*—'On Duties') were in wide use throughout the Middle Ages, it was the Renaissance which saw the beginning of a flood of books on the conduct of everyday social intercourse.[17] In the Renaissance concept of 'courtesy' (expressed in such texts as Baldassare Castiglione's *The Book of the Courtier*[18] or Giovanni della Casa's *Galateo*[19]), the classical doctrines of politeness or urbanity were transformed, not only by the perspectives of medieval Christianity, in which the purposes of daily life were regarded as essentially preparatory to a life beyond, but also by the chivalric codes of the aristocratic courts of the late Middle Ages, particularly those in France. From the sixteenth century, good manners have been the result of the interaction between shifting expressions of the underlying ethical framework of society—largely Christian but on occasion secular humanist—and the particular rituals of belonging and codes of deference of the leading, mostly aristocratic, social groups of the day.

In recent times, commerce and the bourgeoisie have everywhere ousted the aristocracy as a source of power. Their emphases and discriminations on what is decent and proper overlay and distort earlier values although, as we shall see, the quality has by no means entirely lost all its power as a leader of fashions in manners. For the new middle classes of the nineteenth century, the avoidance of vulgarity or commonness gave latterday etiquette its strained and snobbish air. In today's populist democracy it has led to its total disrepute. In

3.10 *Rituals standardize behaviour at crucial moments in social life, such as greetings in encounters with strangers, especially of the opposite sex. And we extrapolate from actual behaviour to the goods which attend it—raising the hat to a lady requires a 'proper' hat to be raised.* (Habits of Good Society, *circa 1860.*)

myriad ways, the world of goods serves to fix the manners and mores of unknown or long forgotten cultures. Unfortunately, the social history of furniture and interior decoration is still largely at the stage of cataloguing changing patronage and stylistic preferences. Rarely is there that detailed examination of the inter-relationship between social usage and useful objects that enables us to grasp for other cultures the equivalent of the many tacit observances we make daily with others in using the equipment of our own.[20]

Consider hygiene. We are accustomed to regard the development of personal cleanliness as one of the greatest boons and characteristic marks of civilization. Yet historically, the varieties of both practical arrangements and social attitude have been infinite. Roman Britons, like other Romans, bathed, in large part, socially. When the Empire fell, the

3.11 *Bernstein's lavatories. A selection of lavatorial imagery in order of ascending 'user-friendliness'. The purely functional toilet leaves the user free from surveillance while the decorated examples require admiring comment of a stranger. Four examples of lavatories furnished by interior decorators in 'ideal homes' (Daily Telegraph Ideal Home Exhibition, London).*

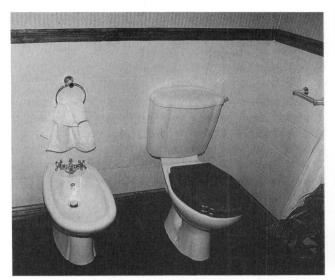

custom ceased in most parts of Europe. Few were as clean for the next thousand years. Throughout medieval Europe, washing was regarded as unhealthy if not dangerous. Consideration for others among the cultivated, who nonetheless stunk, led to the deployment of olfactory countermeasures such as perfume, scented herbs and pomanders. Other bodily functions, such as spitting, have also attracted a wide variety of social regulations, varying from injunctions to strive for modesty and an accurate aim and, where possible, to 'tread out, and cleanse it with thy foot', to the specialized apparatus of the spittoon and cuspidor—devices no doubt favoured by the availability of servants to 'do the dirty work'. Today, we view such objects with aversion. Perhaps it will not be long before similar present-day conveniences, such as ashtrays, are regarded with equal displeasure.

The history of domestic plumbing discloses an equally diverse range of apparatus for the disposal of body wastes.[21] No less remarkable is the range of social attitudes towards this necessary activity, especially in respect of privacy. Privacy is important, because during these vital bodily functions we momentarily abandon the maintenance of expressive control. Our demeanour is no longer a guide to others how we feel. Basil Bernstein has suggested that one can read off significant aspects of family and social structure from the style in which the apparatus of the lavatory is arranged.[22] He postulated a range of four lavatories furnished in four degrees of decreasing formality.

The first is stark, bare, pristine, the walls are painted a sharp white. A square block of soap sits clearly in an indentation in the sink.

3.12 *In real life, many toilets are nearer to Bernstein's descriptions. Thoughtfully provided with reading matter in the form of the* Good Loo Guide, *this example from the home of an art collector in London is also furnished with original watercolours.*

A white towel (or perhaps pink) is folded neatly on a chrome rail or hangs from a chrome ring. The lavatory paper is hiding in its cover and peeps through its slit. In the second lavatory there are books on a shelf and some relaxing of the rigours of the first. In the third lavatory there are books on a shelf, pictures on the wall and perhaps a scattering of tiny objects. In the fourth lavatory the rigour is totally relaxed. The walls are covered with a motley array of postcards, there is a varied assortment of reading matter and curio. The lavatory roll is likely to be uncovered and the holder may well fall apart in use.

3.13 *Royal closet seat, Hampton Court, England. Unlike Louis XIV in France whose quasi-divine standing prevented any misinterpretation of even this extreme public behaviour, English monarchs performed bodily functions in private.*

In Bernstein's interpretation of this array, the four degrees of informality become four degrees of *classification strength*. Strongly classified spaces imply authority as boundaries have to be maintained and the natural entropy of use overcome. Any disturbance to the perfect order implies pollution, and those who use this lavatory are obliged to take especial care in ensuring that no signs of their activities remain. They are brought under the authority of the boundary marker in the very act of being guaranteed the strict privacy of maintained boundaries. In the weakly classified lavatory there are few clearly defined principles of order

to be violated. Indeed, the postcards on the wall might solicit contributions from the visitor, engaging him in dialogue with his host on the matter. The price of this relaxation of personal authority is a diminution of privacy since communication demands surveillance. There is no doubt that this is a plausible interpretation. Immaculate lavatories in a person's home can be menacing. Engaging images on the wall may well facilitate social intercourse in another. But, if Freud and others are to be believed, personal expression in such intimate matters varies widely from individual to individual, being influenced heavily by each particular history of acculturation into hygienic norms in infancy. Besides, other principles of order apart from Cartesian geometry might be in play, principles which someone conditioned to the surgical imagery of the functional lavatory may simply not perceive. We would need much more information about the interpretive systems of both host and guest before we could really claim to know what was going on. Intricacy and informality in an ensemble of goods are relative concepts. Historically, at any rate, they seem to bear no obvious relationship either to privacy or to authority. We have only to remember that Lord Portland, Ambassador to the Court of Louis XIV, was received by His Majesty seated on the closet-stool (incidentally, an elaborately decorated model).[23]

Furniture can be read as the visible expression of social manners only if we have other collateral evidence to confirm or refute our hunches. For example, we know enough about the hierarchic relationships within medieval feudalism to feel secure in our belief that the prestige which is still attached today to a professorial chair in a university dates from

3.14 *The living room of the modern home is often primarily used as a hospitality centre. Popular plan types are those which promote easy face to face conversation with guests. Settees facing each other across the hearth is the most popular layout for the larger home.*

the time when only the feudal lord possessed such an item. Other relationships, for example those between the sexes, are more difficult simply to interpret from the form of a particular artefact or ensemble.[24] We would need to know a great deal about the precise limits currently set upon the public flirtation in a certain period before we could put on a play of the period, in which dialogue took place on a *confident* or an *indiscret*, in a way that would not astonish contemporaries. In more recent times, we have witnessed enormous changes in the allowable public demonstration of gender —good Taste in sexual matters. Adoption of trousers by women has facilitated an altogether more extensive repertoire of acceptable

body gesture. In turn, this has influenced the design of furniture. Much modern furniture is so low that getting in and out of it would be very difficult to effect with decency unless women wore trousers! Differences in the sexual manners of furniture begin to appear, not only between the social classes, but between age groups, as well as between the metropolis and the provinces. Cities are not only the source of civility, but of rivalry, ostentation and exaggeration. Today of course, influences originating in the city spread quickly through the mass media—print, radio and television.

Hospitality rituals still play an important part in determining good manners in a particular ensemble of goods. We need the spaces

3.15 *Placed diagonally in a corner the cocktail bar forces the host to act as a barman with the cabinet between him and his guests. Two examples from different market levels—expensive upper middle class* (left) *and cheap and cheerful working class* (right).

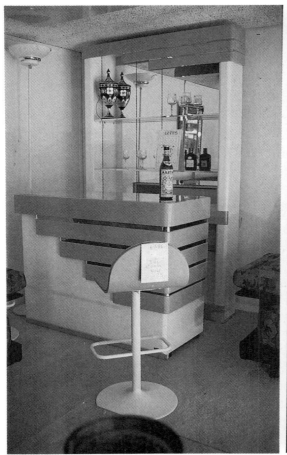

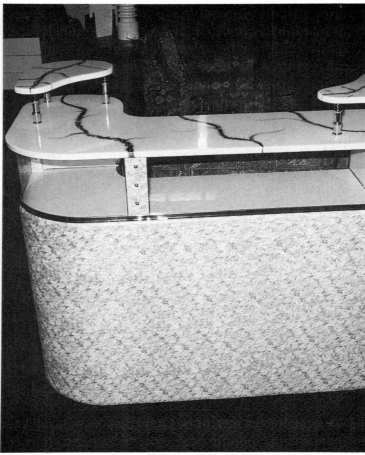

reserved for receiving and entertaining guests to be recognized as such. This entails a certain formality. At the same time they must appear welcoming and inviting. Hard, upright chairs are usually kept for functional or task seating such as dining or writing, hospitality chairs must be relaxing, soft and low (but not embarrassingly so). We must also contrive a natural setting for conversation in their layout. Conversation must be easy. Speakers must be close and face each other. Most guests come in small numbers, usually in pairs, often with spouses. Finally, few nowadays can devote more than a small space to ceremonial purposes. It is the

consideration of good manners towards our guests that induces many to invest large sums in the three-piece suite, an ensemble unknown before the beginning of the century. It is now so universal among the purchases of poorer social groups that proposals to sell seating in forms other than the standard two armchairs plus double or triple settee are greeted with dismay by retailers! A unified design and a formal plan layout—symmetrical, with chairs each side of the fire and settee facing it—gives an appropriately ceremonial and social character. Small occasional tables enable tea to be dispensed to seated guests at their elbows. Decency, in the form of good manners towards guests, overwhelms all other considerations in the furnishing of such spaces, often to the point that they become so crowded with the necessary equipment and symbols of hospitality that physical movement becomes difficult.[25]

There are noticeable differences in the manners of different social groups in their hospitality rituals, especially those concerned with dispensing alcoholic drinks. Those who can afford to keep alcohol in the house generally have some sort of cupboard in which it is stored. Often, this is combined with space for the glasses which traditionally are reserved for particular beverages: beer, wine, sherry, champagne, brandy, cocktails and shorts. These may be displayed either on open shelves or (to protect them from dust) behind glass. In some homes the entire ensemble may be combined into one piece—the cocktail bar. Here the layout mimics that of the public house in which the host faces his guests across a table or a bar. For its domestic setting, the cocktail bar is often located in a corner. An ornamental facade conceals the necessary apparatus underneath a counter-top. When he dispenses hospitality the owner has temporarily to go behind the bar, thus establishing quite a different relationship between him and his guests. An invitation to 'serve yourself' also takes on quite a different significance with this plan-type. To date, the social meanings attached to such specialized manners have little been explored. Why should such formality be observed mostly in lower class homes? Is it simply that the example of the pub is more familiar to certain social classes? Are they mimicking a Hollywood image of high life? Do they have cocktail bars in the poorer homes in other countries? And why do the middle classes deprecate such arrangements here?

On technique

Veracity and demeanour are not the only matters which concern us in our daily symbolic traffic with others. We are no less concerned with technique—the skill embodied in objects or performances. From an appraisal of the level of skill with which something is done, we can discover whether situations are normal—up to scratch compared with some average going rate. Shortcomings are quickly read as symptoms of lack of commitment or concern for us. Easy and masterful performances reassure us. Ineptness and fumbling cause us anxiety. And yet, attitudes to technique are highly variable in different Taste cultures and are sometimes very ambivalent. An excessive display of skill may make us feel inadequate by comparison, although there is more which should be considered. Tradition, fashion, and inevitably, social discrimination, all influence our appreciation of skill, whether it is embodied in a social performance—someone welcoming us and putting us at ease—or whether it is expressed in artefacts themselves—the curves of a particular pot, or merely the felicitous arrangement of flowers in a vase that compliment the ensemble of goods in a living room. Skill in the expressive arts can be demonstrated everywhere. It is also of many kinds. There is sheer manual dexterity—the skill of the juggler or a performance rehearsed to unbelievable heights of physical coordination or speed. There is sleight of hand—the skill of the magician or illusionist who make appearances

3.16 Trompe l'œil *in art has been admired since antiquity when Appeles is supposed to have deceived the birds with the realism of his grapes. Today it is more likely to be found in public places. The blind wall at the end of this New York office building is painted to simulate the real facade.*

deceive. There is the mastery of complexity arising from sheer scale and number of variables held simultaneously in play—the skill of the great orchestrator or architect. Many of the greatest artefacts embody all these skills.

How we react to a particular level of skill depends on how it conforms to our expectations. These are set in part by a very general understanding of the facts of individual maturation and of the stages at which certain skills are mastered. We remember something of our own early development. We have watched the fumbling efforts of countless infants or immature adults to learn or make something. We have all had the shock of discovering that some

people in our age-range or social class are far better than us, displaying skills that are usually evident only in much older people. We acquire a tacit scale of presumed performance levels for a given age—the going rate—which enables us to judge artefacts or performances as childish or, on the other hand, precocious. Whether or not we react with pleasure depends on the information we have. We all delight in a dazzling exhibition of skill, a delight which is probably a projection of the pleasure we feel in our own developing skills, however, we do not want 'to have our noses rubbed in it'. If Mozart had been a cynical and worldly teenager our attitude towards his precocity would be different. Marvellous enhancement in the level of a performance that nevertheless remains (we feel) childlike or pure, is delightful. One who strikes us as 'too old for his age', whose display presumes upon adult experience or attitudes he is unlikely to have known, is correspondingly dubious in our eyes. His technique (while being recognized for what it is) remains disturbing at best. We may find him and the goods he makes or chooses 'too clever by half'.

Our expectations are also set by social and historical factors. In some societies, political and economic conditions are suitable for competitive emulation and striving. Skill is recognized and rewarded with prizes, honours and patronage. At such times, technique in a particular area, for example lifelikeness in sculpture or the illusionistic depiction of three-dimensions in painting, advances with extraordinary rapidity. From their stratigraphical records, archaeologists can discern sudden spurts in the technical and artistic level of goods in all cultures of the world. Classical Greece was obviously such a time. Rivalry between small, independent city states, within a similar overall culture, led to conditions for patronage which quite suddenly produced the great technical 'breakthroughs' that are the foundation of most subsequent Western art and architecture.

As these societies began to keep historical records of their own past, for example in the accumulation of sculpture from different periods in the great temples and public buildings, then the stage was set for a more complicated appreciation of technique. It began to appear to some that the mere accumulation of technical skill or know-how was not in itself a guarantee of the progressive increase of excellence. In works of art, some qualities are patently achieved only at the expense of others. Liveliness and movement in sculpture may be won at the expense of majesty and repose. Some people may come to prefer the earlier modes of expression.[26]

Once a technical breakthrough has been achieved then not to use it suddenly becomes an expressive device. Before illusionistic perspective had been mastered in Renaissance Italy, flat painting was not read symptomatically for its flatness. After the staggering developments of the earlier fifteenth century, not using illusionism to the full became an aesthetic possibility. A conscious choice by an artist to revert to an earlier mode could be read, not as incompetence, but as powerfully expressive—its primitive appearance suggesting other emotional or spiritual forces. When the immediate occasion for such confrontations has receded, it needs the historian to reconstruct the expressive issues that turned upon a particular technique and its renunciation. Both may be so remote from our concerns that, at first sight, we can see no difference in the two styles. For many, at first glance, the frescoes of

3.17 *In naive painting, uncertain techniques such as lack of true perspective and the inability to control a uniform lighting renders the objects depicted curiously concrete and, by contrast with the professional version, the results are often strangely affecting.*

Ghirlandaio and Botticelli both look typically quattrocento. Yet Botticelli's flatter style looks forward to a more consciously mannered use of technique in the service of a heightened spiritual intensity. In contrast, Ghirlandaio's thoroughgoing illusionism already looked somewhat old-fashioned.[27]

In recent times, the adoption of primitive techniques in the interest of heightened emotional expressiveness has been more extreme. Picasso's use of African imagery in his early cubist works depended for its success, at least in part, on the suggestion of savagery embodied in the rude techniques displayed in the masks and totems of primitive tribes. Perhaps we may be able to read African masks directly; we may unconsciously react to the condensed symbols and gestures of such artless productions.[28] However, it is the contrast with the refinement of previous Western high art which gives Picasso's work its cutting edge. It is a similar contrast which gives naive art or craft its appeal. In this case, naivety of the Douanier Rousseau or Grandma Moses variety depends on the contrast between the comparative refinement or artistry of the paintwork with the direct, childlike quality of the symbols and images.

It has long been realized that there are limits to the agreeable perception of mere performance. Excessive skill rapidly leads to showing-off, pointless exaggeration and perversity. Naturalness is a quality also to be prized, and this may be found in the plain workmanship of modest objects or performances. Ostentation and bragging are easily confused in a display of skill or technique. The ludicrous lengths to which refinement in the techniques of display can be pushed have been satirized since antiquity. Equally old is the favourable contrast between the naturalness of the countryside and the artificiality of the city.[29] Jaded appetites have always longed for the almost forgotten simplicities and the songs of experience have ruefully been contrasted with the songs of innocence in most cultures.

Experience is hard to avoid and skill painful to acquire. Neither can simply be forgotten once acquired. This leads quickly to the idea that, when artifice and skill appear artificial, still more artifice could create the illusion of the natural or artless. Thus we have the notion of 'art covering art', the use of skill to conceal just how skilful (and presumably just how calculated and intentional) a performance really is. For Castiglione, therein lies the secret of *grazie*, or easiness:

> to eschue as much as a man may ... too much curiousness (i.e. affectation) and ... to use in everything a certain disgracing to cover arte withall, not minding it ... Therefore that may be said to be a very arte, that appeareth not to be arte ...[30]

Of course, too much art to conceal art is itself an affectation and to be condemned. Best is moderately artful unaffectedness or *sprezzatura*. Sometimes translated as 'nonchalance' (Castiglione's first English translator, Sir Thomas Hoby, called it 'rechlessness'), this is a prime quality of the courtier. Following the universal success of Castiglione's book of the 'gentleman' in all the countries of Europe, it became essential for sprezzatura to be displayed in all social manners from swordsmanship and dancing, to music and painting. In a famous passage, Castiglione refers to some of the more advanced techniques of the art of the day:

> oftentimes also in painting, one line not studied upon, one draught with the pensell slightly drawne, so it appeareth the hand without the guiding of any studie or art ...[31]

This is the value system that makes clumsiness a sin and gaucherie the ultimate social disgrace. Much of Castiglione's thought is based closely upon classical sources. His comments on painting are preceded by a remark that:

> it hath been a proverb among some most excellent painters of olde time, that too much diligence is hurtful and that Appeles found fault with Protogenes, because he could not keep his hands from the table (i.e. painter's tablet or panel) ... Appeles' meaning was the Protogenes knew not when it was well, which was nothing else but to reprehend his curiousness (i.e. affectation) in his works.[32]

Various reasons are given for the adoption of the quality of nonchalance or unaffectedness. In a direct reference to Cicero,

Castiglione points out that, because audiences were fearful of being beguiled by obvious artifice, the ancient orators took care to conceal it, 'dissembling their cunning, made semblant their orations to be made verie simple and rather as nature and truth ledde them, than studie and arte.'[33]

From Castiglione's time, sprezzatura has been preferred to bravura among connoisseurs. To choose the fussy or the over-elaborate is to make oneself out as uneducated in gentlemanly ways. To the aristocrat it is the sign of the bourgeois Taste. In contemporary mass markets the same quality is universally prized and so we speak of 'cool elegance' or the 'discretely casual'. There are innumberable variations on such locutions and on the images which they describe in the worlds of fashion and interior decoration.

Today, the appreciation of technique in everyday things is often embodied in the display of technology. Obvious piling up of complex controls in the knobs and switches of modern hi-fi systems is part of the appeal for many consumers. While its ressemblance to the cockpit of an aircraft may suggest that using the system is in itself a skill and therefore, a challenge, it is safe to assume that, for the most part, many of the innumerable features will never be used. For rival manufacturers the avoidance of technological clutter may be sold as the mark of sophisticated Taste. This dialectic can be seen at all levels, from the digital watch to the high tech office block, such as London's Lloyd's Building which exposes all the technological devices for servicing the building on the outside and ostentatiously displays the cunning of its assembly (or contrivance) in its overt and gadgety detailing (Plates 6 & 7).

3.18 *'Casual' is a category of Taste much prized in contemporary fashion. Deriving ultimately from the Italian Renaissance concept of 'rechlessness', it is expressed in today's costume by natural looking materials, a loose cut and a construction expressed in surface detail. Summer suits for 1990 by Next, England.*

Nor is this delight in the skill embodied in ingenious devices new. Technical artifice has been admired from early antiquity, both in the Western tradition and in China. Indeed, it was in China that techological ingenuity was first put to practical use. In the West, the technology of antiquity was as often as not engaged in for purely pleasurable reasons, rich and powerful patrons supporting the work of the first inventors as a form of amusement, the contrivances which resulted being regarded as pleasing for their curiosity rather than exploited for their wealth-creating potential.

The fascination with ingenious technology is so widespread it is not surprising that when invention began to enter into modern industrial production and technical products began to be widely available, they were seized upon with enthusiasm. Adam Smith satirized early addicts of the exaggeratedly elaborate timepieces that were then becoming available. Their owners (who had previously never bothered about the time) were now in need of costume furnished with special pockets to

3.19 Contemporary toys often exploit the pleasures of ingenious technical contrivances. The dancing flowers jig about mysteriously to the rhythm when music is played. Wonderment at the mystery of 'how it is done' is the main ingredient in this simple but ingenious artefact.

accomomodate the burdens of the newfangled watches. They were clearly not displaying proper gentlemanly behaviour.[34]

But what of the peasant, hitherto unexposed to such temptations? His craft is surely artless and unaffected? Since the beginning of the modern interest in the 'noble savage'—original natural man, unspoiled by civilization—appreciation of peasant or ethnic ware has grown into a popular Taste.[35] In an industrial civilization, an Indian rug is the nearest most people get to the creativity of natural man. Even this has probably been made for export to Western markets, and genuine peasant furniture vanished from the saleroom long ago. From the beginning of the nineteenth century, the imitation of native or peasant crafts by industrial

3.20 Higher up the social scale, expensive Transformers *display amazing ingenuity in the design of the injection moulded parts which can be taken apart and reassembled in many different ways. Their pleasure lies in the creation of a range of vivid images which are 'transformed' when they become parts of a larger assembly.*

techniques has abounded and today the production of simulated ethnic furniture and decoration is enormous. A plain country-style kitchen in natural timber and brown earthenware comes from high technology factories. This is using art to conceal art indeed! How we regard this depends on our appraisal of the amount of effort and skill required to do otherwise. What Castiglione called 'that pure and amiable simplicity which is so acceptable to men's minds' may well entail shopping at Habitat or IKEA! Instead of sprezzatura, we may have to settle for what Robert Venturi proposed as the proper goal for present-day architecture: 'a high standard of ordinariness', in which the undoubted advantages of modern building technology are discretely concealed.

Restraint—rhetoric and moral values

Many years ago, Ernst Gombrich described the influence of classic theories of rhetoric on Renaissance art.[36] Cicero marked varying degrees of artificiality and ornamental effect, from the plain unadorned 'attic' manner to the highly decorated and ornate style. The theory of decorum attempts to set proper limits to verbal display and to relate it to appropriate occasions and suitable messages. A particular style should, of course, coordinate and mutually reinforce along all the various channels of gesture and diction, and these should marry with the choice of figure and literary device. To achieve a convincing rhetorical performance, this is simply sound technical advice. As Gombrich showed however, technical advice is inextricably bound up with moral attitudes, in particular, moral attitudes towards artifice or sham. Cicero, describing a beautiful woman who loses nothing by not being made-up, criticizes the cosmetics and pearls that lead to a too easy seduction of the senses. This argument will be familiar to many contemporary architects and designers for whom 'merely cosmetic' is a term of abuse for works which they see as gratuitously striving for our attention by means of forms deemed to be inessential. Gombrich pointed out that Cicero by no means argued for an exclusively plain style, although it is certainly through his influence that the virtues of a plain and functional style enter into the theory of modern art and design. Those who, like the designers of the Bauhaus, have argued that plain, 'matter-of-fact' imagery (the so-called 'neue Sachlichkeit') is the only morally correct presentation of consumer goods stand in a very long tradition indeed.

In a famous passage, Leone Battista Alberti cites the authority of Plato and Cicero for his view that temples (churches) should be perfectly clean and white.[37] He argued that the structure itself should carry the message. Paintings should be detachable and not painted on to walls. Sculpture—a continuation of the plastic language of the architectural form—is to be preferred to either.

When Alberti writes, denouncing those who lard their buildings with an excess of ornament, sculpture and precious materials, 'Contempt is the best Reward for these wild Prodigals who are ostentatious with such wild Vainglories or rather Follies, and who are thus profuse with the Labours and Sweat of Mankind, about things which are of no Manner (i.e. style) or Use or Advantage to the main Structure, nor capable of raising

3.21 *The 'peasant look' entails the importation of country style historical detailing on the drawer and door fronts in high-technology modular kitchen furniture.*

the least Admiration either for Ingenuity of Contrivance',[38] he is prefiguring the sentiments of subsequent artists and designers who seek to focus the expressiveness of their work on to their skill and artistry in the making of form. What matters is the *Ingenuity of Contrivance*, not extraneous aids—the cosmetics of precious materials or superficial adornment (Plates 8 & 9). It was precisely the contrast of such sentiments with the ecstatic praise of the sparkle of gold by Suger—Abbé of St Denis—that served Gombrich to point out the difference between the Renaissance and the earlier medieval view of expression. It identified the historic shift, whereby renunciation of gratuitous preciousness becomes, what Gombrich called, 'a metaphor of value', a metaphor wherein there is a confluence of

3.22 *Restraint involves the renunciation of extraneous decoration. In fifteenth century Florence it signified moral rectitude. Antinori Palace. G. di Maiano, circa 1465.*

artistic and moral values. This confluence becomes clearer in Alberti's advice on figure composition in the *istoria*—narrative 'history' painting.[39] Sound technical advice on the disposition of figures and props in a painting, to achieve variety while avoiding confusion, mingles with admonitions to strive towards qualities such as dignity, modesty, truth, restraint, discretion, moderation and sweetness—all eminently worthy moral qualities which, in varying degrees, imply renunciation.

Later, Giorgio Vasari picked up Alberti's strictures against the use of too much gold. (In *Della Pittura*, gold was condemned on the

technical ground that it interfered with the modelling of figures in space by means of light and shade.) In his *Life of Cosimo Roselli*, Vasari described how the artist contrived to win a prize for a painting in the Sistine Chapel by seducing Pope Sixtus IV with the lavish use of gold and ultramarine.[40] Gombrich comments that 'it only adds spice to Vasari's story that the Philistine is the Pope himself who thus proves himself inferior in culture to the artists he employs'. We see here one early source for what Gans has called the *creator-orientation*. It is also the classic instance, in Western civilization, of that wilful narrowing of perceptual attention, for which Goffman has coined the term, *negative cultivation*.[41] Subsequently, the confluence of values ensured that incorrect aesthetic preferences were, in themselves, sufficient to mark out the vulgar. Conventions change but, at any time thereafter, we can find colours or forms of a gaudy, naff, plastic or tarty nature—and the Philistines to go with them. Alberti's own precepts were rapidly superseded, even during the fifteenth century. However, his values surfaced again to become the cornerstone of a simplifying classicism—sober, and not infrequently dull—when they were later adopted by the Academies. What began in large measure as sound practical advice, rooted in his knowledge of the actual working methods of his contemporaries, Donatello, Brunelleschi and Masaccio, later became an abstracted set of rules and finally rigidified into a dogma.

In the classic idea of restraint there are no strictures against complexity as such. It is the clash of disparate orders, the confusion of categories, the collision of different levels and manners of discourse, and the juxtaposition of symbols of different degrees of iconicity (or resemblance) to which objections are raised. In seeking to impose these limitations of category it recognizes a limit to our overall channel capacity, a finite limit to what we can take in at any one time. Too many channels dissipate our attention. In particular, they distract us from the intense effort needed to pursue those overarching and interlocking metrical or spatial systems of order that the classic artist strives to attain. Negative cultivation, a renunciation of inessentials (however engaging), is thus a prerequisite for classic art. However, those that follow the path of restraint into ever more abstract metrical orders find that one's range can narrow alarmingly. Such are the extremes reached in an evolutionary history of art, that even reality itself may be deemed an 'inessential'! Not many, it seems, are prepared to consecrate their entire metaphorical life to Florentine painting or Palladian architecture, or even late Beethoven quartets, let alone the canvases of Mondrian. The demands that this degree of commitment to negative cultivation imposes are too great for most, even among the otherwise cultivated, certainly too great for the wider consumer publics which, from the nineteenth century to this day, have numerically dominated society.[42] Nevertheless, a tacit recognition of the perceptual demands placed upon those who speak in a unified, integrated and, therefore, necessarily austere language still enables the classic mode to command universal acceptance as an expression of high moral worth. It is still widely used as the appropriate convention for solemn dignity on the climactic occasions of life, both for individuals and for the state.

3.23 *The clash of orders. If too many different communication channels are used simultaneously then perception becomes overloaded. Sideboard shown in the Great Exhibition of 1851 includes a wide variety of decoration combined with figurative sculpture and illusionist depictions.*

'A sprawling, highly ornamental rococo extravagance'

Throughout history, refinement and restraint (in the sense of the voluntary limitation of the variety of channels of symbolic communication) have been threatened, and often overwhelmed, by the opposite tendencies of extravagance, surprise, exaggeration, primitive sensuality and prolixity for its own sake. Rapid boredom with the objects of present attraction, and the consequent need for novelty and variety of stimulus to maintain interest and happiness, are the hallmark of the child who has not yet learned how to discipline his wandering attention and, through

3.24 *Restraint as the metaphor for moral worth. All over the world, neo-Classical designs are much favoured for state buildings, monuments and other public edifices with up-lifting purposes. Jefferson Memorial, Washington, USA.*

perseverance in a limited focus, penetrate into the complexities of a concrete, framed experience. For him, change is the prime objective. Diversion is the technique for stimulating the visual appetite. What changes is not important, although the simple is preferred to the subtle as novelty can more easily be discerned in simple objects. Broad patterns, bright colours and crude or exaggerated forms have been the staple of regressive or childlike Taste since history began.

Classical antiquity, especially in the later Roman period, was familiar with regressive behaviour, with extravagance, dilettantism, foppery and the need to pile up novelty and diversion to stimulate jaded appetites. Atheneus, in the *Deipnosophists* (the 'dinner-sophists'), describes an extraordinary latter-day symposium given by one Larensis, a proconsul.[43] In place of learned philosophical discussion with the wine after dinner, in the manner of Plato, we are given a rambling account of the pleasures (and perils!) of gourmandizing itself. It includes long extracts of what amounts to the earliest surviving cookery book (a kind of Roman 'Brillat-Savarin'). In other interpolated passages, Atheneus compares the modest diets of the Homeric heroes with the fantastic extravagances and excesses of recent times, where the disputants pour their chamber pots over each other and learned discussion is crowded out by dancing girls and flute players, aphrodisiacs and unguents—not to mention an interminable catalogue of gourmet exoticisms. One of the guests, Cyniculus, a cynic philosopher, attacks all this as base gluttony. He blames it for the corruption of philosophical argument, accusing the company of no longer being capable of correct etymological discriminations. Not only that but, 'Even the perversion of music has increased today, and extravagances in clothes and footwear have reached a climax.'

In Roman criticism of the visual arts, the distraction of a multiplicity of channels was directly implicated with a falling standard of creativity in any one of them. Several writers ascribed what they saw as the falling standard of drawing to an increase in the deployment of colour. Both Pliny and Vitruvius directly blamed colour for the decay of art.

Four colours only were used by Apelles and others in their immortal works . . . while now that purple clothes our walls and India contributes the ooze of her rivers and the blood of dragons and of elephants, there are no more masterpieces, and so everything was better when means were fewer.[44]

Lucian equated lavishness with Barbarism. Describing a hall interior, he wrote:

> Its magnificence was the only reason for surprise. Neither art nor beauty nor right proportions nor the elegance of form gave value to the distribution of splendid metals. Barbarians cannot appreciate beauty, they display the magnificence of their treasures in order to astonish spectators and not charm them because to Barbarians, what is gorgeous is considered beautiful.[45]

Matthew Arnold borrowed the term 'Barbarian' from Byron to describe those who are seduced by the irresistible charms of worldly splendour. Such has always been the attitude of the moralist to the threatening tendency of styles in life, as in art, to evolve in the direction of a plenitude of means.

The abolition of divisions between separate categories of rhetoric (that is, particular manners being reserved for particular classes of subject matter) has also been used to create an emotional effect. In the Christian religion, transcendental mysteries are expressed in paradoxical contrasts between the sublime and the lowly. 'God is born in a stable.' Augustine seized on this paradox, at the heart of the Christian mystery, to detach the Ciceronian categories from their particular subject matter.[46] He related them instead to the relationship between speaker and hearer. According to Augustine, the sublime was for rousing the emotions, the intermediate style was for giving praise or blame, and the lowly or colloquial style for teaching.

In the hands of an inspired preacher, this mixture of styles could send his hearers on an emotional roller-coaster, in which the attachment of everyday symbols to secular values is

3.25 *Prolixity taken to extremes marked many of the artefacts shown in the Great Exhibition of 1851. Piano and side chair show the lengths to which ornamentation and the wilful distortion of form could go.*

lost, leaving a free floating emotional charge to be concretized (or, to use Freud's term, cathected) in the sacred symbols at the centre of the rite. Much later, Romantic art used disparate languages and styles to stir the emotions and cathect them onto new psychological and social values, values which mark the beginning of the modern sensibility: individual liberty and Romantic sexual passion.

Along with a resurgence of interest in Shakespeare—the greatest of those whose art is based on rapid juxtapositions of contrasting manners—complex multichannel forms, such as opera, attained widespread popularity.

In the arts of architecture and design, this explosion of means was soon out of control. The impassioned controversies and quarrels among Victorian Taste reformers following the Great Exhibition of 1851 have been widely documented.[47] Many different 'battle lines' were drawn up including flat-pattern versus three-dimensional representation in ornament; the eternal, underlying geometry of nature versus the contingent accidental details of nature; pictorial illusion versus conventionalized symbol in decoration and congruence of scale in different representations versus consistency of lifelikeness (a problem given a new acuteness by the arrival of photography). All these can be seen as particular revulsions against the plenitude of languages. They typify the unending attempts of artists and critics to re-establish new, even if transitory, integrations in an ever expanding welter of means. Yet, as we may readily observe, most of the population remains immune to these calls to order. In Arnold's day the working class (what he called the populace) possessed little in the way of goods, but as Richard Hoggart perceived nearly a century later—and a visit to any high street shop will show to this day—their sympathies were with the Barbarians.

> I recall now . . . indoors the basic furnishings of the home are surmounted by articles whose main charm is their high colour and suggestions of splendour . . . And the flowers in the box outside are still those which best provide 'a bit of colour'. Plastic gewgaws and teapots shaped like country cottages settle very easily with complicated lace-paper doilies, complicated lace half-curtains, crocheted table runners, family birthday and Christmas cards, coloured wicker shopping-baskets and fancies (curiously constructed and coloured little cakes) for tea.[48]

It has proved extraordinarily difficult for today's designers, once they have been educated into the classic mode of our own modern Academies, ever to undo their inhibitions. The baneful confluence of values ensures that fastidious aesthetic preference for an austere and integrated language flows over into a moral disdain for the vulgar who, lacking the wit or will to understand 'higher' things, continue to wallow in a 'sprawling highly ornamental rococo extravagance'.

Setting a good example

When public money is spent on culture, it is highly probable that much will be made of the moral improvements that accompany enlightenment. It is a rare taxpayer that takes pleasure in the thought that his money is being distributed to finance mere naked hedonism among other social groups. He would more often prefer to retain it in order to finance his own. Where design is concerned, moral uplift must be combined with a commercial payoff. These two objectives are not easy to reconcile. In fact, the morality of culture is not a stable one. A historical perspective shows the varying influence of rival groups. Most important, and underlying all the contingent details of styles prominent at particular moments in time, is the perennial struggle between restraint and indulgence, the endless battle between the Roundheads and the Cavaliers. Roundheads are the cultural puritans who favour gravity, austerity, formal simplicity and emotional restraint. Cavaliers are catholic and their penchant is for exuberance, colour, vivacity, complexity and passion. Styles in the history of high design (as in the history of high art) can be read as the changing fortunes of Roundheads and Cavaliers. In earlier times, a reflection of underlying social and political forces, in our day, the struggle merely reflects the evolutionary selection of images from competing creator groups.

To date, Taste has only been referred to in general terms—the preferences and values of an individual or group. Implicit in this formulation is the existence of a set of choices from various groups of alternative possibilities, for example, patterns for curtains. A would-be Taste educator urges his choices upon his fellow citizens. To be more precise, he urges something similar but not absolutely identical. Few want to people the world with replicas of their own choices. All museums, in practice, proffer examples of their finest pieces in each particular area of choice as type-examples, examples of the greatest art, furniture or decoration. Visual education, in the form of myriads of facsimiles of all types including photographic reproductions, slides, films and videos, is but a technological extension of the great collection, what André Malraux called the 'Museum without Walls'. Inherent to this policy of displaying the finest is the assumption (or at any rate, the hope) that the examples on display will be followed. Practitioners first, and the ordinary visiting public next, will (it is hoped) be infected by what they see and alter, even if only marginally, their own choices and aesthetic values.

There is little doubt that this happens, however, to what extent remains unknown.

Taste bureaucracy is a costly social enterprise in most industrialized countries. The number of visitors to museums (with or without walls) must run annually into billions.[49] Yet the effect of all this effort has never seriously been investigated. It is obvious that what educational effects there are must be pretty marginal. We do not live in a world of discerning connoisseurship, nor do the goods in our shops bear much resemblance to those in the corresponding museums. One obvious reason why this should be so is that museums almost invariably restrict themselves to positive example. By inference they imply that one should admire and perhaps aim to acquire objects similar to those that they exhibit. Yet good Taste is inextricably bound up with bad and there are wrong choices as well as right ones.

The usual name for such constraints on conduct is etiquette. Taste, in this more precise sense, is simply 'consumption etiquette'. Lessons in etiquette invariably follow the same format, some manifestly acceptable instances of correct conduct are generalized into positive recommendations for correct behaviour (or choice).[50] A neutral tone and a particular grammatical style suggests an apparent description of events rather than a direct injunction or admonition to the reader. For example, 'a good hostess brings in the claret after the soup and it passes round the table clockwise'. This form of locution appears to describe a natural event rather than to couch a proposal or to proffer advice. More important, however, than promulgations of what is done, are those on what is not done. Again, the form is similar. Ostensibly it is merely the observation of a fact and not the persuasive urging of precept. These negative features or exclusion rules are imperative in all etiquette, including Taste. Specific

3.26 *Henry Cole followed the logic of what he saw as the task of the museum to educate with the 'Chamber of Horrors' exhibition in the Marlborough House museum. Lamp in metal and glass, the only surviving artefact from the 1852 show.*

rules for right or decent conduct could never be complete enough to define all possible approved arrangements or choices, unknown futures and unforeseeable circumstances entail a generative strategy. Someone's good Taste is therefore of an indefinitely open-ended and promissory character. We believe in it so long as subsequent events do not contradict the initial assumption of appropriateness. Solecisms immediately terminate a promissory behavioural sequence as they invalidate this assumption. Avoidance of solecism is therefore imperative. It is bad Taste that stakes out the margins of particular consumption groups everywhere.

Characteristically, it was Henry Cole who first followed out the logic of the museum in this direction. In 1852, at Marlborough House, he organized an exhibition of bad Taste, vividly to contrast with the good. Known as the 'Chamber of Horrors', it caused a considerable stir. Needless to say, manufacturers whose products were included were not pleased. Nor indeed, were many visitors who, if they were already in possession of similar objects, were confronted with their own bad Taste. It was an experiment that has rarely been repeated.[51] Today, the current orthodoxy in high design (the kind of artefact that easily wins a label—Design Centre Approved) can be described as generalized neo-Classic. Worthy rather than witty, sound rather than sensuous, it is an orthodoxy which is ultimately founded less on aesthetic preference than on moral commitment. It is also an aesthetic of which we are likely to see a great deal more, as museums everywhere enlarge upon their perceived role as public educators and engage in more aggressive use of the artefacts in their collections for didactic purposes.

3.27 *The arts of appearance management. Effective role-play often demands a theatrical setting in which selected goods serve as essential props. A contemporary home office for the professional requires a suitably baronial setting for the personal computer and its associated printer and fax machine.*

The imagery of Greek art, in particular that of the Doric Temple, was understood in moral terms as far back as the fifteenth century. However, it was the German, Johan Joachim Winckelmann who, in the eighteenth century, initiated that form of the Greek revival we call neo-Classicism. Winckelmann saw, in the bleached and apparently undecorated ruins of Greek building and sculpture, an art which was the chaste manifestation of a spirit of calm grandeur and noble restraint.[52] Whether or not this actually was true of Greek art as it was made, such qualities were much to be admired in contrast to the licentiousness and frivolity then reigning. Jacques-Louis David converted Winckelmann's slogan into the official art of the new society ushered in by the French Revolution, and the conflation of aesthetic style with ethical prescription was complete.[53] From the time it became the official style of the French Revolution, neo-Classicism has been favoured by governing bureaucratic élites as both patriotic and responsible. It is easy to see why. To a far greater extent than Cavalier styles, its formal regularity can be generated by rules. Rules are always congenial to rulers. Besides, it is especially suitable to public patronage, for a surprising amount of discreet sensuality can be held decently in check by its austere symmetries on the larger scale. What better for cultural civil servants in a populist democracy who cannot afford to be seen titillating but who, above all, must never bore!

Managing impressions

Of course, it could be argued that this whole discussion of symbolic interpretation of our everyday goods is both cynical and unnecessary. Once we start discussing which effects are most calculated to encourage others to believe us to be unaffected, we are really discussing trickery and sham. But the innocence of the noble savage was always a myth. We always have some flexibility in our role-play, some possibility of role-distancing. One important use of this flexibility is the control of others' feelings, especially their feelings towards us. Goffman developed a penetrating analysis of the many acts and sequences of behaviour that we use to manage our appearances in day-to-day encounters. The title of his classic book, *The Presentation of Self in Everyday Life*, gives the flavour.[54] Most of this behaviour is unconscious. Therefore, the question of whether it is sincere or insincere does not arise in any easy way. In so far as social interaction is creative, articulated occasion by occasion on the basis of interpretive procedures and social norms, it is, in varying degree, under the control of the others in any particular social encounter. There are many shadings between true and false, sincere and insincere behaviour.

Misrepresentation, no less than mystification, is no longer clearly culpable in principle once we accept the dramaturgic metaphor for social interaction. When 'all the world's a stage', there are many occasions when a veridical reading of a particular scene is not crucial. We can accept (because we recognize it for what it is) a degree of artistic licence by the actors. Goffman describes many situations, particularly those involving professional roles —doctor, psychiatrist, nurse, lawyer, bank manager, even plumber or TV repair man— where a degree of connivance at some modest deviation from reality is an essential part of our belief in someone's competence. In fact, we 'put a good face on it', not only on the occasions when we greet our dentist or professor (who engages us with an appropriate manner and *mise-en-scène*) but virtually all the time, and never more keenly than when we are using our domestic setting to front a particular version of ourselves to another.

The use of goods (especially domestic goods) as props—stage properties to dress a scene—is inherent in the arts of appearance management. Without the reinforcement of a selection of objects in a compatible style to provide the backdrop, it is difficult, sometimes impossible, to effect a consistent and coherent role-play. What, though, is a compatible style? It is a commonplace of theatre that a thorough-going consistency in the level of verisimilitude of objects is not a necessary prerequisite for effective dramatic settings. We can watch an actor playing a part, whose face is made up beyond any possible realism, caricatured virtually into a mask. At the same time as we

3.28 *Appearance management is also a key part of the role-play of domestic life, especially in hospitality rituals. The theatre of the lounge,* Ideal Home Exhibition, London, England *(top). Even in the bedroom, managing appearances leads to a celebratory treatment of the centrepiece—the matrimonial bed—with mirrored four-poster architecture,* Scottsdale, Arizona, USA *(bottom).*

identify him as one of the characters, we hold in our minds the memory of his real face (perhaps from the publicity photograph in the programme). He wields what appears to be a real sword. The chairs are also real (or practical, in theatre jargon) but are clearly not genuine period furniture. They are workshop copies. One tree appears to have real branches, but others are made of paper. We notice that other furniture is clearly only painted, as part of the perspective depiction on the flat at the back of the stage. This illusionistic painting is framed with a genuine piece of three-dimensional architecture (but this is only a cutout). The moon is clearly a beam of light projected onto a gauze. We know (because of what has gone before and because of certain carefully constructed incompetencies directed towards us) that the actor is playing a play within a play. As we move our attention from object to object, we continually shift our interpretive-frame as necessary, so that inconsistencies of verisimilitude are not registered. We read each separate level of reality with a separate set of expectations, guided by our overall knowledge of what is going on and by our knowledge of the conventions of the stage at a particular time. Indeed, so powerful is this ability realistically to identify with the action, despite manifest inconsistency in levels of veracity in the setting, that dramatists who wish to remind audiences that they are watching a play have to resort to the most drastic dislocations of the habitual dramatic unities, so-called *alienation-effects*, effects that are themselves soon swallowed up by the audiences' expanding interpretive flexibility.[55]

This is equally true of our living rooms as it is of the theatre. Cissy Jupe displayed just this flexibility in Dickens' schoolroom scene. Her innocent bewilderment at the thought that anyone could not be flexible about the (to her) obvious unreality of printed flowers ironically points out the arbitrary nature of the government inspector's conventions. The arts of appearance management depend upon the conventions of the audience. What counts as an acceptable unity is conventional to a particular group. Protest at the violation of particular conventional selection rules (which are seen as obvious facts) occur at the boundaries of particular Taste cultures. To produce any generic description of the selection rules which are crucial for the correct usage of goods as props in the domestic theatre of different Taste publics is extraordinarily difficult. What seems obvious, even from a cursory survey of the fantastic variety permitted in most domestic settings, is that the stringency of integration demanded by the government inspector (Henry Cole can stand for the bureaucratization of all Taste cultures in the academic mould) is the exception rather than the rule. It does, however, mark out one extremely important boundary, that between creator- and user-orientated Taste cultures— at any rate, as these have evolved over most of the last hundred and fifty years. The Modern Movement in design may have wished entirely to extirpate the arts of appearance management ('mere sham') in the name of a democratically stern and unblinking realism. In fact, it merely forced them underground to work within an unprecedentedly narrow set of images and forms. Spurned by all social classes except a section of the intelligentsia, unadorned realism and naked function have been confronted by the mass market for objects that set out to be intentionally affecting.

Notes and References to Chapter 3

1 E. Goffman, *The Presentation of Self in Every-day Life*, London: Allen Lane, 1969.

2 A. Cicourel, *Cognitive Sociology*, Harmondsworth: Penguin, 1973, reprints the key papers on this theme. See in particular, "Interpretive procedures and Normative Rules in the Negotiation of Status and Role", "The Acquisition of Social Structure" and "Generative Semantics and the Structure of Social Interaction". See also P. J. Warr and C. Knapper, *The Perception of People and Events*, Chichester: J. Wiley and Sons, 1968, for a psychological account, in particular p. 20 gives a schematic diagram of the inferential and feedback processes which underlie interpersonal interaction.

3 E. Goffman, *Interaction Ritual—essays on face-to-face behaviour*, London: Allen Lane, 1972, p. 5, "On Facework".

4 A. Cicourel, *op. cit.*, p. 42 *et seq.*

5 On the eighteenth century interest in such feelings, especially in relation to 'the sublime', see S. H. Monk, *The Sublime*, Ann Arbor: University of Michigan Press, 1960. See also G. Lakoff and M. Johnson, *Metaphors We Live By*, Chicago: University of Chicago Press, 1980, particularly Chapters 6 and 7, for a discussion of personification as an explanatory tool in everyday behaviour.

6 J. Ruesch and W. Kees, *Non Verbal Communication*, Berkeley: University of California Press, 1956, especially Chapters 13 and 14.

7 Ancient attitudes to *trompe l'œil* are variable. On the one hand, verisimilitude in representation art was highly regarded, as evinced by the tale of Zeuxis' skill in painting grapes so realistic that the birds tried to eat them. His rival in illusionism, Parrhasios, so the tale goes, invited Zeuxis to his studio to see his efforts, and when Zeuxis tried to pull the curtain from the front of the picture he found that it was painted (Pliny the Elder, *Natural History*, XXXV, 36). Plato's views on imitation were negative. See K. Gilbert and H. Kuhn, *A History of Esthetics*, London: Thames and Hudson, 1956, pp. 26-34. Also I. M. Crombie, *An Examination of Plato's Doctrines*, London: Routledge and Kegan Paul, 1962, pp. 143-150, 190-194.

8 T. Veblen, *Theory of the Leisure Class*, New York: New American Library, 1953, p. 115.

9 C. Dickens, *Hard Times*, London: Folio Society, 1983 (first published in 1854). When this was written, Henry Cole was at the height of his power as a Victorian cultural bureaucrat. In fact, Dickens is echoing a traditional criticism of the use of figurative elements in applied ornament which goes back at least to Vitruvius who scorned the decadence of fresco painting in almost identical terms. See Vitruvius, *de Architectura*, trans. M. N. Morgan, first edition reprinted, New York: Dover, and London: Constable, 1960, p. 211.

10 W. Morris, "Lectures on Art and Industry; The Lesser Arts of Life" in *Collected Works of William Morris—introduction by May Morris*, 24 Volumes, London: Longman, 1910–15.

11 On the religious and cultural roots of such pronouncements see E. D. Andrews, *Shaker Furniture*, New York: Dover, 1964, p. 9 *et seq.*

12 The slogan is attributed to Adolf Loos. The title of his essay attacking the ornamental style of the Vienna Secession and in particular of Olbrich was in fact "Ornament and Crime". Ornament was supposed to be criminal not least because of the arduous and unrewarding repetitive work it compelled on the craftsmen who executed it—a justification strikingly similar to that of Alberti nearly five centuries earlier. See note 36. Excerpts from Loos' writings in English translation are collected in the exhibition catalogue: Y. Safran and W. Wang, *The Architecture of Adolf Loos*, London: Arts Council, 1985.

13 E. Goffman, *The Presentation of Self in Everyday Life*, London: Allen Lane, 1969, p. 54.

14 E. Goffman, *op. cit.*, p. 183.

15 See J. Ruesch and W. Kees, *op. cit.*, p. 36.

16 See J. Wildeblood and P. Brinson, *The Polite World*, Oxford: Oxford Univeristy Press, 1965.

17 Cicero, *On Duties*, trans. T. Cockman and W. Melmoth (1753), republished London: Dent, (Everyman), 1942.

18 B. Castiglione, *The Book of the Courtier*, trans. Sir Thomas Hoby, London: Dent, (Everyman), 1928.

19 G. della Casa, *Galateo—or the Book of Manners* (1558), trans. R. S. Pine-Coffin, Harmondsworth: Penguin, 1958.

20 A useful exception is M. Harrison, *People and Furniture—a Social Background to the English Home*, London: Ernest Benn, 1971. For example, Harrison quotes an early treatise on manners 'Les Honneurs de la Cour' on the design of sideboards (buffets). We learn that buffets for ladies have two shelves, countesses three, princesses four and queens five!

21 This topic has been entertainingly reviewed by L. Wight, *Clean and Decent*, London: Routledge and Kegan Paul, 1960. Public interest in these matters is reviewed by L. Lampton, *Temples of Convenience*, London: Gordon Frazer Gallery, 1978.

22 B. Bernstein, *Class, Codes and Social Control*, London: Routledge and Kegan Paul, 1971, Volume 1, p. 184.

23 L. Wright, *op. cit.*, p. 102.

24 For an account of the recent social history of soft furniture, see K. C. Grier, *Culture and Comfort—people, parlours and upholstery 1850–1930*, Strong Museum, Rochester, New York and Amherst: University of Massachusetts Press, 1989.

25 Little useful research has been undertaken in this area. An exception is R. Macdonald's paper presented to the International Conference on Environmental Psychology, Guildford, England, 1979. The author discusses findings on the interrelation between changing economic conditions, technology and social life in the uses of internal spaces and furniture of working class homes in Liverpool, UK. See also R. Macdonald, *Architecture and Behaviour*, 1, 1980–81, pp. 49–63.

26 Pliny comments on this most clearly in relation to painting, noting that earlier paintings which used only four colours were better than those of more recent times, since the plenitude of technical means distracted attention from the artistry itself. See Pliny the Elder, *Chapters on the History of Art*, (Eds.) K. Jex-Blake and E. Sellars, Chicago: Ares Publishers, 1982, p. 97. Vitruvius similarly berates the use of expensive pigments which 'present a brilliant appearance even although they are inartistically applied'. See Vitruvius, *op. cit.*, p. 213.

27 The issue of the correct use of perspective in large wall paintings, especially those which included an illusionistic architectural space, was partly an aesthetic and partly a religious matter. Once perspectival illusion was mastered, the issue then arose of whether the space of the picture be integrated with that of the real architectural frame so as to give the illusion of looking out from the architectural setting into a another 'real' world. This is related to another issue to do with the coherence of the perspectival point of view. Should the point of view be chosen so as to represent what a real spectator of the depicted scene would see? The trouble with this point of view is that it entails a low horizon and thus gives the painter the task of filling a large area above the horizon with sky—which is not very interesting to the viewer. In the case of Botticelli, the free use of mulitple viewpoints in his later works, in the interest of a heightened emotional intensity, was connected with his involvement in the religious currents of the time, currents which led to the Counter-Reformation and, in art, to mannerism. See A. Chastel, *The Studios and Styles of the Renaissance*, London: Thames and Hudson, 1966, p. 209 *et seq.*

28 A. Ehrenzwieg, *The Hidden Order of Art*, London: Weidenfeld and Nicolson, 1967, argues for the importance of the 'unconscious' perception of condensed symbols in art.

29 L. B. Alberti, in dealing with the location of the gentleman's villa in the countryside, away from the noise and smells of the city, quotes Martial, 'You tell me Friend, you much desire to know, What in my villa I can find to

do? I eat, drink, play, bathe, sleep, eat again, Or read, or wanton in the Muses Train'. (*Ten Books on Architecture*, IX, Chapter 2, trans. J. Leoni, (Ed. J. Ryckwert, London: Tiranti, 1955, p. 198). See also R. McMullen, *Roman Social Relations*, New Haven: Yale University Press, 1981, p. 28 *et seq.* for a review of Latin sources which deal with the relationships between town and countryside.

30 B. Castiglione, *op. cit.*, p. 46.

31 B. Castiglione, *op. cit.*, p. 49.

32 B. Castiglione, *op. cit.*, p. 48.

33 B. Castiglione, *op. cit.*, p. 46.

34 Adam Smith, *Theory of the Moral Sentiments*, (Eds.) D. D. Raphael and A. McFie, Oxford: Clarendon Press, 1976. (Text from the 1790 edition of Smith's works.)

35 J-J Rouseau, *Essay for the Academy of Dijon*, 1750, and later *Discourse on Inequality*, 1754.

36 E. H. Gombrich, "Visual Metaphors of Value" in *Meditations on a Hobby Horse*, Oxford: Phaidon Press, 1963, p. 12.

37 L. B. Alberti, *op. cit.*, p. 149.

38 L. B. Alberti, *op. cit.*, p. 205.

39 L. B. Alberti, *On Painting*, trans. J. R. Spencer, London: Routledge and Kegan Paul, 1956, p. 76 *et seq.*

40 G. Vasari, *The Lives of the Most Eminent Painters, Sculptors and Architects*, London: Dent (Everyman), 1963, Volume 2, p. 54.

41 E. Goffman, "Symbols of Class Status." *British Journal of Sociology*, 12, 1951, pp. 294-304.

42 The extremities to which a cultural Puritanism, hostile to any kind of illusionism in the visual arts, may go are brilliantly satirized by T. Wolfe in his essay "Up the Fundamental Aperture" in *The Painted Word*, London: Bantam Books, 1976.

43 Atheneus, *Deipnosophists*, London: Heineman, 1927–41, Volume 13, 94c *et seq.*

44 Pliny the Elder, *Chapters on the History of Art*, (Eds.) K. Jex-Blake and E. Sellars, Chicago: Ares Publishers, 1982, p. 97.

45 L. Venturi, *History of Art Criticism*, New York: E. P. Dutton, 1964, p. 57, notes that contrary views were also present, such as those of Plutarch, who asserted that colour was superior to drawing because it permitted a greater illusion.

46 This point is made by M. Douglas, *Natural Symbols*, London: Barrie and Jenkins, 1970, p. 96.

47 Two books which describe these controversies, setting them into the context of the history of industrial design in the United Kingdom, are F. McCarthy, *All Things Bright and Beautiful*, London: G. Allen and Unwin, 1972, and R. Stewart, *Design and British Industry*, London: J. Murray, 1987. Both are retrospects from a 'functionalist' point of view.

48 R. Hoggart, *The Uses of Literacy*, Harmondsworth: Penguin, 1959, p. 119.

49 D. Horne, *The Great Museum*, London: Pluto Press, 1984, discusses the logical end to this process, the synthetic representation of all and any history as a planetary tourist attraction.

50 Extracts from Victorian texts on etiquette considered as rule-systems are included in Mary Douglas' book of readings, M. Douglas, *Rules and Meanings*, Harmondsworth: Penguin, 1973, pp. 216, 219.

51 The material from the Chamber of Horrors itself has been dispersed. However, the Victoria and Albert Museum possesses contemporary examples of the kind to which Cole was objecting. Examples include illusionistic wallpapers similar to those satirized by Dickens. See the catalogue of the first exhibition in the Henry Cole Wing of the Victoria and Albert Museum, s. Lambert (Ed.), *Pattern and Design*, 1983, p. 120. More recently, the Boilerhouse Project Gallery at the Victoria and Albert Museum held an exhibition on Taste which displayed artefacts in bad Taste on dustbins while those held to be in good Taste were shown on plinths in the form of classical columns. The exhibition was equally controversial. The curator of this exhibition also published a set of essays on Taste. See S. Bayley, *Taste*, Boilerhouse Project, Victoria and Albert Museum, London, 1986.

52 J. J. Winckelmann, "Reflections on the Painting and Sculpture of the Greeks, with instructions for the Connoisseur, and an essay on Grace in Works of Art" in *Winckelmann, Writings on Art*, (Ed.) D. Irwin, London: Phaidon, 1765.

53 See L. Ettlinger, "Jacques-Louis David and Roman Virtue." The Fred Cook Memorial Lecture, *Journal of the Royal Society of Arts*, London, 1967.

54 See in particular, E. Goffman, *op cit.*, p. 183, "The arts of impression management".

55 This idea is particulary associated with the theatre of Berthold Brecht. See R. Gray, *Brecht the Dramatist*, Cambridge: Cambridge University Press, 1976.

4. Taste and the Professionals

4.1 *Contemporary public sculpture is the result of corporate patronage and the particular decisions are made within an artistic bureaucracy which has little regard for popular Taste. This leads to the strangest disjunctions between the artwork and its context. Streetscape with sculpture, Chicago, Illinois, USA.*

Creators and curators

There is one group that can be expected to take a quite exceptional interest in matters of Taste. All modern societies support a variety of specialists whose function is to produce symbolic imagery or, if not themselves producers, to urge, persuade and advise the wider public on the appropriate consumption of symbolic goods. Such specialisms have been characterized as *curator-professions* (the term is Erving Goffman's).[1] The term curator implies one who exercises a permanent stewardship over a particular set of images and is wider in its scope than 'creator', which it includes. As professional custodians of social values, members of curator-professions resemble theologians, *chefs de protocole* or Kings of Arms of the Heralds College, all of whom preside in perpetuity over the circulation and legitimation of symbols and metaphors. Like them, curator-professions form part of the various 'establishments'—groups whose prejudices and preferences are disproportionately influential, not so much because of the nature of those values, as of the social position occupied by those who urge them on the public.

Although they include many of the actual creators of symbolic imagery (of whom the purest would be the fine artists) and are, to the wider public, closely identified with the interests of creators rather than consumers, curator-professionals operate in the real world of commerce and politics and as such, their values rarely coincide exactly with those of purely creative spirits. (The struggles between individual genius and entrenched Taste bureaucracy is part of the stock in trade of the cultural historian.[2]) To this extent, the notion (put forward by Gans) that there is but one creator-orientation is an oversimplification, an abstraction which conflates many different and only partly congruent points of view. Such viewpoints are inextricably bound up, not only with the values of the producers as individual members of their particular Taste publics, but with the values that arise directly from the many differentiated roles within the structures of professional organizations. These differentiated roles are associated—as in other social organizations—with differential rewards in terms of money, status and power, to form a powerful and largely autonomous reward system within which the curator-professional articulates his individual life career. The reward systems of curator-professions have little been studied, especially in those professions most closely associated with the production of the artefactual world. Even less is known about the perceptions of them among those who aspire to become curator-professionals. And, further to complicate matters, the creative vocation is the subject of a powerful mythology, fostered by many works of art in which the creative way of life with its splendours and miseries, is romanticized as the chief subject.[3]

The Industrial Revolution gave the impetus for the rise of the curators to their present prominence. Unlike the Renaissance, the Industrial Revolution was not at first a revolution in forms of life, a shift in individual and social attitudes expressed in new images and new kinds of goods. Steam and the division of labour merely created a revolutionary increase in productivity. What goods might be produced was in no way implicit in the discoveries of the great engineers and inventors. Existing products could now be turned out by the million and existing preferences could be shared by the mass of new consumers, at least

4.2 A Committee of Taste—*a painting by Balthasar van den Bossche, Petworth House, Sussex, England shows a meeting of connoisseurs at the end of the seventeenth century.*

4.3 *The Townley Collection of Park Street, London, England is a good example of an early private collection which formed part of the foundation of the British Museum. Zoffany's painting of Townley's rooms is in part an artist's compilation, grouping together works which were in other parts of the house but it nevertheless gives a good impression of what it must have looked like.*

in facsimile or mechanical reproduction. This incredible increase in production demanded equally dramatic increases in markets to absorb the goods produced, hence the preferences of such markets were all important. Matters of Taste, which had previously been the philosophical hobby of noble or cleric, became the urgent concern of commerce. At this period however, competition was exclusively concerned with small-scale objects such as textiles and ceramics. (Competition in capital goods and technology came later.) There was little to distinguish products like these from the consideration of their usefulness. One pot or plate might be just as practical or durable as another. What made it sell was its appearance. The Industrial Revolution also coincided with the rise of the nation state, and the fortunes of industry were won or lost in international competition for markets. England was the first country to experience the revolution in productivity. It was, therefore, the first to come up against the concept of markets and, in particular, the problem of competition from Europe, notably France.

Raising the nation's Taste

In the United Kingdom, in 1835, the House of Commons, worried by the impact of foreign competition on the sale of British goods, set up a Select Committee (this was extraordinary given the overwhelming economic power of the country at the time).[4] Its purpose was 'to enquire into the best means of extending a knowledge of the arts and principles of design among the people (especially the manufacturing population) of the country

and also to enquire into the Constitution of the Royal Academy.' After many struggles, a national system of education in design, based on approximately twenty 'branch' schools linked to a 'normal' school located in Somerset House in London, was established. In time, this system became enriched by a network of art museums in most provincial towns. Private collections of wealthy aristocrats had already evolved into two great metropolitan museums—the British Museum and the National Gallery. Following the 1851 Exhibition, the South Kensington museums were set up as the centre piece of a vast social apparatus aimed at edifying the general public on matters of Taste.

Motives for all these private and public efforts were hopelessly mixed-up: philanthropic—a desire to extend the benefits of civilization to the masses, patriotic—a desire to demonstrate not only the power but also the culture of the country or even of a local town, commercial—a desire to raise the standard of competence of the practitioners (artists were the first to be admitted to the great royal and private collections of earlier centuries) and beyond these, to improve the discrimination of the masses who, for the first time in history had acquired enough wealth to exercise some individual choice in the marketplace for the new mass-produced consumer goods. From its beginning in 1835, the history of education in art and design in the United Kingdom has been a series of responses to external commercial challenges to its manufacturing industry. And to this day, that response has been a twofold attack: one effort designed to raise standards among designers through specialized education in schools, and the other, through increasingly sophisticated exhibitions and

4.4 *Sir John Soane's collections were acquired by the architect for the purposes of study by his students and assistants. It remains largely unaltered to this day.*

displays, to raise the level of Taste among the public at large.

Historical accounts of the early years of the public involvement in matters of Taste make entertaining reading. Scandals, purges and the clash of passionate opinion abound. This is hardly surprising given the reformer's view of his daunting calling as crusader or missionary, fighting the infidel or evangelizing the heathen. Commercial shortsightedness and sheer greed was one enemy. Manufacturers resisted contributing to the system, even though it was aimed at ensuring their long-term survival. And, even while the gospel of beauty was spreading, economic vandalism was destroying much of the traditional British scene under metal, brick and soot. Dedicated amateurs of whom John Ruskin was the superhumanly energetic prototype, relentlessly struggled against the crass, the ignorant and the selfish. Henry Cole, on the other hand, ruthlessly fought to bring order to the public interest in Taste and thereby established a truly modern cultural bureaucracy. Statistics from the early years of these crusades are amazing. Ruskin's lectures were attended by thousands. Attendance at Cole's South Kensington museums ran

to more than twelve million by 1873 when he finally retired.

Today, propaganda for good Taste is financed by central government on a substantial scale. But what are the best examples of industrial artefacts? What exactly is meant by raising the nation's Taste? Or indeed, which direction is up? These and many more questions were implicit from the moment when the connoisseurship of a cultivated minority became mixed-up with the commercial life of modern manufacturing nations. They are debated in democratic institutions as alert to partisanship and personal bias as they are keen to protect the taxpayer's money. Because, before the bureaucratization of Taste got under way, to be cultured was to be rich, it was inevitable that the administration of the new organs of culture, whether schools or museums, should be in the hands of the wealthy.

The first modern collections were those of aristocrats and rich merchants.[5] It was among such circles that the debates of connoisseurs and critics, the dilettanti and the cultural voyagers of the grand tour took on substance in the branch of philosophy that had just been named aesthetics. Throughout the nineteenth century and for the greater part of the twentieth, cultural politics has remained the preserve of the upper, affluent classes. However, highminded and disinterested they may have been in their proselytizing, the values that they sought to spread among the masses were naturally their own. Quite unconsciously, good Taste was taken to be the preferences of a (classically) educated and wealthy élite. Even the huge quantities of exotic and ethnographic material which accumulated during the era of colonial expansion by the European powers were assimilated to this particular viewpoint.

129

Most of the museums for pure art even today embody this perception of Taste. This is also true of official support for other cultural activities. In the United Kingdom, while small sums are hesitantly disbursed to support popular arts such as street theatre or even jazz, most government money is still spent on essentially aristocratic or *haut-bourgeois* Tastes.[6] Most other industrialized countries follow similar policies. (Some may, usually for nationalistic or political reasons, occasionally give a higher level of support to supposedly folk and vernacular activities or to local rural or peasant arts and crafts.)

When Arnold Ross invented the terms 'U' (for the upper class) and 'non-U' (for all the rest) he coined a distinction that became a craze.[7] For a while, it was universally used to denote any behaviour or choice that was socially exclusive or excluded in the practices of any social group. In popular publications and the mass media, aristocratic values are still seen as the paradigms of good Taste. Royalty and the titled gentry are the objects of a curiosity amounting to an obsession. Much of this is directed towards what they do with their money, that is to say their consumption choices or Tastes. A new hat for the Princess of Wales will clear the front pages of the mass circulation dailies in the United Kingdom of all except news of a major war or natural disaster. Yet the very success of those early efforts at raising the nation's Taste along essentially aristocratic lines laid the foundations for developments on very different directions.

Private involvement in matters of Taste is essentially limited and fitful. Founding great collections of old masters is one thing, missionary work in the marketplace quite another. Once a cultural bureaucracy based on education and museums had been set up, it was soon apparent that not only was it self-propagating but that, given the sheer scale of the operation, professional values would rival and eventually supplant all others. We can clearly see in the debates and polemics of the time that by the mid-nineteenth century, what constituted an approved good Taste was already powerfully influenced by the 'New Men'—Establishment artists and critics. Values and preferences of an Establishment of curators and creators are set against those of users—whether these are aristocratic or otherwise. Not that these new Establishments were united on any simple aesthetic platform. Factional in-fighting was the very stuff of nineteenth century art history in countries such as England and France that had got involved in the public patronage of the so-called 'industrial arts'. Yet slowly but surely, the curator interest increased in power so that Establishment artists, keepers and critics became, not estranged and alienated, but confident and assertive—almost philosopher-kings, even if only civil servants in rank.[8]

Artists, intellectuals and the marketplace

There are several stages in the evolution of a full-fledged curator-profession. To begin with, cultural élites of all kinds form part of the wider intelligentsia.[9] Their rise is an intrinsic part of that of the intellectuals as a distinctive social group. From their earliest beginnings in the salons and coffee houses of the eighteenth century, through their massive expansion in the nineteenth, buoyed-up on the rising flood

4.5 Sentimental genre scenes dominated the commercialized art world of galleries and specialist publications in the nineteenth century. The Widow and Uncle Toby *by C. R. Leslie is a typical example from the 1840s.*

of cheap printing, to their present secure anchorages in the various institutions of higher learning, the intellectuals have progressively established a distinctive set of life styles, and a strong if unspoken *esprit de corps*. They have also acquired a definite expectation of a prescriptive role in the determination of the manners and mores of contemporary society. Current methods of patronizing erstwhile independent creative artists entail that they too become assimilated into the institutions of the intelligentsia at large.

As the intelligentsia (including artists) depends on the productive surplus of others, it cannot help but, in one way or another, be

beholden to those others. In early times, those others were usually personal patrons, rich individuals. At first, these were invariably aristocrats but later they were drawn mostly from the ranks of successful commercial entrepreneurs or bankers (or often their wives). In our day, patronage is usually indirect, mediated through one of the agencies of the Taste bureaucracies themselves—the advisory committees on business sponsorship, the boards of the great foundations, the mandarin and often obscure functionaries of semi-government and the so-called quangos such as the arts, crafts and design councils in the United Kingdom and their equivalents in other countries.[10]

From the beginning, it was obvious to the intellectuals that the advantage of personal security was often paid for by a loss of personal independence, an infringement of the very creative freedom which, on the surface, patronage seemed to provide. Some could manage the ticklish social relationships with demanding and often fitful patrons and still remain creatively free. Others could not. Later, commercial publishers or picture dealers seemed to offer an escape from an all too close relationship with an individual patron. Often though, the bookseller or art dealer as an intermediary had little interest in quality. Laments about the inexorable debasement of standards in the interest of ever larger sales were first heard in the eighteenth century. 'Grub Street' is a haunting symbol of the fate of the unsuccessful commercial writer.

Much the same is true of the commercialization of the visual arts. A proliferation of cheap prints, invariably of mawkish religious subjects or sentimental genre scenes, showed artists all too painfully what was really popular marketplace. Those few committed picture dealers who backed artists such as the Impressionists, when others did not, have become, in some cases, cultural heros in their own right.[11] Artists reacted predictably. If it would not sell anyway, why not paint what you liked and damn the public! From here to *épater les bourgeois* is only a short step. The hostile relationship between high art and popular Taste has long since become the staple of cultural history. Naturally, amid all this hostility and exploitation, some artists banded together for comradeship and mutual support. Groups and movements could raise a little money to put on an exhibition or publish a manifesto and thereby achieve what isolated effort, however vigorous, could never do. For the most part however, artists and writers have not progressed from such informal gatherings and coteries into that full-fledged collective that is meant by the term profession. A romantic individualism effectively inhibits long-term collective action.[12]

For a long time, much the same was true of the applied artist. Mass production of gimcrack artistic objects by newly mechanized craft processes presented the same temptations and trials that faced writers or painters. For every Wedgwood or Doulton who patronized artists of merit, there were dozens of proprietors interested only in sales with inevitable results in terms of the debasement of images.[13] 'Commerce versus quality' was a dilemma that tormented the applied artist from the beginning. However, it was only later in this century that applied artists began to make effective progress towards the control of their working conditions by the establishment of professional alliances. Only when this was achieved could they

4.6 *Gimcrack pottery was turned out in huge quantities. Invariably breaking all the rules for good form as espoused by aesthetes it nevertheless satisfied an eager market.*

hope to confront the hostile forces of the cultural marketplace.

The rise of the professionals

In preindustrial societies, the guilds exercised significant control over the provision of important services. These ranged from specialized personal services such as medicine and the law, to the myriad craft activities that furnished the tangible items of the artefactual world. Guilds varied a great deal in terms of their productive efficiency and the extent of their monopoly control. Often they were not accorded particularly high social status nor could they always guarantee a certain economic reward. This was especially true of those creative activities which we rate highly today.

Some of the lowly rankings given to painters and sculptors which we value highly strike us as extraordinary.[14] Yet they were not thought surprising at the beginning of the Renaissance. At the onset of the Industrial Revolution, the outdated structures of the remaining guilds were finally destroyed by powerful market forces. Only gradually were the surviving agencies of control of a few specialized personal services, based on the ancient institutions of higher learning, subsequently transformed into modern professions. Doctors and lawyers were the first to be given those significant responsibilities in law which are the mark of a mature profession.

Although an adequate definition of a profession is hard to achieve, the salient features of professional groups are easy to describe. Professions are coherent and formally structured associations of individuals who provide a specialized service. This service is usually based on considerable learning and often esoteric expertise. It is this expertise which, in an obvious case like medicine, protects the public from danger. However, precisely because of the esoteric nature of medical expertise, there is little the lay public can do to protect itself against abuse or incompetence. Recourse to the courts entails calling as witnesses persons with precisely the same expertise as that which is being challenged. This is true in many other fields, such as engineering or architecture and, of course, the law itself. Perhaps less obviously the same is true in matters of Taste. Who is to challenge the expert in art history who unscrupulously or incompetently agrees to the faulty attribution of a work of art, thereby increasing its market value a hundredfold? Such problems may even arise where the esoteric knowledge concerns the nature and

practice of art itself—as demonstrated in the celebrated case of *Whistler versus Ruskin*.[15]

Emerging professions gradually acquire the capacity to enforce a code of practice upon their members.[16] At first, this is done informally—a kind of blackballing from the club—or the discreet and covert blocking of preferment. Eventually, this responsibility is ceded formally by the state to professions established in law as corporate bodies. In the United Kingdom, this is done by the institution of the Royal Charter. Charters give a quasi-legal standing to what were in the beginning merely clubs. Instead of facing litigation or prosecution, an aberrant professsional is arraigned by his peers who can punish proven abuse or incompetence by striking a member off the roll, thus denying him his livelihood. Naturally enough though, with this power goes the ability to control financial rewards and social status. In order to maintain the quality and disinterestedness of the service (so it is argued) free competition for clients, at whatever rate is determined by the market, must be prevented. All professions therefore seek centrally controlled scales of fees, based on standard charges for particular services.[17] The reward system of members of a mature profession is thus based upon a high and exclusive social status, a fixed and favorable income resulting from the elimination of competition in scales of fees and the power which flows from a monopoly of competence. Within professional organizations and the bureaucracies which sustain them, these reward systems are clearly understood. 'Getting-on' in professional terms is no mystery to the novices. Students soon learn about the various ladders to reward. Their perceptions of their future professions in terms of an anticipated or virtual eer is an immensely important factor in motivating their efforts in particular directions in their chosen field.

The professionalization of Taste

There is rarely anything in the definition of a profession's central concern to suggest clear demarcations and precise boundaries. This is especially true in times of rapid social and technological change. Where exactly an architect's responsibilities should end, and those of the civil engineer, planner or interior designer begin, cannot be decided in any theoretical way. In practice, the issues are settled by continuous and often acrimonious negotiation involving disputes between rival professional cliques. Today, centuries after the notorious struggles between the physicians and the surgeons which delayed the introduction of modern scientific medicine by decades, proper architects are struggling to prevent interior designers (or interior architects as they are called in Europe) from usurping their positions.[18] Attempts to achieve a united engineering profession have been marked by factional in-fighting of sufficient ferocity to frustrate legislation, while the efforts of designers to have their professional name restricted to licensed practitioners have been thwarted by the engineers who assert that they also design![19] In each case, a professional bureaucracy is fighting for its survival. Conservatism is built-in to the very concept of a professional organization dedicated to maintaining universal standards in perpetuity.

All this may be more or less convincing in the case of those professions which are concerned with activities that are really dangerous or damaging. But what about those activities concerned with the production of the artefactual world and thus, in large part, with matters of Taste? What about interior or furniture design, graphics or fashion? Is a 'proper' profession desirable in these cases? By exaggerating the problems, arguments could be presented to justify codes of practice for wallpaper suppliers or the purveyors of bathroom or kitchen appliances, or even perhaps, for the makers and designers of high fashion apparel. If not danger, at least embarrassment and expense could easily be caused to unlucky clients by any of these services if provided in a faulty manner. But what if technical competence can be assured? Suppose that the wallpaper really is suited to the steamy kitchen, the plumbing actually works and the dress really is machine washable? What do we say about standards of service when our complaint is simply that the product is ugly, or even merely dull or unexciting?

These issues do not arise in the case of the older professions but they are crucial with respect to the latest aspirants to professional status covered by the various aspects of the word 'design'. It is at the point where standards of service rest on Taste that the institutions of professionalism are least convincing. We need not be surprised therefore, that emerging Taste professions—which is what design really is—mention little about aesthetics and a great deal about technology, ergonomics and marketing, for it is here that the extrapolation from engineering or architecture is most persuasive. Yet, in the end, design is about Taste and it is precisely in the symbolic expression of values that the difference between clients and their professional servants are most difficult to pin down, and where the imposition of values which ultimately derive from the reward systems within professional bureaucracies are most difficult to accept.

The professionalization of Taste has followed the same competitive pattern that has marked the emergence of other professional groups. To begin with, like everyone who rendered a service, artists were subjected to the values of the guild. First among these was the notion of obedience and the mechanisms of apprenticeship. Writing at the start of the Renaissance, Cennino Cennini, after presenting his credentials by reference to his chain of decent from Giotto, begins his *The Book of the Artist* by praising those who enter the profession because of a sense of enthusiasm and exaltation over those lesser mortals who only do it for money ('poverty and domestic need'). Then follows his prescription for beginners:

> You therefore who with lofty spirit are fired with this ambition, and are about to enter the profession, begin by decking yourselves with this attire: Enthusiasm, Reverence, Obedience and Constancy. And begin to submit to the instruction of a master as early as you can; and do not leave until you have to.[20]

Conditions for contracts were often amazingly onerous by modern standards. Even famous artists such as Ghiberti were bound by conditions pertinent to a humble artisan. At this period, many activities which subsequently became the province of separate professions were barely distinguished in the organization of the workshop or *bottegha*. As work came in, an individual might turn his hand to the building of a church, or to sculpture or painting, gilding or carving gesso. But, by the time that the High Renaissance had established the

artist as a man above mere trade, there were familiar arguments about relative status. Leonardo da Vinci, in his *Paragone*, argued for the primacy of painting over sculpture.[21] When, later, academies began to be formed, modelled on the first—the Academia di San Lucca in Rome—their internal organization mirrored, not only contemporary philosophical judgments, but also the current victories and truces in the perennial conflicts between the various creator groups.[22] Like other groups, artists struggled for monopoly power to regulate entry and eliminate unfair competition. Sometimes it was in the interest of centralist states to give it to them, since they were thereby co-opted into the propaganda service of the government. When, therefore, the first efforts were made to professionalize those industrial artists who were engaged in the manufacture of consumer goods during the confusion following the Industrial Revolution, the main opponents were naturally the already established fine artists.

England had, at that time, no equivalent to France's centralized Taste bureaucracy. Nevertheless, the Royal Academy attempted to extend an effective cartel to ensure that decorative artists did not use their skills to become 'proper' artists 'by the back door'. Persistent struggles and intrigues defined the hierarchy of prestige within painting—traditionally ranked from history painting at the top to still life at the bottom—at a time when social change meant that there was no longer a guaranteed flow of commissions for the history painter in the decoration of churches and public buildings. New organizations, to provide what is now called 'industrial design', were viewed by the Royal Academy as a clear challenge. This was especially true of education, for he who controls education controls entry to the profession and hence the kind and amount of competition. Contemporary truces between rival educators included the agreement to restrict the training of potential industrial artists to the drawing of plant decoration while, for the chosen few fine artists, there was the traditional inculcation into the skills of drawing from the model in the life room. Such practices were difficult to defend and, precisely because of the high prestige thus accorded, there was a constant creeping spread of fine art among those supposedly devoted to no-nonsense industrial activities. This is a perennial problem in British art education.[23] The battles and scandals of the nineteenth century, so vividly described by Quentin Bell, have their contemporary counterpart in renewed government pressure on design education to work ever more closely with (and for) industry, while there is the ever-present threat that many schools of fine art will be closed altogether.

Faced with entrenched opposition from older established professions, applied artists naturally tried to set up rival organizations themselves. In England, these attempts have been inextricably mixed up with confused and ambivalent attitudes towards industry itself. Men such as William Morris and Charles Ashbee were capable of generating enough passionate inspiration in their followers, for what were essentially unworldly and Utopian fantasies, to ensure that such fundamental questions as the proper relationship of art to craft and of both to industry have remained unresolved to this day.[24] Various arts and crafts movements came and went. However, it was not merely the question of appropriate technology that was at stake. The tension between

an individual's creative autonomy and his submission to the marketplace, or as Gans put it, between the creator- and the user-orientations, was, and is, the main concern.

Design as a profession

The recent history of those who have come to be called designers typifies the process of the professionalization of Taste. In the United Kingdom, the first modern organization of would-be Taste makers was the Design and Industry Association. It was founded in 1915, inspired by the outcome of the Deutsche Werkbund in Germany and similar societies in Austria and Sweden. The DIA had the broad objective of fostering good design and included industrialists and other interested parties as well as practitioners. Professional status for the 'industrial artist' was the narrower objective of the Society of Industrial Artists (later to include 'Designers'), the SIAD, founded in 1930.[25] Its declaration of policy of 1932 began with the assertion: 'the future of the Creative Industrial Artist and Designer lies in his attaining professional status as in the case of the Architect, the Engineer, the Solicitor, the Surgeon etc.'.

Although it had friendly relations with the DIA, its real model was the Royal Institute of British Architects. However, given the wide range of activities that could be characterized as industrial art or design, and the equally large range of professional involvement and remuneration, the chances of obtaining a 'closed' profession were recognized at the time as negligible. Nevertheless, the next forty years were characterized by familiar debates about scales of fees, contractual obligations and the control of education that mark each succeeding aspirant to professional autonomy. Currently, the Society has a Royal Charter which, while it does not grant the designers the same sort of powers that are enjoyed by the RIBA (the engineers have seen to that!), nevertheless grants it status as the official voice of everyone engaged in all branches of design. Recently, the name has been changed to the Chartered Society of Designers. However, from the start, the CSD has been riven by the emergence of a new power group from within.

With the explosive growth in the commercial activity of design there has been a consequent increase in the size and wealth of the larger design practices, a dozen or so of which are now quoted companies on the stock market. Their interests are no longer those of the freelance creative artist, applied or otherwise, but of all 'big' business. Fed up with what they saw as the parochialism of the old SIAD, they decided to set up a group of their own, the Design Businesses Association. After a lot of in-fighting and negotiation (the independents saw them as 'share-pushers with no interest in quality') they have finally agreed to become part of a restructured CSD, which will now be heavily influenced by their voice. Needless to say, the first urgent items on the new agenda were the restriction of competition (in the elimination of so-called speculative pitches for new business) and the control of salaries, which the intense demand for experienced staff has bidded up to unacceptable levels.[26] The tone of the debate is becoming increasingly 'hard-nosed', with an undisguised contempt for the 'airy-fairy' (creatively adventurous) as against the commercially proven. Macho catchphrases imported from advertising are increasingly deployed as evidence of realism. (A rash of new designer magazines has appeared to support these attitudes—and the advertisers who inspire and fund them. Weekly announcements of stock market ratings and new client accounts and billings, presented in the form of glamorous, 'personalized' gossip, have displaced older comment modelled on criticism in the visual arts.) To complete the process is the change of name which, by abandoning reference to its origins in the arts, is a token of the achievement of a mature and confident profession in its own right. Similar histories can be traced in other industrialized countries. The irony is that, while some of those who run the society may be great creative performers in their own right, as with the architects, a professional label of competence is no guarantee at all of aesthetic sensitivity or artistic flair. Nor are these qualities to be defined too rigorously by what is, in effect, a self-perpetuating oligarchy, depending for its survival on increasingly heavy subscriptions from its members. Once properly organized with full-time salaried officials and expensive headquarters, none of the Taste professions can be too fussy about Taste!

A complete account of the curator-professions would have to include, not merely the creator groups, but also a whole galaxy of organizations concerned with the distribution of culture. In the United Kingdom for example, these range from the various councils whose remit is the education of both manufacturers and public into good design, to small private clubs and associations. There are also special interest learned or quasi-learned societies such as, to take but one small area, the Museums Association, the Society for Education in Museums and the Society of Museum

Designers and others concerned with the museum world. (Together these have even created a new '-ology', so-called museology.[27]) These and others of their kind are often ephemeral. Many die having made little headway in the struggle for professional autonomy. Others are the fledglings that will grow into powerful monopolies in later years. (Museums form a powerful and extremely expensive cultural pressure-group with their own Byzantine internal hierarchies.) In each of these curator groups the reward systems are defined within a professional bureaucracy.

Alongside these various ostensibly disinterested organizations, there exists a luxurious fringe of commercial imitators. It may seem a big step from the curator of a large museum who, with his board of trustees, chooses which artefacts to present as exemplars of Taste to the huckster outside the museum entrance who sells postcards and plastic replicas of the great works therein. Even more so perhaps to the advertising hack who plagiarizes and satirizes the museum to sell cigarettes, or the furniture salesman who dresses his store with cheap reproductions of Constable or Peter de Hooch (Plate 10). Yet each of them is concerned in his own particular way with the distribution of value judgments about Taste. And, even in these apparently absurd corners of the cultural marketplace, we can discern the omnipresent drive, first for respectability, and then the subsequent attempt to confront market forces with a united group that can impose a degree of monopoly control. Salesmen and advertisers also have their codes of ethics elaborated within bureaucracies such as the Institute of Practitioners in Advertising or the American Marketing Association. Even the humble salesman, pushing his designer double-glazing, aspires to membership of a bureaucracy which displays its respectability by imitating the forms of the older more established professions.[28] Professionalism as the ultimate value has some dubious overtones!

Educating the Taste makers

All professions, to ensure that their claim to a monopoly of competence is valid, seek to control the educations of beginners. Apprenticeship, and other traditional methods of handing down knowledge and skill, have long since ceased to be adequate preparation for professional competence in areas which involve scientific or technological learning. Instead, a long and demanding theoretical education is required. To a lesser extent, this is true of creator professions based ultimately on the exercise of Taste. Part of the charter of each new profession invariably deals with standards of entry and hence with education. Most professional bodies have directly concerned themselves with teaching. Many have specific branches of their bureaucracy dedicated to this end. Historically however, the prevailing pattern of educational development in industrialized countries has been the progressive incorporation of erstwhile professional institutions dedicated to specific vocations into the general education of society—usually in schools and universities. To ensure that standards of entry into the profession are upheld, there are frequently elaborate systems of dual examination in both academic and professional matters where these have ceased to be identical.[29]

When professional education was still in the hands of practitioners, there was little difficulty in ensuring that the training of novices was sufficiently vocational. Indeed, the usual complaint was the opposite—that professionals as educators had little interest in any matters beyond the crudely practical. As soon as the educational system itself is professionalized, there are invariably complaints from practioners that educators are failing to equip their students for the realities of professional life. Schools and colleges are accused of developing a closed system of their own, an ivory tower in which the life style encourages otherworldly attitudes which effectively prevent students from coping with the hard facts of life in the real world.

Except for the very smallest academic institutions, unique social structures and ways of life soon develop. Indeed, they are essential if the institution is to survive. Some students, long before they graduate, are attracted to the life style of the professional teacher and practice their profession perfunctorily if at all before returning to teach. Naturally, such practices are vigorously condemned by practitioners. However, the extent to which they themselves are prepared to devote time to teaching varies a great deal. Not only is teaching poorly remunerated compared with practice, but there are also varying perceptions of teaching itself as a *declassé* activity, not to be engaged in except at the risk of being thought a professional failure. ('Those who can, do. Those who can't, teach.' is a slogan still widely heard among the realists of design practice. Current variations are 'Design or resign!' and 'Make art or depart!') These strictures are much less harshly felt in other professions. No one thinks it a disaster to be seen as a professor

of medicine for example. The obloquy that attaches to the teaching of design probably stems from memories of the disrepute of the Academy in the case of the fine arts. During the nineteenth century, the teaching of applied arts in the schools of design was often in the hands of talentless hacks who obtained a sinecure through influence or taught private pupils by the hour for paltry sums. Moreover, the fact that many of the greatest painters of the later nineteenth century, particularly in France, were either self-taught or had at best a rudimentary education in one of the *academies libres* became the foundation of the twentieth century myth of the artist as unaided discoverer, as well as to the belief that art itself is more or less unteachable. Designers were struggling to achieve professional status at precisely the time when this myth passed into the hands of a commercialized *avant-garde*, newly recruited into the art schools.

In the United Kingdom at any rate, the history of the education of creators—both pure and applied—has been one of drastic reforms and purges visited every ten years or so upon a system that constantly ossifies by virtue of its own internal rigidities. Frequently, that enduring Platonism, that sees the pure as necessarily superior to the merely applied, finds expression in the hierarchy within the schools of art and design. Although much modified, the current system in the United Kingdom is still more or less the one set up two decades ago by Sir William Coldstream, a notable painter.[30] All students of design were required to undertake a component of fine art which was regarded as a kind of civilizing leaven, or more precisely, as the fountainhead of cultural values which would nourish applied artists in Taste. Removal of this requirement, which had no reciprocal entailment upon the fine artist, was seen as a notable victory by the emerging profession of design. (Where attempted at all, educating Taste from a consumer's point of view has hitherto been left to the training of teachers in the home economics department—one of the lowest subjects in the academic pecking order.)

Naturally, varying perceptions of these implied prestige rankings among the arts and crafts, and their relation to those of the design profession, exert a powerful influence on the imagery produced. Not least is the ambiguous colouring given to the notion of professional 'service' by the conflation of artistic impulses, impulses which are reinforced by their high prestige, with technocratic or commercial attitudes to design. To the extent that individuals regard themselves as artists (or more likely, covertly aspire to be artists), they are not strictly speaking offering a service. Instead of finding fulfilment in solving the client's problems, they are more likely to be concerned with getting their ideas through or past the client. As they see it, the thrust of creative invention starts with them and not *vice versa*. Both impulses can usually be seen variously at work in any commercial enterprise. Some theoreticians of the design process have tried to distinguish between demand-pull and invention-push in innovation and further to identify where each might be expected to succeed. In reality, it is the clashes and compromises that result from the rivalries of many competing creator groups—each struggling to survive in an only partly tamed market for their services—that determines what is offered to the businessman. 'What the consumer wants', where this can be determined, is only one factor in this complex game. Of course, the salesmen

4.7 *Design education has itself become a high-profile professional activity. Exhibition of work by students of design from Kingston Polytechnic, London, England in the Boilerhouse Gallery at the Victoria and Albert Museum.*

of the design practices vigorously assert the opposite but, even in the most commercial of offices, there is always a tension between what could have been and what finally was accepted. In a way, this subversive aspect of the designer's motivation can be seen as the institutional embodiment of altruism and of intrinsic values in society, without which the lowest common denominator of pecuniary lust would be the only determinant of Taste. Whatever subsequent transformations they may undergo by virtue of the pressures and erosions of commercial life, it is these early perceptions of what counts as creative integrity, formed during the educational stage of professionalization, that endure to inspire (and sometimes haunt) the designer—that equivocal figure that Wright Mills calls 'the man in the middle'.[31]

Ivory towers and real worlds—reward systems in curator-professions

Curator-professions are now so firmly established that the normal expectation of anyone entering one is a lifetime career on the typical

Plate 2. *The prototypical 'front room'. Frequent exposure to particular goods and their arrangement into characteristic settings reinforces the prototypical categories of the parts of a 'proper' home.*

Plate 1. *Standardized houses built for lock-keepers on the Brittany canal are personalized with lovingly tended gardens.*

Plate 3. *The symbol-limit. To many of a more Puritanical temper this suite of Italian dining room furniture would seem 'over the top'—but it nevertheless sells in significant numbers.*

Plate 4. *This Hollywoodian 'camp' fantasy is realized in the hilltop swimming pool at Hearst Castle, San Simeon, California USA. Real and imitation classical elements combine in a stage set, calculated to enhance the narcissism of those who once disported here in the 1930s.*

Plate 5. *A photomural of the Pacific seashore on the end wall of the bedroom purports to give the illusion of a window looking out on a real scene. Used here in combination with real (and incongruous) props such as skis and cuddly toys. Bedroom in Dayton, Ohio, USA.*

Plate 6. *The visible expression of technology in architecture. Lloyds Building, London by Richard Rogers displays its servicing equipment and its supporting structure on the outside.*

Plate 7. *Invisible technology in architecture. A sleek all-over surface conceals all. Kenzo Tange's office tower in Chicago uses technology to conceal technology—at the cost of a lack of a personal identity.*

Plate 8. *Brunelleschi was the key figure in the rediscovery of the language of Classical architecture in the early Renaissance. Simple rhythms, symmetry and the absence of decoration distinguish the portico of the Pazzi Chapel, Sta. Croce, Florence.*

Plate 9. '*The ingenuity of contrivance'—the visible expression of the construction itself, then becomes the carrier of meaning. Brunelleschi's interior of the Pazzi Chapel as a metaphor of value.*

Plate 10. *Even the humble copy-artist aspires to recognition as a proper professional. Sunday morning pitch on the railings at Hyde Park, London.*

Plate 11. *Legitimate Taste. Even at its lightest,* le goût *is concerned with formal values. Fragonard's* The Swing, *Wallace Collection, London.*

Plate 12. *Barbarous Taste. In contrast,* le goût barbare *is only concerned with superficial appearances. The doll who rides the swing oscillates eternally over the staircase of the Madonna Inn, San Luis Obispo, California, USA.*

Plate 13. *The domestic kitchen as a 'tool for cooking'. This kitchen design for her own flat by architect Eva Jiricna, uses open industrial* storage racking and bins, and contract rubber flooring to produce an image of food preparation as efficient work.

Plate 14. *In contrast, commercial kitchens hide the storage and technical equipment behind ornamented cabinet fronts and bland 'work-surfaces' which disguise the cooking apparatus of oven and hob.*

Plates 15. *Nordic restraint in the studio and home of designer Antti Nurmesniemi, Helsinki, Finland.*

Plate 16. *'Peaky' distribution in an interior. Geometric and figurative paintings and sculpture, together with pieces of furniture of both* *formal and informal designs from all periods are combined in an easy variety. Living room from the house of a collector, London.*

Plate 17. *Anti-design? A stylistic frisson comes from the deliberate use of aggressive forms and alien materials in what might be expected to be a 'soft' context such as the bedroom. Wardrobe in flame-cut steel by Ron Arad, of One-Off, London.*

Plate 18. *Pseudo-rustic batch-produced furniture echoes the hand-crafted styles of earlier folk decoration. German 1970s.*

Plate 19. *Overall incrustation of ornament in a rococo church renders the structure all but invisible. Rottenbuch, medieval interior remodelled by J. Schmuzer, circa 1740.*

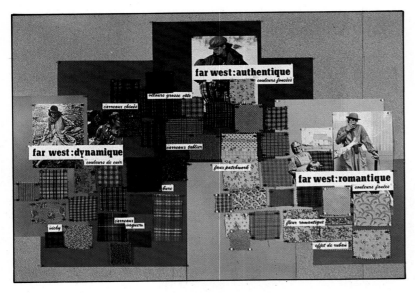

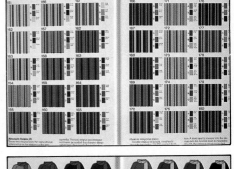

Plate 20. *The International Colour Authority issues annual forecasts of both colour and imagery in the field of dress and interior decoration products. Generic concepts such as 'Far West' suggest broad thematic approaches to form and texture.*

Plate 21. *Colour combination and colour coordination. The surrounding context of other colours makes a great difference to the perceptual appearance of a colour. Textile designers make use of systematic variations to explore the 'look' and 'feel' of colour combinations.*

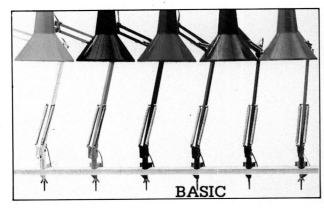

Plate 22. *Stylistic prediction in consumer goods, according to Promostyl in the 1980s.*

Plate 23. *When council estates are privatized, their new owners often seek to personalize them with decorative detailing outside, symbols which allude to the individuality and luxury within. The culture soon spreads to those who remain council tenants. Harold Hill Estate, Romford, England.*

Unfolding of the Water

Watery Radiance

Plate 24. *Russia has long been a major supplier of down-market imitations of traditional forms of interior decoration. Display of Russian goods at a trade fair in Lahti, Finland.*

Plate 25. *Semantic translation from poetry into abstract colour compositions. Sequences of related images from a poem are rendered into a simple composition selected from predetermined colour scales. Colour compositions from Wallace Stevens'* Sea Surface Full of Clouds *by Vicki Powell, Kingston Polytechnic.*

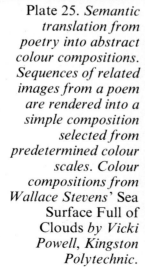

Water Glooms

Summer Hued the Deck

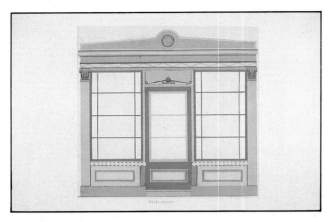

Perfumerie

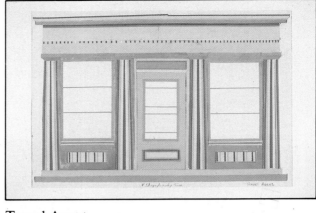

Travel Agent

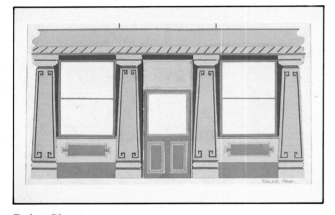

Paint Shop

Ski Shop

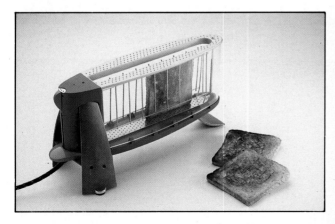

middle class pattern—at least as far as economic rewards are concerned. At the outset, few aspirants to a career in, for example, interior design or the museum service or fashion marketing, will have much concrete idea about the details of how this will unfold but they all take for granted a rising resource trajectory of economic reward and, in consequence, prestige. Although they have been little studied and are rarely discussed in public, the reward systems of the curator-professionals exert a powerful influence on their ideology and hence on their view of what is Taste.[32]

Each dimension of social inequality—economic reward, status and power—is given a different priority among the curator-professions at large from that which commonly motivates the rest of society. In particular, the effects of status and power are usually considered as major factors in determining how a particular career in one of the curator-professions will be regarded. A legendary indifference to mere money is the hallmark of the true curator (of whom the creators are an influential subclass). Power, in this present instance, resides not so much in the ability to exert coercion on others as to resist it on oneself. Autonomy, the ability of the freelance to do 'his own thing', is often the most highly prized reward of all and much economic reward will be sacrificed to obtain it. Status, the ability to attract social honour or deference is, in the curator-professions, highly correlated with power in this sense of creative autonomy. The particular trade off between these three variables will naturally depend on the particular organization in which the curator works.

For the most part, the non-commercial or disinterested parts of the curator-professions are organized along civil service lines. Museum curators, teachers of industrial art or the administrators of a cultural foundation or a national design council can rely on a progressive career structure based on incremental increases in salary for years of service. This is usually overlaid on a recognized promotion ladder to higher grades in the particular service. At the higher levels there is also the graduated apparatus of prestige (offices, official cars) and the conventional symbols of deference such as carpets or private toilets. Naturally, power in the sense of autonomy is relatively curtailed within a bureaucracy. But by the same token, power in the sense of coercion over others is relatively enhanced. The ability to exert authority over those lower down the hierarchy gives satisfaction to many who have long since abrogated their own creative autonomy. And there are salaried creators in the various bureaucracies as well as administrators. For example, official architects and designers (who have their own professional bodies) have the same prospects and career structure as others in the state service although they rarely reach the very highest offices, which are reserved for an academically educated governing élite.[33] Those initially attracted to these branches of the curator-professions by such privileges as comparative security of tenure compared with their freelance colleagues will naturally be selected for advancement by virtue of qualities favoured in any bureaucratic system: patience, loyalty to existing values and diplomatic tact rather than flair, willingness to take risks and aggressive individualism. Such factors are powerfully influential in determining the character and quality of official Taste—whether in patronage or creation—which is rarely noted for its sparkle. They also influence the nature of the relationship between the officials of the various establishments and the remainder of the curator-professionals who offer their services in the marketplace.

Many different systems exist for the remuneration of those who provide services concerned with the exercise of Taste in the artefactual world. These range from salaried positions in large private practices—organizations which can sometimes rival in scale and complexity a small governmental bureaucracy—through various forms of partnership and association in which participants receive profits from a creative business, to the single freelance operating on his own and receiving what income he can command by virtue of his reputation. Prospects for economic reward depend crucially upon whether or not an individual receives a share of the profits of a business. For example, although a designer may accrue quite substantial increases in salary as he rises to a senior position in a large practice, it is only when an individual becomes a partner or shareholder in a successful creative business that his resource trajectory begins to rise steeply.

Creative businesses (and to a large extent curator businesses such as advertising and marketing) are risk businesses—especially those that depend on flair or an eye for future trends and the caprice of fashion. There is, therefore, a trade off between the security of the salaried officials who exist on an annual income, however modest, and the total uncertainty of the freelance, whether operating alone or in partnership. Creative businesses have to survive in a particularly uncertain world. This overriding objective influences the structure of their organizations and through these, the values of those who work in them.

This is especially true when creative businesses reach a larger size and have to support, out of their creative income, non-creative but essential employees such as secretaries and librarians and also feel compelled to maintain expensive premises and equipment. Ostensibly the business is based purely on creative innovation yet, paradoxically, it is beset by exactly the same anti-creative pressures as any other business. There is a market for the services of creator professionals and any business is perceived to be positioned at a particular point within it. Those who founded the practice will have done so by laboriously building a particular image for the firm and the kind of work that it does. If existing clients are not to be lost, this can only slowly be shifted. While the founders remain in charge this need not be a problem. When the business gets large however, employees, who have all been trained to be individually creative and to prize the values of autonomy, have to submerge their creativity in that of the office which, by this time, may have become thoroughly routinized. Measures such as crediting the individuals who actually did the creative work on a new building or product attributed to the organization do little to assuage the alienation and boredom of those who work in a plan factory. Frustrated assistants have the option of leaving to set up their own businesses (and thus repeating the cycle) or else adapt and survive by deriving satisfaction from the office organization and its smooth running. Operating a large creative machine, for which true creativity is reserved for a few individuals, may become the sole reward for the true pro! Ironically, this is the fate that befalls most principals. Few have time to do much creative work themselves so demanding does the organization become. They

4.8 *Easily recognized variations on some generic idea are the staple of advertising campaigns. While they undoubtedly enhance public awareness they are also profitable for design businesses to produce. Examples from a campaign for Silk Cut cigarettes showed how the repetition of not-quite-recognizable pixilated images reinforces the message of the advertiser.*

may 'knock off' a sketch or concept drawing but their true function is to bring in new clients without which the business would fail. Many envy their assistants! All these problems are exacerbated now that Taste is 'big' business, with companies beholden to the shareholders and a stock market demanding, not just survival, but constant and increasing growth.[34]

Such mundane imperatives are rarely disclosed to the outside world, eager to believe in the bubbling mysteries of creation behind the closed doors of the drawing-office or studio. Yet they have a profound influence on the values of those who create the artefactual world. For example, because of the omnipresent pressures on cash flow, there is a built-in drive to go for large buildings or long production runs. Few can make a living out of small-scale interior design projects for instance. Within the realm of large-scale jobs, there is an equally strong drive towards repetition or near-repetition. An initial investment of design time and effort can be paid for over a long production run of identical modules. It used to be said that high-rise buildings were desirable because their stacking of identical floor plans generated considerable profits for their designers once one plan was agreed, fees being nevertheless a function of overall construction costs.

A library of standard office details— routine solutions to common problems within the stereotypical imagery of the practice—is a feature of many large design organizations. These may be much thumbed drawings or, in newer offices, purpose designed software stored on the firm's computer. Doubtless these are useful to ensure coherence and reliability but they can be a daunting experience to the novice aspiring to be creative. In the field of consumer goods, there are similar economic imperatives to go for thematic integration in the form of a programme or collection. Once the client has agreed the theme then the variations follow easily and profitably. Graphic designers and advertising men are always on the lookout for the leading idea or salient image that can be used to generate many easily recognizable variations. Hence the importance of stereotyped structures (such as joke forms) which can be used again and again while employing ostensibly different material, as seen in innumerable magazine advertising campaigns and television commercials.[35] In the world of apparel, the dramatization of annual themes plays much the same role for the professional fashion designer. Once a leading idea is accepted, it assures cash flow into the office. These economic determinants of Taste operate at the production end of the consumption cycle, influencing what gets offered to the entrepreneur and, through him, to the marketplace. There are parallel economic factors operating at the distribution end of the cycle, where consumer demand is expressed as but one important input to retail institutions, institutions that also have to operate in a structured way. We will turn to these institutions of Taste in the world of fashion later.

For most individual creator professionals however, economic rewards are not the most powerful incentive—provided that a satisfactory minimum standard of living can be assumed. For them, status or prestige is the most important consideration.[36] This may be defined as recognition of, and deference towards, their achievements by other professionals. The power of being recognized as truly creative is so great an incentive that even the curators, who are strictly speaking custodians of existing cultural values, strive to demonstrate their own creativity. Art historians who function as media critics or museum directors constantly engage in the attempted fabrication of history through imaginative thematic exhibitions, critiques and 're-hangs'.

Prestige among professional groups may be acquired in a number of ways.[37] The primary and traditional route to prestige is to seek prestigious clients. Studies of traditional professions have clearly demonstrated the importance that the prestige of the patron or client has for the career of the aspiring professional. To be surgeon or lawyer to the king attracts greater prestige than the same office performed for the mere duke or lesser noble. Similarly, to be a painter to the Pope himself is better than to be painter to a cardinal or lesser prelate. In our times, a designer who works for IBM or Exxon or a major bank is accorded more deference by his peers than one who works for the local hairdresser or shoe shop. For contemporary Taste professionals, the prestige of clients lies only partly in size and wealth. IBM is wealthier than the corner shop and because there is more money to spend there is more chance that the designer can produce a memorable result. However, there are many companies that are large and wealthy but do not have a high status as perceived by the Taste professions. The prestige of clients derives in part also from their occupational status, all callings being part of traditional and universally understood prestige rankings. Educational foundations and banks are invariably perceived as more prestigious than betting shops, abbatoirs or waste disposal organizations, no matter how wealthy the latter may be. It follows that to design a building or some equipment for the former gives a higher prestige than does the latter.

These status rankings of clients' occupations derive in part from attitudes to technology. Some technologies are cleaner or more spectacular than others. Computers or space travel are therefore areas for which it is better to design than car-breaking or industrial bakery. Among designers at the present time, capital goods appear to be more prestigious than consumer goods. To design a tiny part of a new high speed train is more prestigious than to design a whole saucepan. This is partly because, in the former case, the designer is dealing with other professionals who act as specifiers and serve as a cushion between the creator and the unenlightened marketing man or shopkeeper. Blue-chip clients for a professional design practice would ideally combine size and wealth with technological respectability. Equally important though is the need for the clients themselves to serve high status end users. This is the difference between, for example, IBM or Herman Miller in the USA and a downmarket or dime store such as Woolworth's. In any sector of marketed goods, there are areas which are more exclusive than others. So, to design furniture for Cassina in Milan is more prestigious than for instance, MFI or Courts in the United Kingdom.

In this instance, the status of the client is only partly a matter of money—although there is obviously little scope for the exercise of Taste when everything has to be designed down to a price. The status of the final customer is also important. It is desirable to have one's work seen in the best surroundings by persons with high social status as this in itself confers status on the designer. Most designers flee from the heterogeneity of downmarket Taste publics and consumers—and the consequent capri-

ciousness and cynicism of those that serve them in the retail trade.

An interesting connection between status and economic reward was explored most characteristically by Thorstein Veblen. According to Veblen, the most important matter in the determination of a person's status is his or her ability to waste economic resources. Waste, the difference between mere subsistence and decently honorific display, is universally admired. Indeed, on this view, the whole panoply of otherwise pointless exaggeration seen in goods and social practices can be explained in no other way. Veblen's own presentation of his case is difficult to evaluate as it is written in a style of relentless irony.[38] It seems nevertheless to contain a wide measure of truth (and in fact, his ideas can be expressed in more neutral and general sociological language). From the viewpoint of the creator professional the Veblenesque perspective is important as the embodiment of waste in ostensibly useful artefacts is precisely the task for which his talents are called. Within some otherwise useful artefact—be it a large building or a tiny object—it is our recognition of the ability of the client to afford, and the ability of the creator to exercise the display of, waste that gives it status in our eyes. Display of waste often involves the incorporation of purely symbolic elements extraneous to the function of the artefact concerned. Equally often though it involves the incorporation of surplus usefulness—the over-lavish provision of space or height in a building or the technologically difficult (and hence expensive) use of minimal or 'pure' forms or, in the case of goods, the provision of exotic functions that will be seldom if ever used. Oscar Wilde's epigram, 'all art is useless', can be given a further twist if we say that, 'only art is useless'. Art is therefore the embodiment of waste in its purest form. In the ultimate, Taste is waste and hence, *pace* Veblen, attracts the highest prestige! This prompts the drive of all creative designers towards the practice of pure or fine art. Design education in particular has an abiding tendency to drift towards art, much to the chagrin of business and government interested in the quickest return on outlay.[39]

Therefore, the most subtle (and seductive) ingredient in the prestige accorded to a creator professional comes from the scope that his clients allow him to behave as an artist and to express his personality through the medium of the client's business and its customers. At this point, power—in the sense of personal autonomy in symbolism, and the ability to impose this on a wide public—interacts with prestige or social honour. As in other fields of coercion, high status accords to he who can exert the widest influence. For designers, such autonomy is easiest to achieve in fields such as fashion where images date quickly and the technological investment needed to launch a new model is low. Aggressive publicity, involving the identification of a named designer by labelling each item, can be an important selling factor. Once a creator can achieve this, then his ability to exert further pressure on the producers to follow a creation-push rather than a demand-pull policy is enhanced. At the other end of the scale, the prestige of an architect can depend on a tiny but intensely personal *œuvre*. If he is lucky with an early patron and simultaneously with a sympathetic editor, an architect can achieve, through exposure in publications circulating among his peers, a worldwide reputation for creativity on the basis on just one building, a building that the

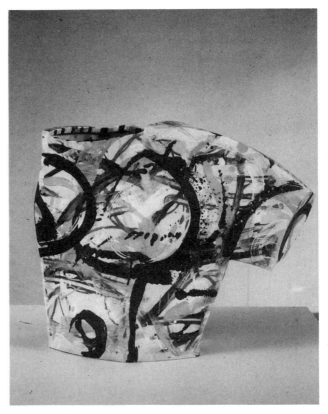

4.9 *In contemporary Western culture, useful objects are rarely given the same high status as 'useless' art objects. In recent years however, several ceramicists have successfully crossed the dividing line between 'pottery' and sculpture. Their work attracts the kind of pecuniary value hitherto reserved for the fine arts. Alison Britton's sculptural ceramics transcend genuine utility while continuing to echo the forms of the vessel.* Brown torso pot *by Alison Britton, 1986.*

rest of the world has never seen! (His actual livelihood must necessarily come from elsewhere, often from university teaching or private means.)

Given these paradoxes and the accidents of fortune in obtaining contacts with clients of different degrees of wealth and social standing, it is not surprising that there is no obvious correlation between economic reward and prestige among creator professionals. Principals of large practices may be both eminent and rich. On the other hand many of the most prestigious practices are small and their proprietors, however well-regarded by their peers, exist on income supported from sources outside of the practice of their profession.[40]

Similarly, the aspiring creator professional may well discover that some of the most prestigious practices pay the lowest wages to their assistants since their status ensures that there will always be a large number willing to work for whatever is offered. Those so exploited nevertheless feel that it is worth enduring low pay for a while, both for the experience—some of the charisma may rub-off—and in the belief that, once they are able to say that they have worked for a famous practice it will enhance their credibility. Indeed, the newcomer to the profession may find out the hard way that some of the most prestigious offices are somewhat unbusinesslike affairs which, while they may be lit by the glow of global publicity are economically very precarious. To work for one of these may excite the envy of other aspirants but it is unlikely to bring in big or steady money.

At the extreme, the prestige of certain curator-professionals may become so great that they are able to usurp some of the status that properly attaches to members of a higher social class. This is particularly true of the highest reaches of the creator professions. The disdain of an artist such as Michelangelo for his Papal patron was legendary and it heralded a tradition of strained social relationships in which, to use Goffman's words, 'it becomes possible for the improper expectations of the curator to be realized and for the status and security of the patron class itself to be correspondingly diminished'.[41]

Goffman's observation was made long before it became commonplace for royalty to hobnob with fashion models, interior decorators and society photographers. Today, even the directors of museums can usurp something of the status of the patron class in those sections of American society in which the ability to donate astronomical sums is the ultimate social cachet. Merely by inviting such donations—and thereby assuring only the most exclusive company at the associated social gatherings—the museum director can control membership to this most exclusive of clubs. Aspirants to the curator-professions soon discover these facts of life, not least through the publicity which surrounds the parties, museums and galleries at which the representatives of the higher social classes may be met.

Power, the last of the external reward systems is, in its positive aspect at any rate, the least important, especially in the creative branch of the curator-professions. Once power in its negative sense of freedom from coercion is assured, most curator-professionals are comparatively indifferent to the satisfactions of its exercise on others. Until recent times creative businesses were usually quite small. In most cases the original founders are usually still active as principals or partners and are active (if not always full-time) in their creative role as designers.

With the present dramatic increase in the size of creative businesses there is a need for a much more formal management structure with a group of personnel dedicated to the function of management control. Once a creative business grows into a publicly quoted company then its share value becomes very sensitive to the perceptions of the stock market of the quality of its executive control. Some curators are tempted by the rewards that flow from the exercise of authority. Particularly in large industrial corporations, the executive role may be highly prized as a means of escape from the frustrations of trying to be creative in an essentially conservative business bureaucracy. Most of their colleagues, while nevertheless maintaining a healthy respect for the powers of patronage they carry, do not regard such offices as particularly prestigious. Much the same is true of advancement in the creative bureaucracy itself. Those who emerge as officers of their creative institutions are rarely those who are regarded as the most creative or talented. Most young creator professionals would rather end up with a medal for creative merit from their professional institution than become its president or secretary.

When they start out on their careers, few curator-professionals have any clear idea of the complex and shifting trade-offs between money, status and power which motivate the established institutions and the individuals within them. These matters quickly become clear during the educational stage when novices compare their lot with that of the other professionals they meet. Even before graduation, the first harsh choices have to be made, choices which will influence their whole future career trajectory and which may effectively pre-empt all other choices. A stint at a high salary with a company car in a large commercial organization is rarely followed by a period of freelance work in which radically innovative but uncommercial ideas are exposed in élite and prestigious 'little magazines'. It is much more likely that the contents of such publications will come from thinkers who have always remained on the margins of true professional life unable to adapt to the harsh economic realities of commerce. We should remember though that the internal reward system of the lonely but satisfied artist warmed by the regard of a few discerning colleagues is not to be underrated. There is a virtual life career in belonging to a secret freemasonry of lofty souls—the truly creative—which can go on even after death as demonstrated by the continuous rediscovery of 'new' artists and designers from the past.

The age of innocence for the novice is soon over, however. The facts of life in any of the creator or curator-professions are soon assimilated by a few lessons in the hard school of commercial cost-cutting or bureaucratic infighting. In consequence, the myriad posts in companies and offices, agencies and practices are readily ranked into hierarchies of desirability as perceived by the juniors of the profession concerned. These rankings in turn influence the type and calibre of applicant for positions within the profession. Widely discussed in private, they rarely figure in any official account of the workings of the Taste professions. Yet, insofar as they determine the character of the debates which set the agenda for the practical realization of matters of Taste in the real world of commerce, they are absolutely crucial.

Out of this uneasy amalgam of high ideals, lofty theories and secular reward systems of an unashamedly mundane character comes what we may call the ideology of Taste at any particular time. Of course, these discordant and often paradoxical accommodations between aspiration and fact are not peculiar to the curator-professions. In more muffled and muted ways they operate in all social organizations however small or primitive. The competitive struggle for recognition within the rules of one of the curator-professions undoubtedly focusses the issues and exacerbates the dilemmas. It is an irony as well as a commonplace that often the last place that one of Duveen's 'rightly constituted minds' is likely to be found is in one of the professions devoted to matters of Taste!

When we come to look at the structure of Taste in modern society we shall see that these ideological factors combine to isolate the Tastes of the curator-professions from the Tastes of the multitude—at both the highest and at the lowest social level. Artists have long been used to this situation. Designers, the new *Wunderkinder* of modern consumer societies who have so recently graduated from the status of commercial artists, still find it puzzling. They must necessarily present themselves as servants of public Taste. On any given assignment they must espouse another's ideology and attempt to identify with a different Taste— that of the client and his customers—even when they find it alien to their own. Yet here is the paradox. It is only as individuals that they can create but only as professionals that they can succeed. No wonder that there is a high level of anxiety among professional designers.

Notes and References to Chapter 4

1 E. Goffman, "Symbols of Class Status", *British Journal of Sociology*, 12, 1951, p. 294.
2 This tradition of art history emphasizes the fact that many artists subsequently recognized as great were rejected by the art 'establishment' of their day. According to this reading, the rejection of Courbet at the 1855 Great Exhibition, the famous 'Salon des Refusées', the 'scandal' of Impressionism, the fact that Gauguin and Van Gogh became lonely outcasts and died in poverty, was evidence enough of a virtual conspiracy against genuine originality. The logic of this position is that, for artistic creativity to function at all, artists must be in conflict with society. See W. Hoffman, *Art in the Nineteenth Century*, trans. B. Battershaw, London: Faber and Faber, 1960, for a reading of nineteenth century art history in terms of the social alienation of the artist, with the alienated artist as 'Great Hero'—Don Quixote, Wandering Jew, even the Messiah himself—becoming the subject matter of painting and sculpture.
3 W. Gaunt, *The Esthetic Adventure*, London: Jonathan Cape, 1975, gives a survey of Bohemian tendencies in nineteenth century art and life.
4 On the workings of Mr Ewart's Select Committee see Q. Bell, *The Schools of Design*, London: Routledge and Kegan Paul, 1973, p. 51 *et seq.* and S. Macdonald, *The History and Philosophy of Art Education*, London: University of London Press, 1970, p. 60.
5 A. Wittlin, *Museums in Search of a Usable Future*, Cambridge, Mass: MIT Press, 1970 p. 75 *et seq.*
6 For discussions of public policy towards the funding of the arts in the United Kingdom, see J. Minihan, *The Nationalisation of Culture— the development of state subsidies for the arts in Great Britain*, London: Hamish Hamilton, 1977. For the United States, see D. Netzer, *The Subsidised Muse—public support for the arts in the United States*, Cambridge: Cambridge University Press, 1978.
7 N. Mitford (Ed.), *Noblesse Oblige*, London: Hamish Hamilton, 1956.
8 Peter Murray has documented some of the recent stages in the rise of art history as a cultural industry in which graduates look forward to employment in one or other of the cultural bureaucracies. P. Murray, "Whither Art History." *Bulletin of the Association of Art Historians*, Number 9, October 1979.
9 L. A. Coser, *Men of Ideas—a sociological analysis*, New York: Free Press, 1965.
10 In the United Kingdom, these institutions as public bodies publish annual reports which give breakdowns of their budgets. Staffing costs are usually the largest item. This is probably true elsewhere.
11 The career of the Paris picture dealer, Durand-Ruel, is noteworthy. His story is interwoven

with that of the Impressionists and post-Impressionists. See J. Rewald, *The History of Impressionism*, New York: Museum of Modern Art, 1973 and J. Rewald, *Post-Impressionism—from Van Gogh to Gauguin*, London: Secker and Warburg, 1987.

12 See J. Rewald, *op. cit.*, for the rise and fall of artistic groups in Paris during the final decades of the nineteenth century.

13 Josiah Wedgwood's patronage of artists like Blake and Flaxman was notable. See W. Mankowitz, *Wedgwood*, London: Spring Books, 1966 for a catalogue of the various stages of the development of Wedgwood's wares. See E. Meteyard, *The Life of Josiah Wedgwood*, (1866). Facsimile reprint by London: Cornmarket Press, 1970, for details of Wedgwood's relationships with his artist collaborators.

14 On the status of artists in the Renaissance see M. Baxandall, *Painting and Experience in 15th Century Italy*, Oxford: Oxford University Press, 1976. On artists contracts during the Renaissance see D. Chambers, *Patrons and Artists in the Italian Renaissance*, London: Macmillan, 1970. The financial position of artists is discussed in R. and M. Wittkower, *Born under Saturn*, New York: Random House, p. 253 *et seq.* "Between Famine and Fame."

15 J. M. Whistler, *The Gentle Art of Making Enemies*, London: Heinemann, 1890, reprinted New York: Dover, 1967.

16 See M. Sarfatti Larson, *The Rise of Professionalism—a Sociological Analysis*, Berkeley: University of California Press, 1977.

17 See M. Sarfatti Larson, *op. cit.*, p. 40. In the United Kingdom at the present time, the system of fixed scales of fees is gradually being eroded by anti-monopoly legislation. Architects, for example, may no longer charge 'scale fees'. Nevertheless, the need to regulate income is a constant preoccupation in new, emerging professions. Typical of these is the Design Business Group of the Chartered Society of Designers.

18 For an account of earlier professional struggles see P. Elliot, *The Sociology of the Professions*, London: Macmillan, 1972, p. 14 *et seq.* Rivalry among professional cliques and the accusation of encroachment and charlatanism are not new phenomena, see W. J. Goode, "Encroachment, Charlatanism and the Emerging Professions." *American Sociological Review*, 25, December 1960, p. 903.

19 Nevertheless, the new Charter of the Society of Industrial Artists and Designers was considered an important step along the road. See J. Holland, *Minerva at Fifty—the Jubilee History of the Society of Industrial Artists and Designers*, Westerham, Kent: Hurstwood Press, 1980, p. 35. The subsequent dropping of the reference to industrial artists is a further step down the road to professional respectability.

20 C. Cennini, *The Book of the Artist*, trans. D. Thompson, New York: Dover, 1954, p. 3.

21 J.-P. Richter, *The Literary Works of Leonardo da Vinci*, Oxford: Phaidon, 1969, Volume 1, pp. 52-68. The argument is an attempt to justify painting over sculpture because it is nearer to literature which was already accepted socially as a respected liberal art and therefore a proper activity for a gentleman.

22 For an account of the early history of academies see N. Pevsner, *Academies of Art*, 2nd edition, New York: Da Capo Press, 1973.

23 Q. Bell, *The Schools of Design*, London: Routledge and Kegan Paul, 1963, p. 253 *et seq.*

24 For a pessimistic view of the legacy of this tradition see M. J. Wiener, *English Culture and the Decline of the Industrial Spirit 1890–1980*, Cambridge: Cambridge University Press, 1981.

25 For an account of the foundation of the SIAD (now the CSD) and its subsequent history see J. Holland, *op. cit.*

26 The debates which led to the setting up of the design business interest as a separate section of the CSD are described in *Design Week*, 26th September 1986.

27 See P. Vergo (Ed.), *The New Museology*, London: Reaktion Books, 1989.

28 See P. Elliot, *op. cit.*, p. 113, on the manner in which new professions such as life insurance salesmen emulate the structures and practices of the older more mature professions.

29 At the present time, architects and surveyors are able to enforce this system in the United Kingdom. Designers with graduate status are able to join as 'diploma members' without further formal examination. Full membership depends on the production of evidence of professional achievement in the form of completed works in the field.

30 An account of the reforms which were set in train by Sir William Coldstream's committee is given in D. Warren Piper (Ed.), *Readings in Art Education—After Coldstream*, London: Davis Poynter, 1973.

31 C. Wright Mills, *Power, Politics and People*, Oxford: Oxford University Press, 1963, p. 374.

32 The nearest to a systematic account of rewards in one of the curator-professions in the United Kingdom was undertaken in the field of the crafts. A. Bruce and P. Filmer, *Working in Crafts—an independent socio-economic study of craftsmen and women in England and Wales*, London: Crafts Council, 1983.

33 In the United Kingdom at the present time, the positions of 'official' architects and designers has been markedly worsened as the result of the desire by the Conservative government to 'privatise' or put out to tender as many services as possible—including specialist creative services. Private design practices and consultancies have correspondingly benefited from this policy.

34 In 1988 there were over a dozen large design firms in the United Kingdom which were registered companies on the London securities market. *Design Week* publishes weekly stock market ratings and the total market capitalization exceeds £500,000,000.

35 Visual puns like those used in cigarette advertising by Benson and Hedges or beer advertisements for Fosters Lager are good examples of the near repetition of standard joke forms. For a structuralist reading of the 'hidden' import of stereotyped forms in advertising design see J. Williamson, *Decoding Advertisements*, London: Marion Boyars, 1978, Chapter 3 and especially p. 85 *et seq*.

36 A. Bruce and P. Filmer, *op. cit.*, is a pioneering sociological study of the way that different perceived reward systems operate in the field of the crafts. No similar study exists for the professional designer but many useful parallels can be drawn.

37 See E. Goffman, *British Journal of Sociology*, 12, 1951, p. 294.

38 T. Veblen, *The Theory of the Leisure Class*, C. Wright Mills (Ed.), New York: New American Library, 1963.

39 In the United Kingdom this tendency has resulted in the discrimination between art and design departments throughout higher education to the detriment of the fine arts, where reduced funding is the norm. Compared to practice in many countries of continental Europe however, the United Kingdom is still relatively well-endowed with educational resources for fine art. It should be noted that the pre-war German Bauhaus, which is still the model for most contemporary design training, while it was staffed by many eminent artists, did not in fact teach fine art as such. See H. M. Wingler (Ed.), *The Bauhaus*, Cambridge, Mass: MIT Press, 1969, for full documentation of Bauhaus teaching and practice.

40 *Design Week* has conducted surveys of 'top' design practices by peers. See *Design Week*, 25th March 1988.

41 E. Goffman, *op. cit.* For Michelangelo's relationships with Julius II see G. Vasari, *The Lives of the Most Excellent Painters, Sculptors, Architects*, London: Dent (Everyman), 1963, Volume 4, p. 121 *et seq*. Michelangelo's temperamental conduct in walking-out on Pope Julius because he was kept waiting for an appointment is often cited as one of the key incidents in the transformation of the artist from humble servant to haughty master.

5. Them and Us

5.1 *High art is legitimate art as seen in museums or in important public places. The standing male figure typifies what people expect to see in museums worldwide. Connoisseurs will note the formal nuances, the subtlety of the modelling and the balance between gravity and liveliness in the oft repeated pose.*

Lansdowne Hermes (unknown Roman copy of a fourth century BC Greek original). Collection of the Santa Barbara Museum of Art. Gift of Wright S. Ludington.

Taste cultures and Taste publics

Philosophical discussion concerning matters of Taste, not only in the sense of discrimination in the various fields of the arts, but in the wider sense of the proper conduct and manner of life, goes back into classical antiquity. Aesthetics, as a formal philosophical discipline, predates the Industrial Revolution. Yet it is only with the Industrial Revolution that we recognize characteristically modern debates about what constitutes good Taste in a consumer society. They coincide with the curator-professions—the burgeoning ranks of salaried Taste bureaucrats in the museum services and educators concerned with raising the quality of industrial artefacts together with the perceptions of those who were to consume them. Also during this period—roughly the last hundred and fifty years—sociology as a discipline has been striving to establish an objective and scientific account of modern society in all its aspects—including consumption.

When sociologists address themselves to patterns of cultural preferences—to matters of Taste—they are faced with a fundamental tension between what is supposedly observed fact and what are personal, yet apparently transcendental, values. In most sociological writings on Taste, there is an uneasy relationship between descriptions of Taste—neutral accounts of observed social patterns of preference and judgment usually measured statistically—and normative prescriptions inherent in the concept of Taste as it is used elsewhere. Ostensibly, the sociologists' account of Taste is value-free or non-partisan, neither endorsing nor contesting a particular pattern of preferences. Such an account implies a concept of Taste that is purely relative. A particular Taste is merely the particular symbolic currency that happens to be valid among members of a particular social group at a particular time. In this context, good Taste is a meaningless concept. Many would go further and say that in a democratic, supposedly pluralist, society, it is not only meaningless but repugnant and insulting as well.

As it exists in ordinary language (leaving out the elaborations and refinements of aesthetics and etiquette), the concept of Taste is intractably linked with the notion of discrimination, not only in the sense of perceiving and marking differences, but also in the sense of selective preferment, a judgment involving acceptance or rejection. Both acts entail some kind of scale along which they can be made, therefore, in this context, Taste is not relative but absolute. Moreover, in the sequence, 'good-better-best', our language itself presents us with a scale of increasing exclusiveness. There may be many 'good' but fewer 'better'. There is only one 'best'. So persuasive is this structural feature of our language that it is remarkably difficult to find genuinely neutral labels to describe the preferences of particular social groups.

Most existing categorizations of Taste imply a hierarchy and tacitly endorse the preferences of those at one end or the other—mandarin or populist. Many sociologists writing about contemporary cultural values incline towards the populist end of the scale.[1] An interest in, and identification with, popular culture (for example, football or jazz) may indeed be a useful corrective to an exclusive preoccupation with high culture. Certainly, many arguments from the mandarin end of the scale about the allegedly dangerous corruptions threatened by popular culture have a quaint, even offensive, ring. Moreover, they are usually confined to issues concerning the mass media and rarely consider the field of consumer goods. Much sociological material concerned with the physical artefacts of consumer society is either vacuous or evasive, concealing partiality with irony.

The first great modern writer to tackle the problem of cultural values in an industrial society was Matthew Arnold.[2] An aggressively confident member of one of the new curator-professions—journalistic social criticism—he was certainly not evasive about his values! In *Culture and Anarchy*, written as early as 1869, Arnold clearly sets his own aesthetic and intellectual values ('sweetness and light' or 'culture') against what he saw as the crass in all the social classes in the England of his day.

Arnold felt that the aristocrats of the time lacked that dedicated and systematic aversion to true culture that would qualify them as genuine 'Philistines'. Although they still showed some signs of sweetness, at least in their good manners, they rarely followed the light due, Arnold declared, to feebleness of spirit. They had been 'lured off from following the light by those mighty and eternal seducers of our race which means for this class their most irresistible charms—by worldly splendour, security, power and pleasure'.[3] Their disinterest in the light was not so much 'perverse as ... too natural'. They were therefore to be called 'Barbarians'. Manufacturing and all it stands for ('mere machinery') was naturally numbered among the Philistines but Arnold also included that part of the working class concerned with financial betterment through trade unions and other means—especially those aiming at supplanting the middle and aristocratic classes in power. Finally, there

was 'that vast portion lastly of the working class which is raw and half-developed, has long lain half-hidden among its poverty and squalor, and is now issuing from its hiding-place to assert an Englishman's heaven-born privilege of doing what he likes'. These Arnold called the 'Populace'.

Thus the behaviour of all classes was denounced equally and, moreover, denounced in the name of an intellectual and cultural élite. To Arnold, a passion for 'sweetness and light' was innate, to be found like genius, but rarely and in all classes. 'Natures with this bent will emerge in all classes ... and this bent always tends to take them out of their class and to make their distinguishing characteristic not their Barbarianism or their Philistinism but their humanity.'[4]

Arnold, like Thorstein Veblen, wrote in a highly rhetorical style, shot-through with sustained sarcasm. He was certainly more interested in vehement denunciation than careful definition. In selecting his targets, he chose the old divisions of social class as categories for the anti-culturists. In so doing he conflated two separate issues—the demarcation of socioeconomic groups (class) and the delineation of patterns of normative and symbolic association (culture). If we identify the salient characteristics of Arnold's categories of anti-culturalists: self-indulgent frivolity and vapidity (for the Barbarians), cheerfully ignorant and abrasively assertive insensitivity (for the Philistines), and a crude, mindless and brutal hedonism—'the trampling of the swinish multitude'—(for the Populace), we can see that, in principle, these characteristic patterns of behaviour could be displayed by individuals from any social class. No doubt, given the importance of education, home background and

5.2 Middlebrow art is often a 'watered down' version of high art, especially of its more engaging bourgeois varieties—canvases by Renoir or Bonnard of happy outdoor compositions with people enjoying themselves in homely ways are always popular. Blunting the formal rigour of the high art from which it is derived draws particular scorn from highbrows.

wealth in the determination of value systems, together with the differential availability of these resources between the various socioeconomic groups, Arnold could be confident of a good deal of overlapping between class and culture. Nevertheless, class and culture are in principle different concepts. It is important therefore to base discussion of their interdependence upon genuinely independent definitions. (This was precisely the circularity in the distinction between 'U' and 'Non-U' behaviour which enjoyed a vogue in the 1960s.[5]) With this proviso we can identify four main subcultures in Arnold's pungent classification—the Enlightened, plus the Barbarians, the Philistines and the Populace. Arnold

further refined this system by subdividing each anti-culture group into a strong and weak version—'the sterner self of the Populace likes bawling, hustling and smashing; the lighter self, beer'.

Many less aggressively contentious classifications exist. One which emerged into everyday speech in the first decade of this century is that of 'highbrow', 'middlebrow' and 'lowbrow'.[6] This is a good example of a hierarchic system as 'high' is usually thought to be superior to 'low'. Given its origins in the populism of the United States, highbrow appears ironically as a term of opprobrium. However, from the viewpoint of many highbrows, to be middlebrow is much worse than to

157

be downright lowbrow! Nevertheless, the height of the metaphorical brow does clearly distinguish between patterns of preferences and values, and does not muddle these with class. Highbrows can come from any social class while many among the most affluent and powerful are proud to be lowbrows. However, there is no explicit account of the particular kinds of judgment or behaviour that would characterize a person as a highbrow or a lowbrow. This vagueness is not surprising, for what constitutes a particular brow is ever-changing and dependent on the flow of fashion at each level. In essence, the metaphorical height of the brow is but an ironic and slighting reference to what is taken to be real or legitimate culture—Arnold's 'sweetness and light'—or, at any rate, to its current and local manifestations, especially when these are endorsed in public by those whose right to do so is suspect.

An explicit (but not entirely dissimilar) tripartite classification clarifies this previously oblique relationship.[7] Edward Shils distinguishes three levels of culture 'which are levels of quality measured by aesthetic, intellectual and moral standards'. These are 'superior' or 'refined' culture, 'mediocre' culture and 'brutal' culture.

According to Shils, 'superior or refined culture is distinguished by the seriousness of its subject matter, i.e. with the centrality of the problems with which it deals, the acute penetration and coherence of its perceptions, the subtlety and wealth of its expressed feeling'. Superior culture 'embraces the great works of all the various arts and sciences, philosophy and letters'. Shils underlines the fact that the superiority of such cultural products is in no way connected with social status, either that of

5.3 *Popular Taste is satisfied by different subjects and more sharply contrasted visual stimuli. Amusing situations in which familiar subjects are treated in odd or striking ways are treated in a broad manner which puts little emphasis on formal relationships whether of shape or colour*. Bulldogs playing snooker, *Sunday sale at Hyde Park Railings, London, England.*

the producers or of the consumers, 'but only with their beauty and truth'.

Mediocre culture consists partly of poorer, less original or less demanding exemplars from the genres approved by superior culture, together with items from 'relatively novel genres not yet incorporated into superior culture such as musical comedy'. Brutal culture, while it may include diluted or bowdlerized works from the other, higher genres, also includes 'games, spectacles (such as boxing and horse racing) and more directly expressive action with a minimal symbolic content. The depth of penetration is almost always negligible, subtlety is almost entirely lacking, and a general grossness of sensitivity and perception is a common feature'. Shils simply assumed that there were publicly agreed criteria for such aesthetic and moral judgments and further, that appropriately qualified and discerning experts might be called upon to make them. His position is therefore based firmly on a transcendental view of the nature of aesthetic and moral quality in artefacts and, consequently, on a detached view of the sensitivity of their consumers to them.

158

5.4 Hierarchies of Taste according to Jay Doblin. A two-dimensional matrix plots cost on one axis against 'level of discrimination' on the other. The cells are occupied by categories of Taste. Doblin's categories are characterized by typical instances of goods familiar in the USA. Although we may well agree with him in most cases, Doblin's examples, as indeed the categories themselves, are subjective impositions on the data.

	Low discrimination	Medium discrimination	High discrimination
high price	⊙ rock stars FLASH ⊙ Dallas, Excalibur	⊙ HRH, Rolls Royce RICHTRAD ⊙ Tiffany, Gucci, Rolex	⊙ MOMA PRO ⊙ Hasselblac, Steinway ⊙ Bauhaus
medium price	BADMASS ⊙ Coca-Cola ⊙ Ford Pinto	GOODMASS ⊙ Polaroid ⊙ TV	CLEAN Herman Miler, B&O, Porsche Honda, Apple, Sony Braun
low price	TRASH Enquirer ⊙ ⊙ ghetto	DISPOSABLE Gillette ⊙ Kleenex ⊙	VERNACULAR ⊙ NY Times ⊙ naturals

Firmly in this tradition is the schema of Jay Doblin, doyen of American marketing professionals concerned with design.[8] According to Doblin, all products can be placed within a two-dimensional map with the axes of price and quality. Quality is simply assumed to be an affair of discrimination. 'Discrimination is the ability to distinguish badly designed products from those which are well designed. It is helpful to categorize degrees of discrimination, so the horizontal scale is divided into three segments; low, medium and high discrimination.' Plotted against the price variable this leads to the nine cells shown in the diagram (Figure 5.4). These are clearly value-laden (for the most part pejorative) concepts. Doblins actual values will be accepted by many mandarins (including most designers) but they are clearly personal judgments which are simply assumed to be universally valid. The schema can be put to work in showing the relationship of different current industrial products to each other and, by implication, the relationship of their users to each other. Many, however, will find this type of sweeping asseveration cynical and socially provocative.

We can compare this standpoint with that of Pierre Bourdieu, who also follows a conventional tripartite classification, describing three *universes* of Taste.[9]

legitimate Taste, that is to say, the Taste for legitimate artefacts which are represented ... by the Well-tempered Clavier, the Art of Fugue, the (Ravel) Concerto for the Left Hand, or in painting Breugal or Goya, and with those, the most assured aesthetes can associate the most legitimate among works of art on the road to legitimisation, cinema, jazz or even Chanson (as here Léo Ferré, Jacques Douai).[10]

Second, there is:

middle Taste which combines minor works in major art forms such as ... the Rhapsody in Blue, the Hungarian Rhapsody or again in painting Utrillo, Buffet or even Renoir, and the major works in minor art forms such as in Chanson, Jacques Brell or Gilbert Becaud.[11]

And, finally there is:

popular Taste represented by a choice of 'light' music or by good music devalued by vulgarisation such as the Blue Danube, la Traviata, l'Arlesienne and above all by songs totally stripped of any ambition or artistic pretension such as those of Mariano, Guetary or Petula Clark.[12]

Clearly these systems of cultural classification are very similar to those of Shils. Bourdieu, however, drawing from his extensive researches into the correlations between people's professed allegiance to one or other of these universes of Taste and their socioeconomic status, arrives at a very different conclusion. Bourdieu is concerned to defend the

159

choices of those who prefer middle or popular culture from pejorative and supercilious criticism. As he clearly shows, the choice of a particular universe of Taste is determined by level of education and by other class variables such as wealth and home background. In reality, the choosers have little choice in the matter at all. In addition, the whole notion of a pure, transcendental faculty of Taste is denounced as illegitimate and irrelevant. Bourdieu sees it as a pernicious by-product of illicit categorizations, generalizations and conflations, all of which are, in reality, merely theoretical abstractions deriving from the mindlessly ecumenical attitudes of curator-professionals, especially those in museums.

In grouping together a disparate collection of 'pietas and fetishes, crucifixions and still lifes', a museum deprives each of their individual *raison d'être*, gratuitously substituting an abstract aesthetic categorization that is meaningless, both to their makers and to their original users. Against this culture of what he calls 'pure Taste', he sets 'barbarous Taste' (Plates 11 & 12). *Le goût barbare* manifests precisely that diverse but secure anchorage in the factitiousness of secular life that the museums (and, by extension, all of the curator-professions) deny. He calls this an 'aesthetique anti-Kantienne'. In support of this contemporary defence of secular values, Bourdieu goes back to a controversy in French artistic life of more than a century ago, when Pierre-Joseph Proudhon fought to establish a social (or socialist) realism in art in place of what he saw as the self-absorbed and narcissistic irrelevance of '*l'art pour l'art*' or 'art for art's sake'.[13]

A few years earlier, a similar distinction was made (in somewhat less dramatic terms) by Herbert Gans in his essay contrasting high and

5.5 *Museum art. By removing works from their original cultural settings and thus stripping them of their original cultural identity, the museum fosters a lifeless and often abstruse aestheticism. 'Academic' art is bloodless and toys with ideals instead of communicating meanings that everyone can feel.*

popular culture.[14] In discussing those abstract and formal concerns which are most clearly important in the appreciation of high culture (the kind of structural intricacies which Bourdieu epitomized in the *Art of Fugue* for example), Gans suggested that these concerns were the hallmark of those who shared the orientation or perspective of the makers of cultural artefacts. While it is most obviously important in the appreciation of works of high culture, a disposition to enter into an intense concern for the technical and formal complexities involved in the making of cultural artefacts is rarely absent from the coteries who surround

5.6 *In constrast, realism focusses on the here and now. Unedited or idealized versions of demotic subjects capture the spirit of a person and a place where academic idealizations never can. Pierre Bourdieu cites the views on the need for a realist painting of the philosopher J-P. Proudhon, seen here in the painting by Courbet.*

the makers of any level of cultural product however brutal. While Gans makes much of this distinction between what he calls respectively a creator-orientation and a user-orientation, it is really a matter of degree. At one end of the scale of vicarious involvement in the processes making cultural products are those who are so deeply involved with a subject that they often know more about it than the creators themselves. In this innermost circle of initiates are other creators, sympathetic critics and academic students of a particular artist or genre. Further out from the centre of involvement is another circle of more casual buffs or fans, well informed on technicalities, but more concerned with the analysis of discrimination

itself and the pleasures which particular cultural products afford. These semi-committed legions in turn fade into those—the majority—who consume cultural products entirely for personal pleasure and have little interest in technical or formal matters. Given these facts it is not surprising that:

high culture pays explicit attention to the construction of cultural products, such as the relation between form, substance and method, and overt context and covert symbolism . . . The (high) culture's standards for substance are less variable, they always place high value on the careful communication of mood and feeling, on introspection rather than action and on subtlety so that much of the culture's content can be perceived on several levels. High culture fiction emphasises character development over plot and the exploration of basic philosophical, psychological and social issues with the heroes and heroines of novels and plays often modelled on the creators themselves.[15]

Yet critical expertise is rarely entirely lacking even from the most uncritical consumers. The distinction between creator- and user-orientation has been used to distinguish the mode of use of rock music among various youth subcultures. 'Bike-boys' or 'rockers' are user-orientated and enjoy EP singles played repetitively for dancing. Those who associate more closely with the 'hippy' life style prefer to listen to music which is less dance-orientated and to identify clearly with the artists.[16]

Fiction and the movies provided the characteristic examples which helped Gans demonstrate his creator versus user dichotomy. However, the same point can be made in the area of household consumption goods. Ideological prescriptions in design, such as functionalism, truth to materials and design for need, all represent varying embodiments of the interests of creators. Even when apparently pursuing sensuous enjoyment, contemporary design is apt to consider space and form at a level of abstraction far removed from most consumers' awareness, except perhaps those from the high culture Taste public.

Gans developed his description of culture in the United States by adapting Lloyd Warner's system of socioeconomic groups to label the various Taste publics.[17] He proposed 'high' culture, 'upper middle' culture, 'lower middle' culture, 'low' culture and 'quasi-folk low' culture. While his own cultural allegiances remained undisclosed, Gans was at pains to stress that the scale from high to low had no pejorative implications for those at the low end. This system is, of course, as crude and sketchy as earlier ones. In particular, it fails to include special cultures such as those which derive from ethnic or religious origins. Youth culture also fits badly into this system. (There is considerable controversy over whether youth is, despite all the commercial propaganda, really a culture at all.)

Even assuming that these and other reservations could be alleviated by improvements to the existing schemes for classifying culture, there remains a worrying suggestion of circularity. That whole populations of individuals should apparently divide into three or four social classes is remarkable enough. That the teeming manifold of symbolic creation and consumption should also be capable of classification into a similarly small number of culture groups and, moreover, a classification which is structurally similar (an élite, a would-be élite, and the remainder) seems more than mere coincidence.

It is tempting to read across parallel divisions in the two systems and see not correlation but cause. Given such parallelism, many would see decisive evidence that cultural patterns are determined by social structures. A more disturbing possibility is that one or even both systems are over-schematic, unwarranted impositions on the data. Perhaps they are not real at all, but artefacts of experimental method or even figments of the sociologists' imagination! Systems of socioeconomic stratification have often been researched and there is no doubt that they are real in the sense that they represent operational concepts in daily use by subjects. But what of Taste cultures? Compared with research into stratification from a socioeconomic standpoint, very little effort has been invested in this area.

A basis for classifying patterns of living was provided by the so-called life style research into 'attitudes, interests and opinions' (AIO) developed in the field of marketing. Life style groupings were able to connect, by means of statistics, related sets of allegiances and aversions to ideas, values, symbols and modes of conduct.[18] Such patterns can fairly easily be extracted from the raw data of replies to questionnaires by the mathematical tools of factor analysis. It is difficult to label these factors in a usefully descriptive way that sums up the correlations empirically disclosed but which is also creatively suggestive. Such stereotypical descriptions have got to be pregnant with other possibilities if they are to have any validity beyond each experiment. Those so stereotyped must be able to recognize themselves in the statistical mirror. Yet, because the values sampled can only represent a tiny fraction of the range of possible values and then only at a particular time and place, the mirror must also be a metaphor. We must be able to see beyond it in order to imagine what a particular life style category would imply when it encountered new ideas and situations. Formulating such generic descriptions involves an imaginative act by the investigator. It is very difficult, not only for descriptions of life styles in the technical sense of the marketing professional, the problem is the same for any kind of style. Labelling styles in art and artefact is no less tricky than it is in life.

The nature of styles

Most of the theorizing about the nature of styles—collections of characteristically inter-related symbols and forms—has come from the history of art. Much of this activity is academic, the product of the endless debates among curator-professionals about taxonomy, an inescapable activity whenever there is a need to complete a museum collection, write a catalogue or educate students. In recent periods, the practice of art itself has become infected by a knowledge of its own history and the erstwhile categorizations of academics have become slogans for rival schools of artists. Descriptions of styles in art are often expressed in contrasting pairs of thematic labels—the familiar -isms—including Classicism versus Romanticism, Idealism versus realism and Impressionism versus Expressionism.

Critical terms of this kind are first arrived at by a process of ostensive definition. Certain examples of artists or works, it is considered, exemplify the particular traits to be described in the most striking way. By an effort of critical imagination—both analytic and sensitive to feeling—these traits are given a physiognomic interpretation. This is usually an abstract description of their forms connected to an account of the emotions they induce. For example, Classic art would ostensibly be defined by pointing to its various great exemplars such as Raphael or Poussin, Greek sculptures of the third and fourth centuries BC, the architecture of Palladio and the verse of Corneille or Racine.[19] It would physiognomically be defined by identifying the pervasive patterns of symmetry such as regularity of rhythm, characteristic range of relative sizes between parts and wholes, absence of sharp discontinuities of scale or shape and, in a more general way, by the feelings of stillness, clarity and authority that these forms characteristically stir in us.

Difficulties arise when categories thus defined are used in areas away from their origin. Although some works (for example, those of the early eighteenth century) may still be felt to be, in a certain sense, Classic, to embody the principles of Classic form to a certain extent or even, to resemble Raphael or Poussin in many ways, the reservations expressed by such circumlocutions show our unconcealed dissatisfaction with these stylistic labels used literally. They clearly fail to fit the actual eighteenth century artefacts before our eyes. Subsequently, various caveats arise to handle these 'not-quite' situations. We speak of *proto*-Romantic or *quasi*-Realist. Later, more drastic prefixes, *neo* or *post*, transform the original categories still further. We may even find ourselves talking of hybrids between opposites such as Romantic-classicism!

When holistic labels for styles are used to describe broader themes in cultural history, paradox—even absurdity—is seldom far away. Ernst Gombrich has devastatingly condemned writers such as Arnold Hauser who found his stylistic generalizations falling to pieces under the load of historical particulars, which committed him to tortuous hybrids such as Baroque-classicism.[20] Similar categories and problems are seen in the discussion of modern artefacts, for example in the controversies among architectural critics about whether a particular building is an example of post- or merely late-Modernism! Perhaps Gombrich's strictures are too severe. We all use such abstract descriptions not as discreet categories or boxes into which new artefacts either do or do not fit, but rather as metaphorically suggestive scales or continua, planes of contrast and correlation in which traits may vary. They provide us with a kind of metaphorical space in which we can move and adjust our critical interpretations as the need arises.

Two main problems arise when we try to refine the concept of style. In the first instance, there is the problem of deciding which particular objects are to be regarded as centrally significant and representative examples of a particular style, spontaneously agreed and accepted by everyone who gives the matter serious thought. How does this collection of representative objects—which is usually called a *canon*—first become established? The earliest occasion that we are able to witness the establishment of canons arose from the activities of what was one of the world's first collections of curator-professionals—the staff of the great library at Alexandria.[21] Greek literature had been transmitted verbally until quite late. Although a decree of the fourth century BC laid down that an official copy of each play performed should be deposited in the public archives, there can be no assurance that such texts were authentic or accurate records of the author's intentions. It was only when large numbers of such manuscripts were accumulated in the library at Alexandria and the job of cataloguing and authentication was undertaken that standard editions could be published together with treatises on the texts. The books were arranged in various classes such as drama, poetry, history and law, and the authors grouped into canons or lists as typical representatives of the particular class.

This procedure of establishing canons or lists spread from cataloguing into criticism. From their original purpose in establishing definitive standards of authenticity, the use of canons developed into a method of characterizing particular manners or expressive qualities, notably in the art of rhetoric. Lists of individual orators were compiled as representative of particular manners. A similar development took place in the visual arts with the work of Xenocrates and other Greek scholars that was subsequently incorporated into Pliny's much later writings on the history of art in his *Natural History*.[22]

Obviously criticism occurred before such published canons became available. In any precanonical critical activity, much depends inevitably on ostensive definition—pointing to particular cases and individuals. However, in the case of style, ostensive definition depends on eliciting agreement by virtue of the compelling obviousness and pertinacity of the cases to which attention is drawn. It is in this way that we arrive at the general consensus 'that so-and-so is a classic artist'. Nevertheless, even before the publication of canons and the establishment of published criteria of judgment, there must clearly be some widespread currency of related ideas and standards so that the connection being pointed to can immediately be recognized. Such a common currency is easiest to achieve within a particular genre, especially one in which there is a sense of historical continuity and precedent. In such cases, public recognition of a new work as canonical can follow immediately, without prior technical analysis or criticism. In 1311, when Duccio's *Maestà* was carried in solemn procession from his workshop to the Duomo in Sienna, the crowds who followed were not sophisticated critics but neither were they unaware of previous works in the tradition of medieval church art. No doubt there was an element of sheer awe imposed by the scale and grandeur of Duccio's masterpiece which influenced the immediacy with which the work achieved recognition. No doubt too an important transference took place between the purely religious and more secular aesthetic emotions. Perhaps some such transference occurs in the initial stages of the establishment of any new stylistic canon. This is probably true at all levels from high art to jazz.

Before a style has coalesced around certain issues explicitly recognized as salient, a particular idiom may have no definite boundaries. Eventually though there is an Alexandrian period, a stage of recording, comparing, evaluation and analysis. Even then however, there is rarely agreement on the precise criteria for admission to the canon of a particular style. In this sense, a stylistic canon is similar to a club. There may be club rules pertaining to membership, but these may be loosely drawn, leaving much to precedent and interpretation. Nevertheless, individual cases may cause great disputes. Moreover, a newly admitted member may be such a powerful personality that he shifts perceptions about what is salient for a particular style from inside the club. In the process, the whole centre of gravity of a particular style may be altered. Even the most hallowed stylistic paradigms or archetypes shift as the canon grows. Moreover, disputes about membership, even of such well established canons as those of Classic art are more frequent than is commonly supposed.[23]

An important ambiguity in the notion of a canon arises in its transition from a concept concerned with authenticity to one concerned with critical judgment. In popular, and even technical usage, these two senses coexist somewhat uneasily. Even in the collection of manuscripts at Alexandria, judgments about quality could not be ignored. A canon of a particular class contains not merely typical exemplars but those which are considered the

5.7 *Canons are created and reinforced by frequent inclusion in museums. Chairs are widely exhibited as exemplars of particular styles. Classic twentieth century chairs on display in the Design Museum, London, England.*

best. A list of trivial works would not serve the function of establishing a definitive historical corpus of literature. The modern usage of the word 'canon' occurs most often, not in discussions of literature, but of sacred texts, in particular the Bible. Whether a particular text is to be regarded as canonical in a Biblical sense is decided not by any perception of immediately compelling aesthetic or other qualities, nor by past or present renown, but by historical fact so far as this can be ascertained. On the other hand, art historians usually use the word with an emphasis on its modern sense—a standard or criterion of quality or excellence. Gombrich, in his famous dialogue with Quentin Bell uses it to mean the corpus of all works that are great.[24] More often though, both senses are indicated. A canonical work of a particular style is not only quintessential of a particular manner, but outstanding in quality. So pervasive is this ambiguity in regard to the definition of Classic art that the word 'classic' has itself come to mean canonical. We may speak of a classic instance, a classic try in a rugby match or even a classic piece of kitsch.

It seems extremely unlikely that the categorizations which lead to a particular canon could ever arise spontaneously. The claim that certain instances of a particular activity are so immediately compelling that everyone agrees that they are canonical is probably overstated, even in the case of Michelangelo. Few of the crowds who shuffle through the Sistine Chapel can have any really decisive opinions on the matter. For all practical purposes, judgments about the inclusion or exclusion of works from a canon are made—as they always were—by an élite. Naturally, their judgments must be vindicated by a wider public if a canon is to endure. Nowadays, the construction and custodianship of canons is in the hands of a bureaucratic élite—the curator-professionals.

This is as true of rock music—where stylistic categorization is in the hands of professional journalists and publicists—as it is of high art. In activities such as rock music or sporting spectacles, the connection with the creators on one hand and the consumers on the other, is both shorter and more immediately responsive. In the case of great art this is not so and the curator-professionals who determine

5.8 *In the context of a display of classics, merely to present a relatively ephemeral artefact in the reverential apparatus of plinth, lighting, caption and catalogue is to ensure inclusion of a new work into the canon. Thus legitimated, it then becomes an icon for students and other designers. Gerrit Rietveld's* Blue and Red Chair *has long been a key icon for twentieth century designers.*

such matters are largely insulated within institutions of scholarship.

This is a matter of little public concern except perhaps with respect to incompetence. Experts in a museum might advise on the expenditure of public funds on a forgery or, on the other hand, they may fail to recognize a work in the saleroom as canonical and hence valuable. A similar example would be failure to recognize a particular building as canonical of a particular style and so prevent its destruction by property speculators. More serious issues arise when we take the matter of canons out of the rarified air of high art and into the wider realms of the consumer society. Can there be a canon of good design? Should bureaucrats in the museum service pronounce on matters of style? In the United Kingdom, where in the one-time Boilerhouse of the Victoria and Albert Museum, controversial exhibitions of proper Taste and good design were the order of the day, recent developments seem to indicate that today's mandarins lack none of the ambition of Henry Cole![25] This tradition has been continued in the permanent collection of the new design museums. The fact that large amounts of public money are spent defending a canon of good design that is recognized by only a tiny fraction of the population and resented by a majority suggests that the issue is by no means purely academic.

The second set of problems in the characterization of styles concerns description. How do we formulate descriptions of a canon for a particular genre of art or class of goods beyond the binary systems of the familiar -isms mentioned earlier? Some recent developments inspired by the study of language are interesting here: an early application of the science of information theory involved an attempt to use statistical methods to describe styles in order to solve difficult problems of authenticity. Suppose we are presented with previously unknown text alleged to be written by Shakespeare. Is it real Shakespeare? Is it a compilation or a workshop job? Or is it simply a fake? Once adequate computing power became widely available, it became possible to search for statistical regularities in the frequencies with which particular words are used.

Regularities in samples of Shakespeare known to be authentic can be compared with an unknown sample. Phrases, idioms or even longer-range syntactic structures can also

167

statistically be described and compared with those in the new piece. Known as *stylometrics*, this laborious procedure can give useful insight into the structural habits of artists, including those who use media other than the written language.[26] Suppose we are presented with a previously unknown painting by Van Gogh. How do we determine whether or not it is a forgery? Traditionally, scholars who have made a prolonged study of Van Gogh's work inspect the new picture and pronounce it as canonical or not (sometimes *œuvre* catalogues are drastically rewritten!).[27]

A stylometric approach would list all the salient features characteristic of Van Gogh's authentic works. Features such as brushwork details, compositional devices, types of canvas and colour usage would be given variable scores depending on a judgment of their relative importance in the known canon. Each known work could be run against the maximum possible total score and the average score calculated for a genuine Van Gogh. Skilled forgers often match Van Gogh in one or two of the variables but rarely in many. All works which fall substantially below the mean for a genuine Van Gogh can be regarded as forgeries. By using works for which we have unimpeachable evidence of authenticity we can construct a statistical boundary for the Van Gogh canon.[28]

Recent technical advances in computing and data storage have made considerable strides towards the realization of such an approach in practice. Most modern museums have started to compile descriptions of all their works into massive databases which are linked into national and international networks. These descriptions (which at present depend on skilled human observers using elaborate

5.9 *To design an artefact that becomes a new icon is the greatest success a designer can attain. Presented in museum surroundings three kettles, created for Alessi by Richard Sapper, Michael Graves and Aldo Rossi.*

checklists to enter the data) can be refined and sophisticated at will. Once a truly universal database of descriptions exists, it can be searched for any pattern or ensemble of features which might be deemed to characterize a given artist's style.

Eventually, more of this task can be left to the computer itself. Images can be taken with a high-resolution camera and recorded digitally. This digital image can be searched automatically for clusters of patterns and features in much the same way that is now done for identifying patterns in fingerprints. At the present time however, matters such as the formal description of texture—crucial in identifying a given artist's hand—are formidably difficult.[29]

In principle, this method can be used anywhere. However, once we begin to consider style in more holistic or global terms—for example, post-Impressionism—the number of pertinent variables which would fingerprint canonical works becomes very large and the problem of scoring each across different artists very complex. Presumably though, the expert in art history performs this kind of scoring operation when he makes his intuitive judgments of quality. Making the process more explicit may be an aid to reliability. In the end though, we must recognize that style is a 'fuzzy' concept, defined from the centre by canonical instances. Computerized definitions of style

5.10 Identification of patterns of brushwork will eventually be aided by computer pattern recognition programmes which pick-up characteristic textures and 'fingerprints'. X-ray photographs (real and fake) of Van Gogh's brush work.

offer, not necessarily a more precise understanding of the boundaries of a particular style, but rather a deeper understanding of the dimensions of typicality or belonging in any particular instance.

Another approach to stylistic description involves the analogies with language developed by structuralist writers such as Roland Barthes and Claude Levi-Strauss. We may take recent criticism in the field of architecture as an example. During the last few years the once monolithic ideology of design—functionalism—has crumbled. Instead of one Modern Movement we now have many, all competing.[30] A recent survey by an architectural magazine listed eleven current -isms, each described by a separate contributor.[31] These various -isms ranged from Classicism, high-tech, structural rationalism, humanism and organic architecture to commercial packaging, neo-vernacular and Rationalism. Each contributor proceeded along the lines previously described. Canonical works were selected and displayed in photographic form. Generic descriptions were extracted from them and these descriptions related back to the global concept suggested by the -isms in the chosen title.

An interesting rejoinder came from a correspondent who pointed out that although they were presented as a simple list, all the various -isms were themselves structurally interrelated and could be put into one all-embracing schema. In many cases, different contributors cited the same architect, sometimes even the same building, as canonical works for different -isms. However, this need not necessarily lead us to see the whole enterprise as risible or that the whole categorical system is the nonsense that Gombrich imputed of Hauser's generalizations. Polysemy is an essential feature of category labels if they are to be useful beyond the first few works at the centre of any particular canon.

Using the analogy of the colour wheel, in which the perceptual relationships between different hues are described by placing them in spectral order on the circumference of a circle, David Capon drew up a schema for previously listed architectural categories. He suggested that there were three primary categories from which the Classical/Rationalist family of concepts were drawn and that an underlying tendency towards analysis and simplicity may be traced within them.

Taking the triangle of primary colours (red, blue and yellow), Capon demonstrated the varying interplay of mathematical purity (blue), technological appropriateness and efficiency (red) and typological historicism (yellow) characteristic of the primary group. From these primary categories, three secondary categories can be formed from which the Expressionist/Romantic family of concepts are drawn—'in them we see a tendency away from the rational towards the ineffable and the complex.' This secondary triangle (orange, green and violet) demonstrates 'the interplay

Classic—Louis Kahn. Library at Exeter, New Hampshire, USA

Organic—Lucien Kroll. Residences for the Medical Faculty, University of Louvain, Belgium

5.11 *The many styles of modern architecture in 1982. In a survey of current approaches to contemporary architecture, the* Architects Journal *asked a series of critics each to characterize one style. The styles were illustrated with buildings which the contributors regarded as canonical.*

Collage—Richard Meier. Athenaeum, New Harmony, USA

Neo-Vernacular—any shopping centre influenced by the Essex Design Guide, England

Functionalism—Martec International. Middlesex Polytechnic, London, England

Structural Rationalism—Norman Foster. Sainsbury Centre, University of Norwich, England

Humanist Housing—Darbourne and Darke, Marquess Road, London, England

Rationalism—Aldo Rossi. School at Fagnano di Olona, Italy

Commercial Packaging—Mies van der Rohe, Court Building, Chicago, USA

Dutch Functionalism—Herman Hertzberger. Music Centre, Utrecht, The Netherlands

Participation—Lucien Kroll, University of Louvain, Belgium

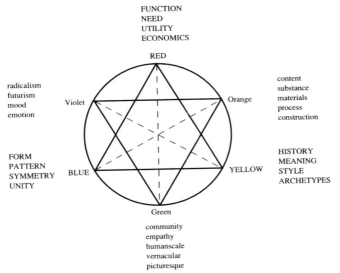

FUNCTION
NEED
UTILITY
ECONOMICS

RED

content
substance
materials
process
construction

radicalism
futurism
mood
emotion

Violet

Orange

FORM
PATTERN
SYMMETRY
UNITY

HISTORY
MEANING
STYLE
ARCHETYPES

BLUE

YELLOW

Green

community
empathy
humanscale
vernacular
picturesque

5.12 *Suggested structural diagram showing the inter-relationship between the previous styles as instances of combinations of broad theoretical positions. The colour circle with superimposed triangles of primary and secondary colours is used to highlight relationships which would not ordinarily be seen as related. After David Capon, letter to* Architects Journal.

of content, substance and material' (orange), 'community and communication' (green) and 'politics, emotion and decision-making' (violet) which characterizes the secondary Romantic group. Capon remarks, 'there is no approach which cannot be seen as a compound of these concepts'. However, he goes on to doubt whether such stylistic chemistry is really worthwhile. Capon probably acquired his idea from Edmund Leach who used the analogy of the colour wheel to explain the basis of structuralism in a popular monograph on Levi-Strauss.[32] Leach also considered the profitablity of such taxonomic juggling because, although it was intellectually satisfying, there was no way of knowing how real it was on any particular instance or occasion. Presumably, like other conceptual tools, it must be for the users to decide when and whether a particular system becomes too complex or, on the other hand, too neat and simple.

In 1969, Charles Jencks attempted to show how various architectural critics and historians have derived their particular critical categories from simpler primary historical *mythemes.*[33]

As with Capon's colour circle analogy, there is no reason to suppose that any one of the architects or critics cited ever thought in this way. We must once more be aware of the distinction between performance and competence. Taxonomic enumeration in schemas of this kind only touches competence.

Regardless of the eventual judgment on such efforts, they do attempt to grasp at the notion that any description of style must grapple with those relationships of contrast and correlation located in the deep structure of works (whatever this metaphor may mean in particular instances!). The telltale caveats—'in a certain sense', 'in many ways', 'quasi', or the paradoxical conflations such as Classic-baroque signal that a particular label is to be used metaphorically. And metaphor is inherent in changes in the deep structure relations between concepts.

For Bourdieu however, such stylistic categorizations are rather more than convenient and creative fictions and much, much more than the abstract theoretical frameworks which define competence. He sees in them the source

5.13 *Cartoon and caricature is often a good way of capturing the essence of an style. Osbert Lancaster's cartoon history of architecture* From Pillar to Post *is brilliantly updated by Louis Hellman in a survey of the modern architectural '-isms'. In many cases his images are only very slightly exaggerated.*

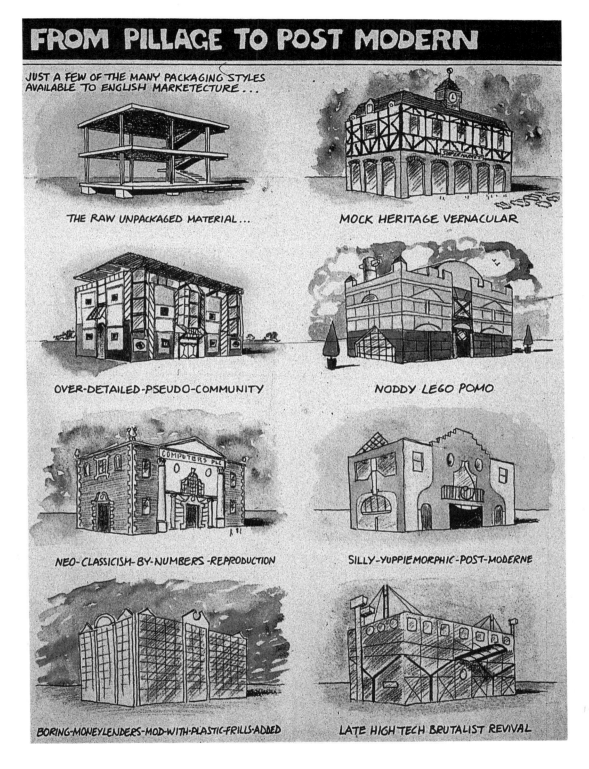

FROM PILLAGE TO POST MODERN

JUST A FEW OF THE MANY PACKAGING STYLES AVAILABLE TO ENGLISH MARKETECTURE...

THE RAW UNPACKAGED MATERIAL...

MOCK HERITAGE VERNACULAR

OVER-DETAILED-PSEUDO-COMMUNITY

NODDY LEGO POMO

NEO-CLASSICISM-BY-NUMBERS-REPRODUCTION

SILLY-YUPPIEMORPHIC-POST-MODERNE

BORING-MONEYLENDERS-MOD-WITH-PLASTIC-FRILLS-ADDED

LATE HIGH TECH BRUTALIST REVIVAL

HISTORIAN	MYTH	MYTHEME A - MYTHEME B	RESOLUTION
PEVSNER	SPIRIT OF THE AGE 'the style'	RATIONALITY - EXPRESSIONISM clarity - fantasy standardization - ornament *Sachlichkeit* - confusion social responsibility - art for art	GROPIUS
GIEDION	SPIRIT OF THE AGE 'balanced outlook'	TRADITION - SCHISM balance - imbalance unified artist - dissociated society cons. facts - trans. facts	BAUHAUS
BANHAM	FUTURISM 'entirely radical'	FUTURIST DYNAMISM - ACADEMIC CAUTION change - symbols technology - convention speed, danger - stasis mechanization - classical trad.	NO resolution presents opposites
SCULLY	EXISTENTIALISM 'image of democracy'	ROMANTIC CLASS - ROMANTIC NAT. Baroque order - fragmented eclecticism Rationalism - continual flux	CORBUSIER Kahn

5.14 *Architectural history itself relies on a limited range of interpretational schema or 'mythemes' according to Charles Jencks. The great historians of twentieth century architecture are related by the use of binary oppositions of their global interpretations or 'myths'.*

of all those baneful aesthetic impositions on reality which mark out bourgeois culture.[34] He asserts that, in this culture, each object loses its factitiousness and, cutoff from its anchorage in a particular place and time, becomes merely an exemplification of an abstract aesthetic category.

The bourgeoisie lives its cultural life in a world of abstractions, a world in which the concrete content of particular experiences is all but eliminated to be replaced by an obsession with form. Generalization and categorization on matters of style become a substitute for direct experience. Bourdieu argues that this way of thinking is rooted in bourgeois educational practice. It therefore plays an important part in creating an intellectual apparatus for the domination and control of the working class, not by a monopoly of power in the place of work, but by continuously setting the patterns of proper consumption through its pur-ported monopoly of those cultural processes which legitimize symbols. The bourgeoisie intellectualizes all consumption into approved aesthetic patterns of symbolic decency, patterns which are constantly redefined in order to maintain its own cultural superiority. Such patterns are ignored or rejected by the traditional working class who have not been subjected to bourgeois education. For them, Bourdieu asserts, aesthetics in the bourgeois sense does not exist. Symbols are admired for themselves and are not actively contrasted or correlated with others. At most, they are instruments of a generalized pleasure. Bourdieu mounts a powerful defence of working class culture against the charges of kitsch by pointing out that the supposedly transcendental categories (or deep structure relations) against which kitsch objects stand out as comically-maimed metaphors, simply do not exist for such consumers.

174

5.15 *Constant redefinition of patterns of symbolic decency within professional coteries leads to 'deconstructions' of existing styles. Unexpected juxtapositions of features that would previously have been regarded as incompatible are the hallmarks of many varieties of contemporary design, the point of which is usually lost on their ostensible consumers. New public housing apartments behind a restored medieval facade, Cahors, France.*

Styles, life styles and the structure of society

There are clearly great difficulties in describing those pervasive patterns of form and symbol we call style. Great care is required to avoid circularity or the projection of the investigator's own categories into other cultures, cultures in which such categories are not recognized. Even greater care is required in explaining the relationship between particular styles and the social orders in which they prevail. How do particular styles come to occupy a certain place? Why should certain periods and places, certain peoples and groups be concerned so exclusively with a limited range of stylistic traits, traits that enable us to attribute an object to a particular time and place? To answer this question involves negotiating some taxing puzzles in the logic of historical and sociological explanation.

Two strategies have been adopted in the attempt to account for the linkage between particular styles and the nature of the society which gave birth to them. The first is to push the problem one stage back. A particular style and the detailed nature of the social order are both seen as separate but parallel expressions of an underlying historical consciousness. As this consciousness evolves so do its separate expressions. It is from this evolving core that we acquire our sense of the unity of style in a period and its appropriateness to its age and to a particular social order. Alternatively (and this theory is related to the first), we may consider that the economic conditions of society are fundamental and that they determine everything else, including the consciousness of individuals and groups, especially those groups who share a common functional position in the economic order of society—the classes. Individual makers of the artefactual world express their class-consciousness and thereby articulate the underlying economic order in visible form.

Stemming from the philosophies of Hegel and Marx respectively these approaches have inspired many social histories of consumption goods, from interior decoration to fashion in dress.[35] Both, however, are dangerously vague and often logically circular. Again, it is to

175

Gombrich (following the example of Karl Popper) that we owe the exposure of the fallacies and illusions which this *geistges-chichte* brings to the serious study of symbol and style.[36] Fundamentally, all such explanations of the relation of style to society involve the multiple meanings and ambiguities expressed in words such as determine, express, mirror, reflect and inflect. No real account is given of how an individual designer or architect comes to acquire his internal representation of the social order so that he can express it in his works. Until this problem is solved we are back again with the dialectics and naivety of the cultural historians who assert that rigid societies patronize hieratic styles. Clearly, such oversimple, linear theories will not do. Correlations of this kind can be refuted by a single historical example which does not fit the rule. And, in any case, correlation is not cause.

An ingenious attempt to find a way round some of these difficulties was provided by Basil Bernstein.[37] His central idea was to locate the mediating step in the transmission of stable patterns of culture from one generation to the next in the style of child-rearing adopted by parents in the different social groups. Such differences between the practices of role-centred families (basically working class) and those of person-centred families (basically middle class) arise by virtue of differences in the work experience of the two groups. According to Bernstein, each different manner of socialization is associated with different styles of linguistic conditioning. These profoundly affect the child's acquisition of his own language. Thus, by virtue of differences in the very language that they learn, children from different classes are predestined to reproduce the social patterns which condition their

parents. And so the existing structure of society prevails across the generations.

Bernstein was able to show some significant differences between working class and middle class families, both in their styles of acculturation and in the range of linguistic features that their children were able to deploy. It would be surprising if he had not. However, it is his interpretation of such differences that is fundamental to the theory. He characterized them as deploying contrasting types of *code*. The concept of a code was never very clearly defined but it appears that in describing the two types of code, structural differences of a quasi-grammatical kind are salient. Structures within an individual's code are the microcosm which mirrors and then transmits the macrocosm of the social structure at large.

Working class children (he asserted) were able to command only a restricted code—metaphorical, affirmative and grammatically simple. Middle class children were able to use this code but were also able to use an elaborated code with an abstract vocabulary and a more complex syntax. Restricted codes were locally focussed. They lock their user into the here and now. Elaborated codes by contrast enable their user to visualize himself outside the situation. He could, by using appropriate grammatical transformations, rewrite a particular action scene internally, thus enabling him to conceive it as at least potentially different. Schools are the other main agency of socialization. Bernstein claimed that their traditional style of curriculum organization and internal control—with sharply divided subjects and a hierarchic authority maintained by middle class professionals using elaborated codes—further reinforced the different world views already well formed within a child's first language usages. Because they operate at a high level of abstraction, Bernstein's ideas are of great general use. Bernstein himself suggested that notions of restricted and elaborated codes might be applied to other fields, for example, art forms such as music, or even household goods.[38] (Bernstein's hypothetical bathrooms were considered earlier.)

Mary Douglas has developed this aspect of Bernstein's early work into a parallel system of classification which is of such a general nature that all types of society and all of their symbol systems can be tied together into one schema. Bernstein's own theoretical variables have changed a good deal over the years. His later version contrasts languages (and social groups) in terms of the relative strengths of *classification* and *framing*. Classification strength is concerned with the degree of categorization of, for example, knowledge, curricula, spaces in a house and types of furniture. Framing is a measure of the degree of control over allowable interrelations within a class. Douglas, stretching these basic dichotomies to develop a generalized anthropological theory, proposed instead, the variables, *grid* and *group*.[39] Grid is the classification variable describing the degree of partitioning—of concepts, symbols, ensembles of goods and behavioural customs. Group describes the pressure of the partitioning between individuals and collectives within the total social structure. In fact, group is derived from the original distinction (which Bernstein borrowed from the sociologist Emile Durckheim) between societies which show organic solidarity (*gemeinschaft*) and those which show mechanical solidarity (*gesellschaft*).[40] Aided by a graphical representation on a two-dimensional map, she was able to generate in some detail

speculative interpretations for symbol-systems in all societies. It is difficult to determine the exact status of such grand theorizing. Some critics dismiss the whole account of society in terms of just these two types of solidarity as 'mere German sociological romanticism'. Historians, who must deeply respect local detail and particular circumstance, may be equally derisive in dismissing such ambitious and necessarily generalized cross-cultural comparisons as impossible. The anthropologist, however, may well argue that this is precisely the issue with which he or she is concerned!

Let us concede that the Douglas schema is an advance on the mere dialectical coupling of parallel contrasts in styles and societies of the kind that Gombrich so convincingly dismissed. With two independent axes of variation we are no longer in the crude world where rigid societies have to favour rigid styles.[41] Moreover, Douglas is quick to point out that hypothetical comparisons of different styles must be limited to 'a particular social environment'. To avoid the use of those theories which can immediately be refuted by a single counterinstance, we have to restrict our predictions to 'relevant' comparisons.[42] But how do we know what is relevant? And how do we delimit 'a particular social environment'?

Further analysis of the terms will not solve this problem for it is inherent to the method. It must therefore be tackled as a problem of method and treated as a practical, operational matter of research technique. Linguists and social scientists, anthropologists and art historians must decide on appropriate operational standards of relevance in selecting their material. To attempt to understand what members of other cultures consider relevant, we must participate in and identify with that

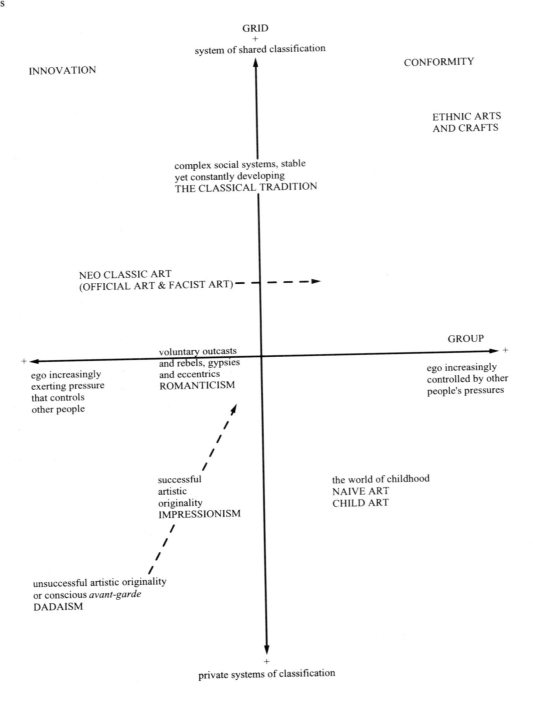

GRID
+
system of shared classification

INNOVATION

CONFORMITY

ETHNIC ARTS
AND CRAFTS

complex social systems, stable
yet constantly developing
THE CLASSICAL TRADITION

NEO CLASSIC ART
(OFFICIAL ART & FACIST ART)

GROUP
+

voluntary outcasts
and rebels, gypsies
and eccentrics
ROMANTICISM

ego increasingly
exerting pressure
that controls
other people

ego increasingly
controlled by other
people's pressures

successful
artistic
originality
IMPRESSIONISM

the world of childhood
NAIVE ART
CHILD ART

unsuccessful artistic originality
or conscious *avant-garde*
DADAISM

+
private systems of classification

5.16 *Grid and Group. Mary Douglas extended Bernstein's ideas into a general explanatory schema for anthropological interpretation. The 'Grid' axis refers to different levels of discrimination in concepts and the 'Group' axis to the extent of personal autonomy in a society. The various artistic styles in the diagram have been added by the author from the suggestions given in Douglas' text.*

culture. This is precisely the nature of interpretation we have conceived in terms of negotiated creativeness—the creative act of relating one's own frames of reference to those of others.

In fact, the greatest difficulty with theories that appeal to linguistic conditioning has been the problem of establishing adequate operational definitions of codes for professional linguists. No one doubts that differences exist between the language uses of different classes. But no convincing general description of these differences in terms of linguistic structures has yet been devised. In particular, the notion of linguistic deprivation implied into the terms 'restricted' and 'elaborated' has never been adequately defined.[43] Language is such a universal instrument that it has yet to be shown that there are social differences in the distribution of linguistic competence. This is a crucial point. Differences in competence would be equivalent to a piano with some notes missing. Such a piano could only play limited melodies. In practice it seems at least as convincing to cast explanations for apparently limited utterances in terms of performance, referring perhaps to the social context of the particular linguistic exchange (for example an unfamiliar formal social setting for an interview with a strange middle class researcher) or, better still, to the particular conversational tasks that the different social classes are habitually required to perform.[44]

We face the same intractable problems when we consider the language of goods. Are class differences in presentational behaviour and patterns of symbolic consumption merely matters of usage and habit, differences at most perhaps of dialect, or are they more fundamental differences, differences of language that leaves the lower classes conceptually and expressively impoverished from their earliest infancy? Do lower class consumption patterns (or Tastes) involve merely differences in symbolic performance or are there differences in competence with all the overtones of limited capacity that the term implies? Working class Taste in consumer goods is as visibly different from that of the middle classes as is their speech. Do we infer from this that the working class is in some way mentally different or is it again merely a matter of context?

Even to ask such questions in a democracy is to offend many people deeply. Elitism or snobbery are the obvious countercharges to the superiority implied by the words elaborated or restricted—for all Bernstein intended them to be neutral, technical terms. He himself has been violently (and perhaps wrongly) attacked, not least because he has been thought to imply that working class speech is in some way worse than that of the middle classes.[45] William Labov, in his description of Negro demotic speech, stressed the richness and vividness of the constant use of metaphor which, at the very least, substituted for the missing syntactic complexity. Conversely, middle class speech was attacked precisely for its circumlocution and its structural evasions which lead to important sounding but empty utterances.[46]

Presumably, the most desirable kind of speech would employ both sets of forces as occasion demanded (Shakespeare would be a good example). But what of the language of goods? Is anyone in the field of Taste prepared to praise the richness of imagery in a working class home above the elaboration of theme and formal structure in a refined bourgeois home? True, there are many fictional denunciations of the emptiness and bleakness of environments dominated by good Taste—in the films of Antonioni for example. Equally, the clutter of the working class domestic interior is often used as a symbol of homeliness and good nature in many television series. Yet how valid are such generalizations? No one has comprehensively investigated the stylistic preferences of the classes since the pioneering works of F. Stuart Chapin and Dennis Chapman.[47] Particularly lacking is a study based on existing and widely used systems of classification. This is important, for without it cross-cultural comparison is difficult. The nearest we have is the study of French consumption preferences mounted by Bourdieu in 1979. Even here though we have to make do with a system of social classification very much Bourdieu's own. Moreover, he makes no mention of previous attempts to correlate demographic and life style measures as developed within the American tradition of market research.

Bourdieu's work is based on a large-scale social survey in which respondents were asked a series of questions about their preferences in various areas of culturally important consumption. These were chosen on the basis of previous investigations in order to highlight Bourdieu's theoretical preoccupations.[48] First was a group of questions concerned to measure an individual's acquaintance with legitimate culture—his knowledge and use of established works of serious or high culture in fields such as music, painting, theatre and books. As a knowledge of high culture is not the same as any genuine aesthetic disposition, Bourdieu's second set of questions addressed this topic. Aesthetic disposition was measured by the capacity to envisage the abstract (formal) or symbolic possibilities in various items suggested as potential subjects for a

photograph. A third battery of questions concerned the consumption of middle culture—knowledge of popular songs, radio and television programmes and film and television stars. Final questions concerned the expression of what Bourdieu termed ethical attitudes. In particular, attitudes to personal presentation in dress and body-imagery and to social presentation in matters such as language and domestic milieu, together with preferred methods of entertaining, choosing and receiving friends. The questionnaire also included questions regarding socioeconomic status, measuring age, sex, income, extent and level of education and also included similar questions about the respondent's father and grandfather.

Bourdieu's objective in the analysis of the data was to establish correlations between the choices of particular sets of goods and practices with the socioeconomic position of various groups. It could thus be demonstrated that possession and display of such goods acts as a symbol system, a system which immediately signals to others the ownership of particular kinds and amounts of resources. Cultural symbols are used by everyone in delineating the recognizable boundaries of social groups.

In setting up his system of social stratification, Bourdieu eschewed the conventional methods which aggregate different types of resource such as wealth and education into a one-dimensional ranking, the so-called *social-scales* or *indexes of status*. For him, such scales are crude fictions.[49] They have an objective validity only to the extent that people really do recognize an interconvertibility between their various constituents. Only if a society recognizes a trade-off between the various kinds of resources in the marketplace can a scale based on one resource serve to index the whole. This in turn depends on the current state of competition between the various factions which are uppermost in possession of each significant type of resource.

Significant resources—which include both the resources acquired during a person's lifetime and those he has inherited—are of three kinds: economic, cultural and social. All three types of resource simultaneously demonstrate a person's position on a social map. Moreover, the social map must consider not only the magnitude of these variables at a given moment in time, but must also take into account a person's social trajectory—his past career and his normal expectations for the future (what Lee Rainwater called his actual and his virtual life careers).

Bourdieu manipulated the conventional socioeconomic variables to construct a three-dimensional social space. The three axes represented the total volume of a person's resources (the most important variable demarcating the major division of class), the structure of these resources and his social trajectory. Analysis showed that within any particular level of overall resource (or social class) economic and cultural resources have a mutually reciprocal relationship. Bourdieu plotted these in opposite directions along the axis at right angles to the total volume of resources. As three axes cannot easily be represented on a two-dimensional page, the third variable, social trajectory, was represented as a series of vertical indicators plotted locally at points on the page.[50] These were in the form of histograms giving the relative proportion of the social class of origin. A series of vertical and horizontal arrows indicated a significant (at least 25%) change in the size of a particular

group over a six year period. This gave rise to a map showing the relationship between different occupational groups in terms of the significant resource variables (Figure 5.17).

When the salient preferences of each group (as indicated by replies to the questionnaire) were extracted statistically, a series of homologous maps of different Tastes were superimposed on to the social spaces. Bourdieu calls this the *life style space* (the upper and lower case legends to Figure 5.17). Represented in this way, the social space is merely an abstract theoretical scheme, a map which gives an overview of all the points surveyed by the sociologist. Individual subjects (including the sociologist) cannot see the system from outside. They cannot have an objective view of the map. Figures in the social landscape can only see a partial and incomplete view which depends on their position on the map. Nevertheless, the entire system is manifest in their perceptions insofar as the system of social relationships marked out by the different forms and levels of resources is a system within a set or matrix of concrete possibilities and impossibilities. Both social role and the possession of resources are intrinsically relational concepts. Likewise is the concept of life style and Taste—that ensemble of consumption goods and symbolic practices which is the normal prerogative (and duty) of the incumbent of any particular role.

The particular facts of life prevailing at any point in the social space condition a set of habits and propensities or dispositions which, to use Bourdieu's terminology, activate and direct generational schemas. These internal mental schemas generate both the normal practices and patterns of consumption (goods and settings) and one's perceptions about

181

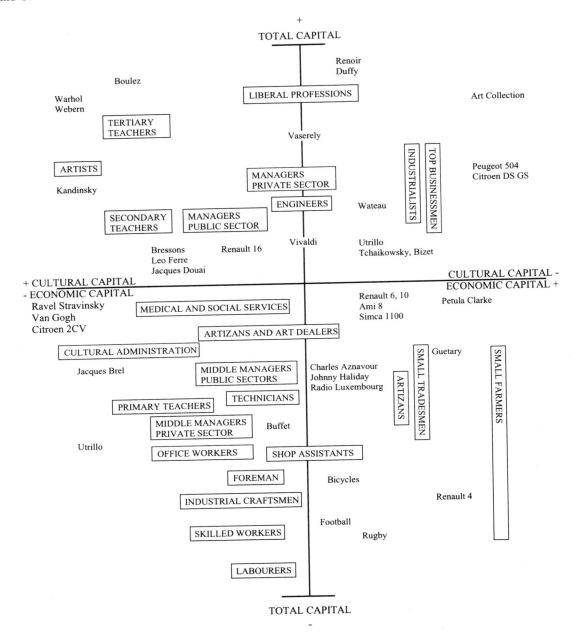

+

TOTAL CAPITAL

Renoir
Duffy

Boulez

LIBERAL PROFESSIONS   Art Collection

Warhol
Webern

TERTIARY
TEACHERS

Vaserely

ARTISTS   Peugeot 504
                                                               Citroen DS GS

Kandinsky   MANAGERS
                   PRIVATE SECTOR

                   ENGINEERS   Wateau

SECONDARY   MANAGERS
TEACHERS   PUBLIC SECTOR

               Renault 16   Vivaldi   Utrillo
Bressons   Tchaikowsky, Bizet
Leo Ferre
Jacques Douai

+ CULTURAL CAPITAL   CULTURAL CAPITAL -
- ECONOMIC CAPITAL   ECONOMIC CAPITAL +
Ravel Stravinsky
Van Gogh   MEDICAL AND SOCIAL SERVICES
Citroen 2CV
                                        Renault 6, 10   Petula Clarke
                                        Ami 8
                   ARTIZANS AND ART DEALERS   Simca 1100

CULTURAL ADMINISTRATION

Jacques Brel   MIDDLE MANAGERS   Charles Aznavour   Guetary
                   PUBLIC SECTORS   Johnny Haliday
                                        Radio Luxembourg
                   TECHNICIANS
PRIMARY TEACHERS

MIDDLE MANAGERS   Buffet
PRIVATE SECTOR

Utrillo   OFFICE WORKERS   SHOP ASSISTANTS

               FOREMAN   Bicycles

               INDUSTRIAL CRAFTSMEN   Renault 4

                              Football
SKILLED WORKERS
                                   Rugby

LABOURERS

INDUSTRIALISTS   TOP BUSINESSMEN

ARTIZANS   SMALL TRADESMEN   SMALL FARMERS

TOTAL CAPITAL

-

5.17 *The social space and the life style space. The socioeconomic groups are shown in capitals. The characteristic life style indicators are shown in lower case. Axes represent economic resources (income, access to pensions, progressive salaries) and cultural resources (indexed by the number of years in education of both subject and his or her parents).*

5.18 *Intellectualizing consumption. A strategy open to members of social groups with a relatively high educational endowment. Humble artefacts, often displayed in inventive new contexts are preferred to more expensive items the purchase of which would put unacceptable strains on an individual's life style. Rocking chair made out of tractor seats, wall decoration of bent metal. Interior from Arcosanti, Arizona, USA.*

them.[51] Normal practices and perceptions interact to form a given life style. (The concept of generational schemas has much in common with Aaron Cicourel's ideas about interpretive procedures although, unlike Cicourel and Bernstein, Bourdieu does not limit conditioning to infancy.)

Like the social order by which they are conditioned, customs and dispositions (*les habitus*) are also structured. So, in turn, are the generational schemas. An individual's perception of a normal ensemble of goods and practices can thus be generated in previously unknown situations with novel consumption goods. In this way, the social order is replicated in the relations of correlation and contrast between different life styles, even in rapidly changing historical and economic circumstances, where technology presents endlessly novel and unpredictable possibilities for consumption. Differentiation is intrinsic to the very concept of both social and life style space although it is by no means implied that individuals are aggressively (or even consciously) pointing to these differences as Veblen alleged. By resting his system on the positional nature of the concepts themselves, Bourdieu is echoing James Dusenberry, who showed that mere awareness of a set of relations (in his case a rank-ordering of goods into a hierarchy of desirability) was enough to generate interdependent utilities.[52] Rather sadly perhaps Bourdieu rarely uses familiar terminology or refers to any work outside his own immediate circle. Nevertheless, his system has the potential for elaborating Dusenberry's approach on a multi-dimensional basis.

Because the ensembles of practices and Tastes for different kinds of goods which constitute a particular life style are each

congruent with the social space derived from the distribution of different kinds and amounts of reward, they are all homologous with each other. Bourdieu, however, does not press this aspect of this schema very far. Unlike Bernstein and Douglas, he does not attempt to devise an all-embracing system for characterizing the syntactic and semantic structures of the ensembles themselves. There is nothing similar to Bernstein's classification or framing strengths or Douglas' grid or group. Instead, Bourdieu points to obvious antitheses arising from inequalities in the distribution of resources, both in terms of overall levels and their composition, and to social and psychological strategies for dealing with them. Using these he could deduce some plausible systems of binary oppositions which characterize particular Tastes along the structuralist lines discussed earlier in the work of Barthes and Levi-Strauss.

The contrast between those who live with large overall levels of resource (both economic and cultural) and those who live with very little is perhaps most obvious.[53] Between these opposing groups there is a contrast between luxury (and freedom of choice) and necessity. There are two methods for dealing with this latter situation. The first entails making a virtue out of necessity, of drawing pleasure and pride in making the most of things and refusing to be drawn into invidious comparisons with groups and life styles to which one cannot realistically aspire. This involves the familiar narrowing of focus of comparison onto one's immediate social milieu to which theorists of relative deprivation (for example Robert Merton and Walter Runciman[54]) have previously drawn attention. It implies a denial of the validity of the whole basis of luxurious Taste and the concern with choice, arrangement, variety and novelty. The second strategy concerns displacing the focus of mutual comparison away from the global amounts of resources onto particular limited areas of resource where one may be (relatively) more advantaged.

Bourdieu's schema, which distinguishes the relative distribution of cultural capital (derived largely from education) from purely economic capital, serves neatly to demonstrate an obvious mode of displacement which is available to those with a (relatively) high cultural endowment at whatever global level of capital. This is to subject consumption to greater intellectual study. It involves a shift of attention away from sheer quantity onto quality and, in particular, away from substance and experience onto form and analysis. From this point of view, mere quantity in consumption, even of luxury items and ensembles, comes to signify the gross and the coarse—the gourmand rather than the gourmet. Conversely, abnegation, self-denial and restraint come to signify nobility, dignity and virtue. Low status is attributed to the former and high status to the latter characteristics.[55] Many societies have subcultures within

them (for instance, that concerned with Classic art) which manifest this displacement. It was this displacement that Goffman termed negative cultivation. Negative cultivation is not only an effective psychological stratagem for maintaining self-esteem within a system of publicly marked differences in resources or capital, coincidentally it is also a psychological preconditioning of the appetites essential if one is to achieve the necessary variety in levels of stimulation and arousal (fasting and feasting). This is the best strategy for the maximization of pleasure given the limits imposed by the inverted U-shaped curve of arousal (the Wundt curve) to which David Berlyne has drawn our attention.[56]

A good example of these two strategies working together is found in the social distribution of styles of consumption of the most basic commodity of all, food—the archetype of Taste. It has been known for many years that as incomes rise, people spend a relatively smaller amount on food (this is known as Engel's Law). Furthermore, many researches have shown pervasive differences in diet among different social groups, not only in relation to the raw materials consumed but also in the way they are cooked and served. Bourdieu, following Levi-Strauss, displays his own research findings on the life style map. Laid out in this way, the structure of gastronomic possibilities clearly shows the two strategies—making a virtue out of necessity and negative cultivation. The former appears in the vertical comparison between the diets of labourers and those of businessmen, while negative cultivation is shown in the horizontal comparison between the diets of businessmen and those of the intellectual professionals. A complete interpretation of the findings involves not only

5.19 *Pierre Bourdieu's diagram shows characteristic differences between the classes which can be explained by the demands of the situation in which they find themselves. The family supported by manual labour requires a large supply of calories, the intellectuals turn food into an art form and everywhere the status of the wife and hence her ability to spend time in food preparation is crucial to styles in food.*

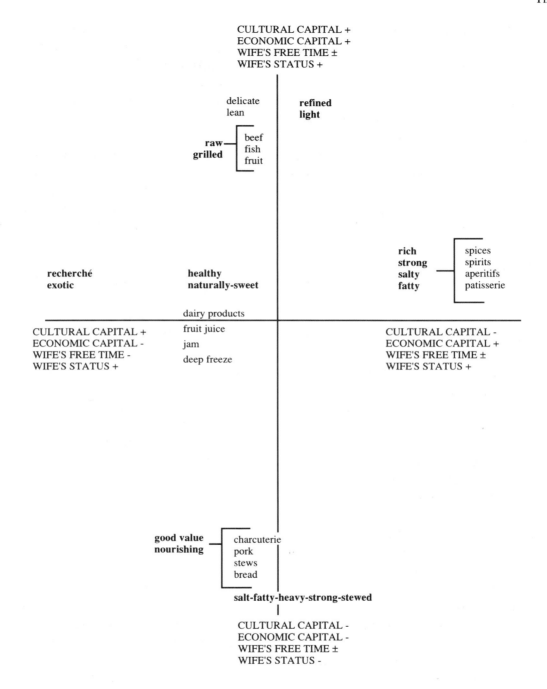

CULTURAL CAPITAL +
ECONOMIC CAPITAL +
WIFE'S FREE TIME ±
WIFE'S STATUS +

delicate
lean

refined
light

raw—
grilled

beef
fish
fruit

recherché
exotic

healthy
naturally-sweet

rich
strong
salty
fatty

spices
spirits
aperitifs
patisserie

dairy products

fruit juice

jam

deep freeze

CULTURAL CAPITAL +
ECONOMIC CAPITAL -
WIFE'S FREE TIME -
WIFE'S STATUS +

CULTURAL CAPITAL -
ECONOMIC CAPITAL +
WIFE'S FREE TIME ±
WIFE'S STATUS +

good value
nourishing

charcuterie
pork
stews
bread

salt-fatty-heavy-strong-stewed

CULTURAL CAPITAL -
ECONOMIC CAPITAL -
WIFE'S FREE TIME ±
WIFE'S STATUS -

the different distribution of the two species of capital but also (and plausibly) the status of women in the different social groups and their willingness and ability to devote time to methods of food preparation.[57]

This basic interpretive schema, together with various supplementary rationales can be used to explain the rest of the findings, whether in the fields of legitimate culture or high art, or in the humbler fields of middle culture. Results here are more or less congruent with those demonstrated in the study of food, and the same psychological strategies and social factors provide plausible explanations. However, the generic adjectival descriptions (refined-nourishing, rich-exotic) which mark out the poles of the two axes of gastronomic style were provided by the analyst after the study had taken place in order to summarize objective differences in the distribution of various types of food. In the case of interior decoration, these stylistic adjectives were given in the questionnaire itself. Therefore, it is difficult to know how a concept such as comfort—which was universally admired at all social levels—was interpreted by respondents from different social groups. The results are, in consequence, less clearly defined.[58] In this particular aspect of the enquiry, there is an obvious, if unacknowledged, affinity with the earlier works of Chapin and Chapman whose questionnaire design was attacked for similar reasons. Certainly, the vagueness which characterizes enquiries about the consumption of goods concerned with the physical environment of the home—which is in marked contrast to the subtlety of understanding displayed in relation to high art—is remarkable. It is also regrettable given the enormous economic importance of the market for those goods which make up the

5.20 *Traditional high tea in a working class home with cold ham, eggs, kippers or haddock provided cheap calories for the labouring man in the 1930s.*

physical fabric of people's lives. Design as an aspect of Taste has yet properly to be recognized by the sociologist.

Despite these reservations, Bourdieu's approach does enable plausible explanations of the many relationships between styles and the structure of society to be marshalled into a satisfying schema. By not laying too much emphasis on the structuralist categories themselves and relying on widely accepted behaviour maxims as supplementary explanations in particular cases and instances, Bourdieu takes a position on the social determination of style which is subjectively satisfying and usefully suggestive. However, two important points must be understood when we attempt to evaluate the significance of structuralist interpretations (of whatever kind). Both are obvious but the very persuasiveness of social and psychological interpretation makes them easy to forget. In the first place, we consume goods for many reasons which operate to varying degrees on any particular occasion. Many of the satisfactions we enjoy in consumption arise from intrinsic and not relational properties. Sweetness in cakes and pastries from the patisserie is an enjoyable

Taste in its own right without having to contrast it with the fancies of other social groups. Not all consumption is symbolically significant in a particular context. In this respect, socioanalysis is similar to psychoanalysis. Freud's notion of multiple causation or, as he called it, *over-determination*, is a necessary adjunct to all explanations of the relationship between styles and societies. Compared with the simpler models of causation familiar from the natural sciences, it is obvious that structuralism has a limited use as a predictor of human behaviour. It seeks to explain too much.

In the second instance, even where relational properties are observed, whether consciously or subconsciously, not all relationships are considered simultaneously. Each individual is in the social space, not outside of it. What he observes depends not only on the view from where he stands but also on the depth and range of his focus. For the most part this is necessarily limited. For example, within the life style space concerned with legitimate art, it could be argued that a complete understanding of the meaning of Bach's *Art of Fugue* would take into account its relation to a multiplicity of works within the total domain of musical composition and consumption. In practice this is not done. To a devotee of Bach, the *Art of Fugue* may well be compared with the *Well-Tempered Clavier*. Indeed, an important part of the pleasure in listening to a particular piece of music may well be the evocation of echoes of another work in the mind of a consumer. Only slightly less remote musical comparisons may serve to anchor a mood or locate a particular frame of mental receptiveness. But no one compares Bach with, for example, Françoise Hardy although the latter may well be compared with Petula Clark in much the same way as the two works of Bach.

To the extent that relational or positional considerations are active in the perception and appreciation of styles we necessarily limit their range in any particular instance. Quite possibly someone may admire both Bach and pop music. On each occasion however, a different set of relational properties will be considered. The mental activity of focussing selectively on a limited range of positional relationships may be thought of as involving a small sliding window which can be moved about over the social or life style space to isolate a finite, limited area at any one time. The Bourdieu schema demonstrates the familiar fact that individual stylistic preferences are transposable anywhere within the universe of possibilities framed by the life style space. Wherever the sliding window comes to rest, predictable stylistic preferences within the window mark out the underlying orthogonal structure of dispositions (*les habitus*). If we know someone's preferences in a certain field of high art (Bach rather than Beethoven) we can predict with some degree of certainty what he will choose within the possibilities of contemporary pop music.

The apparent paradoxes concerning the nature of Taste—is it relative or absolute—which has beset aesthetic discourse since the eighteenth century may now finally be resolved. From an analytic point of view, outside of the life style space, Tastes are clearly relative. They are part of a matrix of differences which embraces all social groups in the homologous social space. From within the life style space however, Tastes necessarily appear to be absolute. This is not only because the view into the life style space is necessarily focussed and

187

limited. It is also determined by one's own location in the social space and, equally important, by the relation between this point and the point which describes the location of the relevant reference group—usually the dominant, upper middle class, group. The line joining these two points describes a vector which forms the operative axis for mutual comparison, the axis along which judgments of Taste—good and bad, high or low—are inevitably made.

Notes and references to Chapter 5

1 For example see, K. Roberts, *Contemporary Society and the Growth of Leisure*, London: Longman, 1978.

2 M. Arnold, "Culture and Anarchy" *Collected Works*, R. H. Super (Ed.), Volume 5, Ann Arbor: University of Michigan Press, 1962.

3 M. Arnold, *op. cit.*, p. 140 *et seq.*

4 M. Arnold, *op. cit.*, p. 145.

5 A. Ross, "U and Non-U" in N. Mitford (Ed.), *Noblesse Oblige*, London: Hamish Hamilton, 1956, p. 11.

6 See R. Lynes, *The Tastemakers*, London: Hamish Hamilton, 1954, p. 310.

7 E. Shils, *The Intellectuals and the Powers*, Chicago: University of Chicago Press, 1972, p. 232.

8 J. Doblin, "Discrimination: the special skills required for seeing, and the curious structure of judgment." *Design Processes Newsletter*, Design Process Laboratory, Institute of Design, Illinois Institute of Technology, Chicago, Illinois, Volume 2, Number 4, 1987, p. 1.

9 P. Bourdieu, *La Distinction*, Paris: Editions du Seuil, 1979.

10 P. Bourdieu, *op. cit.*, p. 14.

11 P. Bourdieu, *op. cit.*, p. 14.

12 P. Bourdieu, *op. cit.*, p. 16.

13 P. Bourdieu, *op. cit.*, pp. 50-52.

14 H. Gans, *Popular Culture and High Culture— an analysis and evaluation of taste*, New York: Basic Books, 1974, p. 71.

15 H. Gans, *op. cit.*, p. 14.

16 P. Willis, *Profane Culture*, London: Routledge and Kegan Paul, 1978, p. 62 *et seq.* and p. 106 *et seq.*

17 W. Lloyd Warner and P. S. Lunt, *The Social Life of a Modern Community*, New Haven: Yale University Press, 1941. W. Lloyd Warner, M. Meeker *et al*, *Social Class in America*, Chicago: Science Research Associates, 1944

18 See Chapter 1, Note 27.

19 The account of Italian Renaissance art in H. Wolflin, *Classic Art*, Oxford: Phaidon, 1959, centres on the treatment of just five great masters—Leonardo, Michelangelo, Raphael, Fra Bartolomeo, and Andrea del Sarto.

20 E. H. Gombrich, "The Social History of Art" in *Meditations on a Hobby Horse*, London: Phaidon Press, 1963, p. 86.

21 *Oxford Dictionary of Classical Literature*, compiled and edited by P. Harvey, Oxford: Clarendon Press, p. 418. See also K. Gilbert and H. Kuhn, *A History of Esthetics*, London: Thames and Hudson, 1956, pp. 97-99.

22 Pliny the Elder, *Chapters on the History of Art*, K. Jex-Blake and E. Sellers (Eds.), Chicago: Ares Publishers, 1982.

23 The Rembrandt Research Project has reduced the canon of the artist's works which are regarded by contemporary scholars as authenic by half! For a discussion on the idea of a canon see E. H. Gombrich and Q. Bell, "Canons and Values in the Visual Arts—a Correspondence" in E. H. Gombrich, *Ideals and Idols*, Oxford: Phaidon Press, 1979, p. 167. The perceptual processes by which styles are gradually perceived differently in the light of new emerging images is discussed in greater detail in Chapter 7.

24 E. H. Gombrich, *op. cit.*, p. 167, continues the discussion of whether there can be an absolute standard of excellence or whether standards are merely relative, a theme of his Romanes Lecture, "Art History and the Social Sciences" in *Ideals and Idols*, Oxford: Phaidon Press, 1979.

25 See S. Bayley (author and editor), *Taste—an Exhibition about Values in Design*, Boilerhouse Project, Victoria and Albert Museum, 1983.

26 For a description of the use of stylometrics in literature see R. A. Wisbey, *The Computer in Literary and Linguistic Research*, Cambridge: Cambridge University Press, 1971 and J. Spencer (Ed.), *Linguistics and Style*, Oxford: Oxford University Press, 1964.

27 There have been drastic changes in the size and content of the recognized *œuvre* of Rembrandt. See S. Alpers, *Rembrandt's Enterprise—The Studio and the Market*, London: Thames and Hudson, 1988. The invention by Bernard Berenson of the entirely fictious 'Amico di Sandro'—a supposed working colleague of Botticelli, with a similar but ostensibly different style—is a notorious example of the pitfalls which attend the use of connoisseurship alone in defining the boundaries of a canon.

28 It is important to note that this boundary is statistical. Canons are good examples of so-called 'fuzzy' concepts, defined from the centre with a scale of diminishing typicality or 'belonging' towards the fuzzy boundary. Stylometrics may however diminish the fuzziness somewhat and, in many cases, that is well worth the effort. An easy introduction to the topic of concepts and their representation is I. Roth and J. P. Frisby, *Perception and Representation—a cognitive approach*, Milton Keynes: Open University Press, 1966, especially Chapters 5, 6 and 7 and notes. An example of how the fuzziness of verbal colour concepts can be measured is given in Jhy-Ping Hsu and Tsao-Hung Wei, "Classification of Colours through a Fuzzy Statistical Experiment." *Colour Research and Applications*, Volume 14, Number 2, 1989, p. 64 *et seq.* In principle this approach could be extended to other fuzzy concepts including style.

29 For details of work in this area see the CHART (Computers in the History of Art) Newsletter, Department of the History of Art, Birkbeck College, London.

30 The work of Charles Jencks has been influential in categorizing recent architectural styles. See C. Jencks, *The Language of Post Modern Architecture*, London: Academy Editions, 1978.

31 *Architects' Journal*, 20 January 1982, p. 45. The rejoinder by D. Capon appeared in *Architects' Journal*, 17 February 1982, p. 24.

32 E. Leach, *Levi-Strauss*, London: Fontana, 1970.

33 C. Jencks, "History as Myth" in C. Jencks and G. Baird, *Meaning in Architecture*, London: Barrie and Rockliffe, The Cresset Press, 1969, p. 145.

34 P. Bourdieu, *op. cit.*, p. 31.

35 For example see A. Hauser, *Social History of Art*, London: Routledge and Kegan Paul, 1951.

36 E. H. Gombrich, *In Search of Cultural History*, Oxford: Clarendon Press, 1967.

37 Bernstein's many essays on this topic are collected in B. Bernstein, *Class, Codes and Social Control* (3 Volumes), London: Routledge and Kegan Paul, 1975.

38 B. Bernstein, *op. cit.*, Volume 1, p. 223.

39 M. Douglas, *Natural Symbols*, London: Barrie and Jenkins, p. 77 *et seq.*

40 The terms 'organic' and 'mechanical' solidarity were first used by E. Durckheim in his review of A. Schaeffle's article, "Bau und Leben des Sozialen Korpers" (1885). The concepts were developed in his *Introduction to the Sociology of the Family*, 1888. His thought converged on that of F. Tonnies whose *Gemeinschaft und Gesellschaft* he reviewed in 1889. See M. Traugott (Ed.), *E. Durckeim on Institutional Analysis*, Chicago: University of Chicago Press, 1978.

41 M. Douglas, *op. cit.*, p. 84.

42 M. Douglas, *op. cit.*

43 The issues and evidence were reviewed most clearly by A. D. Edwards, *Language and Social Class*, London: Heineman, 1976, p. 81 *et seq.*

44 G. E. Eastehope, A. Bell and J. Wilkes, "Bernstein's Sociology of the School". *Research Intelligence*, July 1975.

45 For example H. Rosen, *Language and Class*, Bristol: Falling Water Press, 1972.

46 W. Labov, "The Logic of Non-Standard English" in P. Giglioli (Ed.), *Language and Social Context*, Harmondsworth: Penguin Press, 1972.

47 F. Stuart Chapin, *The Measurement of Social Status using a Social Status Scale*, Minnesota: University of Minnesota Press, 1933. D. Chapman, *The Home and Social Status*, London: Routledge and Kegan Paul, 1955. Exceptions include the study by E. O. Laumann and J. S. House, "Living Room Styles and Social Attributes" in E. O. Laumann, P. M. Siegel and R. W. Hodges (Eds.), *The Logic of Social Hierarchies*, Chicago: Markham Publishing Company, 1970, p. 189.

48 P. Bourdieu, *op. cit.*, p. 587.

49 P. Bourdieu, *op. cit.*, p. 117 *et seq.*

50 P. Bourdieu, *op. cit.*, p. 140.

51 P. Bourdieu, *op. cit.*, p. 191.

52 J. S. Dusenberry, *Income, Savings and the Theory of Consumer Demand*, Cambridge, Mass: Harvard University Press, p. 19 *et seq.*

53 P. Bourdieu, *op. cit.*, p. 198

54 See R. Merton, "Reference Group Theory and Social Mobility" in R. Bendix and S. M. Lipset (Eds.), *Class, Status, Power*, London: Routledge and Kegan Paul, 1970, p. 510, and more generally, *Social Theory and Social Structure*, New York: Free Press. Also, W. G. Runciman, *Relative Deprivation and Social Justice—a study of attitudes to inequality in 20th century England*, London: Routledge and Kegan Paul.

55 P. Bourdieu, *op. cit.*, p. 201 *et seq.* For a discussion of the high status attributed to those who acquire negative cultivation see E. Goffman, "Symbols of Class Status." *British Journal of Sociology*, 12, 1951, p. 294.

56 D. Berlyne, *Conflict, Arousal, Curiosity*, New York: McGraw-Hill, 1960, p. 200.

57 P. Bourdieu, *op. cit.*, p. 293.

58 P. Bourdieu, *op. cit.*, pp. 275-277.

6. High Art, Big Design . . .
and What Sells

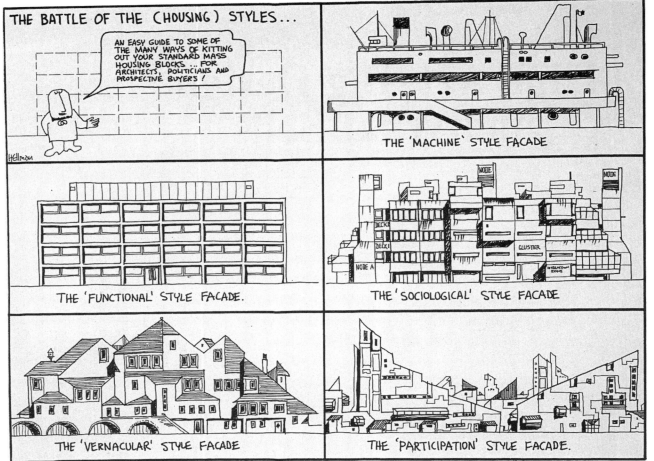

6.1 *Louis Hellman's* The Battle of the (Housing) Styles. *Hellman's acid caricatures of current styles which professional architects (us) consider appropriate for mass housing (them) point out the gap between popular desires and the images that the professionals think they need.*

Legitimacy, quality and value

Ostensibly, modern consumer societies are both open and pluralistic. They are open in the sense that all social roles (and the life style obligations which go with them) are supposed to be available to those with talents and energy. They are pluralistic in that many different subcultures are considered to be tolerated, even respected. In practice neither of these claims is true. Many social roles and, therefore, particular life styles, are only accessible to those with certain kinds of economic and cultural capital. Moreover, not all life styles are equally valued. One particular life style, together with its appropriate consumption package, is universally prized. This is the upper middle class life style normally only accessible to those with sharply rising resource trajectories. In closed societies, its adoption by upstarts is prevented by means of exclusive customs and taboos (supported on occasion by sumptuary laws). However, in open societies, this life style is universally promoted as the only 'proper' or 'decent' one. The Taste of the dominant class is promoted as the only legitimate Taste. Bourgeois life styles are held out as the universal exemplar for all. Therefore, those that do not conform to this pattern are regarded as illegitimate or vulgar. Between the decent and the vulgar are those who aspire to legitimate culture but who have yet to be accepted. They are regarded as pretentious. These qualities—vulgarity and pretentiousness—are in turn projected onto the corresponding life style. Such one-sided judgments need be neither aggressive nor even conscious. Indeed, the concept of legitimacy in culture is so closely bound-up with the life style of the dominant social group that the conflation of the two issues is unnoticed, buried deep in language itself.[1]

The first canons of literature were drawn up by an early cultural élite. Interestingly, the word 'canon' in Greek is itself a homonym or pun. In Greek, 'kanon' means a ruler or measuring stick.[2] The verb 'kanonikos' is to measure with a ruler. Hence, the first textbook on proportion in sculpture by Polycleitos was called by him, *The Canon*.[3] However, even at this time the word signified in its other sense of 'to rule'—to regulate in the sense of to make the rules, to control or dominate. So familiar is this ambiguity that we often forget that a ruler is a pun. No doubt this metaphorical extension dates from earliest civilizations. Those who ruled controlled the distribution of significant goods, notably land, by measurement. In Latin, the same metaphor is seen in the words *regula* or *norma*. Indeed, many other words involving standards of judgment and assertions of legitimacy in the field of Taste convey this double meaning.

The several senses of the word 'canon' have drifted apart in Modern English. There is the abstract sense concerned with authenticity and quality within a particular corpus—'a standard of judgment or authority, a test or criterion or means of discrimination' —which is still commonplace.[4] There is also that sense more overtly concerned with social control which is nowadays used only in the language of the church. Yet these two senses still endure and often fuse—especially in critical discourse. This elision plays an important part in enabling those from the dominant social group to assert their particular life styles as the only true and authentic ones, while persuading both themselves and others that these represent detached and disinterested standards of value. Rulers thus set the rules. This is true of good Taste, the rules for 'correct' consumption, which are framed, not overtly as prescriptions, but covertly as canons. Quality and legitimacy are thus conflated. Particular artists—for example, Mozart, Michelangelo or Chippendale—are not only supreme in quality but are considered the truest examples of their particular art. From the perspective of the dominant social group, all other works are seen as corrupt or deficient versions of the 'good'. Those who inhabit the opposite pole of the social space rarely share this view, not because they are unable to perceive that such works are great, but because they do not make the conflation of quality with truth or legitimacy embodied in the concept of a canon.

From the earliest days of large-scale marketing—an inevitable consequence of large-scale production—strenuous efforts have been made to equate quality in goods with the consumer preferences of the quality. In this way, goods can be given a symbolic value in excess of that which could be derived from mere function. Consumers have been only too willing to pay. Josiah Wedgwood was a key figure in this process.[5] He usually appears in histories of design as a pioneer of modern ceramic manufacturing techniques and the enlightened patron of artists such as John Flaxman who produced the designs for many of the wares. Wedgwood is, at the very least, a pioneer of modern marketing. It is to him that we owe a great deal of our understanding of the relationships between markets for a given type of design imagery and particular socioeconomic groups.

Following precedent in other areas, Wedgwood went all out to obtain aristocratic patronage for his new products. This social group

6.2 The Pegasus Vase *by Josiah Wedgwood, jasper ware modelled by Flaxman after a Greek vase in the British Museum. Presented to the museum by Wedgwood in 1786. Wedgwood established his reputation with characteristic pieces. The presence of works of this kind in the national museum acted as a powerful endorsement of Wedgwood's reputation.*

followed the monarch. Wedgwood began by contriving the commissioning by the British Crown of complete services of massive size, thereby impressing kings and queens in other European countries. He succeeded in this as a result of skilful lobbying and the exploitation of personal contacts with the court. He then made sure that the facts of this patronage were widely advertised by means of display in purpose built premises in the centre of fashionable London.

At this stage the exclusiveness of the clientele was stressed. Pains were taken to ensure that his Soho gallery in London avoided the

6.3 *Josiah Wedgwood's* Queen's Ware *of the 'Lag and Feather' design*, circa *1790. The name was authorized by Queen Charlotte in 1765 and served as a powerful marketing tool for what was in modern parlance an exclusive 'brand'.*

stigma of being seen as a mere shop. Penetration of aristocratic circles was soon complete. However, Wedgwood's new assembly line for the manufacture of pottery produced wares in such numbers that the aristocratic market soon became saturated. Wedgwood had to look to other markets, and where better than to the new upper middle class thrown up by expanding trade and industry. Once a given ware had been in production for some time, the initial investment, both in the moulds and other physical plant and in the financial and artistic contributions, had been paid off. He could afford to sell cheaply and in high volume. But how?

By coining names such as *Queen's Ware* for his new ceramic bodies, Wedgwood skillfully placed brandnames suggestive of royal patronage into everyday circulation.[6] He could now offer goods which had previously been the exclusive preserve of the aristocrat to a new and potentially enormous public. Wedgwood thus pioneered the technique of trading downmarket in a society divided by a hierarchy of class. Nowadays, Wedgwood is in turn a name suggestive of high quality and ancient lineage combined.

The dominant social group today consists of, not only those with what Pierre Bourdieu called economic capital, but also those who possess cultural capital—artists, academics and others from the curator-professions. Their voices have been the loudest in attempting to establish and promote good design in the field of consumer goods. There has always been a tension between the intelligentsia and its patrons which is made explicit in the rivalry to promote canons of excellence in the world of goods. Those who were born into a world of legitimate goods (legitimate because they were the possessions of those who were themselves legitimate rulers) had no need of the academic activity of classification and comparison with which the philosophers of Taste sought to define their subject. Rulers confer legitimacy by mere possession. They have no need of rules, merely an ability to perceive a certain *je ne sais quoi*. A visit to any downtown shopping area or bourgeois appartment will show that this ancient dichotomy still prevails today. (Bourdieu sarcastically uses the old eighteenth century distinction between *les doctes* and *les mondains* to underline this point.[7])

In fact, obtaining and maintaining agreement on a canonical set of examples is vastly more difficult in the field of design for everyday artefacts than in the case of works of art. The number of objects with some claim on our attention among the plethora of industrially produced consumer goods is infinitely greater. Daily, secular use of our domestic goods leads us to a more fickle judgment of their merit. Fashions and fads expire far more quickly in design than in even the most transient *avant-garde* art. For some art historians these difficulties are insuperable, leading them to deny that the history of design is history at all

195

in the serious sense that the history of art is. Certainly, it is difficult to compare the histories of, for example, quattrocento wall-tombs with 1950s table-lamps. Nevertheless, despite these protestations, attempts are constantly made to define—and then defend—a canon of design. It is a natural preoccupation of museum directors who would like to extend their historical collection towards the present. We see today in the history of design, a repetition of that process of 'professionalization' which took place in the study of art during the nineteenth century when collectors and amateurs gave way to curators and scholars. Today, 'inadequate' connoisseurship and 'personal' Tastes once more dissolve into a canon defined under the influence of comparison, criticism and cataloguing. Museums build up design collections which their keepers try to complete. Thematic exhibitions endorse the museum curators' judgments. Once all this reaches the textbook stage we have the historical tradition laid down for design just as it was for art. Alongside high art we now have what I call by analogy, *big design*.

As far as the applied arts of the remoter past are concerned, this history is comfortably similar to that of the history of pure art, not least because most artefacts are hand-made craft items, often unique and made for specific patrons. In more recent times, the differences have become much sharper. When one particular object—for example, a teacup—is selected for a modern museum's collection, there may already be millions in circulation. In these cases, the modern museum can create canonical works—'contemporary classics'—simply by exhibiting them! Such is the authority and prestige of the great museum that endorsement by selection is enough to give almost any object

6.4 *Canons in creation. In modern museums even ephemeral goods are treated with the reverence normally reserved for major art objects thus legitimizing their inclusion into the company of the great.*

a reputation as a key work in some particular historical story.

In the United Kingdom, the Victoria and Albert Museum has this power. The Museum of Modern Art (MOMA) in the USA can also create masterpieces of modern design at will. Writers of design history thereafter document their sequences from museum catalogues! Unfortunately, the judgment of curators in the field of modern design is both cautious and capricious. Victor Papanek makes much of the fact that out of 397 twentieth century classics selected by the Museum of Modern Art in New York in 1934 only one, a range of chemical glassware, survives in use today. Similar results followed later exhibitions in 1939 and 1950. As Papanek notes, 'When we are dealing with the Taste-making apparat of the Museum of Modern Art, a score of three successes and 510 misses is far from reassuring.'[8]

Despite this appalling record, the preferences of the dominant social group, especially those with high cultural capital, are still officially promoted as the exemplars of good design. Characterized by an asceticism deriving from negative cultivation (itself often a question of making virtue out of necessity) and

6.5 *An alliance with rock music gives designers an opportunity of wide exposure in lifestyle magazines. Jon Wealleans flat for the manager of pop group* Led Zeppelin *shows how charismatic consumers act as the flag-carriers for advanced styles.*

emphasizing internal formal relationships, often formal minutiae (the product *par excellence* of the academic's trade of classification and analysis), good design is in striking contrast to that prevailing in the popular marketplace for consumer goods.

By virtue of that conflation of legitimacy and quality implicit in the notion of a canon—especially a canon physically embodied in a national collection of artefacts—what is not canonical is by implication bad design. To avoid reaction from populist sentiment, the starkness of this cultural exclusion is frequently camouflaged by more or less irrelevant references to performance criteria deriving from the technical specifications of goods. From the viewpoint of the academics in the cultural élite, bad Taste is seen, not as Bourdieu's 'refusal', but as a deficit, an unfortunate disadvantage or deprivation, calling for remedial efforts to spread enlightenment. This is not always cynical. Many individuals, for

example Herbert Read, have devoted their lives to cultural proselytizing at considerable personal cost. In recent decades, this effort has received government support. Considerable outlays of public money have been disbursed to support the efforts of education departments in the various agencies (such as the Design Council) which operate in this field.

There are obvious parallels here with earlier efforts at remedial education programmes for deprived social groups, for example those directed towards urban blacks in the USA during the 1960s. It is difficult to assess the impact of these efforts. Good design would appear to be more abundant now than in the days when Nikolaus Pevsner lamented the state of industrial art in Britain. On the other hand, IKEA and Habitat notwithstanding, good design is still a small fraction of the total market. Indeed, even in ostensibly successful modern design countries, such as Finland, the market for good Taste may be declining in favour of bad reproduction and traditional styles. In any event, propaganda for good design is often more effective when designers themselves act as charismatic consumers. Trendy designers frequently infiltrate the publicity apparatus surrounding stars of films, television, pop music and fashion. Publicity photographs of fashionable designers' pads in the mass media are an effective generator of imitation and the consequent diffusion of a particular concept of good design. (This version is usually considerably more eclectic and romantic than that favoured by official good Taste.)

Given the complexity of the constant shifts in concepts of quality among the dominant groups, and their equally complex structural relationships with the concepts of other

197

6.6 Wassily *armchair by Marcel Breuer, the archetype of Bauhaus style. This never widely popular chair has gyrated widely in price over the six decades since it was designed.*

groups, it is obvious that an adequate description of value needs to embrace considerably more than mere emulation and exclusion within a linear hierarchy of social class (*pace* Thorstein Veblen). Even using Bourdieu's rather simplistic mapping of life style spaces on to the social space, we can see that movement through the social space is more complex than mere vertical mobility. Over time our social trajectory can be sideways or diagonal as we exchange one kind of capital for another.

As we progress along a particular social trajectory so we move congruently through the corresponding regions of homologous life style spaces. These will be defined in terms of the particular cultural artefacts available at each moment in time. A comprehensive theory of fashion would depict, not images trickling down a hierarchy of social groups, but individuals and groups moving past evolving sets of goods in each particular region of a given life style space. At a given moment in time, different sets of goods, by virtue of their structural relationship to other goods previously encountered, will appear as canonical and hence act as salient indexes of quality for each social group. Value, in an economic sense, depends on the fluctuations in saliency for each group. The focus of saliency is often very narrow. Goods can cease to be salient—go out of fashion—over comparatively small ranges of features. Conversely, previously unnoticed

6.7 *Down-market imitations of the original Bauhaus designs abound now that the copyright has expired. Poor construction (the wicker seat is now machine-made in one piece and is impossible to replace) has meant that Bauhaus soon comes to signify 'cheap and nasty'.*

nuances can suddenly become prized and hence increase the value of goods. The vagaries of the art market and the market for antique furniture have often been remarked.[9] Price fluctuations in cultural artefacts are subject to constant scrutiny once they become vehicles for investment and speculation. There are well-defined secondhand markets for goods of every kind, however humble.

Distance from saliency among the dominant social group is the prime determinant of price. Michael Thompson has vividly described the fluctuations of value which mark the cycles of use, rejection and reuse which transform everyday objects from quality items to rubbish and back again.[10] Such transformations are social in origin and can only be understood as part of the migrations of people in the social space. There is no exemption from social revaluation, even in objects which are strictly intended for utilitarian purposes.

The case of the famous Marcel Breuer chair—*Wassily*—is instructive. Originally designed at the German Bauhaus in 1926, it was envisaged for mass production using the then revolutionary new material, chromium-plated steel. However, the chair was never really popular as it was considered uncomfortable to

sit in and was soon out of production. Its worth was merely its secondhand value, reflecting a demand for the originals as archetypes of early Modernism by 'in-touch' designers or architects. In the 1960s, an Italian firm, Cassina, recommenced production with hide seats instead of the original canvas. This time they were purchased as exclusive icons for top executives and their price increased by over threefold to about £200 over the following ten years. In the 1970s, 'knock off' versions began to appear. These were slightly different in scale and detail to evade the copyright restrictions. Value-engineering dictated the use of cheaper chrome and the new, reconstituted, leather. Shorn of other characteristic detail they became dramatically cheap, coming down at one point to about £30! Lawsuits were fought between the imitators and the owners of the copyright for the original designs. Along with Breuer's *Cesca* cantilever dining chair they changed from being high class hardware for the executive suite or office foyer to symbols of suburban domestic modern living. Fifty years after the conception of the original massmarketed steel chair, *Wassily* finally achieved a modest success in that target area. It was only fashionable among the lower middle classes for a short while and is now once again found only in the upper middle circles. Doubtless its latterday owners neither know nor care that it was named after Wassily Kandinsky, long dead artist colleague of Breuer in the 1920s.

Designers and their colleagues are in a good position to profit from the price fluctuations of goods which derive from social changes. By virtue of their professional acquaintance with changing symbols, they can adhere at an earlier stage to a new trend, buying before the market has registered a new vogue and prices outrun their resources. Invariably, given time, economic capital will dominate cultural capital. But curator-professionals are in a good position to keep ahead of price increases as their knowledge of the symbolic traffic between emergent and declining social groups facilitates an opportunistic purchasing strategy. Taken over a period when, as typical upper middle class professionals, they enjoy a rising resource trajectory this opportunism enables them to enjoy a life style in terms of durable consumption goods that is far higher than their actual income would suggest.

In contrast, the dominated social group—roughly identified with the working class—is generally deprived of both economic and cultural capitals. They have less money but (crucially) less knowledge of dominant culture and its developing history. What to the curator-professional appears as a plenitude of different symbols each claiming legitimacy from one dominant group or other, to the uninformed appears as one single monolithic life style. Decency to them is all that is sponsored by the dominant culture. Consequently, they are unable to make the differentiations that would enable them to benefit from the anticipation of price fluctuations arising from social change. Combined with a flat resource trajectory which gives no advantage to a purchasing strategy of gradual upgrading, their perception of a cultural uniformity among the higher social groups condemns the lower social groups to the purchase of expensive but vague imitations of the dominant life style. Hence those baneful categories of the popular furniture store—the 'traditional' that derives from no known historical tradition but doffs its hat to them all and the 'contemporary' which owes no identifiable debt to any current design or designer. It is not only in a strictly functional sense that 'the poor pay more' (Caplovitz).[11]

Professional ideology and good design

What then can we deduce from our previous account of the structure of curator-professions (including design) and of the various reward systems that operate within them? Obviously, there are limits on what can usefully be deduced from any account of social structures. Such deductions from the general to the particular can never be definitive, whether they concern matters of style or the specific content of individual artefacts or works of art. Nevertheless, given our knowledge of people's general behaviour—the so-called *behaviour-maxims*—together with our familiarity with contemporary social structures, we can begin to understand the prevailing ideologies of design. We can thereby account for the pervasive divergences between the images and styles favoured by the curators and those admired by the consumers whom they ostensibly serve. In turn, we can give a more detailed account of Herbert Gans' notion of a creator-orientation (developed from the realm of fiction) and relate it to the world of goods.[12]

Firstly, designers as a group have a vested interest in the processes of symbolic appropriation among consumers (of which the trickle-effect is one example) as it necessitates the continuous marginal differentiation of products. These 'new' products provide the designers' livelihood. However, while the endless marginal differentiation of products may be in the interests of designers as a whole, individual designers and practices may have a stronger interest in reducing marginal differentiation (competing brands and products) or, at any rate, controlling it through the use of product themes or programmes or other generic motifs and devices. This is because genuinely new designs cost time and money to produce. The exigencies of value-engineering bear on new ideas just as they do on new products. Generic concepts enable standard procedures developed by a particular designer or practice to be used and reused so that adequately novel variations can be generated cheaply. In addition, the family resemblances thus produced can easily be recognized by other professionals if not by the layman. This produces a measure of publicity and security in a notoriously uncertain business. Given the competitive nature of professional life it follows that the greatest market-power (and with it prestige and pecuniary rewards) usually goes to those who succeed in imposing their particular generic concepts on the rest. In a sense they set the major agenda which the rest then follow with minor variations until the theme is exhausted. When this happens, the time is ripe for a new stylistic shift which ensures that the process is repeated. Once a powerful design concept is established it is obviously in the interest of everyone to work within it. It gradually becomes the only 'decent' way of doing things.

There is a considerable similarity here with the institutions of scientific research described by Thomas Kuhn.[13] According to Kuhn, so-called 'normal science' involves the progressive expansion and development of the hypothetical implications of a particular master concept or *paradigm*. The paradigm (once it is universally accepted by professional scientists) provides the leading metaphor, the extensions of which suggest sensible and

proper problems on which the 'normal' scientist works. Competition among these scientists is inspired by the esteem granted to the increasingly well-crafted and finely honed solutions to normal problems. It is this progressively focussed craftsmanship which ensures the systematic exploration and eventual exhaustion of the paradigm.

Craftsmanship, and the pride and satisfaction it creates, is a major theme of all professional institutions, including those of the curator-professions. In preindustrial societies, craftsmanship and the social structures of the guilds which maintained it were often able to guarantee a man a certain minimum independence from the untrammelled workings of the marketplace. However, once societies became industrialized, the ruthless division of labour destroyed these time-honoured defences, devaluing work into fragmented and meaningless toil. Only the professional groups have inherited a certain independence from the marketplace and a degree of control over the planning of their working lives. It is among these groups that craftsmanship is most admired. Indeed, it has become a leading component of the ideology of professionalism, even in professions such as design where direct involvement in manual labour is rare. (A superfluous craftsmanship in designers' drawings is universally esteemed among the professionals however.) Vicarious participation in manual craftsmanship is probably a significant factor in the romantic enthusiasm of many designers for what I have called the *tool-aesthetic*—the elevation of the appearances of hand-tools and primitive machinery as the paradigm for the imagery of *all* designed objects. On the other hand, those whose working lives are dominated by the division of labour and who are forced to perform fragmented and trivial tasks are notoriously unimpressed by the tool-aesthetic, however elaborate the technological support equipment at their workplace.

Those who have newly emerged into a fully professionalized activity such as design see in the craftsman's tool a pregnant metaphor for many activities of daily life that are not usually related in any way to work, producing slogans such as 'a house is a machine for living-in' (Le Corbusier)[14] and, by extension, the idea that a chair is a 'tool' for sitting on. They hold that, like simple tools, familiar consumption goods such as houses and chairs should express their function in simple and expressive components which are direct analogies to blades, handles and other similar devices (Plate 13). In this respect the professional is unique. To most consumers, the tool (as a preindustrial craftsman would have conceived it) is a meaningless concept when applied to consumption goods. For them, the freedom which the professional finds in work can only be found in leisure. This is where the industrialized proletariat are at one with the leisure class in both its aristocratic and bourgeois versions. The consumption goods of the working man embody work in the form of expressive symbols of idleness, of easement from toil, not the mastery of it as expressed in the form of good tools (Plate 14).

Only in hobbies (which are a kind of quasi-craftwork distinguished by personal autonomy over its extent and content) does the concept of craftsmanship as an essential, integrating factor in the good life lead to the connoisseurship of tools. Only, for example, in their fishing or skiing equipment, pleasure boats or sports gear do we find among the working class the love of a good tool that the

6.8 *Austerity in the peasant cottages of the Mediterranean littoral provided a potent source of inspiration for the austere images of Modernists such as Le Corbusier.*

curator-professional would wish on them everywhere, even at their ease in their homes.

Another significant factor which arises from the professionalization of expressive symbols comes from the exercise of negative cultivation. Pointing out that in many societies avocational pursuits such as the cultivation of the arts, sports and handicrafts have been accorded high status, Erving Goffman noted that prestige was accorded to experts and to expertise where this was known to require concentrated and single-minded attention over long periods of time.[15] An interesting case arises when this prestige is accorded to the cultivation of Tastes themselves—to connoisseurship. This lies in the quality of restraint, on which so many societies have set a high value. 'Here social use is made of the discipline required to set aside and hold in check, the insignificant stimuli of daily life so that attention may be free to tarry upon distinctions and

6.9 *Mies van der Rohe. Corner detail of faculty building for Illinois Institute of Technology. The rationale for the radical minimal forms of Mies' functionalism came apart when the fire officer insisted on the cladding of the supporting columns with concrete. Mies designed an external steel cladding for the corner post which gives the appearance of a load-bearing column to what is in reality a decorative surface.*

discriminations that would otherwise be overlooked.'[16] Restraint, as we have seen, involves the purposive and studied attenuation of attention from many items routinely embraced under ordinary circumstances. Goffman's example involved Zen philosophy as expressed in the Japanese tea ceremony where selective withdrawal of attention amid simple and austere surroundings enables the free play of the mind to dwell on otherwise overlooked detail, the minutiae of the craquelure on a raku teacup for example.

We have already considered negative cultivation as a mark of prestige within the Euro-

pean tradition of art appreciation. Ernst Gombrich has drawn our attention to the importance given to restraint in the use of expressive language by Roman rhetoricians such as Cicero.[17] During the early Renaissance such sentiments were echoed by Leone Battista Alberti. Later, Giorgio Vasari, noted that newly 'professionalized' quattrocento painters had already begun to despise rich materials—and even the Pope who was seduced by them. While, in the eighteenth century, Johan Winckelmann discerned in the stark white remains of Greek sculpture and architecture a simplicity and restraint expressive of calm grandeur and nobility.[18] These qualities became the hallmarks of the neo-Classical style that superceded the elaborations of the rococo which were in turn perceived as frivolous.

Of course, restraint is not reserved merely for upper class pursuits and Tastes. Austere white forms are found in many peasant cultures and have been much admired by designers as symbols of a dignified way of life. And simplicity, even ruthless austerity, has been very much the touchstone of good Taste among curator groups in the present century, especially those concerned with design. Our twentieth century equivalent to Zen might perhaps be encapsulated in the *dictum* (borrowed from Flaubert) of the architect Mies van der Rohe—'God is in the details'. Certainly, the attenuated and symmetrical long-range order in the architecture of the Miesian tradition does enable the mind to dwell on minutiae that would otherwise be overlooked—for example, the famous detailing of the steel frames so often photographed.[19] Negative cultivation in one form or another has been the central theme and inspiration of many important twentieth century aesthetic movements including purism and minimalism. Particularly in their most radical forms these movements have little appeal to most consumer groups. Without the sanctions and supports of religion, the spiritually demanding exertions of such a disciplined withdrawal of attention are rarely practised except in élite groups. Conversely, religion in the form of a fundamentalist Lutheran puritanism has been influential in the cultures which have given rise to the so-called classics of simplicity, notably in North America (Shaker furniture), Holland (the de Stijl movement), Germany, (the Bauhaus and later Ulm) and Scandinavia (Nordic restraint, a byword among designers and often attributed to a cold climate, almost certainly owes more to the strength of Protestant beliefs than it does to snow-covered birch forests or frozen lakes!).

Established institutions for a particular curator-profession actively foster a conscious awareness of the history of the profession—especially in education. Novices are acquainted with certain valued traditions and the ways in which earlier masters excelled. Within these traditions, competition and rivalry among professionals may be justified by appeal to certain master works or famous forbears. Polarizing issues within the context of normal professional life naturally arise as preferred dimensions of rivalry, dimensions along which 'one-upmanship' or 'topping' may occur. Especially in mature curator-professions—for example, architecture—a large penumbra of fringe activities develops including education, the publication of books and periodicals and critical enquiry within the framework of meetings and conferences. Within these essentially impractical activities which yet relate to the central concerns of the profession, negative

6.10 *Formal austerity and the refined use of a single material are typical of the work of many Nordic designers. Sauna by Antti Nurmesniemi, Finland. (See also Plate 15.)*

cultivation itself becomes the object of competition and rivalry. In a purely theoretical formulation, for example, an ideas competition in a didactic journal directed at other professionals employed almost exclusively as teachers, negative cultivation can be taken, by the processes of competitive topping, to the very limits of abstraction. Following this, practical realizations in the real world come to be seen as, at best, partial and incomplete versions of the pure formulation embodied in theory. From this perspective, the 'complexities and contradictions' of ordinary consumers seem bizarre exaggerations and excesses, superfluities in need of explanation and justification.[20] Needless to say, all the different parties regard their particular level of restraint—or lack of it—as entirely normal and proper.

Negative cultivation, the selective attenuation of attention, is the essential prerequisite for the development of elaborate thematic construction. Without it, the cacophony of

204

6.11 *Architect Allan Philips' home is a rigorous and didactic exercise in austerity and the use of surprising triangular geometry to make a statement.*

stimuli at the edges of attention would be so great that specific themes would have to be aggressively obvious to be noticed. Tunes that need to be played loudly to overcome the background noise must be simple as well, hence those who have yet to acquire the power of negative cultivation are considered by those that practice it as lacking in descrimination and having motifs that are course, crude and obvious. Those who have acquired the power of negative cultivation also have the possibility of that subtle combination of negative and positive cultivation we have called *sophistication*. Once established professional institutions exist to sanction and support particular symbolic usages, then licensed competition

among curator-professionals becomes channelled into particular forms and specific subjects which can only be appreciated by the initiated, often only by those who are versed in the theory and practice of the professional activity at its highest level. Conceptual elegance, formal refinement, structural rigour, boldness or subtlety in the integration of symbol and nuanced ambiguity of expression, in general that controlled balance of negative and positive cultivation embodied in sophistication, all may be savoured by the cognoscenti for themselves. The professionals are thus the very ones who learn to benefit most from that regime of fasting and feasting—the peaky distribution of stimulation which David

205

Berlyne recommended as the optimum balance between pleasure and comfort (Plate 16). Not surprisingly, the institutions of the curator-professions promote and sustain a highly elaborated or private language based on a specialized use of what are ostensibly public symbols. Within this private universe of discourse, all manner of combinations may be allowed—we may have anti-art, or even anti-design. Those who are accustomed to this private language often find more conventional usages weak or less meaningful however coarse or crude they seem to the otherwise refined! Popular Taste, when savoured by those accustomed to pungency and austerity, seems by contrast flavourless or bland—a critical terminology quite meaningless to those whose preferences are so described.

In general, the regulated competition of curator-professionals takes place within a reward system that accords high prestige to those who deploy what is called a *hard-edge* version of the currently approved repertoire. A hard-edge to a particular Taste implies that prominence or saliency of particular aspects is achieved by a negative cultivation of other aspects which has been taken to the extent of an aggressive indifference so that the whole appears *abrasive* or *raw*—qualities which are much admired by the initiated (Plate 17). (A milder indifference to wider considerations would be regarded as *cool*.) Again, this is a critical vocabulary, incomprehensible to those who are not part of professional coteries.

Considering all these themes together, it is not difficult to see why there is an abiding tendency for the forms favoured by designers to converge on a mainstream imagery that may be regarded as a generalized neo-Classicism. Neo-Classicism in nineteenth century architec-

6.12 *Rojii Suzuki, Edge Building, Tokyo, Japan. Ruthless austerity in the concrete finishes is combined with surreal 'impractical' elements such as the staircase that goes nowhere but simply vanishes into a wedge-shaped split in the facade.*

ture involved the restatement of Greek style architecture, particularly that of the classical Doric Temple. However, the sacred imagery was adapted to suit secular purposes and to express feelings quite different from religious awe or devotion. Following its adoption as the house style of the French Revolution, neo-Classicism became the favourite idiom for the expression of the power of the state (or even of individuals). Conceived as the embodiment of reason, it was particularly favoured for legal and administrative architecture and civic buildings such as town halls, universities, libraries and museums—in general, for all solemn and dignified social purposes. Such functions, however, usually required specialized and complex accommodation quite unknown to Greek temple builders and thereby entailing different detailed planning. The architecture of the temple provided a frontal colonnade for use as a dominant symbolic facade, axial plano-symmetry for the major spaces and extreme simplicity in the overall large-scale form.[21] Equally important in this secular reinterpretation of classic temple architecture was the large separation in the

206

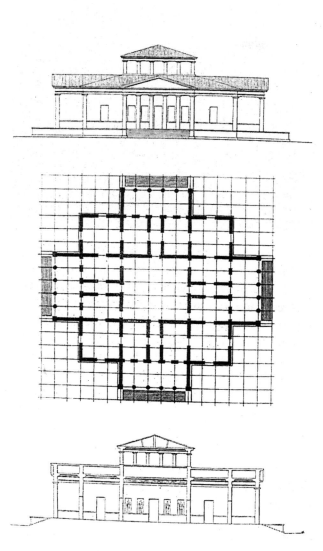

6.13 What came to be known as beaux arts *concepts (axial symmetry and geometric rigor of the large scale form and localized decoration) are epitomized in the great collections of plans and elevations of historic prototypes by the architect J. N. L. Durand.*

found in the Greek temple including doors, windows and staircases. Without specific prototypes to follow, neo-Classical architecture resorted to a radical simplification and removal of the decorative adornment which had been exploited in previous styles. What remained was austerely geometric. Usually the materials were modern, stone was cut by machine and plaster immaculately replicated by mould, adding to the starkness and unusual clarity of outline. It was also an architecture conceived, not as the Greeks originally built it—colourful and dramatic—but as Winckelmann had spoken of it—monochromatic and chaste.

In the two centuries since the beginning of neo-Classicism there has been endless repetition and variation of this particular range of devices within the overall formal paradigm. In modern times, these have been expressed in ever simpler and starker terms ending in a plain, undecorated geometry echoing the original temple only in the formal closure of the overall form and the deep structure relationship of parts to whole. Particularly since the Bauhaus, the conflation of architectural philosophy with that of product design has meant the wholesale adaptation of the neo-Classical formal organization to other uses. So that one may now speak of a neo-Classical radio set or chair, as well as a building. It has become a favourite idiom for a wide range of product types with which professional designers now earn their living. The austerity well suits those educated in the ways of negative cultivation, especially in its contemporary form with an emphasis on abstract spatial relationships. Assertive prominence of a large scale bespeaks a determined and immediately obvious adherence to a formal paradigm conventionally expressive of reason and dignity.

hierarchy of scale between the dominant symmetrical statement of the building as a whole and the next level of detail. Neo-Classical structures had also to accommodate a great variety of particular features which were not

207

6.14 *The Classical forms have been adapted to an infinite variety of new uses since the nineteenth century revival. Stanley Tigerman's new working of the classic idiom houses an electricity substation in downtown Chicago, USA.*

On the other hand, the sharp separation of scale between the overall form and the next level of detail makes it peculiarly suitable for the development of programmes—themes and variations which are easily readable as homologues by the client and his customers. And, of course, from the point of view of ease and cheapness of production, the neo-Classical relationship of parts to wholes is especially conducive to the 'bodywork plus tuning' strategy as one technology can be used to manufacture the large-scale form which can be varied with a tuning of minor additional components plugged in.

This is all far removed from the Hegelian or Marxist deduction of the neo-Classical style as the proper expression of a particular social order. Nevertheless, it is useful to observe that its formal structures, which arise from the confluence of what Capon called the primary triangle of intellectual forces, are particularly congenial to those who, educated into contemporary professional ideology, are faced with the practical problems of earning a living in the cultural marketplace.

Popular, vernacular and pop

The adoption by a dominant social group of simple and austere styles is quite common.

6.15 *Commercial Classicism in furniture. Spanish mass-produced cabinets* 1990.

supposed to have prevailed. (We have seen this tendency in later Roman writers and it has been common ever since.) Where style is borrowed from a contemporary culture, the problem of invidious comparison arises. It is important for the culture of the dominant group that their Tastes are uncorrupted by features drawn from their immediate social inferiors. They would otherwise become *déclassé*. This may only be avoided by borrowing from remote social groups at the antipodes of the social space. Direct comparison with them is so implausible that it may be ignored. Aristocrats or curator-professionals may occasionally play at peasant life in search of stylistic innocence as the supposedly uncorrupted simplicities of poverty-stricken rustics could never seriously damage their status by virtue of its very remoteness from serious comparison (Plate 18). This may be called the 'Marie Antoinette ploy'.

There is a long artistic tradition of adoption of styles from remote cultures. Greek, Roman, Etruscan and Egyptian architecture, African, Asian and Polynesian fetishes, the early paintings of the Italian and Flemish Renaissance—the so-called primitives—have all provided the prototypes for a return to austere styles in art.[22] Occasionally, such adoption of styles has been justified by the theory of a stylistic fall from grace, a catastrophic dissociation of the sensibility ending a supposed 'age of innocence'. Many of the same processes may be observed in design—as it is perceived by the curator-professionals.

Preindustrial artefacts and the utensils of primitive tribes seem to them to possess an unspoiled directness and simplicity, a fact which explains their important place in the prehistory of Modernism in design. Vernacular

Indeed, such periodic symbolic renunciations provide an important series of visible markers—end points of the swinging pendulum of the dialectic of style displayed in all chronological fashion sequences. Although austerity may result from the progressive purification of an existing style within legitimate culture, a return to austerity usually involves the conscious borrowing of forms from styles which are already austere. These may be from remote periods in which simpler ways of life were

6.16 *The deep structure of Classicism remains even when the decorative elements are stripped away and the structure is suspended rather than architectonic. Crown Hall, home of the architecture school, Illinois Institute of Technology, Chicago, USA, Mies van der Rohe.*

(native or domestic) artefacts are carefully distinguished from those manufactured for general consumption which are held to be corrupted by their imitation of the styles of the dominant culture group. No matter how wide their circulation among the peasantry or industrial proletariat, artefacts cannot retain their innocence once they allude to the styles of legitimate culture. A somewhat paradoxical distinction must therefore be drawn between the truly vernacular and the merely popular.[23] Only the former may be imitated as popular culture is merely a corrupt version of legitimate (authentic or true) culture.

Prior to the mid twentieth century such conventional rules sufficed to maintain stylistic boundaries and to direct down-market adoption of styles into the safe channels of the remote and the rustic. In more recent times however, they have been challenged by an aggressive intruder in the form of an institutionalized artistic *avant-garde*. Radically contesting all socially-determined limits to legitimacy in art, the *avant-garde* eventually had no choice (given the competitive processes of topping) but to confront art with anti-art, good Taste with bad Taste, and legitimate or high culture with popular or mediocre culture. This challenge was mounted, not by asserting the equality (or even the supremacy) of popular culture against the claims of high culture, although such populist sentiments are

6.17 *Popular and vernacular. E. Schaefer's account of the rise of Modernism separates out the functional from the merely popular. One of Schaefer's illustrations of the vernacular—the sleigh—and the context from which it was selected, the Art Journal Catalogue of the Great Exhibition.*

ART-JOURNAL ILLUSTRATED CATALOGUE.

The contributions of our fellow-subjects in Canada are not without a considerable portion of interest, but they are chiefly of a character which does not come within the scope of our plan of illustration; indeed, are not of a description to admit of it, even with less limitation. The wealth of Canada lies in her agricultural and mineral productions, of which she contributes to the Exhibition a large variety of examples. Among her textile fabrics are several specimens highly creditable to her manufacturers, and there are some engineering objects worthy of notice, especially a powerful and most elegant fire-

community exhibit no little taste, and spare no expense, to put their carriage and all its appointments, into suitable condition. The

harness of the horses is generally very gay, and beautifully ornamented; while the fur robes in which the riders envelope themselves

to exclude as much as possible the severity of the cold, are often very costly. There are

some choice specimens of all these objects in the Canadian department of the Exhibition,

engine. We have selected, from the few productions that we deem would make effective engravings, a SLEIGH, of elegant proportions, manufactured by

which are worthy of minute inspection. The rides and drives round about Quebec, Montreal,

Toronto, &c., are, during the winter months, quite lively with the showy equipages, and

Mr. J. J. SAURIN, of Quebec. "Sleighing," as it is termed, forms one of the principal amusements of the Canadians of all ranks, who can afford to keep one of any description, and the wealthier part of the

musical with the bells suspended from the heads of the horses. The FURNITURE, also engraved on this page, is manufactured by

Messrs. J. & W. HILTON, of Montreal. They are made of black walnut, boldly carved, the chairs are covered with crimson and gold damask.

211

6.18 *The populist advertising signs of Las Vegas were recognized as a lesson that could be learned from by architect Robert Venturi.* Learning from Las Vegas *is a key work in the retreat from functionalism towards a symbolic and expressive mode of architecture.*

common enough, but by adopting the hitherto despised forms of popular culture as the very subject matter of art itself. The movement which made this final step immediately became dubbed *pop art* or simply *pop*.

This is not the place to retell the history of pop or of how the heroes on both sides of the Atlantic—Hamilton and Paolozzi, Lichtenstein and Warhol and their friends and admirers—changed the course of art history.[24] They asserted that anything can be the subject matter for art, even the mundane and the commercial, even kitsch itself, in fact, especially kitsch. Soup tins, comics, Marilyn Monroe, Jackie Kennedy and Hugh Gaitskell, the 1956 *This is Tomorrow* exhibition and the

alliance with 'big money' rock music, have all been the familiar staple of the culture historian for twenty years. Equally familiar is the spin off into related areas of sixties fashion, decoration and design including Lord Kitchener's Valet and Hung on You, the record sleeve for Sergeant Pepper, the shop front for Granny takes a Trip, leopard skin mini cars and juke boxes auctioned at Christies, paper furniture decorated like Smarties and packaging which looks like a pop painting of packaging. This hugely energetic and disparate movement has achieved a change in the way we look at all our goods, both high and low.

Its ubiquitous technique is irony, in devices of which it is inexhaustible. Yet soup tins or

6.19 *Populist elements in a new post-Modern development in Venice, California, USA. The Disney-like figure in garish plastic wags his leg ceaselessly over the entrance to an otherwise elegant block of shops and apartments.*

malignant in its tone, it was nonetheless a class phenomenon—an aggressive rebellion by scholarship boys against the stuffy and boring upper class establishment which ruled their cultural lives at the time. Reyner Banham is said to have described it as 'The Revenge of the Elementary Schoolboys'. Whatever the subconscious motives, it was clear that by the end of the 1960s, pop had become a highway between the innumerable culture groups that formed what was called the *new class*. And, as John Russell noted, the traffic was, for the first time, two-way. Before that, highbrow had simply provided the cultural plunder needed for commercial reprocessing into lowbrow. Now, while the lower class or user-orientated consumer could swing along with a rock version of Mozart's *G Minor Symphony* in the hit parade, the cultural élite could indulge in artful quotations from kitsch decor or pin up comics. Pop's original source was Dada, the conscious and brutal rejection of established values and beliefs through the rape of hallowed symbols. While less passionate and more cool than Dada, pop's insouciant equivocation and studied ambivalence towards issues of stylistic consistency that had previously been matters of profound moral commitment succeeded no less effectively in the complete rupture of the metaphorical linkage between images and traditional class values.

pin ups were always treated artily (highbrow) even when the superficial message was one of bland acceptance of its lowbrow character. Even when an item of kitsch was physically incorporated into a pop work, some familiar formal device from the world of art provided quotation marks to signal the necessary ambivalence towards the material.

Although, when compared with the American variety, English pop was distinctly less

The pop revolution is surely final. Popular can clearly be transmuted into pop *ad infinitum*. But what about the reverse process? Can pop ever become popular?[25] This question has harassed a good many architects, designers and artists over the years since the heyday of pop. There is no doubting the influence of pop on advertising and the mass media. But what of the marketplace? A great deal of theoretical argument and rhetoric concerning the conversion of pop into popular has circulated among professional coteries, most especially in education. Some of this has a vaguely populist (often left-wing) inspiration. Most persuasive has been the writings of the American architect Robert Venturi who has combined the subtle analysis of symbol systems with a sharp eye for concrete visual examples culled from contemporary popular culture in the United States. Two famous titles—*Complexity and Contradiction in Architecture* and *Learning from Las Vegas*—give the flavour.[26] It was Venturi's assertion that 'Billboards are nearly alright!'. Architects, he said, should not build isolated statements that registered only the slogan 'I am a monument!'. They should concentrate instead on providing a high standard of 'ordinariness'. In this way, they could resume their place among popular culture and be genuinely 'popular'. Most people, especially designers and architects whose living depends on it, like to be liked. So what is the difference between designer's ordinariness (there is no doubt that this would be of a high standard) and mere ordinary ordinariness? Venturi's *œuvre* consists for the most part of single buildings for individual private or corporate clients. By definition these are not popular, although liked by their owners and renowned among curator-professionals. How far his elegant, wry ironies ('The commonplace made uncommon.') could ever become truly popular—for example by featuring in the catalogues of the speculative developer or builder—remains to be seen.

Much the same is true of the furniture that was produced in Italy by Ettore Sottsass and his friends in the Memphis group.[27] More brutally ironic, their imagery, which in recent

6.20 *Popular art into high art. Typical 'over-decorated' interior with busy patterns running everywhere.*

6.21 *Ironical recycling of busy decoration in this original etching, the work of Memphis artist and designer George Sowden.*

6.22 *'Granny's curtains'. The introduction of alien down-market floral decoration into otherwise high design. Settee by Paolo Deganello.*

years has enjoyed a considerable vogue among students and teachers of design, juxtaposes judiciously chosen 'nasty' (nice) decorative surfaces from kitsch furniture of the 1950s and 1960s. Memphis furniture is extremely expensive at present and this alone would be inhibitive to most consumers. However, in the form of photographic images circulating in the journals of the curator-professionals, it still exerts a considerable influence. Recently, a very prestigious (and expensive) UK design office has used 'Memphis' imagery in the design of household goods for the UK store, Woolworths (from whom some of the imagery was probably borrowed in the first place). Why should Woolworths not recycle their own imagery? How will these subtle interchanges of legitimacy in popular imagery affect secondhand prices (or the value) of existing artefacts? It is too early to say, although massive publicity will ensure that popularized pop will make an initial impact. Whatever the final outcome in the marketplace, designers have certainly come a long way with such contortions. The stern and unbending ethic of functionalism seems remote indeed.

Notes and References to Chapter 6

1 For an introduction to the many technical issues surrounding the social creation of exchange values see A. Appadurai, *The Social Life of Things*, Cambridge: Cambridge University Press, 1986. Although most of the essays concern anthropological studies, there is much to interest the student of contemporary consumer societies.

2 *Intermediate Greek-English Lexicon*, Oxford: Oxford University Press, 1968, p. 399.

3 See R. Brilliant, *Arts of the Ancient Greeks*, New York: McGraw-Hill, 1973, p. 172, and M. Robertson, *History of Greek Art*, Cambridge: Cambridge University Press, 1975, p. 328 and 674 (notes). For the literary sources of information on the canon see J. J. Pollitt, *Sources and Documents—The Art of Greece 1400–31 BC*, Englewood Cliffs: Prentice-Hall, 1965, pp. 88-92.

4 Oxford English Dictionary

5 For an account of Wedgwood as a pioneer of modern marketing see N. McKendrick, "Josiah Wedgwood: an 18th century pioneer of salesmanship and marketing techniques." *Economic History Review*, XII, 1960, pp. 408-433.

6 The name was authorized by Queen Charlotte, wife of George III, to whom Wedgwood had supplied a tea service in 1765.

7 P. Bourdieu, *op. cit.*, p. 74.

8 V. Papanek, *Design for the Real World*, (2nd Edition), London: Thames and Hudson, 1972.

9 G. Reitlinger, *The Economics of Taste*, Volumes 1, 2 and 3, London: Barrie and Jenkins, 1961, 1963, 1970, document the rise and fall of prices of pictures and art objects over two centuries.

10 M. Thompson, *Rubbish Theory—the creation and destruction of value*, Oxford: Oxford University Press, 1979.

11 See D. Caplovitz, *The Poor Pay More*, Glencoe: Free Press, 1969 and F. Williams, *Why the Poor Pay More*, National Consumer Council, London: Macmillan, 1977.

12 H. Gans, *Popular Culture and High Culture—an analysis of Taste*, New York: Basic Books, 1974.

13 T. S. Kuhn, *The Stucture of Scientific Revolutions*, Chicago: University of Chicago Press, 1979.

14 This now famous phrase is Le Corbusier's. See Le Corbusier (trans. F. Etchells), *Towards a New Architecture*, London: Architectural Press, 1927, p. 245.

15 E. Goffman, "Symbols of Class Status." *British Journal of Sociology*, 12, 1951, pp. 294-304.

16 E. Goffman, "Symbols of Class Status." *op. cit.*, p. 294.

17 E. H. Gombrich, "Visual Metaphors of Value." *Meditations on a Hobby Horse*, Oxford: Phaidon, 1963, p. 16.

18 See D. Irwin (Ed.), *Winckelmann—writings on art'*, London: Phaidon Press, 1972, for essays on Winckelmann's thought and a selection from his most important writings.

19 See D. Spaeth, *Mies van der Rohe*, London: Architectural Press, 1987, p. 130, for Mies' comments on the aesthetics of structural steel detailing. Books on the architecture of Mies van der Rohe usually include very detailed section drawings of curtain walling—an architectural feature that is seen by most people as virtually featureless. Often the apparently minimal rationality is a contrived effect since the use of exposed steelwork is limited by fire regulations.

20 The phrase 'complexity and contradiction', so provocative at the time it was written, is Robert Venturi's. It was used as the title of his early attack on the minimalism of the Modern Movement in architecture. The book is now seen as a seminal work in the theory of post-Modernism. See R. Venturi, *Complexity and Contradiction in Architecture*, New York: Museum of Modern Art and Chicago: Graham Foundation for the Arts, 1966.

21 J. N. L. Durand, *Precis des leçons d'architecture donnée à l'Ecole Royale Polytechnique, Paris 1821–3* and *Recueil et parallele des édifices de tout genre anciens et modernes*, Paris: L'Ecole Polytechnique, 1801, are two classic expositions of the geometric basis of neo-Classical architecture.

22 The best source for the ideas of the pre-Raphaelites is the artists themselves. A useful collection of essays is J. Sambrook (Ed.), *Pre-Raphaelitism—a collection of critical essays*, Chicago: University of Chicago Press, 1974. On the Egyptian Revival see R. C. Carrott, *The Egyptian Revival—its sources, monuments and meaning 1808–1858*, Berkeley: University of California Press, 1978, and J. S. Curl, *The Egyptian Revival: an introductory study of a recurring theme in the history of Taste*, London: Allen and Unwin, 1982. On the use of 'savage' and 'primitive' sources by twentieth century artists see R. Goldwater, *Primitivism in Modern Art* (revised edition), New York: Vintage Books, 1967, W. Rubin (Ed.), *Primitivism in 20th Century Art: affinity of the tribal and the modern*, New York: Museum of Modern Art, 1984, and M. Bell, *Primitivism*, London: Methuen, 1972.

23 Erwin Schaefer is forced to resort to this distinction in his account of the sources of modern—functionalist—design. See E. Schaefer, *The Roots of Modern Design—functional tradition in the nineteenth century*, London: Studio Vista, 1970.

24 Good accounts of the history of pop art are L. Lippard, *Pop Art*, London: Thames and Hudson, 1967, and C. Finch, *Pop Art—Object and Image*, London: Studio Vista, 1968.

25 Good reviews of the interaction of pop art, pop music and various genres of consumer artefacts include T. Hine, *Populuxe*, London: Bloomsbury Publishing, 1987 (consumer imagery in the United States), and N. Whitely, *Modernism to Mod*, London: Design Council, 1987. T. Polhemus, *Pop Styles*, London: Vermilion, 1984, provides a survey of the confluence of pop music and the fashion industry.

26 R. Venturi, *Complexity and Contradiction in Architecture* (Museum of Modern Art Papers in Architecture Number 1, New York, 1966. Second edition, London: Architectural Press, 1977). R. Venturi, D. Scott Brown and S. Izenour, *Learning from Las Vegas*, Cambridge, Mass: MIT Press, 1972.

27 The work of the Memphis Group has been discussed by B. Radice, *Memphis— researches, experiments, results, failures and successes in modern design*, London: Thames and Hudson, 1985. A similar Milanese *avant-garde* group, perhaps even more provocative in its use of popular sources is Studio Alchimia. See K. Sato, *Alchimia— never ending Italian design*, Tokyo: Rikuyo-sha Publishing, 1985, Studio Alchimia's own review of some of its ideas is in P. C. Bontempi and G. Gregori, *Alchimia*, Milan, 1985.

7. Fashion

7.1 *Rages and crazes.*
Extreme emotions are
often aroused by a
new craze. In the
post-war period of
Paris, the stylistic
exaggerations of the
New Look provoke an
assault on the wearer

Stability and change in symbolic forms

Incessant change in the symbolic expression of individual and social values—including, importantly, critical judgment or Taste—is a fundamental feature of human life. Many of the mechanisms which produce this chronic instability in cultural codes have already been described. At root there is the tension between individuation (as a particular person) and identification (as a member of a group. A person only comes to know who he is—'I'—in his transactions with the group—'the others'. Conformity with the norms of the group—'what is decent and proper'—is the price paid for the comfort of belonging. But, as we have seen, comfort is not the ultimate goal for the human organism. We do not seek permanent comfort or rest, but pleasure. And pleasure is not associated with comfort itself but arises in the process of moving towards and away from it. Too much comfort is boring. Spontaneous activity which seeks to avoid boredom by means of the stimulation of novel experiences is part of everyones mental functioning. Abundant laboratory evidence exists which corroborates the inverted 'U'-shaped relationship between pleasure and novelty implied in the commonplace that, beyond a certain point, 'familiarity breeds contempt'.[1]

In static, closed societies powerful mechanisms exist to dampen spontaneous instability in symbolic norms. But in open societies, societies which are nevertheless stratified by the imperatives of class, status and power, these two mechanisms—the dialectic of 'I' and 'other' and the spontaneous pursuit of novelty—drive the great engines of stylistic change that provide much of the demand for industry in contemporary consumer cultures.

Identification with other social groups leads to the imitation of their symbols. Aspiration to join leads to emulation, rivalry and symbolic 'outbidding' or 'topping'. Conversely, a group that desires to maintain its exclusiveness defends its symbols against misappropriation by sudden unannounced and esoteric redefinitions and elaborations in directions which, it is alleged, cannot be matched by the parvenu. To the snob, stigma attaches precisely to those whose efforts at symbolic identification come near enough to show merely that they have 'missed the whole point'.

The structural rigidities of birth and kin, tribe and caste in closed societies, are reinforced by constant conditioning into the separate symbolic patterns proper to different stations in life. There is often an explicit supernatural religious justification for the unchanging scheme of things here below. However, the existence of powerful, often brutal, sanctions against those who infringe exclusive symbolic usages testifies to the enduring dynamic power and disruptive potential inherent in these tendencies to symbolic expansion and appropriation. Many examples exist of societies in which sumptuary laws lay down precise definitions and limits within which supposedly immutable codes for symbolic display may operate.[2] Particular symbols and stylistic markers (for example the colour of one's attire) are exclusively reserved for particular persons or groups.

In some feudal societies, those who infringe sumptuary laws could even be threatened with the death penalty. Over the long term however, even such drastic sanctions as this may be powerless to defend exclusive dominion over symbols. For modern societies, the opposite is the norm—the constant diffusion of symbols by virtue of the unconstrained imitation of the display of various social élites. These élites may be the ancient aristocracies (a royal wedding still has a significant effect on the national economy) or their present day counterparts—the 'robber barons' of capitalism characterized in Thorstein Veblen's description of the leisure class. A complete picture of symbolic diffusion would need to include many other élites such as the *demi-monde* of high society, artistic Bohemia, popular heroes of the media and mass entertainers, international stars of commercial sport and, not least, among the various curator-professions which, in today's society, claim a right to prescriptive judgments on what is proper, 'trendy' museum directors, fashion designers, interior decorators, advertising whiz-kids and their associated journalistic pundits of popular magazines.[3] All these potential initiators of symbolic diffusion function in a blaze of commercial publicity and fabricated human interest. A large segment of the mass circulation press caters for little else than the diffusion of the opinions and preferences of such 'culture heroes'. Although it is certainly not the case that symbolic diffusion can be initiated and sustained at will, it is nevertheless true that much of what currently passes for spontaneous change is in reality the result of a good deal of commercial stimulation. Given the economic importance of a successful shift in symbolism—a 'new look' in women's fashion can be worth billions internationally—it is not surprising that much of the research effort directed towards understanding the diffusion of Tastes is part of a wider effort of marketing research.

There are several separate traditions in diffusion research based on different academic subject boundaries and precise areas of

application. Most concern quite specific innovations, for example, a new brand of breakfast food, or a new approach to agriculture through new seed varieties, or innovations in hygiene such as the acceptance of health-care in developing countries. 'Diffusion' as a technical term embraces all of these phenomena in a more or less value-free way.[4] In contrast, the many terms commonly used to denote shifts in symbolic forms are loaded with value judgments, often pejorative by implication. Popular terms for transient disturbances in the equilibrium of symbols can be arranged along a scale. At one end are 'rages', 'crazes', 'manias' and 'fads'. Next are 'snowballs', 'stampedes' and 'bandwagons', then 'trends', 'vogues' and 'fashions'. At the other end are 'movements' and 'styles' and finally, 'Tastes' and 'customs'. This scale ostensibly refers to different speeds of social change. Crazes and manias are extremely swift forms of symbolic diffusion while styles and Tastes suggest quasi-permanent forms in a more or less equilibrium state. Fashions would come somewhere in between the two extremes.

These popular descriptions also suggest that extremely swift diffusion processes are at once trivial, even ludicrous and at the same time transient—likely to disappear as abruptly as they arose. Using words such as crazes or manias (for example, 'Beatlemania' or the 'craze' for skateboards) suggest an unconscious contagion more or less beyond intellectual or moral control, similar to the blind panic of a crowd.

Stampedes and bandwagons suggest an element of calculation, however slight—at the least an impulsive movement which is informed by some observation of the direction of others, particularly certain significant figures

7.2 *Where chemical reactions are slowed by the process of diffusion through some medium, waves of chemical activity can be generated which provide an analogy to the processes of the diffusion of innovation (such as a new style) in a population. Liesegang rings, showing one of the first published images by R. Liesegang, 1896.*

superimposed on the slower more wide-ranging movements of style. As such, it acts as a legitimate band of 'fringe' deviation within the larger or mainstream Taste concerns of a group. In fashion there is thus a reconciliation of individual freedom with social conformity, at least in the matter of critical judgment.[5]

The diffusion of innovation

Having adopted the neutral terminology of diffusion, we are in a position to borrow analogies and mathematical models from other fields of science in which the concept of diffusion has already been exploited—for example, from the study of chemical reactions.

For any chemical species to react together two things are necessary. Firstly, the reactive molecules have to meet each other. Secondly, once they have made contact, they have to be induced to combine. Consider what happens in the first case if reacting molecules have difficulty in making contact with each other. This might arise if the reacting species were separated by some kind of physical barrier and therefore could not diffuse or move around easily so that encounters were rare. The overall speed of any process is determined by the slowest step—in this case the *diffusion step*. Hence, even if the two chemicals reacted immediately they made contact, the overall speed of the process would necessarily be slow. Similar considerations apply in the second case. Here, mingling might be infinitely fast but the two chemical species may be reluctant to combine. In this case, the *combination step* is the slowest or rate determining step. A complete model of this reaction would include a

who lead the rush to 'climb aboard'. On the other hand, styles and Tastes are terms which imply varying degrees of aesthetic refinement and intellectual calculation—including the ability to perform more or less explicit acts of discrimination and the exercise of critical judgment. As control is held to be superior to abandon, a moral judgment is built into the very terminology of fashion. Therefore, those who quite consciously seek to disrupt a particular symbolic equilibrium resort to strategies which involve deliberate non-rational devices as triggers.

Finally, the scale from crazes to Tastes implies a progressive extension of the scope and scale of symbolic change. A craze is not only abrupt and transient it is limited to one or a very few items or forms. A Taste, on the other hand, not only changes very slowly, but it embraces a wide-ranging cluster of related symbolic allegiances. A common formulation holds that fashion is a minor oscillation mathematical description of both processes and lead to well-known equations for the overall rate as a function of time. In certain conditions a chain reaction can spread through a whole population of molecules. At first sight, a chain reaction seems a good analogy for the spread of fashions, however, there is one obvious difference.

For chemical substances, the disposition to react with other substances is a fixed quantity for any species. By contrast, in the diffusion of fashions, the propensity of any individual to adopt an innovation is not fixed but depends on the behaviour of others and on that individual's knowledge of it. Hence, at any point in time, the process depends on the sequence of what has gone before. Mathematical models which seek to simulate what happens during the processes of fashion innovation need to take the whole history of the diffusion process into account. Somewhat similar mathematical formulations have been devised to describe what are at first sight rather different forms of diffusion—for example, the snowballing of rumours or the spread of an infectious disease during an epidemic. Both of these have also been used as models for fashion diffusion with some success.[6]

A useful model of the diffusion of innovation which has been developed in the field of marketing has as its foundation two processes analogous to those described above. The first is an account of supposed internal changes of an individual as he first becomes aware of a new product or innovation. The second is a description of the processes by which this individual's adoption of the innovation are passed on to others and thus spread or diffuse throughout the whole social system of which he is part.

This first process attempts to take account of the obvious fact that it takes more than mere encounter to induce an individual to adopt an innovation. Like molecules, people may be reluctant to react. It is supposed, therefore, that individuals must pass through various stages before an encounter with an innovation will lead to its adoption. First is an awareness stage at which information about the innovation is received. However, mere possession of information is not sufficient to cause them to adopt. Before this may be achieved, they must pass through successive stages of persuasion, decision and confirmation. In the post-adoption stage, individuals may search for further reinforcement to convince themselves that they had made the right decision. In practice, most of the details of these supposed internal cognitive changes are unknown and can only be accounted for indirectly.

The other base for the theory is more easily accessible to observation and modelling. This involves the various social processes which transfer information about the innovation through various channels of communication to the individuals which make up a particular social group. (These correspond to the ability of one diffusing chemical species to encounter another with which it might react.) For practical purposes 'a particular social group' is simply taken to be a market for a certain type of good. It has been known for many years and has been verified on innumerable occasions, that the curve for the rate of adoption of an innovation is 'S'-shaped.[7] At first, few people adopt a new product but after a while the process starts to speed up and continues to accelerate until the innovation is no longer a novelty, at which point the process slows down and finally tails off.

Two extreme cases can be distinguished. In the first, knowledge of the innovation comes more or less entirely from outside the system—for example, via one of the mass media in a sparsely populated country where interpersonal contact is minimal. The second—the opposite situation—occurs where interpersonal contact is the dominant mode of communication. It is not too difficult to combine these possibilities into one mathematical model which produces the familiar 'S'-shaped learning curve.[8]

Even where there is an input of information from outside the system, much clearly depends on those few individuals who first adopt an innovation. Until adoption is more widespread the cumulative knowledge of the innovation does not reach that threshold beyond which interpersonal contact generates a rapid and accelerating increase. Once this threshold is reached, further knowledge in the system powerfully influences individuals to adopt. Much research has shown that media influences from outside the system are most influential at the first stage where cognitive change and the acquisition of information are important. Conversely, interpersonal contact is most influential at the persuasion stage—the moment when knowledge and awareness shapes individual attitudes.

Following these first innovators come the different groups who progressively join the bandwagon. Conventionally, in modern studies of the uptake of new products, these are divided into 'early adopters', 'early majority', 'late majority' and 'laggards'. (Although a simpler division into 'innovators' and 'later adopters' appears adequate.) Again, much research has verified the proposition that external inputs to the system via the media are more significant for the innovators while interpersonal contact is more influential in persuading later adopters.

While inputs of knowledge to the system (for example, via the media) are usually favourable to a particular innovation, the same cannot be assumed of information generated by interpersonal contact. This depends on individual experience and response and may be favourable, unfavourable or neutral. Correspondingly, among the total population of a particular social system there will be those generating favourable or unfavourable information and those who are passive. A complete mathematical description has to incorporate all these categories into a dynamic model which shows the influence of all the parties as they interact and change their state on the rate of adoption over a period of time. The complexity of this situation is such that, even when depicted in an abstract and schematized way, much computational effort is necessary to handle the calculations. In some cases, plausible simplifying assumptions and reliable information about the mechanisms of transfer between the various states (favourable, passive or reject) enable quite accurate predictions to be made of the rate of diffusion of a particular innovation.[9] Solutions to these special cases are easiest in the case of low risk products—those whose acquisition involves the purchaser in little risk by virtue of their low cost and/or their close resemblance to existing products.

In reality, innovations in the form of new brands or product lines usually show a peak in their adoption curve. Adoption rises to a maximum along the familiar 'S'-shaped curve but then declines, often settling down later to a more or less extended plateau. There is a simple explanation for this peak which involves repeat

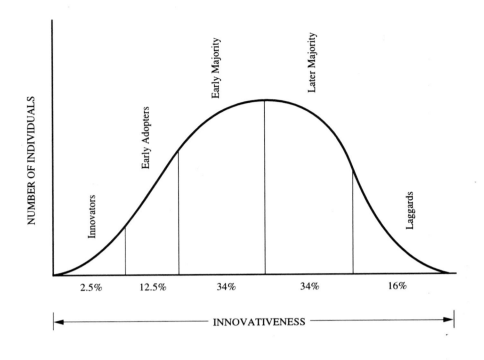

7.3 *Innovators as a fraction of the population. Those who lead are a small fraction of the total population but are crucial in getting a new innovation into circulation.* (*E. Rogers. Simplified version by D. Midgley.*)

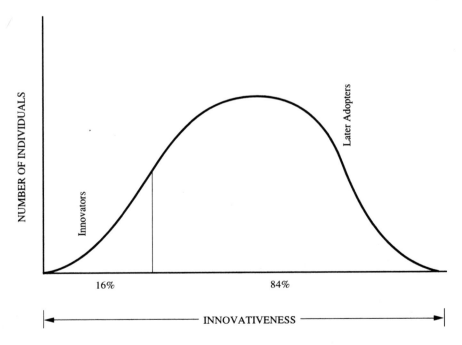

7.4 *Theoretical and observed adoption curves for a consumer product. Computer models of the uptake of a new innovation, for example a new consumer product or brand, can be surprisingly good predictors of actual behaviour when the product is launched. Forecast of the adoption during the launch period is important so that distribution can match sales.* (*D. Midgley.*)

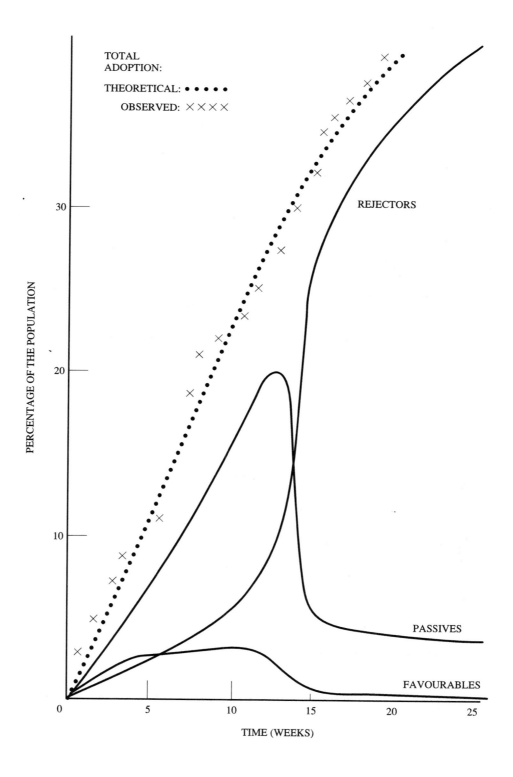

TOTAL
ADOPTION:

THEORETICAL: • • • • •

OBSERVED: ✕ ✕ ✕ ✕

REJECTORS

PASSIVES

FAVOURABLES

PERCENTAGE OF THE POPULATION

TIME (WEEKS)

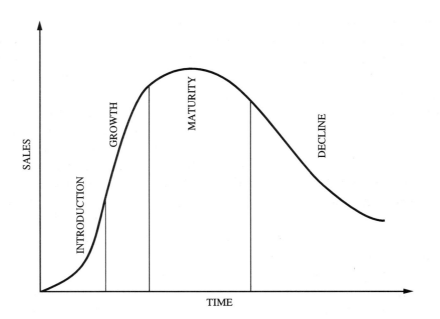

SALES

INTRODUCTION

GROWTH

MATURITY

DECLINE

TIME

7.5 *The product life
cycle or PLC. All
products (and styles)
eventually die after a
period of so-called
maturity. The
biological metaphor
which underlies the
PLC needs careful
interpretation and
there can be several
superimposed cycles
at different levels of
analysis.*

purchasing. Where consumption of a product
is fairly rapid, the innovators will already
be repeating their purchase before the late
adopters have joined the bandwagon. All
new products, however successful, eventually
suffer a permanent decline from their stable
plateau. In marketing parlance, there is a
finite *product life cycle* (PLC). Women's
fashion, for example, would have a short
PLC. Consumer durables have a longer life
in the marketplace. (For a fashion product
which is purchased only once, the product life
cycle is identical with the adoption curve in
Figure 7.5.[10]) Among some marketing men,
there is a belief that the product life cycle
with its characteristic stages is in some way
analogous to the animal life cycle of birth into
a dependent infancy, followed by a vigorous
youth, then a stable maturity and finally
inevitable senility. (It is quite hard to adopt the
biological metaphors as 'jargon' in the course
of everyday conversation without carrying

over unnoticed the concept of the biological
cycle of ageing.)

A closer look at the sales curves of new
products reveals not one life cycle but several
superimposed on one another. Much depends
on the nature of the particular taxonomy of
products used for the survey. Again the biological analogy is not far away. For example,
a common sense division of goods into
'product classes' (for example, non-durable
personal consumer products such as cigarettes), 'product forms' within classes (for
example, filter cigarettes) and finally, 'brands'
within product forms, echoes the familiar
genus, species and variety hierarchy. While
brands have a comparatively short life cycle,
product forms change more slowly and the life
of product classes may be measured in decades,
even centuries. Clearly the particular way in
which the taxonomic hierarchy is constructed
will influence the kinds of cyclic variations
observed. It may also be difficult to divine at

what level decline may be taking place from actual sales curves. Both long and short cycles in women's fashions have often been noted but it is far from obvious that the generic features under scrutiny were always those of particular significance for the users.

Dropping dead in the market—a parable and a model

What finally kills off a once successful innovation? Obviously a successful product which has endured is no longer an innovation but what makes us discard it for another? The standard answers from marketing theory rest on the familiar notion of the person as a bundle of drives which generate associated needs (or desires) the satisfaction of which produces the demand for goods. Products are discarded when they have been superceded by others which satisfy particular needs (or desires) more fully, more effectively or more cheaply—or at any rate persuade the consumer that they do. Alternatively, our desires themselves may have changed and the old product fail to cater for our new requirements. Both of these explanations see the satisfaction provided by the consumption of goods as somehow external to the social system within which they are consumed. What then of fashion itself? Fashion really only satisfies the need to be marginally different from other consumers of the symbols of a particular group.

Clearly the abandonment, no less that the adoption, of an innovation under these circumstances will depend on the consumer's perceptions of others' behaviour as much as, and perhaps more than, any specific needs of

his own. When a particular need is for an exclusive marginal differentiation within a particular domain of symbolism in goods then, obviously, the more those people who already possess a certain symbolic innovation see others acquiring it, the more they will want to discard it. How much this inclination is a conscious matter, an overt attempt to reestablish an invidious comparison, as the crude Veblen model suggests, is debatable. Veblen himself was ambivalent on the matter.[11] Much of his irony depended on convincing us that the most arbitrary and capricious whims were in fact perfectly natural and proper to those who indulged them.

It seems more in accordance with our own introspective awareness of fashion to assume an unconscious or, at best, a barely conscious shift in our perceptions of objects after they appear to become increasingly common. The gradual perception that too many people in one's network of acquaintance have adopted a particular fashion is projected onto the fashion item itself. Moreover, a sense that particular objects are becoming common may well be reinforced by the realization that the increase in demand for a successful innovation has led to a decrease in price due to economies of scale. This is clearly unpleasing to those innovators who bought at a time when costs were spread over the comparatively small numbers sold. For them common signifies 'cheap'.[12]

Where there is an awareness of increasing symbolic appropriation at the lower margin of a particular group, commonness is felt as an increasing banality. At the same time, consumers perceive a diminution of creativeness or innovative drive among the producers of the once novel symbols. Designs for 'new' brands appear to us as increasingly 'facile'. Designers themselves seem increasingly 'slick' producing only variations at the brand level—variations which are perceived as no more than deftly routine. Once a vogue is over, the central or modal symbols appear to us as merely 'quaint'. Time must pass before they can once more be adopted as innovations.

An old-fashioned hat may be discarded immediately, as soon as the thought strikes us that it will no longer 'do'—when it is, as the saying goes, 'old hat'. With more expensive durable products, these changing perceptions may occur with surprising slowness, perhaps over many years. 'Falling out of love' with something we have long considered as dear to us may occur abruptly—on waking one morning—but it may equally be a lingering process taking place unconsciously over time. Old allegiances are gradually forgotten, allowing new ones to be formed which supplant them almost unawares.

The problems of one keen yachtsman will serve as a parable to show how complex these processes really are. For years he was absorbed by the expression of a 'proper' boat which he saw in terms of an image of robustness, an image in which 'beauty' lay in a clean, trim version of a very traditional nineteenth century English pilot-boat hull. Naturally everything was made of solid wood, expressing traditional craftsmanship in elaborate joinery and carefully wrought metal-work fastenings. This made it very heavy and it would only go reasonably fast in quite strong winds and strong winds mean rough seas and the owner was prone to violent seasickness! Still it was a lovely boat, to its owner, entirely beautiful. Needless to say, all other boats, especially modernistic ones of newfangled plastic, seemed to him in the worst possible Taste—cheap and tawdry by comparison.

Transition to a new perception of a 'decent' boat proved remarkably difficult. It meant getting used to the idea of plastic—previously the symbol of all that was cheap and nasty. Worse still, it meant adjusting to the idea of a drastic change of form—from a monohull to a catamaran with two hulls. In fact, the transition took years, including several without a boat at all, years during which both plastic boats and catamarans became increasingly popular. The problem for that once 'traditional' yachtsman was that of adjusting to its novel visual features, such as the startlingly smooth and flowing forms given by the 'liquid technology' of plastic mouldings, and, bit-by-bit incorporating these into a new internalized conception of a 'proper' boat that made it seem every bit as Tasteful as did its wooden predecessor. Presumably the earliest owners of catamarans were not so deeply attached to an internalized image of a 'decent' boat embodied in traditional monohull imagery. Probably many had not owned a boat of any kind before and did not face the problem of liquidating symbolic commitments.[13]

There are innumerable examples of these subtle but sometimes traumatic transitions in everyone's personal experiences. At the level of whole populations, similar considerations apply. David Midgley has given an interesting historical account of the complex interaction between economic, technological and behavioural factors in the sudden extinction of the market for fully fashioned stockings in favour of the seamless variety. Initial resistance on the grounds that the nude look of stockings without seams were in poor Taste were eventually overwhelmed by new consumer groups

7.6 Perceptions of the newness or oldness of artefacts among whole populations also undergo drastic changes. Jaspersen modelled this in terms of the passage of the percept of an object across a 'stylistic trench'.

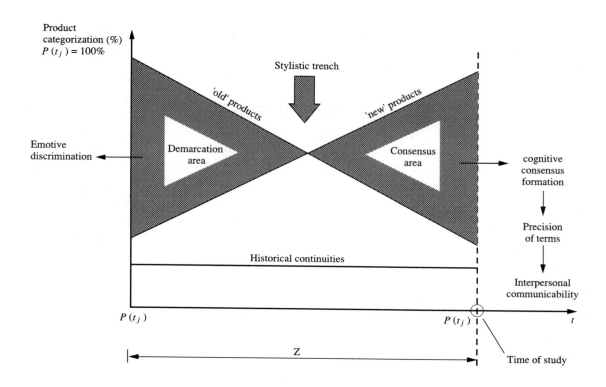

from the youthful end of the market for whom the old proprieties did not apply.[14] For those invested in the technology of seamless stocking manufacture, the diffusion of innovation processes must have been perceived as very slow. For the individual adopter the processes may be traumatically rapid. For those who see their old symbols discredited but can't bring themselves to adopt the new ones, the old love is discarded and that whole sector of consumer activity entirely abandoned. Another fashion is waning.

Obsolescence as a perceptual phenomenon—the intimation that things just don't seem so new and interesting any more—has recently been studied at the level of populations (of people and things) and the observations put into a model.[15] Jaspersen developed a test instrument for measuring the change in the perception of a range of typical consumer products based on aggregating the responses of a group of subjects. A dominant influence was that of the perceived 'newness' or 'oldness' of products which were presented pictorially in the forms they were sold over a period of thirty years. As might be expected, forms which were perceived as 'old' had sharply negative ratings on test instruments which measured emotive response. Another important finding was that current products were assessed more homogeneously than 'old' products. Jaspersen's hypothetical explanation for this concerns the establishment of dividing lines of stylistic feelings through the process of emotive discrimination which allow people to classify their product environment. He called these barriers *stylistic trenches*. Figure 7.6 shows how a stylistic trench divides two zones. In one zone negative emotional connotations lead to an incomplete classification. In the other, products are perceived as 'new' and a cognitive consensus is formed leading to an increased precision of discriminating terms and, therefore, a high interpersonal communicability among those who use the products as a visual language.

Not all products are perceived consciously. Many (if not most) are perceived peripherally, at the edge of consciousness, leading to what Jaspersen called 'an evanescent zone'. A complete model of the phenomena spread over in historical time is depicted in Figure 7.7. On Jaspersen's model, our subjective perception of products in a population changes in three waves according to whether we see them as innovative, contemporary, or old and historical. Products initially perceived as innovative, if they survive in the marketplace, are moved into the consensus zone and, through sharper discriminations, become part of a new product language. In turn, other products are moved to the demarcation zone, pushing out others into the historic zone—the cognitive structure of each of these zones becoming transformed in the process. An important point which manufacturers would do well to understand is that a high rate of stylistic innovation is not necessarily advantageous. There is a law of diminish-

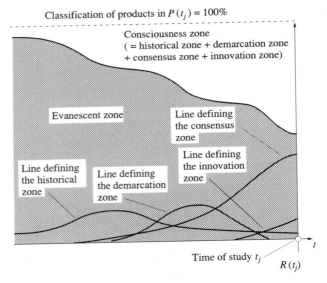

7.7 *Slow changes, first in the awareness of newness and then in the acceptance of novelty, occur until the new image becomes the 'normal' form as modelled by Jaspersen. Curves show the fluctuations in the perception of novelty over time.*

ing perceptual returns as the old is constantly removed from perception at the same time as the new is embraced. The consensus zone is thus not enlarged overall but rather attenuated in time, forcing still faster innovation in order to create perceived newness. Jaspersen's descriptive language is somewhat abstract and there is an obvious objection to the use of design students as subjects as it is well known that concept formation depends a great deal on expert knowledge. Nevertheless, his technique is highly suggestive and could well be extended to larger populations of ordinary consumers. It could also be an important tool in the investigation of the development of product concepts during education including, importantly, consumer education.

Michael Thompson in *Rubbish Theory* developed a similar line of thought using the mathematical theory of the 'cusp catastrophe' to generate models of how the social consensus which gives value to things—emotionally and financially positive (for example, in high art) or emotionally and financially negative (for example, in 'rubbish')—flips from one state to another.[16] As a metaphor, passing through a cusp is not too dissimilar from crossing a trench. However the cusp metaphor has the advantage of being able to model the process of change in more detail.

In their current state, abstract formulations such as those of Jaspersen and Thompson will perhaps seem of marginal interest to the designer or marketing man. However, as we saw in Chapters 5 and 6, the structure of our perceptions of the product environment is also influenced by the structure of the society in which we live. For that reason, these difficult and abstract topics in statistical anthropology are near to the centre of the mysterious shifts in the structure of our stylistic perceptions or Tastes to which the changing environment of products inexorably compells us. Who has not finally parted company with a much loved motorcar, apartment or piece of furniture when its manifest disadvantages compared to a new product environment finally overwhelm our earlier symbolic attachment to it, being subverted by new and more vigorous rivals for our affections.

Fashion and commerce

What sequence of events occur during a fashion vogue? When a particular innovation, or more usually a cluster of stylistically related innovations, is launched, the first consumer innovators buy—usually in comparatively exclusive up-market shops.[17] Their performance is watched closely by volume manufacturers and retailers catering for lower socioeconomic groups. If the up-market innovators are enthusiastic, then frantic marginal differentiation within the same overall style sets in but this time using cheaper materials and techniques. How much variation at the brand level is acceptable within the overall theme is a matter for trial and error. Quite soon a modal tendency is apparent. The more *outré* variations are dropped and manufacturers concentrate on finely tuned variations close to the central tendency. To cope with these familiar facts, the mathematical modelling of the diffusion process needs to be sophisticated quite considerably. Not only is the amount of information in the system increasing rapidly, there is an increasingly sharper formulation in practice (amplified by advertising and journalism) of the precise nature of the innovation itself. There is therefore a large gearing at the production end as manufacturers and retailers step up the supply of the modal forms and eliminate variation away from it.

In an effort to predict the particular form of the vogue and hence anticipate its economic implications, each large manufacturer and retailer constantly monitors sales figures—their own and their competitors. These yield information, not only about aggregate demand, but also about trends—the shift of demand over time. The more sharply the trend is rising, the greater the incentive to produce more brands within a particular modal form. After the initial sales peak, repeat purchasing of variations at the brand level ensures that there is a period of comparatively stable demand. The erstwhile innovation has become a contemporary classic.

At this point, the innovators will notice that the aggregate consumption of the product form is increasing to the point where 'everyone they meet' is now wearing or using one variant or another. Individuals clearly have a sensitivity to the overall statistical density of a particular symbolic display within their own group. Probably the most acutely sensitive 'trendies' are attuned, not just to this overall statistical density of a product form, but also to changes over time. Trendies operate on the first or even second differential of the adoption curve. They notice the rate at which things are becoming too common! At some critical point the 'warning bells' ring and they move on to something less tired. When these effects become significant statistically, positive feedback ensures that the bandwagon goes into reverse with ever increasing speed. Yesterday's high style is something that 'no one could be seen dead in'. Sales curves for this phase of the fashion product life cycle mirror those of the growth phase.

At the first signs of rapid decline, manufacturers may persist blindly with further marginal differentiation within the same product form, perhaps trying out some of the more extreme variants previously held back. At this point in a fashion the clearly perceived lineaments of a style become blurred and the fashion seems to stagnate. Once an unmistakable downturn occurs, everyone tries to clear the stocks which have accumulated along the system by price-cutting in preseason sales.[18] In earlier years, it was possible to 'move' démodé lines by selling them off in the provincial hinterlands where news of the decline had yet to penetrate. With national, even global, publicity via the mass media this strategy is no longer viable. Stocks are liquidated at whatever loss is necessary to make space for the next vogue which has, of course, already been planned on the basis of shrewd observation of the sophisticated up-market outlets.

In areas of consumption which are symbolically sensitive and therefore prone to fashion, the industries have developed institutions for dampening and controlling the instability of demand. At the retail end there are the annual and biannual sales or 'events'—organized at fixed times in the calendar.

Wholesalers or, where organizations are large enough, merchandizing operations within retail chains respond to this seasonal cycle with their own cyclical sales venues, the big trade fairs. These are international events of profound importance to a particular trade. Manufacturers present their new models directly to the buyers at enormous gatherings from which the public is excluded. Buyers give orders for the new season's lines which they have decided should be offered to the public. The ensuing exchange of information and prediction may clarify and endorse the emergence of a definite 'new tendency' in design.

Feeding on this annual symbolic 'stock-exchange' is the world of fashion journalism.[19] From specialist magazines for the trade right down to the gossip column in the mass circulation daily, all journalists are in the business of making good copy out of gossip and prophecy. Fashion journalists cover the great 'events' such as the London Ideal Home Exhibition, the Paris Prêt-a-porter and the Cologne Möbel-Messe. Each must follow the imperatives of journalism: a strong simple story, a single catchy idea and a vivid leading image to hang it on. It is the fashion journalists who provide the first level of abstract description of a new style, trawling the mind-boggling diversity of the great international marts and

7.8 *Those who operate in mass markets cannot afford to be too* avant-garde. *Instead of leading fashion, they follow at a discreet distance. Summer display at a leading UK chain store.*

summarizing their impressions in pithy generalization. Astute manufacturers or wholesalers try to help by feeding them promotional information with their own generalizations couched in clichés which refer to imaginary 'new tendencies'—of which their own products are (needless to say) particularly good exemplars!

Sometimes a new product form is recognized immediately. A new style will be launched with spectacular *éclat* in brands that are instantly recognized as canonical.[20] At other times though the modal tendency may not be overwhelmingly obvious. Fashion is confused and only after much discussion and criticism (associated of course with more or less fitful innovation at brand level) is a line recognized and endorsed by the press and public. Seen as a sequence, the procession of modal forms add up to the larger rhythms of style in dress that have more or less monopolized the word 'fashion'. However, analogous rhythms exist in all the other areas of consumer culture. Backing-up the great trade fairs in finished goods is a further layer of exchanges at the level of semifinished materials including dress and furniture textiles, fixings and finishes. At base, there are the more or less mystical (or at the very least, heavily intuitive) exercises in prophecy which undertake to predict the Tastes and life styles of particular consumer groups a couple of years hence—exercises to which commerce, from manufacturers of dye-stuffs and yarn to garments or upholstered goods and on to the individual High Street retailer, is ultimately beholden.[21]

Many have seen this vast international apparatus of private information exchange as a deliberate attempt to manipulate Taste and thereby 'con' the public into ever increasing expenditure on symbolic obsolescence.[22] Little objective research has been undertaken to evaluate the real efficacy of attempts to manipulate Taste. To the marketing manager attempting to drum up orders it must all seem frighteningly hazardous and uncontrolled. No doubt there is an element of self-fulfilling prophecy—what Karl Popper has called the *Oedipus-effect*.[23] If ICI or Du Pont declare 'next year's colour' who is likely to argue? Yet deliberate attempts at fad creation have rarely been successful.[24] Despite amazing successes such as 'Davy Crockett', novelties are still at

235

the risk end of the market. Inevitably, such risks are far too great for the larger entrepreneurs in the fashion industries. They dare not lead. Instead they have to follow at a discreet (but not too great) distance from the *avant-garde*. Who though are the *avant-garde*? Who are the initiators of Taste and who are their first customers?

Innovators, opinion leaders and gatekeepers

Given the crucial role of those first intrepid individuals in establishing a fashion bandwagon, it is not surprising that much research effort has been directed at attempts to locate them and identify their characteristics. So far as their location is concerned, one obvious consideration is their socioeconomic status. We have seen that the dominant social class does indeed exert a generalized influence on Taste and there is no doubt that the processes of emulation and imitation are real ones. Traditional discussions of fashion, since the time of Veblen and Simmel,[25] have located innovation more or less exclusively in the upper or leisure class and pointed to the 'trickle' effect as a generalized means of transmitting innovations (or at least imitations of them) to lower social groups. While there is plenty of evidence that many innovators are, in one sense or another, upper class, it is clear that social class in itself is quite inadequate as a predictor of innovativeness. In modern societies, Veblen's unidirectional model of invidious distinctions expressed solely in economic terms needs to be elaborated to accommodate many other dimensions on which invidious comparison—and consequently opportunistic

innovation—is possible. There are therefore *status dissenters*, a powerful source of innovation, in many different status groups.[26]

Moreover, research has shown that any adequate model of the communication of innovation has to take into account the fact that information about an innovation into a social system is rarely a guarantee of uptake, wherever it originates. People need to see others adopt it or read or hear of the endorsement of an innovation by others they respect before they will take it up themselves.[27] In marketing terms this has lead to a theoretical distinction between innovators as such and what are termed 'opinion leaders'. If the innovators are essentially 'adventurers', opinion leaders are 'editors', deciding through the power of their leadership which innovations will be passed on to the wider community. In practice, it is not always easy to maintain the distinction as roles may overlap but they correspond broadly to the first two categories in Everett Rogers' classification—opinion leaders are the early adopters who lead the later majority of more or less conformist followers and laggards.[28]

So far as the innovators are concerned, an important finding is that there are few, if any, generalized or, 'across the board' innovators. Innovation in consumption is, on the contrary, very much a matter of the particular product class concerned. There are significant differences between innovators for fashion goods *per se* (clothing and cosmetics) and, for example, consumer durables (large and small) and ordinary supermarket goods (foods and cleaners). Certain correlations are quite strong. In durable goods, the more radical the technological innovation, the more educated are the consumer innovators and the greater their

7.9 *'Clothes not clones'. Innovation in fashion often emerges from the rival gangs in bipolar youth cultures, a fact which is not lost on commerce. Background images of violent clashes between rival gangs seek to give 'street-cred' and individuality to a particular brand of blue jeans, a product distinguished only in detail from its many competitors.*

CLOTHES NOT CLONES

incomes. This is because information about a new product in this category is usually quite technical and, therefore, its appraisal demands a certain level of education. On the other hand, there is some evidence that in the field of men's clothing, where technical knowledge is unnecessary, innovativeness is more likely to be found among the lower social classes where the level of education may be lower. In this instance, fashion may be said to 'trickle-up' or, at any rate, 'sideways'.[29]

Innovativeness in dress is a hallmark of most youth cultures and especially of the more deviant varieties. It is often taken to great lengths and forms part of the rebellious protest of lower class adolescents against their lowly economic and social position. Often such innovativeness occurs within a simple bipolar system of two opposing subcultures such as 'Mods versus Rockers'.[30] Tom Wolfe has elegantly described the extraordinarily subtle discriminations involved and the extent to which innovativeness within a particular style by charismatic leaders is admired by members of a particular lower class youth culture.[31]

Certain personality variables correlate quite highly with innovativeness including a willingness to take risks, positive attitudes to change, the ability to be relatively uninfluenced by others and a high level of cosmopolitanism. As all these attributes can be considered to contribute to an individual's reaction to the risk perceived in a novel situation, it is understandable that personality correlations with innovativeness of low risk products such as ordinary supermarket purchases are much less strong.[32] Qualities such as analytical ability (correlated with education) and willingness to adopt one's own standards are clearly important in choosing a brand of motorcar for example, but unlikely to be influential in routine discussions about a breakfast cereal.

Perceptual attributes are also important. Clearly, to consider an innovation as a risk, one must have perceived it to be significantly novel. Different individuals classify goods conceptually in different ways. Some use 'narrower' categories than others. The 'bandwidth' of the classification system used by individuals correlates with the perception of risk. Those with coarse bandwidths do not register novelty as sensitively as those with narrow bandwidths. Hence they do not react to new products—either favourably or unfavourably.[33]

For fashion goods, where social risks are usually greater than financial ones, correlations with personality variables are somewhat confused. 'Social integration' was significantly correlated with innovativeness but researchers also noted an increased impulsiveness in purchasing. However, innovators are important, not merely for consuming the first batch of a new product thus importing information into a social system, but in communicating their decisions to others. Their example, reinforced by their verbal endorsement and visual display, is crucial in generating the growing aggregate of social information about a new product. Much evidence has been accumulated to show that innovators are also important communicators and therefore important influences on the 'leaders of opinion'.

In formal, operational terms, the concept of 'opinion leadership' is somewhat nebulous. It seems open to doubt whether 'general' opinion leaders exist. Different groups appear to be important in leading opinion in different product categories.[34] Opinion leadership may well arise among innovators who display their innovations very publicly and hence are asked about it by the curious. Indeed, they may well have a psychological propensity to draw attention to their innovation and thereby start conversations about it, perhaps to reinforce their own convictions. This seems likely in the case of symbolic innovations in dress and home furnishings as they concern fundamental norms for proper membership of the group. In other instances though, opinion leaders in a particular social group may not be innovative and dissemination of new ideas or images is slow and difficult. There is no doubt of the enormous importance of direct interpersonal contact and example in transmitting information and generating acceptance of new ideas and products, even though the early model of the communication process, a simple two state model in which opinion leaders obtained their information from the media and in turn disseminated this by example, has been abandoned in favour of more complex multiflow models in recent work.

Opinion leadership is thus obviously closely related to patterns of sociability. In many situations, these patterns are related to social class. In areas such as the consumption of leisure products, however, class bias may not be obvious. For example, a camping or caravan site is a relatively heterogeneous milieu and opinion leaders from several social classes may display the latest specialized equipment to the admiration of novices. One significant set of findings is that both innovators and opinion leaders in the field of fashion are both gregarious and extensively involved in the media exposure of fashion, a key route through which information flows into their social system from outside.[35]

In so doing they were brought vicariously into contact with another social system, that of the fashion creators themselves. Fashion journalism not only purveys information about commercial trends and events, it is concerned to depict the life styles and doings of the first, innovating consumers. And these as a group overlap the world of the creators themselves. Designers often produce their first and most spectacular innovations for themselves and their friends—often out of necessity as initially they have no commercial recognition. At the very least they can dress themselves, or furnish themselves, even house themselves, according to the most radically innovative conceptions of what is good Taste. Their products may be acceptable within this subculture while consciously *outré* as far as the larger community is concerned. Most designers realize the need for publicity and use their own clothes, furniture or house as a platform for disseminating their symbolic innovations. In the world of fashion, symbolic innovations are usually circulating among quasi-professional cliques long before their first appearance in the commercial marketplace.[36]

Opinion leaders are crucial targets for information from outside particular social systems about new products, for example by selective mailings, channelled television commercials or the stratified location of shops and stores. Once they can be persuaded to adopt an innovation it is likely that the network of acquaintance which they dominate will follow their example.

Commercial interests continue to make conscious use of well-known figures who will, it is hoped, be regarded as generalized opinion leaders in order to sponsor new products. This explains the public endorsement of new brands for payment by prominent personages from fields unrelated to the product concerned. Such sponsorship is often done after the product form has reached a stable plateau, when advertisers are aiming to influence 'local' or product specific opinion leaders. By suggesting that a certain prominent figure is adopting a particular product, it is implied that the solid centre of the social system with which he is associated is already committed to the new product. Sponsors are chosen to represent the custodians of the central norms of decency for a particular group and are supposedly removed from overtly commercial considerations. They are the moral 'gate-keepers' of a particular culture. It is they who legitimize the adoption of an innovation.[37] In so far as this technique is effective it may well operate by reducing the perceived risk of the innovation among the hesitant.

The dialectics of display

As fashion is a function of identification and emulation with no obvious limits, it is not surprising that the history of fashion is a story of symbolic rivalry in which excesses are the rule and exaggeration is endemic. Examples of the perversities of fashion are innumerable and have provided the staple for moral critiques of fashion since Biblical times.[38] Taken singly and out of context, each vogue can seem entirely irrational and fashion appear as a series of fatuous caprices and arbitrary fancies. Yet a closer look reveals that the sequence of vogues is not entirely factitious. Behind the apparently irrational lies a kind of rationality. The seemingly illogical is in fact governed by a species of logic—what Ernst Gombrich dubbed—'the Logic of Vanity Fair'.[39]

Outbidding one's symbolic competitors can often be a simple scalar matter. In medieval times, the height of the cathedral nave could be the occasion for a literal 'topping' of rivals in other cities. Similarly, the amount and elaboration of decorative adornment on buildings is a perfect field for incremental outbidding, leading eventually to architecture in which the structure all but disappears under a carapace of ornament (Plate 19). But there are inevitable limits to the possibilities of topping the competition by exaggerating any one dimension of display. Limits to symbolic outbidding may be imposed by extraneous factors. Economic exigencies may ensure that a yet larger pyramid finally bankrupts the state. Given the currently available technology, the cathedral nave may attain a height that overreaches its structural stability and so collapses. In certain cases, there are also social constraints. In dress for example, miniskirts may eventually reach a point where they expose the wearer entirely and overstep the mark of what is socially acceptable. However, such limits may also arise intrinsically, from within the display itself. After a certain point, an exaggerated symbolism may no longer be legible or becomes so distorted that it is misread as deliberate deformity or, worse still, is interpreted as something else entirely. There is a kind of symbol limit after which further increments are dismissed as 'over the top'.

As in a game of cards, the possibilities for outbidding are limited by the hand you are dealt. The analogy with cards may be taken further. In card games, not only are there elaborate rules for sequential moves and an ordinal array in each suit, there are trump cards which out play all other cards in the pack. To the notion of topping we must add that of 'trumping'. When no further topping is possible within the rules of a particular vogue, a skilful competitor may play a trump and thereby alter the rules so that success in attracting attention and admiration lies entirely elsewhere. In a game of cards the circumstances and manner in which trump cards may be used are themselves governed by rules so that 'sideways' switches, at least in their most general form, are themselves predictable. But what of the symbolism of fashion? Is the next move in the game of fashion predictable? Within limits, the answer would appear to be 'yes, it is'.

Gombrich has termed the particular dimensions along which rivalry leads to scalar outbidding as *polarizing issues*.[40] When the possibilities of incremental topping within a particular polarizing issue have reached their economic, technical or socially acceptable limit, it is often possible to see what the next

7.10 *'Over the top' in automobiles. Rear end styling in American cars in the 50s and 60s incorporated the tailfin imagery of the jet fighter. While at the front the exaggerated bulges were patently sexual. Known as 'Dagmars' after a well-endowed television personality of the day, the breasts and nipples in the lighting cluster have no obvious function.*

polarizing issue will be although, fashion being full of suprises, it is equally often not. Yet, to the extent that, with hindsight, a particular fashion switch can be seen to have been an obvious move—albeit one we didn't happen to have thought of ourselves—the social game of 'Vanity Fair' can be said to have a kind of 'logic'. 'Logic' is of course used metaphorically (as indeed is 'dialectic'). The logic of fashion is certainly not an analytical affair. Neither is fashion scientifically predictable by virtue of lawful behaviour accessible to observation and verification. Rather we can understand, and sometimes anticipate, the switch from one polarizing issue to the next by virtue of our own identifications with the protagonists. We can empathetically project ourselves into their place and intelligently imagine, given what appear to be the range of possibilities, what we would do next if we were them.[41] We can do this because of our knowledge of the way that polarizing issues—indeed all issues—are interrelated. Here we come back to the analogies with language that form the basis of the structuralist approach to fashion.[42]

The dialectics of display have some predictive value, not because of the validity of the Hegelian triad thesis, antithesis and synthesis, but because polarizing issues exist in a semantic 'space' that is structured.[43] Once a given possibility has reached its practical, social or symbolic limit, one obvious next move is to switch to the exact opposite. After higher and higher churches let's switch to comparatively low but wide buildings.[44] When skirts can get no shorter, let's move to skirts that trail the ground. After *décolleté* has reached virtual nudity (signalled by one of the periodic 'topless' controversies) let us sheath women up to the neck.[45] Once rococo decoration has reached an extreme confabulation let's switch to plain forms and materials which are used to express a natural character. Conversely, once 'functional' design has reached the limit of all-white Platonic geometry let's go for the opposite, a Baroque particoloured exuberance. These are obvious moves because polar opposites are more closely related concepts than others. If concepts are plotted in a semantic space of however many dimensions, concepts which can be joined by a line through the origin are more closely related than those which cannot, even though their distance apart in absolute terms may be the greater.[46]

A semantic space for a particular area of Taste can be reconstructed by an empathetic entry into the particular symbolic system followed by a rational and exhaustive enumeration of what appear to be the alternative possibilities together with their opposites along the lines staked out by Roland Barthes[47] or Claude Levi-Strauss (procedures which are in fact somewhat similar to the repertory-grid approach of George Kelly).[48] The result is a multi-dimensional matrix of points which can each have two or three values (+ −, or 0). Alternatively, where an allowance is made for scalar quantities such as dimensions of a skirt or proportions in architecture, each alternative can be rated on a scale of however many points seem necessary to accommodate metrical distinctions recognized in practice. Symmetries, complementarities and adjacent empty regions are prima-facie candidates for the 'next move'. In this sense, 'lateral thinking' is much like rational thinking.

It is in such ordered, if still speculative, interpretations that the structuralist technique is most useful as it provides a basis for generating metaphorical extensions to particular patterns of Taste which can be recognized for what they are. Would-be innovators can thereby perceive a historical continuity in the evolution of Taste. This is an important point as fashion changes of whatever kind must be in accord with the felt continuity of the lives of their consumers including their perceptions of the past which, within its horizons, is largely determined by memories of characteristic patterns of Taste. Consumers of new Tastes want to feel they know from where they have originated. And, of course, the explicit reconstruction of an ordered universe of possibilities is an important part of the teaching process in all 'creative' subjects which are dominated by the exercise of Taste judgments—including design of every kind. It is not just apparel which is subject to those fluctuations of Taste we call 'fashion'.

Fashion cycles

As always with structuralist schemas, it is not easy to know to what extent what appears to the investigator to be the ultimate logical structure or 'coding grid' for a particular area of Taste corresponds to any practical or 'effective' grid. One obvious candidate for the presumption of an overlap (or at least a close similarity) between the two is the realm of *colour*. This is in part because of the relative simplicity of the description system of colour. Colours can only vary in three dimensions: hue, brightness and saturation. Therefore, the drifts and shifts of fashions in colour can be represented as a series of movements of points in a three-dimensional coding grid or 'colour space'. It also appears that, as Eleanor Rosch has shown, colours are among the fundamental anchor points which connect our language with external reality. We might therefore suppose that people are especially sensitive to changes in colour, and it is not surprising, given the relative cheapness of dyestuffs in comparison with other technological products which might be used as vehicles for changing Tastes, that so many variations in apparel arise merely from different choices of colours and their combination.

In fact, little research has been performed on the history of such variations in the sense of tracing the drift of dominant colours through the colour space over periods of time.[49] Colours in women's fashions (and, to a lesser extent, in the much less frequently purchased household furnishings) are subject to biannual changes according to season—Spring-Summer or Autumn-Winter. Colours for the latter are invariably darker or more saturated than the former which are usually pale to pastel coloured. There is some practical basis for this variation. In very sunny regions, light colours reflect radiant heat as well as light. Dark coloured materials are thus hot and uncomfortable. Conversely, in winter, light colours require more frequent cleaning. A great deal of the correlation seems to lie in habitual association with seasonal colours in nature—bright flowery colours in spring and summer, sombre and desaturated browns, reds, greens, blues and purples for autumn and winter.

Scales of predicted fashion colours for the following season are available from many commercial sources and usually present a complete range of colours in all the hues.[50] A particular 'collection' for spring fashions will be displayed as a swatch of pale, desaturated colours. No one wants to leave out any hue completely. Indeed, a particular collection is better characterized by what it leaves out than what it includes—so-called exclusion rules discriminating against those considered *démodé*. The practice is to emphasize one or two 'theme' colours for the particular season. Theme colours are presented as stronger, more saturated variations, sharper accents which serve to bias the whole ensemble towards a particular region of the colour space. A cluster of related accents may be given a further set of connections by virtue of some colourless verbal associations which may underlie the entire collection that year, for example, 'Marine', 'Sugar and Spice' and 'Circus' (Plate 20).

Sometimes tentative shifts towards, for instance, an enhancement of the blue-green

7.11 House and Garden *monitored sales figures for different coloured products in the field of home decoration for several decades. The curves showed a wave-like fluctuation in the popularity of the broad colour families.*

Nadine Bertin, Director of the House and Garden Colour Programme. Faber Birren was responsible for the inception of the programme in 1947.

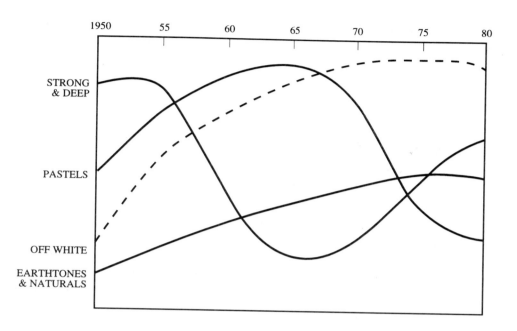

region one year may show progressive increases in saturation in later seasons. Only later will the 'marine' associations be seized on to give a coherence to an increasingly disparate set of colours. After one season in this mature, fully articulated form, the blue-green collection may be abandoned entirely. What follows could be a repeat of this performance at the opposite pole of the colour space in the red-yellow region. However, another possibility is that a much more diverse collection of colours held together by a semantic association such as 'Carnival' or 'Rodeo' may be substituted. Such themes are too specific to allow progressive incremental development and only last one season. Dominant themes in colours are of course developed into characteristic weaves and patterns, themselves integrated into the thematic description. What value there is in all this activity is hard to judge. As the information is highly sensitive and essentially projective, there is little commercial incentive

for retrospective analysis and evaluation in any usefully quantitative way. Nevertheless, the forecasters continue to flourish. Certainly, the commercial reward for giving products the colours that current consumers will find attractive is enormous and anything that can be done to reduce the risk of failure is well worth the cost. Subscribers to some commercial forecasting sources can obtain confidential updates on the current popularity of colours in the collection which run from two years up to just six months before a particular prediction. Little of this material is accessible to detached scrutiny and published appraisals of this approach are meagre where they exist at all.

For this reason, one of the most interesting approaches to fashions in colour is that adopted by the American household magazine *House and Garden*.[51] This involves a continuing study (over a period that now amounts to thirty years) of sales volumes of standard ranges of consumer products concerned with interior decoration. Their surveys show a series of slow wave-like oscillations in the popular appeal of various colours. Cycles range from about twelve to twenty-five years. At first glance it is hard to see any coherent pattern of vibrations. Perhaps the clearest summary of the position is shown in Figure 7.11 where data from the annual trend-curves for many different colours are summarized under four broad headings or 'families'. Each family of colours will have many variants within it. At any one time, colours of quite different hue may be typical of any particular family. It appears that with colour, as with other symbolic goods, there are several cycles superimposed on one another. The hierarchic system of 'colour families', 'generic colours' and 'individual (*House and Garden*) colours' corresponds to the hierarchy of product classes, product forms and product brands. As before, we see individual colours fluctuating in popularity quite rapidly. Many only last one season. However, the generic colours from which they were derived change slowly while the popularity rating of colour families only varies very slowly over quite long periods of time. (Similar fluctuations of colour in female costume have been observed directly by counting samples of the population in a particular street in Tokyo on a regular basis over a period of years.[52]) It is not difficult to construct mathematical models incorporating the concept of feedback which will generate curves similar to those shown in the *House and Garden* survey.

Manufacturers and consumers alike are not only concerned with the shift of Taste embodied in the ebb and flow of one dominant colour over time. Nor is it just apparel in which colours invariably appear as part of an ensemble. Durable goods are often sold in families with a hierarchy of product levels corresponding to the needs of different markets. For example, a tool such as an electric drill may be sold in several different guises ranging from the simple do-it-yourself version sold in volume through the retail trade and by mail-order, where it is visually in competition with other fashion goods, to the professional model which is bought by businesses for their operatives. This hierarchy needs to be signalled visually and different paint colours offer an obvious method. The colour range which is chosen has not only symbolically to express this hierarchy, it must also cohere visually so that the brand may stand out from its competitors. Add to this the fact that decisions have to be made two years in advance of a product launch and the size and scale of the problem is manifest.[53]

Similar problems abound in the field of interior design and decoration and in merchandizing in the clothing industry. It is not surprising, therefore, that what may once have seemed a simple, intuitive matter of Taste has now become a technical task and that 'colour coordination' is now a professional service in its own right (no doubt swept by fashions of its own!). Just how much combinatorial variation is possible within a limited range of colours can be seen in *Showing Your Colors*, a useful guide to colour coordination in dress by Allen (Plate 21). Identical combinations of garments drawn in outline generate widely differing 'looks' when a few colours are permutated on them. In the characteristic manner of fashion reportage which Barthes criticized, each overall look is given a semantic interpretation. 'This section should be a favourite for those women boxed in by the rather strict codes of the office environment. The look is clean and conservative in styling . . . but the use of colour as an accessory creates a business-like but feminine look embraced by a majority of business women.'[54]

If we consider the system of possible variations in a relatively simple item of attire such as the shoe, we can develop the structuralist approach a stage further. The shoe can formally be regarded as a combination of a number of features each of which can have a range of values. A platform of two main components—sole and heel—which can each exist at a number of heights forms the basis.

There is a simple combination rule based on the practical problem of walking, 'the heel must be higher than the sole'. The upper part of the shoe can be divided into three regions—the front or 'vamp', the centre or 'quarters' and the rear or 'heel'. Each of these may be either singly open or closed, or two may be open, or all three may be open—the sandal.

Each of these parts may be expressed in different shapes. The toe or vamp may be long or short and each form may be pointed, rounded or squared. The toe may or may not have a separate cap. Shapes of heels may vary considerably for each particular height, and the point of attachment may vary in its distance from the rear of the shoe. Profiles of the heels differ from the side view—waisted or not—and may also vary in plan—square or circular. Again, there are some simple exclusion rules which restrict particular combinations of shape and height. A particularly narrow waist on a heel of great height may become too flimsy to last. There may be more subtle rules of proportion—a really short heel does not allow enough length to develop a curved waist at all.

Each of the different parts and each different form of the parts becomes in turn a vehicle for subsidiary decoration of all kinds and also a support for variation in colour. A particular shoe may therefore be regarded as occupying a point in a multi-dimensional matrix or space. A particular 'style' (or product form) will occupy a cluster of neighbouring points, a cluster which determines (by contrast with other previous clusters) the particular fashion theme for that season. That points do cluster indicates that, although the theoretical permutations (even when reduced by exclusion rules) are innumerable, most are in fact not used. Styles in shoes oscillate around certain preferred combinations of features interrupted by infrequent excursions into little inhabited regions of the space.

A similar structuralist description can be given to the combinatorial possibilities of the components of costume. Skirts may be long or short, narrow or full. Necklines may be high or low. A low neckline (*décolleté*) may be V-shaped—'plunging', U-shaped or 'horse-shoe', or cut straight across—'bateaux'. Similarly, sleeves may be long, short or three-quarter length, shoulders built-up or allowed to fall freely from the neck.

There has been an interesting attempt to systematize the significant components of the female costume in such a way that any costume may very quickly be given a code that can then be recorded on a computer file.[55] Clearly this will make the logging and analysis of larger samples of costume much easier. As always, each feature, either singly or in combination, can act as a 'support' for further decorative variations. But many combinations are rarely used in practice, certain combinations being consistently preferred above others. In dress, the history of fashion shows the slow movement of such combinations of forms, a total look or Gestalt, subsuming individual, more or less capricious features which can be regarded as transient ripples on the slower rhythm. For example, the silhouette or overall outline of the clothed body can adopt a limited number of contrasting possibilities: it may be plain and symmetrical or complex and asymmetrical. Emphasis may either be at the top, or the bottom, or both (emphasizing the waistline).

Recently, fashions have pointed to the overall Gestalt or look with a suggestive title, for instance, the trapeze-line, the A-line and the tube-look. Again, the fundamental posture of the female body seems to have undergone a progressive shift in its emphasis. A projecting lower half was characteristic of the abdominal 'slouch' seen in the Gothic period. This gradually reversed and in recent times the abdomen is held withdrawn while the breasts are pushed forward to give a more athletic look.

Although this change may initially have been connected with the widening availability of chairs for seating (the 'slouch' being more comfortable for prolonged periods of standing), there is little doubt that even such fundamental features as posture are socially acquired characteristics and therefore subject to changing fashions.[56] Each of the combinatorial structures for the various components marks out a set of possible variations within one or other of the overall Gestalts or deep structures suggested above. As in the case of shoes, there are certain practical considerations which define rules for excluding certain combinations. A short skirt may be any width whereas a long skirt cannot be less than a certain minimum diameter at the bottom lest movement be prevented entirely. These practical difficulties can be overcome by designing skirts with a different length at the front than

the back. While they look long they are nevertheless open to leg movement at the front. Other solutions involve long but split skirts.

It is a matter of empirical (social) trial and error to determine how much emphasis or elaboration a particular component, such as a skirt or neckline, may be given while remaining within the overall Gestalt of the time. As long as this overall Gestalt is maintained, such variation is quite unlimited—the history of costume is replete with examples of exaggeration to the point of perversity. The toes of shoes may reach such lengths that the flopping points require attachment to the hose near the knee. Skirts become so full that movement is impossible or so ballooned with padding or supporting cage that women find difficulty in passing through a door. Neither is male costume exempt from such exaggeration. Slashings of the sleeves and trimmings of the neck or headgear reached (to us) preposterous lengths during the seventeenth century. But what exactly are absurd limits? How far is 'too far'? When is 'over the top'? What controls the symbol limit in the field of costume?

Support for the idea of an underlying (and probably unconscious) Gestalt or ideal silhouette, which persists over time despite extensive variation in component and detail has come from a quantitative analysis of stylistic change in women's evening dress over several centuries. Kroeber collected dimensional data (from fashion illustrations and historic sources) on women's evening gowns and characterized them in terms of six basic dimensions: skirt length, skirt width, waist height, waist width, *décolletage* length and *décolletage* width.[57] He was able to show that despite short-term oscillations of between one to five years each of these dimensions showed an underlying trend which changed but slowly over long periods of time. An average of the wavelengths of each of these cycles is about one hundred years. However, the data showed clearly that different historical periods manifest great differences in the amount of variability compared with the average dimensions over the period concerned. At some times style is stable and although there may be comparatively rapid incremental shifts, such changes are smooth and not marked by abrupt changes and reversals. At other times, fashion is highly unstable and violent oscillations of dimensions are frequent. Moreover, there was a correlation between extreme dimensions and high variability. In the case of four dimensions out of six (the heights and widths of skirts and *décolletage*) there is a strong relationship between large dimension and low variability. The reverse is also true. When the dimension shrinks the variability increases. In the fifth case (height of waistline) a median position is associated with low variability. In the sixth case (diameter of waistline) the correlation is reversed, 'low' values of waist width being associated with low variability.

Kroeber interprets these findings in terms of an underlying Gestalt for the ideal female silhouette which is both long and full in skirt, with both wide and deep *décolletage* and a very narrow waist placed in a median position. When this norm is approached variations away from it are minimal. As fashion swings incrementally away from the Gestalt it is subject to *strain*. In this strained state it is liable to violent swings and abrupt reversals between 'extravagant' manifestations. Kroeber is really using a feedback model in which the perceived mismatch between a particular manifestation and the underlying Gestalt (what is 'proper')

stimulates experimentation. The metaphor of energy implied in the notion of stylistic strain or of an equilibrium Gestalt form can simply be translated into contemporary language by reformulating it in terms of economic mental codes or 'templates'.[58] Certainly, the model of an underlying equilibrium state from which actual examples diverge with progressively increasing strain does explain the saw-tooth rhythm shown in so many dimensions of fashion variation.

A similar historical survey to Kroeber's, this time based on women's daytime wear, was mounted by Agnes Young.[59] Young discovered that all the apparent diversity of shape in women's skirts could be reduced to variations on three conical forms, 'full backed', 'tubular' and 'bell shaped'. Apparently, each one of these forms is prominent in turn. There are three cycles per century.

Full backed	1760–1795 (36 years)
Tubular	1796–1829 (34 years)
Bell shaped	1830–1867 (38 years)
Full backed	1868–1899 (32 years)
Tubular	1900–1937 (38 years)

A complete cycle is about a hundred years—close to Kroeber's findings. There appear to be few attempts to bring Kroeber's investigations up-to-date or to investigate the connections between fashion and other sociocultural indicators in more detail. A notable exception is the work of Carman who extended the work of both Young and Kroeber up to the mid-1960s.[60] He used mathematical techniques to fit sine curves to the data which showed that superimposed on the 'Young cycles' was an oscillation of a much shorter period—about 30–50 years. He ascribed this to institutional factors (in contrast to the more fundamental anthropological factors underlying the cycles of Kroeber and Young) and, in particular, to 'the interaction of a variety of social institutions such as designers, sellers, media, consumers and the adoption and diffusion processes which link them'. The actual period seems to be linked to the human memory span. It amounts to about two generations, after which few remember some once hugely popular but long outmoded fashion. Designers can then judiciously introduce elements from the older style which then appear refreshingly new.

In the recent period studied by Carman the curves fitted the data less and less well. This may be ascribed in part to the fragmentation of social ritual in an increasingly pluralist society. What actually constitutes an evening dress when the variety of social functions—from cocktails with friends to a diplomatic reception—for which it might be required is so great? It is also in part a reflection of the much greater socioeconomic segmentation of the market. Given this fragmentation, the data is necessarily an average, covering progressively wider variations at any one time.

It has often been noted, at least at the level of anecdote, that there are coincidences between periods of extremes in fashion and periods of sociocultural disturbance such as wars and slumps. Kroeber's data certainly indicated periods of stylistic extremes at the time of the revolutionary Napoleonic wars and also at about the time of the First World War. Clearly though, there are no plausible historical explanations for why one war should produce high waisted dresses and another low waisted ones! Rather, as Kroeber argues, we should regard periods of sociocultural stress (by definition periods in which the 'comfort of belonging' is not at a stable maximum) as periods in which the underlying schema or Gestalt is subjected to willing assaults, producing extravagant or absurd variations.

An apparent correlation between the yearly rise and fall in the length of women's skirts in the USA and the annual gross national product of the American economy is also suggestive of the possible influence of institutional factors.[61] Both variables appear to rise and fall roughly synchronously. A dramatic fall in the length of women's skirts from about the knee to the mid-calf in the autumn of 1929 heralded the Wall Street crash a month later! Again, as with Kroeber's observations on the apparent correlation of fashion switches with time of war, it is hard to see any credible mediating factors connecting economic well-being and the amount of leg exposed by women of fashion! A more detailed analysis of the data, plotting changes in length year by year against similar figures for changes in GNP, appears to vindicate Kroeber's approach. Significant changes in economic well-being (up or down) lead to a willingness to experiment with more drastic alterations to the underlying fashion schema. Whether fashion presages or lags economic change cannot at present be determined. However, plausible mediating assumptions of the kind adduced by George Katona in his studies on optimism and affluence would seem adequate to account for the correlation.[62]

Occasionally, it is possible to spot some obvious correlation between a fashion vogue and wider institutional factors. The colour green has been largely absent from the marketplace in textiles for some years. According to the colour prediction experts it is slowly making a comeback. This is put down to a metaphorical identification with 'green' positions in environmental matters. Increasing exposure to green as a symbol and a uniform for political agitation is overcoming resistance in the wider consumer field. However, it is unlikely that the trend will succeed unless it fits in with the whole pattern of colour changes which derives from the structured transformations of colour preferences in previous years. Even the current popularity of simple and restrained packaging is part of the perennial oscillation of Taste between Roundheads and Cavaliers for all its ostensible justification in terms of reducing waste and respecting the natural environment.

What determines a particular Gestalt as the underlying schema within a particular social group and historical tradition is presumably an unconscious trade-off or compromise between eroticism on the one hand and decency on the other in the conduct of interpersonal encounters within particular contexts—the evening social gathering to take Kroeber's example. Psychoanalytic interpretations for the underlying schema of the ideal female body image abound although in the psychology of clothes as elsewhere they have little predictive value. No doubt other cultures and other situations would produce different schema. It would be interesting to see how far this type of detailed stylometric analysis could be carried in other product forms, chairs for example, or even perhaps motorcars.

Beyond the attempted precision of measured data on historic change there are the more or less traditional interpretive categories of style. Time-frames and typologies from the history of art and architecture can equally well be applied to the history of costume. 'Renaissance man' could hardly eschew his own dress

as an arena for expression, especially as his new thoughts were based on his interest in the Classic past—including its costumes. Similarly, we have mannerist costume, Baroque apparel, rococo and neo-Classic dress, Romantic and materialist garb, and so on up to the present day.[63] Obviously the particular distinctive features and the underlying Gestalt or schema which characterize for example, mannerist painting, cannot readily be translated into other media such as building, furniture or costume. What characterizes mannerism in these fields is the presence of certain salient devices or ordered sets of features which are metaphorical translations of those stylistic markers perceived as the determinants of style in painting. This adds up to a much looser typology than the distinctive feature approach attempted by the structuralist. Nevertheless, it is surprising how evocative such metaphorical pointers can be. Impressionist music or punk furniture are immediately recognizable categories. Style changes characterized by such descriptions are roughly paralleled in different fields of consumption, especially at times of sharp reaction which ensue when one style has reached an extreme. However, it is their very adaptability which makes such categories useful in predicting 'what comes next', which is the obsession of commerce and of all those concerned with the fashion business.

A recent example of a commercial service which attempts to use such broad categories for stylistic prediction in the field of furnishing is that offered by Promostyl (Plate 22). A couple of years ago, Promostyl predicted that there would be three new tendencies in styles of furnishing in the following year: Neo-Classic (conventional mainstream modern), Basic (cheap versions of high tech) and New Wave (punk inspired recycling of 1950s style).[64]

Without a great deal more quantitative information such prophecies are hardly a revelation. Nevertheless, an idea of the commercial power of successful stylistic prediction can be gained from the example of Coloroll, until recently, a major United Kingdom supplier of wallpapers and similar home decoration products.[65] This company operated a marketing strategy based on its perceptions of what it called *style waves*. These were seen as operating at several levels with different cycle times. A metaphorical display monitor 'tracks the progress of individual styles as they originate in Fine Art, move through fashion fabrics and enter interiors and then furnishing fabrics'. Beneath this was another metaphorical display which monitors a long wave fashion cycle with a frequency of twenty to thirty years. This apparently oscillates between 'Cottage' and 'Modern' styles.

It is not clear what visual images these generic descriptions connoted to the company but one obvious dimension is the familiar dialectic between Roundheads and Cavaliers—between restraint taken to the point of austerity and indulgence taken to extremes of informality, even an engaging disorder. Overlaid on this is another dimension which embraces time—'Cottage' connoting a nostalgic backward look while 'Modern' suggests futuristic imagery. Superimposed on this is a short wave cycle with a frequency of one to four years 'which reveals the popularity of new style families: geometric, cottage, primary and teutonic show up as the most recent cycles'. The final 'display' shows where each of these different style families is located in the endless drift between different socioeconomic groups.

Designers working for Coloroll were briefed according to these perceived fashion cycles. In a field where good timing is so important, the company claimed that the style wave analysis gave a competitive edge to its new product launches. 'Ignoring convention . . . (the company) . . . positioned these immediately before each peak. Over 90% used to be launched in the Back End . . . (of the season) . . . with no new product for Spring. "We call this surfing the Back Wave".' Sceptics of such generic extrapolations—especially those brought up in the cautious discipline of the history of art—should ponder the spectacular growth which this approach allowed during the 1980s.

Other 'designer' retailers such as Habitat operate with generic categories of furnishing imagery which are similar in their structural interrelationships to those employed by Coloroll. Habitat currently use 'Country House', 'Young + Bright' and 'City'. ('Romantic' does not feature in their more austere taxonomy of style, as it is still influenced by its founder's Modern Movement ideology.)

Just how difficult prophecy in these matters is can be seen by the fact that none of the 'designer' retailers in the United Kingdom foresaw the downturn in the High Street and are currently in severe financial difficulties. (Coloroll was broken up into constituent companies in 1990 and Storehouse, the company which controls Habitat among others, sold off Heals, the prestige furniture retailer, and was forced to close a large percentage of its retailing operation in the UK.) Nevertheless, despite the problems created by too rapid expansion followed by sudden fluctuations in overall demand, the generic categorization of lifestyle images has undoubtedly been a success as an important tool—if only one tool—of fashion marketing in dress and in home decoration.

It has been painfully learned that, in marketing, extrapolation is not prediction much less prophecy. But, of course, all structuralist interpretations and extrapolations fall far short of prophecy. In reality there are too many interacting factors to predict 'what will come next' with anything like total accuracy. Fashion is creative and therefore full of surprising twists and turns. But fashions—shifts of Taste over time—can often be understood better than the apparently arbitrary patterns of preference and prejudice operative at any one particular time. And we are more likely to understand them if we see them not merely from the outside as topping or, to put it more formally, as statistical extrapolation, but also from the inside. After all, it is open to anyone to engage, albeit often only vicariously, in that shared conversation which is Taste, an endless series of rejoinders in a metaphorical language, rejoinders that succeed precisely because they are, to those engaged in the conversation, socially—and therefore stylistically—obvious. This is really what designers do.

Notes and References to Chapter 7

1 D. A. Berlyne, *Conflict, Arousal, Curiosity*, New York: McGraw-Hill, 1960, p. 200 *et seq.*
2 See M. E. Roach and B. Eicher (Eds.), *Dress, Adornment and the Social Order*, New York: John Wiley, 1965, for essays on this topic. See also J. W. Philips and H. K. Staley, "Sumptuary Legislation in Four Centuries." *Journal of Home Economics*, Volume 53, Number 8, 1961, pp. 673-677. Reprinted in L. M. Gurel and M. S. Beeson (Eds.), *Dimensions of Dress and Adornment—a book of readings*, Iowa: Dubuque, 1975, p. 65.
3 Modern mass media need the ready availability of cultural 'pundits' who are able to pronounce on the cultural issues of the day. The transition from academic disciplines such as the history of art to journalistic punditry is eagerly sought and is now advertised as a possible career outlet for those who wish to study the discipline. Sir Roy Strong is an example of one of those who combined the role of director of a great museum (The Victoria and Albert) with a newspaper column on cultural issues of the day.
4 See E. M. Rogers, *The Diffusion of Innovations* (3rd Edition), New York: Free Press, 1983, and E. M. Rogers and F. F. Schomaker, *The Communication of Innovations*, New York: Free Press, 1971.
5 This picture of fashion is that favoured by R. Konig, *The Restless Image—a sociology of fashion*, London: Allen and Unwin, 1973.
6 See E. M. Rogers and F. F. Schomaker, *op. cit.*, p. 48 *et seq.*
7 This goes back at least to Tarde in 1890. See G. Tarde, *The Laws of Imitation*, trans. E. Parsons, Gloucester, Mass: Peter Smith, 1962.
8 E. M. Rogers, *op. cit.*, Chapter 5 and bibliography for a comprehensive review of the topic. A non-technical account of the computer modelling of the diffusion process is given in D. F. Midgley, *Innovation and New Product Marketing*, London: Croom Helm, 1977.
9 A good non-technical account of the statistics of the uptake of a new product is given in D. F. Midgley, *op. cit.*
10 For an account of the use of computer predictions in the fashion industry see G. S. C. Wills and D. F. Midgley, "Management Information Systems for the Retail Menswear Industry." European Seminar on Marketing Research (ESOMAR), Amsterdam, 1974, p. 175.
11 T. Veblen, *The Theory of the Leisure Class*, (first published 1899), London: Allen and Unwin, 1970, p. 60 *et seq.*

12 See E. M. Rogers, *op. cit.*, on this aspect of consumer behaviour.

13 In Europe, innovation in the design of yachts and related pleasure craft has come almost exclusively from the French, a nation that did not sail at all twenty years ago. They were able to build up a massive new industry from scratch using the most modern technology available. Their innovative boats were sold to a new market consisting of a generation who had no previous symbolic commitments to traditional forms. This example is repeated innumerable times in contemporary marketing.

14 D. Midgley, "The Seamless Stocking Saga." in G. Wills and D. Midgley, *Fashion Marketing*, London: G. Allen and Unwin, 1973, p. 415.

15 See T. Jaspersen, "Perception Changes in the Realm of Design." *Environment and Planning B*, Volume 13 (1), January 1986, p. 85.

16 M. Thompson, *Rubbish Theory*, Oxford: Oxford University Press, 1979.

17 There is evidence that measurable differences exist between the patterns of diffusion of innovation for men's fashions and women's fashions. Fashions for women are more likely to emanate from up-market purchasers while men's fashions have a possibility of being influenced by vernacular patterns or 'Street Style'. At the present time however, the fashion media are so quick to publicise new trends that it is difficult to track the processes of diffusion closely. See J. O Summers, "Identity of Women's Clothing Fashion Opinion Leaders." *Journal of Marketing Research*, 7, 1970, pp. 178-185.

18 Seasonal sales and 'events' provide a considerable proportion of the annual revenue of many stores. While *démodé* lines are genuinely discounted, so much custom is attracted to sales that much specially made cheap merchandise is also provided for the occasion, the so-called 'sale quality' goods.

19 Fashion journalism has played an important part in the diffusion of new styles since at least the eighteenth century and many regular publications existed promoting the latest vogue. See H. Freudenberger, "Fashion, Sumptuary Laws and Business." *Business History Review*, 1963. Reprinted in G. Wills and D. Midgley, *op. cit.*, p. 141 and references p. 145.

20 In dress, Dior's 'New Look' of the years immediately after World War II, and the Couréges' mini-skirt of the 1960s are good examples of new images that were instant successes in their canonical form. See R. Konig, *op. cit.*, and R. Broby Johanson, *Body and Clothes*, Faber and Faber, 1968.

21 For example those by Promostyl. See note 64.

22 This is a view taken by critics of the consumer society, for example V. Packard, *The Hidden Persuaders* (originally published 1957), reprinted Harmondsworth: Penguin, 1981, and V. Papanek, *Design for the Real World* (2nd Edition), London: Thames and Hudson, 1985.

23 See K. Popper, *The Poverty of Historicism*, London: Routledge and Kegan Paul, 1957, p. 13.

24 See R. Meyerson and E. Katz, "Notes on a Natural History of Fads." *American Journal of Sociology*, May 1957, p. 597.

25 G. Simmel, "Fashion." *American Journal of Sociology*, 62, 1957, p. 547.

26 See E. M. Rogers, *op. cit.*, p. 252 for a discussion of empirical correlations between socioeconomic status and innovativeness and, in particular, for a review of evidence that there is a linear relation between the two.

27 For an account of a relative failure to launch a new fashion vogue in dress by means of extensive publicity in parallel with the UK launch of the movie *The Great Gatsby*, see J. Dickens and J. Wilkinson, "Gatsby—Great or Small?" European Seminar on Marketing Research (ESOMAR), Amsterdam, 1974, p. 50.

28 See E. M. Rogers, *op. cit.*, p. 241 *et seq.*

29 D. F. Midgley, "Innovation in Male Fashion Markets—the Parallel Diffusion Hypothesis." ESOMAR, Amsterdam, 1974, p. 101. Midgley observed that the exposure to new men's fashions was largely visual, little verbal contact being noted. The effect was also amplified by the highly stratified nature of the UK retail market. An earlier research paper which claims to invalidate the Veblen hypothesis on empirical grounds is C. W. King, "A Rebuttal to the Trickle Down Theory" in the Proceedings of the AMA Conference: Towards a Scientific Marketing, American Marketing Association. 1963. Reprinted in G. Wills and D. Midgley, *op. cit.*, p. 215.

30 See C. Macdermott, *Street Style*, London: Design Council, 1987, T. Polhemus and L. Procter, *Pop Styles*, London: Vermilion, 1984, and P. Willis, *Profane Culture*, London: Routledge and Kegan Paul, 1978.

31 See T. Wolfe, *Electric Kool Aid Acid Kit*, London: Weidenfeld and Nicolson, 1968.

32 For an account of the topic of 'perceived risk', an important research tradition in the field of consumer behaviour, see T. S. Robertson, J. Zielinski and S. Ward, *Consumer Behavior*, Glenvill, Illinois: Scott Foresman, 1984, p. 184 and R. Markin, *Consumer Behaviour—a Cognitive Orientation*, London: Macmillan, 1974, p. 521 *et seq*. A discussion of the usefulness of this concept in the field of fashion is given in D. F. Midgley, *Innovation and New Product Marketing*, London: Croom Helm, 1977, p. 88.

33 See R. Markin, *op. cit.*, p. 248.

34 See E. M. Rogers, *op. cit.*, p. 288.

35 See S. D. Baumgarten, "The Diffusion of Innovations among US College Students." ESOMAR, Amsterdam, 1974, p. 83. Earlier literature is reviewed by D. F. Midgley, *Innovation and New Product Marketing*, London: Croom Helm, 1977, pp. 99-100.

36 For an overview of communications network analysis and the concept of 'weak ties' see E. M. Rogers, *op. cit.*, p. 294.

37 Recent United Kingdom 'gatekeepers' who have endorsed commercial products include the recently retired Commissioner for the Metropolitan Police (motor tyres) and the conductor André Previn (hi-fi units).

38 In the Bible, fashion is singled out for excoriation in Isaiah iii, verses 16-24.

39 E. H. Gombrich, "The Logic of Vanity Fair" in P. A. Schilpp (Ed.) *Essays in Honour of Karl Popper*, LaSalle, Illinois: Library of Living Philosophers, 1974, p. 927.

40 E. H. Gombrich, *op. cit.*, p. 929, quoting J. Gimpel, *The Cathedral Builders*, New York: Grove Press, 1961, p. 44.

41 On empathetic interpretation see T. Abel, "The Operation called Verstehen" in E. M. Madden (Ed.), *The Structure of Scientific Thought*, Boston: Houghton Mifflin, 1960, p. 158.

42 The logic of the distinction between literal and metaphorical interpretation in language is discussed by E. R. MacCormac, *A Cognitive Theory of Metaphor*, Cambridge, Mass: MIT Press, 1985, Chapters 4 and 5 on the Semantics of Metaphor and Metaphor as a Knowledge Process both provide suggestive starting points for an account of interpretation in the 'language of goods'.

43 The treatment of non-verbal meanings in terms of relative locations in a multi-dimensional semantic space goes back to Osgood. See C. E. Osgood, G. J. Suci and P. H. Tannenbaum, *The Measurement of Meaning*, Urbana: University of Illinois Press, 1957.

44 Perhaps this is one of the reasons why, when the time came to build a new cathedral church in Florence, the decision was made to construct, not an even higher nave than those constructed in the previous decades in Northern Europe and Milan, but the biggest span of dome to be undertaken since the Roman Empire. The decision to build a large cupola instead of the normal apse to end the nave was made in the first few decades after 1292, the year in which Arnolfo di Cambio was appointed as the architect. At the time

there was a considerable controversy over the use of Gothic forms in preference to Romanesque ones which overlapped the political controversy of Guelph and Gibelline. See F. D. Prager and G. Scaglia, *Brunelleschi—studies of his technology and inventions*, Cambridge, Mass: MIT Press, 1970. A similar point was made many years ago in the context of modern architecture when, in the 1950s there was a marked swing to a new style of low, rambling 'ranch' house in the US housing market. See D. E. Robinson, "Fashion Theory and Product Design." *Harvard Business Review*, Volume 36, Number 6, 1958. Reprinted in G. Wills and D. Midgley, *op. cit.*, p. 433.

45 See J. Broby Johanson *op. cit.*, for illustrated examples of such swings.

46 See C. Osgood, *op. cit.*, p. 244 *et seq.* for graphical depictions of related and opposing concepts. See also D. MacCormac, *op. cit.*, in particular Chapter 4 for an extended discussion of the vectorial relationships between concepts.

47 For example in R. Barthes, "Le bleu est á la mode cette année" originally *Revue Francaise de Sociologie*, Volume 1, Number 2, Centre de la Recherche Scientifique, 1960. Reprinted in G. Wills and D. Midgely, *op. cit.*, p. 313.

48 See D. Bannister and F. Fansella, *Inquiring Man—the Theory of Personal Constructs*, London: Penguin, 1971, pp. 66-67.

49 An interesting exception comes from Japan. See C. Minami and F. Tsubaki, "The Status of Women's Costume Colours on the Ginza Street." *Studies of Colour*, 26:2, 1979, p. 19.

50 For example those produced by the International Colour Authority, 33 Bedford Place, London WC1, and 343 Lexington Avenue, NY 11016, USA. Colour predictions aimed primarily at the apparel industry are issued to subscribers biannually and two years in advance.

51 N. Bertin, Colour Research Department, *House and Garden Magazine*, NY, USA.

52 C. Minami and F. Tsubaki, *op. cit.*

53 See C. M. Gantz, "Mass Market Colour Selection." *Colour Research and Application*, Volume 3, Fall 1978, p. 137 which outlines the strategy adopted by the Black and Decker company.

54 J. Allen, *Showing Your Colors*, North Ryde, Australia: Angus and Robertson Publications, 1986.

55 R. Holman, "A Transcription and Analysis System for the Study of Women's Clothing Behaviour." *Semiotica*, Volume 32, 1980, pp. 11-34.

56 R. Broby Johanson, *op. cit.*, has many useful silhouettes which emphasize the changing overall Gestalt of fashions.

57 J. Richardson and A. L. Kroeber, "Three Centuries of Women's Dress Fashions—a quantitative analysis." *Anthropological Records*, 2, 1940, pp. 111-153. Reprinted in G. Wills and D. Midgley, *op. cit.*, p. 47.

58 For an information theory model account of mental Gestalten see U. Neisser, *Cognitive Psychology*, New York: Appleton-Century-Crofts, 1967 and *Cognition and Reality*, San Fransico: W. H. Freeman, 1976. For a defence of the idea of 'experiential Gestalts' see G. Lakoff and M. Johnson, *Metaphors We Live By*, Chicago: University of Chicago Press, 1980, p. 77 *et seq.*

59 A. Young, *Recurring Cycles of Fashion*, New York: Harper and Row, 1937.

60 J. M. Carman, "The Fate of Fashion Cycles in our Modern Society." *Science and Technology Proceedings*, American Marketing Society, 1966. Reprinted in G. Wills and D. Midgley, *op. cit.*, p. 125.

61 See R. Broby Johanson, *op. cit.*, p. 216.

62 G. Katona, B. Strumpel and E. Zahn, *Aspirations and Affluence in the USA and Western Europe*, New York: McGraw-Hill, 1971.

63 Many of these archetypes are the subject of new cycles of fashion. See for example B. Baines, *Fashion Revivals from the Elizabethan Age to the Present Day*, London: Batsford, 1981.

64 Promostyl, *The Household Textile Trend Book*, Paris, 1982. Promostyl has existed for over two decades as a commercially successful 'prophecy' service to the fashion industry.

65 *Design*, February 1987, p. 24. Coloroll expanded sixfold in the years from 1982 to 1985 to £35m. Turnover in 1987 was £100m–£120m. Of course, much of the later expansion was driven by acquisition although the launch pad was undoubtedly successful marketing.

8. Quality and Equality

8.1 '*A commitment to a standard of values (or at least personal Taste) . . . that people whose business is counting things and predicting things do not in their natures possess.*'
Advertisement for a hamburger joint, London.

If your game is lightning calculation, quick quantification, then that which cannot be speedily and meaningfully quantified—that is, turned into an efficient market . . . tends to send you back into the grey area of aesthetics, which is precisely what the lawyers and accountants and marketing M.B.A.s sought to avoid when they chose their professions in the first place.

(However) . . . the real challenge of marketing lies in ways of winning the large public over to things that initially seem strange and difficult. But that requires . . . a commitment to a standard of values (or at least, personal taste)—the qualities that artists possess and that people whose business is counting things and predicting things, do not, in their natures, possess.[1]

Quantification or understanding?

These final quotations bring the issue of Taste right up-to-date. Yet, while cast in characteristically acid contemporary terms, they nevertheless echo many of the sentiments of Duveen's bold assertions from the beginning of the century with which we began, particularly the emphasis on a high quality of cultural production based on the exercise of 'good' Taste. And good Taste in those far off days was presumed to embrace complex and subtle perceptions and deep emotional tasks and relate thereby to the most important experiences of life. However, there is an important difference between the views of Edward Duveen and those expressed in the epigraph above. Duveen was writing before the onset of two trends which, throughout the twentieth century and with ever increasing force, have come to dominate Taste as they do everything else: the institutions of mass publicity and of market research. Although, in castigating their baneful effects, the author, Richard Schickel, is referring specifically to contemporary media—in particular, to painting, fiction, television and the movies (Schickel is a noted film critic)—his sentiments would be applauded by many designers, even though their ostensible concerns are with the world of industrial artefacts. It would strike a special chord with those designers who regard design as an important part of culture, continuous with—if not exactly equal to—high art.

As Schickel notes, the coincidental arrival of a new breed onto an increasingly industrialized cultural scene has ousted the exercise of appreciation and critical judgment (together with the artists and designers who exercised it). On one side there are the publicity men—advertising executives and specialists in media hype—and, on the other, market researchers and investment analysts. Given the scale of modern cultural enterprises such as the film industry, few will be surprised that this breed has triumphed and what Schickel calls an unholy alliance between 'big names' and 'big numbers' has bypassed Taste altogether. However, this did not happen overnight. Eight decades have passed between the utterances of Duveen and those of Schickel.

To understand what separates these two entirely different worlds we have to go back to the art and literature of the early twentieth century and look more closely at what happened when the values of a man like Duveen were challenged by the young rebels. In painting, there were the Fauves, the cubists, the Dadaists, the futurists and others to which we referred at the start of this book. Similar groups and movements can be found in writing and in musical composition.

Cultural historians have usually regarded this period of early Modernism as a heroic enterprise, a cultural revolution in which a lonely band of idiosyncratic geniuses overthrew the stuffy Taste of men like Duveen, supplanting it with a radically new Taste of their own—a Taste in which new kinds of critical judgment, more fitting to a democratic, technological age, usurped the traditional 'bourgeois' values they despised. Schickel points out that, in reality, the founding fathers of Modernism were for the most part not isolated and alone and neither were they despised. From the outset they worked within small but supportive critical subcultures and quickly learned to exploit the burgeoning publicity machinery of the twentieth century which, they soon discovered, was not interested in anything except personalities. So the rebels turned themselves into personalities, cultivating the outrageous and the eccentric in life styles that ran the gamut from the vagrant to the grandee but which were never less than topical and hence newsworthy.

Far from creating a new, democratic culture more in keeping with the times, the founders of Modernism set in motion a train of events which has lead to a situation in which, in our own time, increasingly incomprehensible or trivial products are sold on the strength of an increasingly strident personality cult of the artists themselves. Professionally packaged by the dealers, the myth of the artist as a personality rather than a hero becomes the unique selling point of otherwise unmovable merchandise.[2] Given that a radical rejection of traditional values has left us with no other standard by which to judge them, such works

8.2 *The* avant-garde *gallery needs presentation of a high quality in order to build the belief necessary to create and maintain a market. This leads to an impeccable, usually austere, interior design for the gallery space. Artist Deryck Healey's show 'Have I got your number?' at the Salama-Caro Gallery, London, England.*

are inevitably rated by what they fetch—by whatever price modern marketing hype can wring from collectors. And these days collectors are usually guided by curators, the cultural bureaucrats disbursing public funds to which we referred in Chapter 4. The logical end to this process is that the staggering prices paid for such works become the only measure of their value. The price becomes part of the subject of the work.[3]

In Schickel's view, the ultimate example of this process in which pecuniary quantification usurps critical judgment was that of the pop artist, Andy Warhol, who commanded ever higher prices for his studiedly banal works the more he claimed that there was no critical judgment behind them at all. Warhol was even able to assert that, in a sense usually fatal to markets in supposedly 'original' cultural products, his repetitive films, paintings and prints were often not even his but the products of other artistic vagrants associated with his 'Factory'. And his prices increased even more.[4]

Similar inflations can be noted among the 'big names' in other artistic genres such as the movies or television where, in recent times, many stars only play themselves, often owning

8.3 Public art in our time. Whether funding is public or private advice is invariably sought from the 'curators' —critics, historians and teachers—who make up an advisory caste. The result is often puzzling to those who are supposed to benefit. Sculpture by David Mach, Kingston, England.

the production company which is committed to creating 'vehicles' for this purpose.[5] Given that the value of a star is determined by his or her ability to fill seats in cinemas worldwide and that this in turn depends on public perception of the unique personality of the star, the motive for a close alliance between the fabricators of the personality of the star and the accountants who monitor the gross is obvious. Thus the apparatus for inflating personality sits quite naturally alongside another important branch of twentieth century numerology—the statistical sampling used in market research surveys.

In those fields of cultural production where the exercise of individual critical judgment has largely been abandoned in favour of personality and publicity, audience ratings and other kinds of head counting have come to be used, not only to assess likely response to new cultural products, but to predetermine what artists and writers get asked to produce in the first place and, by an obvious extension, which artists and designers get asked to produce them. Those products which can be shown by this method as most likely to guarantee a return on investment receive the most financial

support. This ensues an ever increasing concentration of resources on fewer and fewer artists ('bankable stars') and the reduction of a once diverse cultural industry to a mere handful of products that market research suggests will appeal to (or at any rate not alienate) the largest audience. This unholy alliance between heroic names and heroic numbers is held responsible for the progressive homogenization characteristic of American television and most of the movie industry which is now inextricably interwoven with it. A plethora of channels and stations churn out variations on a few banal archetypal entertainments—comic cartoons, chat shows, quiz games, soap operas and old cowboy films—between which bored and disinterested viewers flit with the aid of their electronic remote control buttons. The captains of this industry are no longer creative artists but the accountants, lawyers and marketing M.B.A.s castigated by Schickel. Their only critical value is publicity and their only Taste that which commands the best ratings.

Designers will find many familiar themes in this. Certainly, the frustration felt by those who find that their creative decision making is circumscribed by the constraints imposed by Philistine marketing departments claiming to measure scientifically 'what the public wants' is never far from the lips of original thinkers in most areas of consumer product design. For, despite some obvious differences (the industries of consumer manufacture are for the most part much less concentrated in the hands of a few 'players'), there are many disturbing similarities between contemporary media and the world of consumer goods. The same unholy alliance of big names and big numbers can be recognized in the growing phenomenon of 'designer products'. For a fee, a big name in the world of design gives his name to items far removed from his or her original field of expertise. From designer clothes to designer accessories to designer luggage to designer perfume to designer cigarettes, such 'spin-offs' are an established trend that enable products to command huge premium prices.[6] But why end here? Why not have designer diets, designer vegetables or even designer manure to grow them in? Such possibilities are only a modest caricature of the trend to the increasing use of personality and publicity as a substitute for genuine creativity. (Consumers addicted to this type of merchandise are known colloquially as 'label-queens'.) Further trivialized by popular journalism, the very word 'designer' (as in 'designer water', the generic soubriquet for bottled mineral water) becomes debased by such personification.

Parallel with this burgeoning exploitation of big designer names is the growing problem of big designer numbers. Many design practices are now big businesses in their own right. Funded through the stock market and thus committed to endless growth, they too are sucked in to the world of cartels and takeovers. What began as a couple artists and a pair of drawing boards is now a huge conglomerate, the result of labyrinthine megadeals in which the motivation is often defensive rather than constructive.[7] Such design companies now have to have their own market research departments, no doubt staffed with those same alien accountants and M.B.A.s that guide the contemporary movie moguls. Even in their own organizations, designers find themselves up against the same imperatives of quantification. (The fact that design is no longer a mere 'profession' but a real 'business' is widely stressed.[8]) But, however much an earlier

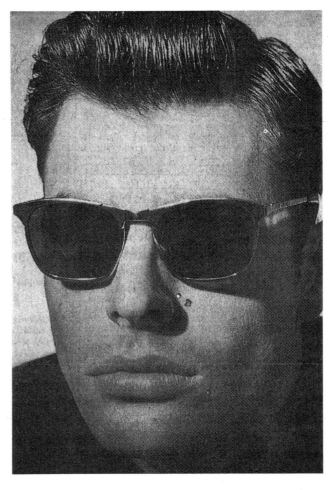

8.4 *Big names in the fashion world can enjoy the benefits of 'spin-off' products which use their name to create 'added-value'. Designer sunglasses by Jean-Paul Gautier retail at twenty times the standard supermarket product.*

generation of designers may rail, it is clear that quantification and prediction are not going to go away. Financial risks in creative businesses are now of the same order as those long since faced by large-scale manufacturers or retailers. These are simply too great to leave creative decisions and critical judgments merely to personal Taste—even that of the founding partners. It is clear that the accountants, lawyers and marketing M.B.A.s are here to stay in design as elsewhere.

So where does this leave individual values and standards of Taste? If consumer choice is

8.5 *Would you employ the professional of today? Louis Hellman's caustic comment on the snappy modern architect as proper businessman juxtaposed with Sir Christopher Wren who had to function without the aid of a marketing department.*

reduced to selection from a few products in mass markets already predetermined by the numbers men, does this inevitably mean the levelling down of culture? Must we accept the same decline in the material world as we have seen in the entertainment field? A glance at any market for consumer goods shows that a strategy of moving down-market is not inevitable and, where it does occur, it is often not sustainable. In many instances (cars for example) the trend is rather the reverse. To move up- or down-market indicates a clear commitment to a particular set of values, values adopted as conscious decisions by those who manage businesses.

From a purely business point of view, the problem is often not one of deciding which direction to go, but how to achieve a given market goal once this is set. And, in most cases, the difficulty which companies encounter is not only a matter of perceived differences between the values of the 'creative' people and those of the numbers men, but that of the languages in which these values are couched. In the management of appreciation and critical judgment or Taste, which has its roots in cultural symbols and myths and its most characteristic manifestations in art, we have an especially taxing instance of the general problem of how to manage innovation in businesses. Nevertheless, in any industry concerned with symbolic products, creative artists and designers on one side and number crunching accountants and marketing M.B.A.s on the other are each likely to be more effective if the barriers to mutual understanding are reduced.[9] Indeed, in

263

countries such as the United Kingdom, where the school system has hitherto separated the culturally inclined from the numerate at an early age, the very survival of manufacturing industry may depend on a more effective, 'holy' alliance between the parties.[10]

To date, there has been no overall theoretical framework for such an undertaking. We can only begin to provide one once we grasp that both approaches are concerned with Taste and that it is merely the different paradigms by which this is understood that are in collision. What is really at issue is a meaningful partnership between two complementary modes of understanding: understanding 'from the outside'—the public world of empirical study, quantification and prediction—and understanding 'from the inside'—of personal engagement in symbolic languages in which each of us is silently uttering his or her messages of individuality and community. What we need is not quantification *or* engagement but quantification *and* engagement.[11] This clash of rival world views is another example of the quintessential *Two Cultures* problem and will only be resolved by a revolution in education. This is also the reason why this book, which aims to contribute to such a revolution, has moved frequently between the languages of both cultures.[12] Any real change will entail a pervasive and long-term transformation in the structure of the educational curriculum which will bridge the gap between the world of symbols and values and that of numbers and predictions.

Taste engineering

Attempts to 'engineer' changes in public Taste by deliberate government intervention have

8.6 *Restaurant interior, Parc des Sciences et l'Industrie, La Villette, Paris, France. While popular for public spaces, neo-constructivism has never caught-on as a style for domestic building.*

not been frequent. While particular patterns of preference and prejudice in aesthetic matters among the populace are often an anathema to governing élites, the practical difficulties of changing them in any significant way are formidable. It is therefore not surprising that most open societies shy away from the attempt. However, in revolutionary situations, the newly successful regime may feel sufficiently confident of its powers to attempt radical changes in the symbolic expression of cultural values which in turn may lead to genuine changes in Taste. For example, the wholesale fabrication of symbols by Jacques-Louis David for the revolutionary government in

8.7 Mussolini's brand of neo-Classicism was also overscale and portentous but executed with a higher level of architectural understanding than Hitler's. Foro Romano, Rome, Italy.

France in the so-called 'Festivals of the Supreme Being' undoubtedly led to the widespread acceptance of the stripped-down Doric of the neo-Classic style in architecture, interior design and dress.[13] The Russian revolution also led to the widespread promotion of a radical geometric abstraction as the official style of the Bolshevik government. This did not prove influential beyond officially sponsored art and architecture and its main consumers at the time were the intelligentsia. It was soon abandoned by Stalin in favour of more traditional images of state power especially an overscale and overblown variant of neo-Classicism. Even so, in particular fields such as graphic art, the new style effected permanent changes in Taste far beyond the borders of the Soviet Union itself.[14]

Nazi Germany also paid a great deal of attention to the possibilities of using 'Taste engineering' as a tool for creating a decisive shift in cultural values, more often than not, falling back on large-scale neo-Classicism in its architecture. Fascist ideology was however both confused and eclectic in its sources and official Taste in the Third Reich embraced other traditional forms including Gothic and various styles of native vernacular in its attempts to create a uniquely fascist culture.[15] The Chinese 'cultural' revolution resulted in attempts to impose a uniform modesty in clothing and presentation in the name of a radical egalitarianism. Even here though it is probable that the ostensible omnipotence of state and the party was, in matters of Taste, limited to more or less public symbolism and overt outdoor display.[16] It is even more difficult to know what goes on indoors, let alone influence it. What the citizen puts on his walls or uses to cover his floors and windows is more likely to be constrained by shortages than controlled by *diktat*.

Curiously, it is in one of the major democracies, Great Britain—that archetype of the open society in which, as Matthew Arnold astringently observed, the Englishman belligerently asserts his God-given right 'to do as he likes'—that we find one of the most extensive interventions in matters of Taste. Unlike the previous examples, this was not a matter of policy—the exertion of state influence in the interests of a political ideology. It was on the contrary an almost accidental by-product of the necessity to solve the problem of desperate shortages of consumer goods caused by world war.

During the Second World War, all furniture and clothing manufacture in the United Kingdom came under government control. There was an acute scarcity of materials and skilled manpower and under Emergency Legislation the production of all artefacts was regulated in style and workmanship.[17] A small group of 'Modernist' designers produced a series of standard types of plain, but well-made furniture and garments which were sold on ration. For six years the population was adorned and all new homes were furnished with the new style, thereby spreading the gospel of 'functional' form far beyond its original coteries of upper middle class devotees of Modernism. Working class families were now also exposed by law to what had been very much a minority Taste. It must have seemed the final breakthrough of the plain, undecorated style for which pioneers had struggled in

8.8 *Ricardo Bofil creates a new kind of classical language using pre-cast concrete units and at the same time plays skillfully with the traditional forms, turning columns into transparent glass walls. Yet the association of neo-Classicism with totalitarianism is so complete that many think of Ricardo Bofil's apartment blocks as threatening, even fascist, although they were created in a democracy.*

vain throughout the 1930s.[18] Alas their hope was not fulfilled.

What happened when the law was eventually abandoned is instructive of the issues that are at stake. In the event, the working classes were not won over by their exposure to the obvious practical merits of 'Utility' despite the fact that rigorous quality control meant that, for many, it was the first furniture or clothing they had seen that was not blatantly shoddy in construction or manufacture. As soon as the legislation was abandoned after the Second World War, Utility was immediately displaced by a resurgence of styles which catered for a much richer symbol laden Taste. Richard

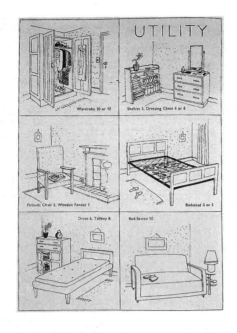

8.9 *Utility furniture—a modern style which was imposed throughout the United Kingdon during the Second World War. Designed under the supervision of Gordon Russell, it was all that could be obtained under the rationing scheme.*

8.10 *In terms of quality, Utility provided many of the working classes with hardier furniture than they could previously afford. The 'Morris' textile was added later.*

Hoggart wrote perceptively about this swift demise just after it happened. Speaking of the working class home he noted:

the older forms may often look grotesque, and the new ones debased, but the tradition is unbroken. The older-style pots and decorated sea-shells are disappearing from the mantle-piece but the replacements are just as vivid. It was not difficult to guess that working-class people would go back, as soon as they no longer had to buy utility furniture to the highly polished and elaborate stuff the neon-strip stores sell. Gone as we have seen is the lush aspidistra in its equally lush bowl . . . But its successors in the window space speak the same emotional language.[19]

Hoggart's vivid autobiographic descriptions can be verified in contemporary photographs. Furthermore, the employment of a rich 'emotional language' did not die with the demolition of the older slums in which Hoggart's generation grew up. People took their familiar interiors with them to their new flats and new towns. This language extended virtually unchanged into the suburbs and survives in diluted form in the High Street furniture shop to this day.

It was not merely the style of an alien social group that was rejected with Utility but the whole artificial distinction between genuine usefulness and superfluous embellishments—a distinction at the heart of the functionalist beliefs. In this, of course, the working class were right. For embellishment—the lush symbols on the aspidistra vase—although a 'written' message, is just as functional in its way as the concavity which keeps in soil and water. Its function, however, is a social one. It expresses in visual form, a value system, an image of an ideal home or an affirmation of worth for someone who occupies a particular (lowly) position in a complex social hierarchy. A glance at a particular set of symbols will tell a man that he is spiritually 'at home' and among his own kind. Friendship, brotherhood and the solidarity of belonging to a group, not to mention the antithetical values of individuality, rivalry and up-staging, are messages of primary importance, well worth the sacrifice of a little extra bodily comfort or durability if the price for that comfort is a 'meaningless' nakedness of form.

In more recent times, the rejection of Utility indoors has been matched by a similar rejection of austerity outdoors. Over the past decade in the United Kingdom, there has been a large scale privatization of public housing leading to a proliferation of new private owners of houses and apartments—most of which had been designed on the best 'functional' principles. Many of these new proprietors immediately demonstrated their desire to be rid of the mass-produced minimalism to which they had previously been restricted, by decorating the exterior of their dwellings with every kind of ersatz period finish and symbolic trim (kitsch) to the dismay of their designers and their erstwhile landlords alike (Plate 23).

China, subsequent to the Cultural Revolution, offered the same example. Once the constraints of an imposed uniformity were removed, there was an explosion of diversity, but diversity along well worn symbolic channels and expressed in the forms of earlier traditions. There seems little doubt that, once the resources become available, there will be a similar rejection of an imposed minimalist uniformity by the newly freed countries of Eastern Europe and the Soviet Union (Plate 24).

8.11 *Pre-fabs. Britain's top Modern Movement designers were employed to create new types of mass-produced industrialized housing. These were provided during and after the Second World War in an attempt to solve the homeless crisis brought about by bombing and neglect.*

8.12 *It was not long before the tiny functional interiors were overlaid with decorative trim reminiscent of earlier forms. Plastic timber beams are stuck onto asbestos cement walls to create the effect of a Tudor cottage.*

Quality in a democracy—the designer's responsibility

Until now we have treated the contentious issues which arise when matters of Taste are involved in the workings of contemporary societies largely as academic problems—the province of theory rather than practice. For example, the question of whether all Tastes are relative or whether there are at least some absolute values—qualities in objects and settings which are to be admired whether they are popular or not—has been discussed historically, most recently in the context of Pierre Bourdieu's somewhat abstract structural schemas. But, although accounts of Taste such as Bourdieu's have satisfying explanatory power, they do not in themselves suggest an agenda for action. There is still a necessary gap between facts and theories on the one hand and values and actions on the other.[20] This gap can only be bridged by an assertion of particular values and a commitment to action by individuals and groups, including designers themselves.

In moving from detachment to commitment, designers have a special responsibility to others. This derives from their privileged position as the creators of all those images on which the exercise of Taste in a consumer society ultimately rests. For, in addition to the material rewards outlined in Chapter 4, they also derive considerable personal satisfaction from the exercise of this creativity in, and for, itself—regardless of any other rewards it may bring. These 'intrinsic' satisfactions form a reward system which is often stronger than the external reward systems—money, status and power—which we discussed in Chapter 4 and which otherwise frame their professional lives. However, designers must recognize that their very existence as professional individuals depends on a division of labour which removes precisely these intrinsic satisfactions from the working experiences of most other people.

Earlier systems of craft production did not entail that sharp division between conception and execution which is the defining characteristic of the practice of design in modern manufacturing economies. A craftsman exercised considerable scope for his inventive skills which were inextricably mingled with his manual dexterity. Mechanization brought a halt to both. Modern conditions of production, far from providing the continuing and often profound emotional rewards of self-expression (one of the reasons that the designer's professional autonomy is so jealously guarded), guarantee that the majority are 'alienated' from the material world which they themselves produce by their work.[21]

If (for the alienated majority) production is removed as a source of intrinsic reward, all that remains is vicarious satisfaction through consumption. In the all-important personal settings which give meaning and continuity to otherwise factitious lives, the only satisfactions available for most people are those obtained through the consumption of goods which embody the creative acts of others. Given this asymmetry in the distribution of intrinsic reward, designers have an obligation to create products and settings which promote the satisfactions that they themselves enjoyed in designing them to the maximum.

However, there is a more important reason for maintaining this challenge, more important even than the obligation to strive for equality in the intrinsic satisfactions of production. Consumption, when based on the supply of goods

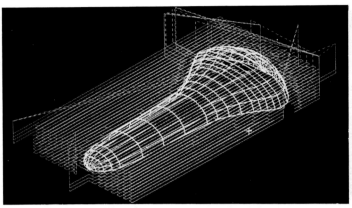 

8.13 *Alienation of the worker reaches its extreme in the use of robots and computerized machine tools. In the case of the computer controlled router, a high speed cutting machine, the design is created elsewhere and stored as software. The machine operative merely has to put the blank wood or metal onto the worktable—endlessly.*

denuded of intrinsic satisfactions, does not and cannot fulfill its promises. In a search for emotional satisfaction, people buy goods characterized by a perfunctory simulation of truly integrated symbolism, goods which quickly exhaust their immediate interest. There is no recourse except further purchase. More and more new goods are acquired in a futile search for a fulfillment that is not to be had and the production system churns endlessly on, creating wants where they never previously existed in order to dispose of ever larger quantities of goods until the very existence of life on earth is threatened.

Whatever turns out to be the ultimate limit to growth, there is no doubt that the present system is ultimately unstable and must one day come to an end. Yet, as we have seen, attempts to engineer new, more austere Tastes or to impose sharply attenuated patterns of consumer behaviour by direct state intervention have had little success. Designers can have little hope of succeeding where dictators have failed. The road to an ecologically sound design lies elsewhere. Working with the grain of the social structure and attempting to redirect human motivations by offering more intrinsically satisfying products to the market is the only

realistic way in which designers can contribute to a more profound and hence more stable material culture.

The goal of a democracy must be to offer equality of opportunity in terms of access to the satisfactions of life, including the intrinsic satisfactions embodied in goods. The designer in such a democracy must offer not the opportunity of *equality* but the opportunity of *quality*, quality in both the perceptions of meanings and values in the surroundings of everyday life in the public environment and quality in the intrinsic satisfactions which contemplation of present possessions offers their owner. Only when we are satisfied with what we have will the drive for progressively more goods finally be abated. How will this be achieved? How can designers enrich the intrinsic quality of life without necessarily promoting the values and symbols of their own subculture or that of the ruling (largely commercial) élite on whom they currently depend for their patronage?

The grey area of aesthetics

What I have called the 'intrinsic satisfaction' of goods is a quality that traditionally fell within

8.14 *Precious things. Mantelpieces traditionally provide a prominent shelf for the display of a variety of objects of varying source, quality and value which remind the owner of who they are. Mantelpiece belonging to a pensioner, Farnham, England.*

the remit of aesthetics, where it was rather vaguely attached to the idea of the 'beautiful'. However, the idea that aesthetics concerns an elusive property of beautiful objects, a property which cannot easily be described but which nevertheless requires proper training of 'rightly constituted minds' to enable perception and appreciation, is nowadays properly questioned. In the pluralist, post-modern world which we now inhabit, exercises in good Taste such as those discussed in Chapter 1 seem quaint indeed. Democratic societies demand that aesthetics is understood in much broader terms than these. Beauty is certainly in the eye of the beholder and Taste cannot be limited to the symbols and values of élites—whether

these are aristocratic or bourgeois or, as many today would wish, professional élites drawn from the cultural bureaucracies.

Perhaps a resolution of these paradoxes of quality and equality would be easier if we start among the consumers themselves rather than with assumptions about aesthetic quality. What gives *them* intrinsic satisfactions? What kind of object or setting do consumers of material culture find most precious? What qualities do these consumers find valuable in their dearest possessions? Most important of all, are there common features in the attribution of intrinsic value by different types of consumer—young or old, male or female, rich or poor? The answers to such questions could form the basis for design interventions which could be directed to raising the intrinsic qualities of goods and settings for all consumer groups from whatever class.

Of course, commercial interests (the accountants and the marketing M.B.A.s) will argue that sales figures in themselves provide us with all the information we require. On this view, what sells is what consumers, at the time they contemplate a purchase, feel is most precious to them. Strangely, little research has been done to verify this assumption, which flies in the face of all we know about an open cultural marketplace dominated by the cult of personality with all its propensity for the stock solution, the immediately seductive, and the easily understood.

Systematic efforts to document the life of goods as part of the myriad settings which people create in order to live their lives have been relatively recent. These are usually confined to unstructured visual records and informal interview techniques. One problem with this approach, especially when poignant quotations from interviews are presented juxtaposed with beautifully composed images, is that it is often difficult to know whether the poetry that emerges from such 'documentation' of the lives of ordinary people would be recognized by the participants themselves. Are these revelations true research findings or are they an artistic creation, the work of those who edit and present the data? Despite these ambiguities, the value of an extensive visual archive is inestimable given that the present disappears so quickly from view. A recent project in the United Kingdom called 'Household Choices' shows what might be achieved.[22]

One of the more objective (because unedited) parts of this project was the investigation by the Tom Harrison Mass Observation Archive of the University of Sussex into which domestic objects people felt most attached to and why. Some twelve hundred respondents where asked to write about their favourite or most precious objects. Although the replies were varied, the proportion who gave reasons concerned with usefulness were very much in a minority. Respondents were overwhelmingly agreed in their attribution of preciousness on the basis of quite personal and intimate associations, for the most part associations with their immediate family. Photographs of parents and children, heirlooms, goods purchased on memorable trips with spouses and leftovers from childhood possessions, were among those goods considered most precious, despite the fact that large sums may have been spent on other items such as leisure equipment, motor cars or home entertainment.

Although it was noteworthy that respondents said very little about interpersonal values at any level beyond their immediate family and job circle, the survey responses (which in

8.15 *Precious things. Middle class manners usually preclude the display of family photographs in the room where visitors are received. Bedrooms suffer no such embargos. Mantelpiece belonging to a writer and artist, London, England.*

general replicates the rather more rigorous earlier studies by Mihalyi Csikszentmihalyi in the United States) nevertheless endorse our commonsense, introspective impressions that intrinsic satisfactions bear little relationship to functional considerations or economics.[23] For most people such goods act as signposts towards a stable personal identity in a mobile—even febrile—society where time flies, families scatter and to buy is to belong. From the designers point of view, these studies document a profoundly unsatisfactory state of affairs in that large investments of time and effort embodied in supposedly functional goods yield only a modest amount of intrinsic satisfaction among their consumers.

8.16 *Memories of private intimacies between spouses or family are cardinal in the selection of precious things. A son long-since grown-up and with children of his own left behind his collection of hippopotami. Home of a design historian, Scottsdale, Arizona, USA.*

Csikszentmihalyi's researches showed that explanations for respondents' attachments to their favourite objects in terms of symbolic relationships alone were not enough. Things were valued for the pleasure that their contemplation gave, even when these symbolic relationships were not obviously in play. Csikszentmihalyi had earlier studied the nature of the intrinsic satisfaction perceived in activities which are engaged in, often ardently or even obsessively, for their own sakes. He called such activities *autotelic*.[24] Mountain climbers, chess players, rock dancers and a musical composer were chosen as representative of various activities which totally engage their protagonists, blotting out all other stimuli from consciousness while they are undertaken. Based on his findings from a sample of those who found their greatest satisfaction in such autotelic activities he singled out a quality of perceptual engrossment that he called *flow*. Flow occurs when people are faced with some kind of environmental challenge based on a clear goal (this is why competitive games are frequently mentioned as quintessential flow experiences) and when they can exercise a level of skill which is commensurate with the particular challenge.

In suggesting a mental model for this process, Csikszentmihalyi refers to the earlier work of David Berlyne which we have already considered.[25] (The title of his work *Beyond Boredom and Anxiety* alludes to that same biological foundation for our perceptions of pleasure that Berlyne set as the basis of his theories on aesthetics.) There appears to be a biological basis for the connection between the sensation of pleasure and a certain threshold of sensory arousal. When this arousal arises from complex cognitive and sensory-motor activity, and especially when arousal arises from an external challenge involving multiple orders which need simultaneous attention, the brain removes it from momentary consciousness. This kind of intense involvement with an external challenge which engages the subject in more or less automatic behaviour and at the same time renders him oblivious to everything else generates a kind of rapture, an intense pleasure coupled with a lowered external awareness—the defining characteristic of flow according to Csikszentmihalyi's subjects.

In addition to these more spectacular examples, Csikszentmihalyi also considered this type of spontaneous perceptual stimulation as it occurs in everyday life. Almost unnoticed in the myriad enactments of secular life are innumerable tiny autotelic activities ranging from idly looking at objects to day dreaming or humming a tune. Modest enough ways of momentarily interesting a person and amounting to reverie rather than rapture, such activities nevertheless shared many of the features of the more deliberate and structured flow embodied in activities such as games, dance or musical composition. They were therefore called *microflow* activities. Denied these under experimental conditions, subjects all reported various degrees of distress.

Csikszentmihalyi suggested one obvious remedy for the emotional poverty of much of daily life which was to encourage the pleasures of flow behaviour, including that which arises from those activities which involve the perception and pleasurable contemplation of goods. Clearly, there has to be a disposition to attend to possessions in this way and many consumers may need some training in this mode of perception—a topic to which we will come in a moment. If a person's possessions are to be capable of stimulating lasting intrinsic satisfaction however, it is clearly desirable that they are designed from the outset, not only to provide the emotional goals and perceptual challenges which stimulate flow, but moreover to be inexhaustible to this kind of contemplation. Designers therefore need to know what kinds of objects have these properties so that as much encouragement to pleasurable contemplation as possible can be 'designed-in' from the beginning.

Given the infinite diversity of goods and the enormous variety of family life and its settings, there can be no question of any universal aesthetic prescription for flow. There are, however, some general pointers which indicate a different direction for design than that which emerges from the paradigms of problem solving or marketing. These signal a return to older preoccupations albeit within a contemporary context. If we ask what artefacts quintessentially present us with symbolic goals, perceptual challenges and invitations to flow behaviour—eliciting both reverie and rapture—the obvious answer is 'works of art'. Works of art are contrived so that they give intrinsic pleasure and are at the same time inexhaustible to our attention. Poetry and music, painting and sculpture, no less than the dance studied by Csikszentmihalyi simply *are* flow. At this level of engagement 'you are the music while the music lasts'.[26] To engage our perceptions at this level, design must at least be art whatever else it may be. It thus follows that the study of art—aesthetics—is far from being a 'grey area'. It must be the central concern of design.

On the face of it though, this view of design as art runs completely counter to the prevailing notion that design should be as literal as possible so that objects are transparent to their meanings. In the traditional theory of design, meaning is largely restricted to an account of instrumentality and an understanding of use. We should therefore draw a distinction between those goods which are primarily tools and the remainder which have broader functions especially where these functions include the facilitation of social intercourse and the maintenance of personal identities. Obviously, in the case of tools, self-evidency—freedom from ambiguity and, in consequence, the prevention of contemplative flow—is an important consideration. Taste has but a minor role to play in such situations. No one wants a surgeon to be distracted by the decoration on

274

8.18 *There is a valid place for the* tool aesthetic. *Few would prefer to be shaved with these highly decorated razors, shown at the Great Exhibition while the decoration on a surgeon's knife would be regarded with even less favour.*

his scalpel and there are equally good reasons for ensuring that the cockpit of an airliner is furnished differently from a living room. In a world of poetry there is a proper place for the plainest prose.

The mistake of the classical theories of modern design was to assume that the prose of the 'tool aesthetic' could be applied everywhere whereas its use should clearly be restricted to certain limited, task-driven situations. However, such situations and the goods that provide their settings are very much in a minority in everyday life. *Taste Today* addresses itself instead to all those other everyday, poetic goods and settings in which symbolic expression and contemplative flow is the kernel of their enjoyment and even a prime reason for their existence.

Design and the poetry of everyday things

Of course, art is many other things besides flow. The perception of art is therefore a commensurately complex process. But to isolate the aspect of flow is to focus for the moment on the aspect of time as a crucial component of aesthetic perception. In fact it is just this component which has so far been neglected in the discussion of Taste. Hitherto, accounts of the perception of meaning in everyday objects—whether the earlier structuralist models discussed in Chapter 2, the more sophisticated versions of Bourdieu, or the recent developments in product semantics—have been essentially static. This is not a criticism. Insights into momentary relationships from so-called 'synchronic' or snapshot views of behavioural processes are valuable enough in themselves.

However, when the perception of meaning in things is viewed exclusively as a synchronic phenomenon, an important component of the pleasure that attaches to those perceptions is left out. It is not only the output of those perceptions, the discovery of this or that meaning, which is pleasurable. It is the process of perception itself. Discernment of symbolic meanings provides those clearly defined goals which are necessary to trigger engagement in flow behaviour. If, however, these goals are too easily achieved, then flow cannot be sustained. We are 'in one side of the percept and out at the other' too soon. For aesthetic flow to be maintained, a significant symbolic goal must exist before us which we feel to be attainable but must always in the end elude us. Works of art embody complex recursive orders which are immediately clear and lead us on to some symbolic goal. At the same time, they are interlocked with one another so that they always fold back on themselves. There is no final end to the cognitive maze. As Wallace Stevens notes in one of the most pregnant utterances in his *Adagia*, 'Poetry must defeat the intelligence almost successfully'.[27] This is the real reason why aesthetic experiences may indeed be perceived as 'initially strange and difficult'. However, aesthetic experiences of this kind are the exact opposite of those purveyed by the commercial *avant-garde* which are strange and difficult only because they are at once banal and obscure.

Today, most designers see in art merely an initial training ground for certain useful techniques, in particular the skills of depiction—figurative drawing plus a little three-dimensional modelling. Artistic values such as the expression of profound human experiences are largely ignored and the 'hidden orders' of art which lead to flow are not considered at all.[28] Indeed, the contemporary gallery scene has moved so far away from the concerns of the public at large, that it would be difficult to do much with most of the art that is currently being produced—even if designers were willing. If design is once more to become an art in a serious sense of the word then it must return to artistic sources outside the reach of today's commercialized *avant-garde*. Given the immense power of the institutions of publicity so eloquently indicted by Schickel, the best hope of change seems to be to influence the motivations of designers during their education.

One example gives an idea of what might be achieved. For nearly two decades the notion that design should be treated as art has been central to the educational philosophy in the design school at Kingston. Applied aesthetics, allied with studies in the social basis of stylistic preference or Taste, has been an essential part of every design student's curriculum, equal in status to workshop and studio technique. Much of this effort has paralleled and sometimes anticipated the work described earlier under the heading of product semantics.

Take, for example, what has been called the *semantic translation*. This is a useful technique for training design students intuitively to grasp those structural invariants or forms, for the most part too complex to be given explicit descriptions, which carry the meanings of works of art. The process of re-expressing a set of meanings embedded in one medium into the forms of another is not new of course. For example, the reinterpretation of musical themes in terms of abstract sculpture dates back to the Bauhaus.[29] In adapting this idea for our own purposes, the importance of flow was recognized from the outset, although it was not called that at the time. Our starting point was a realization of the importance of the way in which the 'hidden orders of art' induce a continuing ebb and flow of perceptual tension and relaxation as we attempt to decode their recursive structures. An early piece of research on flow in music by Rogge gave the us the start towards an awareness of the central significance of this experience.[30] That the experience of music entails the ebb and flow of tension through time, and that the structure of this experience could be carried over into written narrative, gave us the idea that it might be possible to effect a semantic translation of the ebb and flow of tension in poetry into visual terms, for example, an abstract colour composition (Plate 25). At least some of the flow of the original poem might be embodied in the visual expression even though, on the face of it, painting does not exist as a phenomenon in time at all. By arranging the forms and colours of an abstract composition in a particular way (parallel stripes or nested squares for example) it is possible to influence the sequence in which they are attended by an observer. In this way, perception of the colour relationships is spread out over time in a manner similar to the serial process of listening to the music.

Another part of our thinking was the idea that visual meanings, like those in spoken languages, are inherently structured and, therefore, that their perception depends on the establishment of relationships within a set of alternative possibilities. If we provided a set of related poems, comparison of one with another and the perception of similarity and difference between each poem, or between stanzas or phrases from within the same poem, would be more likely to generate an understanding that could be translated into congruent sets of colour compositions than one isolated example.[31] Poetry was chosen in which such alternatives were easily discerned.[32]

Once the ability to carry complex meanings from poetry into abstract visual terms had been achieved, it was a small step to carry it further into a piece of useful design where figuration might not have been appropriate (Plate 26). The effectiveness of this general approach to the education of designers may be seen in the many striking design images which have been produced.[33]

The work of Reinhart Butter, and others in the field of product semantics, although starting from a somewhat different standpoint, also shows what can be achieved by a richer vision of the nature of design. To date, product semantics has not been very concerned with issues of ambiguity and art, or with time and

the flow of attention, but there is plenty of room for these broader themes within the overall theory.[34] There is the beginning of an international interest in these new ideas and practices as conferences, publications and research projects spread a proper understanding of the importance of the subjective and the expressive in the perception and appreciation of everyday objects.[35] The intellectual tools are there for designers who wish to put, not only meaning, but also the intrinsic satisfactions of flow, back into everyday goods and settings (Plates 27 & 28). Designers now have it in their power to repay some of the creative ransom that their profession exacts from the rest of the world which 'consumes' design.

Consumer education and cultural values

What, however, of the rest of the world? What should a democracy do to help its citizens enjoy their goods and settings to the full? How should it provide access for its citizens to a good life which involves not just the purchase and ownership of goods but the exercise of aesthetic perception, critical judgment and emotional engagement that we have called Taste? The democratization of economic resources, especially the wider distribution of access to rising resource trajectories, presents some formidable political difficulties, but what about the democratization of what Bourdieu called 'cultural resources'?

Clearly, little can be done to influence the distribution of cultural resources inherited at birth. A 'good background' is not something that can be redistributed by legislation. This leaves only what Bourdieu called 'acquired cultural resources'—primarily, education. It is education (in all senses of the word) that must bear the burden of redressing the inequalities of distribution inherited with each person's birth into a particular location in the social system. Obviously, anyone may increase his cultural capital through education. Beyond this, however, effective strategies for converting economic resources into cultural resources (and vice versa) can also be taught. In this sense, education offers the promise of escape from necessity into that cultural freedom which comes through the effective exercise of choice. 'Making the best of it' becomes a positive and creative stance far removed from mere passive submission to brute circumstance.

What can be taught that is relevant to everyone and is, at the same time, free from the cultural bias of any particular group? We have previously discussed the Wundt curve and its adaptation by Berlyne to illuminate and explain many familiar facts concerning our feelings of pleasure and well-being and the relation of such feelings to the amount and variety of stimulation from the environment.[36] Rooted in our biological nature, these psychological observations surely transcend cultural boundaries. Yet they are seldom discussed in educational circles. Indeed, apart from Berlyne himself, only Tibor Scitowsky and Csikszentmihalyi have sought to put them to work in wider contexts.[37] Certainly, teaching us scientific observations about our mental make-up does not of itself alter that make-up. Moreover, to be truly universal, educational principles based on science would have to be presented at a fairly high level of abstraction. Nevertheless, when put into particular social contexts, such principles would generate an aesthetics based on universal (culture-free)

8.19 *Self-evidency and beyond. Innovative thinking in design seeks to avoid the world of 'black-boxes' and provide instead products which are not only immediately communicative of their function but which also give pleasure through their sculptural form. Radio alarm clock by Surindarjit Jassel, Kingston Polytechnic, England.*

facts and insights and, at the same time, excised from its traditional attachment to high art.

Theoretically, such a value-free aesthetic education could include, for example, instruction in strategies for effective gourmandizing— the subtle alternation of fasting and feasting and, in general, the choice of 'peaky' stimuli. A crucial topic would be an introduction to the techniques of negative cultivation or the selective attenuation of attention. This would naturally lead to instruction in the techniques for framing stimuli into figure and ground and make manifest the consequent possibilities for

8.20 *Ambiguity, irony and metaphor in everyday objects draws the owner into a pleasurable contemplation which is not easily exhausted. Gentleman's valet by Juan-Antonio Egusquiza, Kingston Polytechnic, England explores the image of the saddle, an easily overlooked aspect of the 'clothes horse', a dead metaphor normally buried in everyday language use.*

shifting the viewpoint or adopting varying or multiple viewpoints that we call ambiguity or irony. Other crucial matters, hitherto only the province of the cultured—for the most part professional—include the cultivation of an understanding of the principles (including, especially, an individual's own principles) of taxonomy in the world of goods and the subsequent progressive development of taxonomic flexibility.

Once this is achieved, the possibility opens up for the gradual perception of structural invariants or 'deep structure' relationships between ostensibly different items or ensembles of goods. These are also topics that are commonplace in the vocational education of designers and artists. Here they are undertaken in a Socratic spirit using the individual student's own concrete content of images and his own current 'attitudes, interests and opinions'. There is no reason why this kind of Socratic exchange should not be extended from design—a part of production—to Taste, the symbolic trafficking arising from consumption. Anything from planning a menu, through choosing an outfit to wear, to setting up home

could be considered in this spirit. Of course, innumerable contemporary magazines, television and radio shows give advice on such matters. Haphazard and casual at best and with no theoretical foundation, such offerings are invariably concerned to sell particular products or life styles. They are indeed part of a system of indoctrination that consumer education, seen as a public service (rather like health education), would necessarily need to confront if it is to be effective.

To be successful, such an education, however firmly based on theory, would have to be grounded in practice, on individual lives as they are lived. The revelation and reinforcement of self through the contemplation of that burgeoning ensemble of goods which constitutes a home is a quintessential example of situated learning—the kind of learning which emerges slowly and unacknowledged from an engagement in practice. We should envisage the proper education of Taste not as an exercise in didactics but as engagement in a kind of 'cognitive apprenticeship'.[38]

Some modest efforts towards this kind of education in matters of Taste were made in the United Kingdom nearly forty years ago. Jack Pritchard described some 'play flats' that were installed in various English primary and secondary schools by a progressive educational authority. Children could gain an introductory socialization into the principles of homemaking by playing with furniture donated by manufacturers or purchased by the school. Pritchard criticized these early ventures on the grounds that the schools did not employ professional designers as experts who could show the children 'proper' Taste.[39] From the point of view presented here, their absence was fortunate as their contribution was unlikely to

279

have been a Socratic dialogue on effective gourmandizing given the didactic and self-confident ideology propounded by designers at the time. But can we really claim that we would do better? Is it realistic to suppose that in practice such teaching would ever concentrate exclusively on cognitive techniques? Many have been sceptical.

Bourdieu, for example, was pessimistic. He insisted that the values of the cultural élite which runs the educational system will always be covertly (usually unconsciously) transmitted as the only legitimate ones in any exchange concerned with Taste. Because of the superior ('bourgeois') status of the teacher and the standing of his institutional position, his values are tacitly endorsed. He confers legitimacy on his own (inherited and acquired) preferences and prejudices simply by presenting them as routine in the course of playing his role as teacher, or so Bourdieu would have it.[40]

Anyone who has ever wrestled with the problems of discussing, criticizing, confronting, endorsing and transmitting cultural values, even in institutions such as schools of design or art which are ostensibly dedicated to the purpose, will know that this is not true. No doubt some of the teacher's own values obtrude in the dialogue on occasion but, like a good psychoanalyst, a good teacher is remarkably self-effacing. Teachers often receive as much (in terms of cultural values) from their pupils as they transmit to them. Just how particular cultural values are socialized as tacit normative patterns within the institutions of Taste such as universities or schools of art or design is little understood and rarely studied. Serious sociological research in this area is long overdue. Almost certainly the difficulties of avoiding indoctrination have been

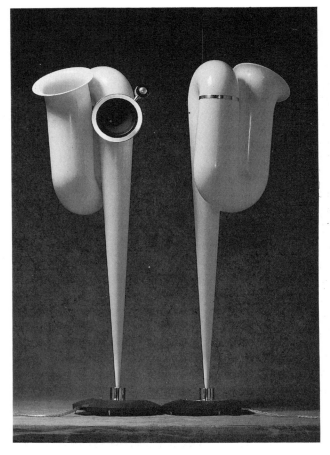

8.21 *Innovative forms are not easy, given our daily bombardment with visual clichés. Usually packaged in rectangular boxes which have no relation to acoustic need, the loudspeakers of the domestic hi-fi set are here expressed with subtle echoes of the plastic saxophone. Speakers by Morten Warren, Kingston Polytechnic, England.*

overstressed. It is possible to teach more people more ways of properly enjoying their goods and settings than is usually supposed. A good teacher plays many roles *vis-à-vis* his pupils, deploying multiple ironies and presentational strategies in order to distance his own preferences and beliefs from the current conversation. Cultural education need not end up as merely a twentieth century version of those earlier upper class tracts on etiquette, or a finishing school which passes on to each new generations the secrets of 'good breeding' or the manners of the dominant élite.

It must frankly be admitted that, in passing the perceptual and emotional trade secrets of professional creators on to wider circles, one may be tempted to emphasize those 'abstract' preoccupations with form which characterize the creative mind. But this need not be seen as the dry and bloodless activity that Bourdieu attributes to the bourgeois museum. Most creators derive the keenest of pleasures from their perceptions of formal relationships. The habit of mind which imposes order on the symbolic tumult of the artefactual world (thereby inducing perceptual flow) gives sensuous, physical pleasure directly, not merely as an added bonus to the superior status that some societies confer on those who adopt it. Nevertheless, it is worth remembering that being continually creative can itself become a burden—as may the activity of creative consumption. In a free society those who prefer to let the opportunity pass must be permitted to do so. Not everyone wants a continuous intellectualizing of their likes and dislikes.

Cultural education is one of the great future challenges for consumer societies as they move into the phase where production no longer dominates all other considerations. If contemporary consumption, in most advanced industrial societies, is largely liberated from necessity and therefore a subjective matter of selective preferences and choices or Taste, then it is remarkable that consumer societies devote so little attention to the study of Taste at the present time. Consumer education deserves a much broader and more serious remit than it currently enjoys. The relatively low status in the academic pecking order that subjects such as home economics currently occupy also needs re-examination. Why should the study of, for example, the history of art be considered superior to the study of domestic science, given their respective importance to the economy and to the individual's enjoyment of the good life? (According to Scitowsky, expenditure on home improvements exceeds that of all leisure activities put together.) What is required is a merger of all the peripheral interests in consumer culture at present scattered about in higher academic institutions (universities and polytechnics). This in turn must be integrated with the many so-called 'vocational' and 'recreational' subjects at other levels—especially those concerned with the pleasant life, from hygiene and hairdressing to handicrafts and home decoration.

Founded on a more adequate understanding of the psychological and sociological determinants of well-being, a cultural education of this kind could provide for each citizen what is currently only enjoyed by small élites—a gourmet's guide to his or her own particular corner of consumer society. Indeed, taken to its limit, the distinctions between producers and consumers and between design education and consumer education begin to dissolve. Instead of designers acting as prepackagers of meanings for the multitude, they would play the role of 'cultural enablers', assisting people to move forward in their own lives. This is already happening in the office environment where the interaction of equipment, software, work practices and employee life styles is complex and continuous. In this sense, office workers are already becoming what have been termed *prosumers—builders of their own life-support systems.*[41] There is no inherent reason why this approach should be limited to designing the workplace or facilitating the use of high technology. There is every reason to extend it into the enhancement of the settings of everyday

281

life—although this radical enlargement of the notion of participation would no doubt put new and taxing strains on the relationship between designers and those who work in the quantitative disciplines ('the accountants and the marketing M.B.A.s') which would need to be overcome in turn.

There are certainly dangers in too much Taste, in becoming too self-aware or too absorbed in providing intellectual analyses of consumption. The passion for the raw experience of here and now, that Bourdieu so admired in the social realist Proudhon, is not without point (and, of course, art itself constantly returns to the contingent and the actual—'not in ideas but in things').[42] In becoming too self-consciously 'Tasteful', the settings for everyday life can become too abstract and ultimately unsatisfying. For most citizens of contemporary consumer society, however, there are huge territories to be explored before this particular perceptual frontier is reached.

In the meantime, unsatisfied and thus unfettered, consumption has begun to threaten the future of life itself. But, if the proper exercise of Taste adds to the enjoyment of what we already have, then it may thereby help to attenuate, if only slightly, the present drive towards the accumulation and final waste of ever more goods. It could even be the arts and acts of appreciation, appreciation in the fullest sense of the word as we have used it here, which helps us to preserve the possibility of life on earth.

8.22 *Still useful goods become worthless when people tire of them. The result is the waste which threatens the planet—everywhere. Wrecked car body, Little Colorado River Gorge, Painted Desert, Arizona, USA.*

Notes and References to Chapter 8

1 R. Schickel, *Intimate Strangers, the Culture of Celebrity*, New York: Fromm International Publishing Corporation, 1986, p. 341. (Although I have separated the two passages for the present purpose, they do in fact run continuously in the original text.)

2 See Tom Wolfe, *The Painted Word*, London: Bantam Books, 1975. Also Robert Hughes, *The Shock of the New*, London: BBC, 1980, for accounts of this aspect of the history of *avant-garde* art.

3 This process is of course merely a contemporary version of that described so caustically by Thorstein Veblen in *The Theory of the Leisure Class*. See T. Veblen *op. cit.*, p. 87 on 'pecuniary canons of Taste'. For an introduction to the anthropology of value see A. Appadurai, "Commodities and the Politics of Value" in A. Appadurai (Ed.), *The Social Life of Things*, Cambridge: Cambridge University Press, 1986, and particularly the discussion and references to the work of J. Baudrillard on the 'tournament of value' which obtains in the institution of the art auction.

4 For a critical evaluation of Warhol's own obsession with celebrity and the impact of the publicity cult surrounding his 'Factory' upon his assistants ('a desert of destroyed egos') see P. S. Smith, *Andy Warhol's Art and Films*, Ann Arbor: UMI Research Press, 1986.

5 See R. Schickel, *op. cit.*, p. 118 *et seq.*

6 Yves St Laurent, Giorgio Armani and Calvin Klein are just a few of the fashion designers who have lent (or rather sold) their names to this mode of merchandizing.

7 The takeover bid by the advertising agency Saatchi and Saatchi for one of the four major United Kingdom clearing banks could well have succeeded but was finally blocked by the Bank of England!

8 This issue has been discussed in more detail in Chapter 4.

9 There are, at least in the United Kingdom, considerable pressures from a concerned government to bring this about, however, the issue is seen from one side only (there are no visually trained persons in government and precious few in business). Only in a few pioneering instances are business students even perfunctorily introduced to the culture of design. The London Business School has been a pioneer of this effort and it has now been joined by a few Polytechnics, notably Kingston. In the United States, the Design Management Institute, Boston, Mass., has been one of the leaders in interdisciplinary efforts in this field.

10 This is why the battles to include design and visual literacy into the new 'core curriculum' are crucial.

11 This confrontation goes back to the early days of sociology. Understanding 'from the inside' is very similar to *verstehen* while quantification and prediction—understanding 'from the outside'—is the English equivalent of *begreifen*. See T. Abel, "The Operation Called Verstehen." *American Journal of Sociology*, Volume 54, 1948-49, p. 211. Reprinted in E. H. Madden (Ed.), *The Structure of Scientific Thought*, Boston: Houghton Mifflin, 1960. Abel's point that the operation of *verstehen* is most useful at the 'hunch-making' stage of science parallels my stress on its use in design and in the consumers vicarious engagement in design through the exercise of Taste judgments.

12 For the original 'Two Cultures' dispute see C. P. Snow, *Two Cultures—and a second look*, Cambridge: Cambridge University Press, 1964, and the rejoinder by F. R. Leavis, *Two Cultures?*, London: Chatto and Windus, 1962.

13 See D. L. Dowd, *Pageant Master of the Republic—Jacques-Louis David and the French Revolution*, Lincoln: University of Nebraska Press, 1948.

14 See C. Gray, *The Russian Experiment in Art 1863-1922*, London: Thames and Hudson, 1971, and C. V. James, *Soviet Social Realism*, London: Macmillan, 1973.

15 See J. Willet, *The New Sobriety—Art and Politics in the Weimar Republic*, London: Thames and Hudson, 1978, for an account of the artistic situation in Germany in the pre-Hitler period. See B. Hinz, *Art in the Third Reich*, Oxford: Blackwell, 1980, for the art and architecture of Nazi Germany.

16 See A. Hsai, *The Chinese Cultural Revolution*, London: Orbach and Chambers, 1972.

17 See F. MacCarthy, *All Things Bright and Beautiful*, London: G. Allen and Unwin, 1972, p. 140, and D. Joel, *The Adventure of British Furniture*, London: E. Benn, 1953, p. 129 *et seq.* for a brief history of 'utility' furniture. See also "Utility or Austerity" in *Architectural Review*, Volume 93, 1942, pp. 3-4, and M. Bruton, "Utility: strengths and weaknesses of government controlled crisis design." *Design*, 39, September 1974, pp. 66-69.

18 So confident were the Modernists that success was finally theirs that, in 1953, the Design and Industry Association organized an exhibition called 'Register Your Choice'—a small display at Charing Cross Station in London which contrasted two fully furnished room sets. They were fitted out 'with modern English furniture, one showing pieces and fittings which proved best-sellers and the other showing pieces and fittings which the DIA considered to be a good design. Neither room was to be a caricature and both rooms were to cost the same'. Visitors voted by very nearly three to two in favour of the 'good design' room. There was real hope that 'this country would no longer have to go to Scandinavia or the Continent for its modern inspiration'. See *Design and Industries Association Yearbook 1953,* pp. 15-16 (Mass Observation Report on the 'Register Your Choice' Exhibition).

19 R. Hoggart, *The Uses of Literacy*, London: Chatto and Windus, 1959, p. 119.

20 The duality of facts and values is a central theme in the social philosophy of Karl Popper. See K. Popper, *The Open Society and Its Enemies*, London: Routledge and Kegan Paul, 1945 and 1957.

21 This difficult and highly metaphorical notion has long been a popular locution with those who have pondered the problems of art and design in industrial societies. See for example H. Read, *Art and Alienation*, London: Thames and Hudson, 1967, and T. Maldonado, *Design, Nature and Revolution—towards a critical ecology*, New York: Harper and Row, 1972. For a clear explanation of the notion of alienation and its relation to the possibility of an integrated lifestyle in which people are happily reconciled to their own cultural productions see A. W. Wood, *Karl Marx*, London: Routledge and Kegan Paul, 1981, especially p. 28 and 37 and notes. See also H. Arendt, *The Human Condition*, Chicago: University of Chicago Press, 1958, especially Chapter 4 on 'Work'. The views of William Morris on the need for an integrated life style in which creative activity is intermixed with necessary journeywork echoes the earlier thoughts of Marx on alienation. Morris came to his thoughts independently through his own experience and was unaware of Marx's work which was not published until much later. See K. Marx, *The Economical and Philosophical Manuscripts MSS of 1844*, D. J. Struik (Ed.), London: Lewis and Wishart, 1973, especially p. 106 *et seq.* See also I. Meszaros, *Marx's Theory of Alienation*, London: Merlin Press, 1970, p. 190 *et seq.*

22 'Household Choices' is a project operated jointly by The Victoria and Albert Museum and the London and Middlesex Polytechnics together with a network of universities and polytechnics. Many students and researchers have contributed to an exhibition and a publication. See T. Puttnam and C. Newton (Ed.), *Household Choices*, Hainault, Essex: Futures Publications, 1990.

23 See M. Csikszentmihalyi and E. Rochberg-Halton, *The Meaning of Things—Domestic Symbols and the Self*, Cambridge: Cambridge University Press, 1981.

24 M. Csikszentmihalyi, *Beyond Boredom and Anxiety*, San Fransico: Jossey-Bass Publishers, 1975.

25 In particular, D. E. Berlyne, *Conflict, Arousal, Curiosity*, New York: McGraw-Hill, 1960 and D. E. Berlyne (Ed.), *Studies in the New Experimental Aesthetics: steps towards an objective psychology of aesthetic appreciation*, New York: Hemisphere Publishing, 1974.

26 T. S. Eliot "The Dry Salvages" from *Four Quartets*, London: Faber and Faber, 1946.

27 See W. Stevens, *Opus Posthumous*, New York: Knopf, 1957, p. 171.

28 See A. Ehrenzweig, *The Hidden Order of Art—a study in the psychology of artistic imagination*, London: Weidenfeld and Nicolson, 1967.

29 See H. Wingler, *Bauhaus*, Cambridge, Mass: MIT Press, 1969, pp. 440-441.

30 See G. O. Rogge quoted in P. R. Farnsworth, *The Social Psychology of Music*, Ames, Iowa: Iowa State University Press, 1969, p. 87. In her researches, subjects were played various musical themes and asked to make a semantic translation into a story which, in their opinion, described the experience of the music. A second group then read these stories and gave them adjectival descriptions according to their understanding of the overall mood. When other subjects again were asked to correlate the stories with the musical pieces, it was found that their performance was markedly superior to those who attempted the correlation with the aid of the adjectival descriptions of mood alone. Somehow the stories, however simplistic, were carrying over some pattern of the changing tension and relaxation of the original music. This was lost when the experience was reduced merely to one of meaning.

31 The influence here was E. H. Gombrich—although with his well-known aversion to abstract art he would hardly have approved of what we were doing. See E. H. Gombrich, "Communication and Expression" in *Medita-*tions on a Hobby Horse, London: Phaidon Press, 1963, p. 56.

32 For example the repeated stanzas with variations of colour and image in Wallace Stevens' "Sea Surface with Clouds" in *Collected Poems*, New York: Knopf, 1955, p. 98.

33 See P. Lloyd Jones, "The Failure of Basic Design." *Leonardo*, Volume 2, 1969, pp. 155-160. for an early attempt at a critical appraisal of theories of design then current which anticipated later practical work in design education. See also "Form and Meaning in Colour" in A. Harrison (Ed.), *Philosophy and the Visual Arts*, Dordrecht: Reidel, 1988, for an account of semantic translation in the field of colour and "Drawing for Designing." *Leonardo*, Volume 17, Number 4, 1984, pp. 269-276, for a discussion of generative techniques and metaphorical transformation in three dimensional form.

34 For example the remarks of H-J. Lannoch, on the need for works to be ambiguous and contradictory—what he calls the 'resistance of form'. H.-J. Lannoch, "Towards a Semantic Notion of Space." *ICSID News*, Number 3, 1989, p. 1.

35 The 1989 International Conference on Product Semantics at the University of Industrial Arts in Helsinki was a landmark.

36 D. Berlyne, *Conflict, Arousal, Curiosity*, New York: McGraw-Hill, 1960, p. 200.

37 T. Scitowsky, *The Joyless Economy—an enquiry into human satisfaction and dissatisfaction*, Oxford: Oxford University Press, 1976.

38 On situated learning see J. S. Brown, A. Collins and P. Dugald, "Situated Cognition and the Culture of Learning," *IRL Report No. 88-088*, Institute for Research on Learning, Palo Alto, California, 1989.

39 See J. C. Pritchard, "Raising the Standard of Furniture" in *The Studio Yearbook of Furnishing and Decorative Art*, Volume 43, 1953-1954, p. 7-13.

40 P. Bourdieu, *La Distinction*, Paris: Les Editions du Minuit, 1979, p. 448 *et seq.*

41 The phrase is John Rheinfrank's of the Exploratory Design Laboratory, Fitch RS, Worthington, Ohio. He has been largely responsible for this shift of emphasis in the designer's role in relation to the users of hardware and software in the office environment in his work for the Xerox Corporation. See for example, J. Rheinfrank, "On the design of design" paper presented to the conference *Product Semantics 89,* University of Industrial Arts, Helsinki, Finland. Also "Animating Interfaces" paper submitted to the *Conference on Computer-supported Co-operative Work*, Association for Computing Machinery, Los Angeles, California, 1990.

42 The expression was the lifelong motto of the poet William Carlos Williams.

Name Index

Where references to the note sections are provided the relevant page numbers are followed by 'n'.

Subject Index

Where references to the note sections are provided the relevant page numbers are followed by 'n'.

Subject Index